M000315131

Cultures of Yusin

perspectives on CONTEMPORARY KOREA

SERIES EDITORS: NOJIN KWAK AND YOUNGJU RYU

Perspectives on Contemporary Korea is devoted to scholarship that advances the understanding of critical issues in contemporary Korean society, culture, politics, and economy. The series is sponsored by The Nam Center for Korean Studies at the University of Michigan.

Hallyu 2.0: The Korean Wave in the Age of Social Media
  Sangjoon Lee and Abé Mark Nornes, editors

Smartland Korea: Mobile Communication, Culture, and Society
  Dal Yong Jin

Transgression in Korea: Beyond Resistance and Control
  Juhn Y. Ahn, editor

Cultures of Yusin: South Korea in the 1970s
  Youngju Ryu, editor

Cultures of Yusin

South Korea in the 1970s

Youngju Ryu, editor

UNIVERSITY OF MICHIGAN PRESS

Ann Arbor

Copyright © 2018 by Youngju Ryu
All rights reserved

This book may not be reproduced, in whole or in part, including illustrations, in any form
(beyond that copying permitted by Sections 107 and 108 of the U.S. Copyright Law and except by
reviewers for the public press), without written permission from the publisher.

Published in the United States of America by the
University of Michigan Press
Manufactured in the United States of America
Printed on acid-free paper
First published November 2018

A CIP catalog record for this book is available from the British Library.

Library of Congress Cataloging-in-Publication data has been applied for.

ISBN: 978-0-472-07396-2 (Hardcover : alk paper)
ISBN: 978-0-472-05396-4 (Paperback : alk paper)
ISBN: 978-0-472-12415-2 (ebook)

This work was supported by the Academy of Korean Studies (KSPS) Grant funded by the Korean
Government (MOE) (AKS-2011-BAA-2102).

Contents

Introduction

Youngju Ryu

The cover image of this volume is an architectural detail from a building constructed in 1976 that now houses the Human Rights Center of the Seoul Metropolitan Police, photographed by Kim Myung-shin. Nestled in a forest of prime commercial real estate in Namyŏng-dong, halfway between the Yongsan and Seoul train stations, the black brick building was once known by a more ominous name, Ch'ianbonbu taegong punsil (Office of Communist Affairs) in the National Police Headquarters. A few exterior details still attest to those bygone days—vertical slits across the fifth floor that serve as windows, an outdoor kiln used to burn legally sensitive documents in the days before the invention of the shredder—but it is on the inside that the true frightfulness of that past becomes fully visible in one historically preserved cell.[1] Corresponding to each of the vertical slits on the fifth floor was an interrogation cell outfitted with a small cot, a metal desk nailed to the floor, a flushing toilet, and a tiled bath. In these cells, torture specialists worked over their detainees for confessions, frequently false, and other information deemed important for national security by the government. After days filled with electric and water torture, in addition to "lesser" forms of cruelty such as joint dislocation and group beating, detainees would inevitably emerge from these cells as self-proclaimed North Korean spies or conspirators against the nation.

Knowledge of what went on in these cells was first publicized in earnest in 1985 when a prominent activist named Kim Geun-tae (Kim Kŭn-t'ae) managed to expose in great detail the variety of torture techniques he had been subjected to during twenty-three days of confinement, but the most famous victim of Namyŏng-dong is probably Pak Chong-ch'ŏl, whose death while undergoing water torture galvanized the democratization movement. The public outrage that followed his death set the stage for what Bruce Cumings has called the "June breakthrough" of 1987, which succeeded in wresting the promise of direct presidential elections from the Chun Doo Hwan (Chŏn Tu-hwan) regime's ever reluctant hands.

The featured detail on the cover is of the Namyŏng-dong building's spiral staircase, which connects the ground floor directly to the fifth floor with no landings in between. According to Kim Myŏng-sik, the staircase was designed to maximize the sense of disorientation and fear that the detainees would feel prior to being interrogated: "Climbing the spiral staircase without pausing on any landing, the blindfolded victims would have had a difficult time remembering what direction they came from or the floor they were on. . . . And without any ceilings between the first floor and the fifth, reverberations of the footsteps combined with the barking of the interrogating officer would be magnified to the extreme, causing the victims being dragged up the stairs to feel intense fear. Architecturally considered, this is an exceptional space, one that could hardly have been created without a particular purpose in the architect's mind."[2]

The creator of that exceptional space was Kim Swoo-geun (Kim Su-gŭn), undoubtedly the most famous architect of the modern Republic of Korea (ROK) and one of the trio of men discussed in Se-Mi Oh's chapter in this volume on the development of Yŏŭido. Kim's SPACE Group Building, completed in 1977, was voted the greatest architectural accomplishment of twentieth-century Korea in a 2013 survey of architecture specialists.[3] Less well known, however, is the fact that this widely touted masterpiece of multilateral space and human scale was constructed at nearly the same time as the torture headquarters of Namyŏng-dong and that the two buildings share several key architectural features, including the flat-textured black brick facade, patterns of ornamental brickwork, protruding vertical window frames, entry from the side, reinterpretation of the courtyard, and even the spiral staircase. What Kim Swoo-geun's admirers have touted as his mastery of "continuity in space" in reference to the SPACE Group Building became, as Kim Myŏng-sik's analysis of the spiral staircase indicates, a means of disorienting political detainees prior to their torture sessions.[4] "The contrasts of narrow and broad, high and low, closed and open" that rendered the interior of the SPACE Group Building so diverse and interesting for the architectural critics facilitated in the case of the Namyŏng-dong building the psychological isolation of the torture victims and the spatial separation of the regular administrative functions of the police from its more extraordinary use of power. Not surprisingly, though quite conspicuously, the Namyŏng-dong building is absent from the list of works featured on the home page of the Kim Swoo-geun Foundation, but the architect Cho Han has called the building "the little stepbrother" (*ibok tongsaeng*) of the famed masterpiece.[5]

This architectural tale is a dense text, possibly a cautionary one, for a volume seeking to examine the 1970s in South Korea through a cultural lens. An understanding of Kim Swoo-geun's deep complicity with the authoritarian regime must inform any pat characterization of Kim as "the father of modern Korean architecture"; striking the Namyŏng-dong building from a website, for example, will not make it go away. Nor can the question of how to evaluate the Namyŏng-dong building formally as a materialization of that architectural and spatial philosophy, which Hyung-min Pai (Pae Hyŏng-min) has described "a commitment, not to a transcendent whole, but to discordant parts that the parsing of Korea's dense modernity reveals," be dismissed on purely moral grounds.[6] The artificiality of isolating Kim Swoo-geun the architect of the SPACE Group Building from Kim Swoo-geun the architect of the Namyŏng-dong building applies more broadly to much of the 1970s' cultural production, especially that of a more popular nature.

But at a more basic level, the tale of the two buildings also suggests the deep indebtedness of the subsequent Chun Doo Hwan (and Roh Tae-woo (No T'ae-u)) regimes to ideologies, institutions, and infrastructure consolidated during the 1970s. Indeed, it would not be an exaggeration to say that South Korean society as we know it today was born in the 1970s. This is a polemical statement to be sure, given that every decade of the country's existence since its founding in 1948 was dramatically, and often cataclysmically, paradigm shifting. As is well known, the 1950s in Korea saw the catastrophe of war and national division. The 1960s began with a student revolution that ousted the sitting president, followed the year after by a bloodless military coup d'état that put Park Chung Hee (Pak Chŏng-hŭi, 1918–79) in power for the next eighteen years. The 1970s came to an end with Park's assassination at the hands of his chief intelligence officer, only to give way to another military coup. From 1980 to 2010, South Korea underwent several additional transformations of national scale, including democratization, globalization, and neoliberalization. And in 2017, the Candlelight Revolution that led to the impeachment and imprisonment of Park Geun-hye (Pak Kŭn-hye) put an end to the nostalgia for the political economy of the 1970s once and for all, as I discuss in the conclusion of this volume.

The degree, however, to which the polemical claim found endorsement among Korean people was reflected in the consistency with which Park Chung Hee topped the list of Korea's greatest presidents in national polls until recently. This assessment of Park as a "great" president reflected the view widely shared by both supporters and critics alike that the Park era was foundational and formative in a way that no other period in modern Korean history can quite match. To use a sports analogy that has a special resonance in the Korean historical context, we might say that although the physical stadium Park built may have given way to ravages of time in the nearly forty years since his death Koreans are still playing the game according to the rules he set.[7] It is in this light that we can understand the historian Park Tae Gyun's (Pak T'ae-gyun) suggestion that for the "archetypes" (*wŏnhyŏng*) essential to understanding the peculiarities of contemporary Korean society we must look to the Yusin era.[8]

In its narrowest sense, Yusin refers to "October Yusin," the extraordinary political sequence of autumn 1972 that marked the beginning of the second half of Park Chung Hee's rule. On October 17 of that year, Park announced in a special presidential address four emergency measures that would bring the normal operations of the entire South Korean government grinding to a halt. These included the declaration of emergency martial law, the dissolution of the National Assembly, a partial suspension of the constitution, and a ban on all political activity. Ten days later, on October 27, the partially suspended constitution was replaced with the Yusin Constitution. Devised by a small team of men working behind closed doors under Park Chung Hee's personal direction—the ironic name given to the secret operation was Project Good Harvest (P'ungnyŏn saŏp)—the new constitution granted the president unprecedented powers over the entire election process. The presidential term limit was removed altogether, allowing Park, who had already amended the constitution once before to seek a third consecutive presidential term, to remain in power. The task of electing future presidents was entrusted to a newly created political body called the National Conference for Unification (T'ong'il Chuch'e Kungmin Hoeŭi), whose chairman was Park himself. This body was also responsible for selecting the delegates of Yujŏnghoe, a quasi-political party that was allotted a third of the seats in the new National Assembly, from the pool of candidates that the president had the power to nominate. Since the ruling Republican Party (Konghwadang) already belonged to Park by any meaningful measure, what the constitutional change meant in effect was that Park now personally controlled not only the entire presidential election process but two-thirds of the National Assembly as well. Completing the president's control over all branches of the government, the new constitution also gave Park the power to appoint and dismiss all judges, including the chief justice of the Supreme Court.

The executive apparatus for maintaining Park's iron rule came from the presidential authority to issue sweeping "emergency decrees" (*kin'gŭp choch'i*). During the next several years, Park declared nine presidential emergency decrees in all and placed the entire Korean society under lockdown, turning even the mere act of criticizing the government into a capital crime. In what is undoubtedly the most egregious application of the decrees, the Park regime executed eight men within thirty-six hours of sentencing on the trumped-up charge of plotting to overthrow the government. The 1975 case, known as the People's Revolutionary Party Incident (Inhyŏktang sakŏn), resides in the annals of modern Korean history as an example of "judicial murder" (*sabŏp sarin*) and a particularly scandalous instance of state terror. It would take more than thirty years for these men's names to be finally cleared in court.

The declaration of October Yusin in 1972 is said to have surprised even the members of Park's inner circle. Park, after all, had taken pains throughout the 1960s to preserve the outward appearance of electoral democracy, even after first grabbing power by storming the capital in the company of tanks. To be sure, the so-called free elections were rarely free of massive fraud in South Korea—even the very first presidential election in 1948, monitored by the United Nations no less, had been marred by irregularities big and small—but it had still been a broadly accepted minimum requirement for remaining within the American boundaries of the "Free World" in the post–World War II era. As such, electoral democracy had been a powerful source of legitimation for a state competing with its northern counterpart for regime supremacy. The Yusin Constitution challenged this acceptance, stripping Korean electoral politics of even the veneer of democracy.

Much of the existing English scholarship on the Yusin era has attempted to shed light on its political economy, starting with why Park sought to formalize his dictatorship in 1972, more than a full decade after his rise to power. The answer typically invokes three interrelated factors, as Won Kim's chapter outlines. The first concerns the geopolitics of détente and the changing terms of US-Korea relations in the wake of the Nixon Doctrine. The 1969 declaration by President Richard Nixon signaling that the United States would be scaling back its involvement in Cold

War theaters around the globe and seeking instead diplomatic solutions such as normalization of relations with Communist China was, at one level, a pragmatic response to the economic crisis brought on by the escalating costs of the Vietnam War. In South Korea, however, Nixon's declaration that the United States would "look to the nation directly threatened to assume primary responsibility of providing manpower for its defense" could not but precipitate an acute sense of security crisis, accompanied as it was by the reduction of US troop levels in Korea and increasing tensions in the US-ROK alliance. At the same time, the Nixon Doctrine was a signal that the United States would be less than enthusiastic to intervene in Korea's domestic affairs. What resulted was the opening up of a "breathing space" for authoritarian politics.[9] According to Tae Yang Kwak, Yusin was born within this space as "a gambit born of desperation," a systematic attempt to shore up the Park regime's authority at a time when the boundaries of the "Free World," within which South Korea had existed as an anticommunist garrison state supported economically and militarily by the US, became subject to redefinition.[10]

The second commonly invoked factor is the complexity of inter-Korean relations. In the late 1960s, North Korea engaged in a series of provocations that brought the peninsula to the brink of war, including the hijacking of the USS *Pueblo*, an attempted commando raid on the presidential residence, and guerrilla warfare in Ulchin and Samchŏk. And yet, in the historic Joint North and South Korean Proclamations announced just a few years later on July 4, 1972, the two Koreas reached a basic agreement concerning reunification. Though appearing to be part of the global détente and at the strong urging of the United States, the inter-Korean dialogue was motivated in the South by the Park regime's anxiety about the security crisis that the Nixon Doctrine had unleashed: the withdrawal of twenty thousand US troops from South Korea by 1971 and the rapprochement with China, combined with the earlier United States' refusal to engage in military reprisals in the wake of North Korean aggression in the late 1960s. The Park regime saw inter-Korean dialogue as a means of containing the North Korean threat at a time of increased South Korean vulnerability. The new external uncertainties introduced by the dialogue also provided the Park regime with both the motivation and the pretext for tightening internal control. As Kim Chihyŏng has observed, the word *reunification* appears no less than eighteen times in the presidential address of October 17, 1972, in which Yusin was billed as "an urgent reform that would support the maintenance of South-North dialogue and enable us to respond actively to the rapidly changing political climate all around."[11] Prior to the national referendum that ratified the Yusin Constitution, the Park regime led the public to believe that "voting for the reforms was a vote for reunification, and voting against them was a vote for permanent division."[12]

The third factor was domestic. As the Park regime prepared in the early 1970s to launch the third Five-Year Plan for Economic Development and the "Big Push" toward heavy and chemical industrialization—a drive that Park saw as requiring an unprecedented level of coordination among all sectors of Korean society—it encountered troubling signs of domestic unrest. A crisis had emerged in government-business relations regarding how to finance economic growth. The self-immolation of a garment worker named Chŏn T'ae-il in 1970 had galvanized a labor-student alliance within the growing dissident, pro-democracy movement. Years of rapid urbanization had led to a housing crisis in Seoul, and the ill-conceived and terribly executed plan to relocate residents of the city's shantytowns to the so-called Grand Kwangju Complex in Kyŏnggi Province led to an uprising in 1971. Above all, however, it was Kim Dae-jung's (Kim Tae-jung) strong run in the presidential race of 1971 that reinforced a sense of crisis in the Park regime. Despite the massive amounts of money that the Park campaign had poured into the race and quite a bit of election rigging as well, Kim carried the capital city of Seoul and came close to defeating Park overall. In addition, Kim's party received over 42 percent of the votes and became a formidable minority in the National Assembly.

Whatever Park Chung Hee's motivations might have been for embarking on the Yusin reforms, there is no denying the fact that their implementation created a police state in South Korea. While the most spectacular displays of state power occurred during exceptional exercises of political violence such as judicial murder, its penetration into people's everyday lives took the form of what Hwang Pyŏng-ju has called "the politics of prohibition" (kŭmyok ŭi chŏngch'i). National security, argued Park, was not simply a matter of defending the country from external threats. At a time of great uncertainty and renewed crisis brought on by the Nixon Doctrine and the opening of inter-Korean dialogue, any divisiveness within the country could jeopardize its overall security. Vietnam and Cambodia had fallen prey to communism because their peoples had failed to "unite as one" (ch'onghwa tan'gyŏl); what would keep South Korea from going their way but the vigilance and discipline of the Korean people? "Political instability or social chaos, fragmentation of the national opinion, the loosening of social discipline, decadent customs and trends, and various other antisocial absurdities make us vulnerable. . . . It is imperative from the point of view of national security to boldly rid our society of these ills so that not even a trace remains."[13]

In a more expanded sense, then, Yusin refers to the system of total social control that the Park regime created during the seven years in which the constitution stayed in effect. The regime issued and reinforced detailed prescriptions about the kinds of activities, and even practices of thought, in which Korean citizens must not indulge. Plainclothes police and military personnel became permanent fixtures on college campuses as student protest was suppressed by liberal applications of anticommunism and sedition laws. The resurrection in 1975 of the Patriotic Students Corps (Hakto Hoguktan) transformed the student association into a paramilitary organization devoted to the dissemination of Yusin and anticommunist ideology.[14] A labor relations law revised in 1973 and again 1974 paved the way for a crackdown on the labor movement and surveillance of union activities. Censorship of what the public could read, hear, and see extended from the pages of daily newspapers to reels of film to broadcasts over the airwaves. The list of banned songs—characterized as depressing, decadent, or otherwise socially undesirable—grew long during the Yusin era, along with a list of *kŏnjŏn kayo*, wholesome songs at least one of which every musical record had to include in order to be approved for the public. Consumption of foreign or luxury goods became strictly forbidden. Even "minor offenses" (*kyŏng pŏmjoe*) came under the purview of state control with a law passed in 1973. As a striking image in Joan Kee's chapter reveals, government control over South Korean society extended even to the amount of leg a woman could show below the hem of her skirt.

These draconian measures were rationalized as being what the extraordinary times required. Over and over again in his speeches, Park Chung Hee stressed that this was a time of unparalleled crisis and that the very survival of the nation was at stake. We might then ask, given that it was launched by means of a *special* presidential address, sustained by frequent exercises of *emergency* decrees, and brought to an end by no act of law or eruption of popular will but by a shiny bullet "shot through the heart of Yusin" (the famous words of Park's assassin when asked why he had killed his commander in chief), what makes the Yusin era "archetypal"?

The well-known answer is that Park Chung Hee's "developmental dictatorship" gave birth to some of the most distinctive and enduring features of South Korean politico-economic culture, among them the dominance of business conglomerates (*chaebŏl*), export-oriented growth, and the un-equal industrialization of the country along the East-West axis that helped to produce the regionalist topography of contemporary South Korean electoral politics. But the above question also leads us into the realm of what Hwang Pyŏng-ju has called "the politics of desire" (*yongmang ŭi chŏngch'i*) and the mechanisms of consent formation that a heavy empha-sis on the coercive state can sometimes occlude. Let's take as our example the signature mobilization campaign of the Park Chung Hee period: Sae-maul (Saemaŭl) Undong, the New Village movement. "New Village" evokes tableaulike images in black and white of villagers engaged in col-lectivist work projects. Whether as Atarashiki mura, the utopian com-mune launched in 1918 by the Japanese intellectual Mushanokōji Saneatsu, or Xin xiangcun jianshe, the New Rural Reconstruction movement led by Wen Tiejun in China today, New Village has been the name in East Asia used to describe collective responses to crises confronting the countryside as a traditionally agrarian society undergoes modern industrialization. Unlike the above two movements, however, Saemaul Undong in South Korea was launched as a government initiative from the start whose roots lay in the rural campaign undertaken in Korea during the colonial era by Governor-General Ugaki in order to combat the growing popularity of the Left in the impoverished countryside. Begun in the early 1970s under the slogans "Let us live well!" and "Let us modernize our homeland!" the Sae-maul campaign yoked individuals' basic desire for a better, more affluent life explicitly to the national agenda of rapid development.

During the initial phase of the Saemaul movement, rural communities were exhorted to help themselves by modernizing their physical environ-ment, replacing thatched roofs with "modern" slate tiles made with asbes-tos and government-issued cement, for example, or widening village roads and paving them over as communal work projects. The movement quickly evolved, however, into a nationwide campaign with a heavily spiritual em-phasis, "a revolution in consciousness" (*ŭisik hyŏngmyŏng*) and "the foun-dation of the national spirit of the Korean people" (*kungmin chŏngsin ŭi kijo*), according to Park Chung Hee.[15] Thus, when Korean citizens got up at the crack of dawn and began their day by sweeping the sidewalk to the beat of a Saemaul song playing over the neighborhood public address sys-tem, a song whose words were written by none other than President Park himself, they were not simply keeping their communal environment neat. Through these individual practices of diligence and cooperation, they were actually bettering themselves spiritually and bringing about a brighter future for their nation. The power of the Saemaul rhetoric lay in its ability to give each individual action a national significance and to integrate every individual movement into the choreography of the national body. The statist corporatism of Saemaul provided, in Park Chung Hee's own words, the "training and practice ground (*silchŏn tojang*) for the actualization of the ideology of the October Yusin."[16]

Indeed, the Yusin system shared several key features with fascist experiments of the twentieth century elsewhere in the world: a corporatist philosophy that sought to integrate every member of society organically around the state, an emphasis on collective action achieved through discipline and mobilization, and maximization of efficiency achieved by the willingness to sacrifice individual liberty for the "greater good." What stood in the way of the pursuit of such efficiency was, of course, democracy. From early on in his rule, Park Chung Hee publicly questioned the suitability of Western liberal democracy on the "inhospitable" soil of South Korea, impoverished and divided; his slogans, such as "democracy Korean style" (*Han'gukchŏk minjujuŭi*) and "ethnonational democracy" (*minjokchŏk minjujuŭi*), were qualifications that challenged the universality of American democracy while still remaining within the American boundaries of the Cold War world order. In the "breathing space" that opened up following promulgation of the Nixon Doctrine, Park dispensed with this American universal altogether, no longer feeling the need to go through the "wasteful" motions of democratic procedure. The United States had never been Park's model for economic development anyway. The inspiration had come not from across the Pacific or Atlantic Ocean but from across the East Sea.

Seen in this light, we can understand the October Yusin of 1972 as the crystallization, as well as an outright declaration, of the vision of modernization that had guided the Park regime from the start. Han Suk-Jung (Han Sŏk-chŏng) describes this vision as "high modernism" characterized by economic development, heavy industrialization, construction of railroads, urban planning, and improvement of hygiene, all under the terribly efficient and strong-armed direction of the militarist state.[17] That vision of planned economic development and modernization had come to Korea from Japan, as practiced in its purest form in the puppet state of Manchukuo (Manchuria) in the 1930s and 1940s. Park Chung Hee had spent five years in Manchuria (1940–45) as a young low-ranking military officer, and he watched this developmental model unfold firsthand. Han Suk-Jung notes that so many of the Park regime's personnel—not only in the military but in the economy and across education—were Koreans who had gained their valuable first experience in management on the lower rungs of Manchukuo's bureaucracy as "clerks, military officers, policemen, prison guards, physicians, teachers, and even labor supervisors."[18] It is no accident, then, that on grabbing power in the 1961 military coup, the first country Park Chung Hee visited was Japan, where he was greeted by none other than Kishi Nobusuke, the architect of the Five-Year Plan for Manchukuo focusing on heavy industry. In response to the hospitality the so-called Kishi Line of Japanese bureaucrats showed him during this visit— support that would continue throughout Park's rule and be reciprocated with much gratitude by Park in turn—Park Chung Hee is said to have promised that he would do his best "with the heart of a patriot who dedicated himself to the Meiji Restoration."[19] As is well known, the word meaning "restoration" in Japanese is *ishin*. In Korean the Chinese characters that make up the *ishin* of Meiji Ishin are pronounced as *yusin*.

Like its predecessor in Manchukuo, the Yusin regime was militarist, constructionist, mobilizational, anticommunist, organicist, and biopolitical—in short, fascist in a broad sense, though of the military-bureaucratic regime type rather than the single-party regime type of Germany and Italy.[20] If, following Janet Poole, we understand fascism at a more basic level as "the desire for a kind capitalism without capitalism . . . the dream of capitalism without its excesses," then Yusin was engineered on the back of the belief that capitalism's excesses were enabled by liberalism and individualism, that is to say, the twin pillars of democracy.[21] The solution to this problem was for the state to monopolize the fruits of capitalism and direct them toward further and further development. Capitalism's excesses would not have a chance to take root in society then, simply because there would be no excesses to speak of at the level of individual Koreans. "Growth first, distribution later" (*sŏn sŏngjang, hu punbae*) proclaimed the Park regime in the 1970s as the export-oriented development of light manufacturing industries in the 1960s began to pay dividends. Keeping those dividends from being distributed and channeling them toward heavy and chemical industries, the Park regime kept the people in a state of perennial need and thus mobilizable toward national ends. The very brutality and oppressiveness of the Yusin regime meant that even more attention had to be paid to spiritual reform and ideological inculcation in order to keep popular discontent from boiling up and derailing Yusin's political economy. And yet, as the media scholar Yu Sŏn-yŏng has argued, the Park regime's "hypernationalization project" was deeply riven and highly unstable, lacking both the theory and the executive capacity to create the kind of suturing emotional politics that characterized the fascist cultural policy of the National Socialists in Germany, for example. It was because the subtler mechanisms of persuasion and consent formation had not fully succeeded, or remained unavailable from the start, that the kind of brute, heavy-handed, and highly visible apparatus of censorship used by the Yusin regime became necessary in the first place. The Yusin Constitution of 1972 may be seen as a response not only to the crises in the economy, domestic politics, and international relations, as adumbrated above, but to a crisis in the cultural project of hypernationalization brought on by the regime's inability to establish a seamless three-way equation among the regime, the state, and the nation.[22]

Given these inner dynamics and outer manifestations of Yusin, culture emerges as an absolutely crucial and fascinating battleground for understanding South Korea in the 1970s and during the Park Chung Hee era more broadly. This central insight about the importance of culture serves as the common point of departure for the essays gathered in this volume. Bound up with articulations of national identity, culture was the locus of self-conscious recuperations on the part of both the state and those who sought alternative narratives out of the past and into the present. As is always the case, these recuperations were necessarily accompanied by active repressions and erasures. Culture was also the site of intense orthopractical inculcation and mobilization of the masses by the state, both in tandem with and in tension against forms of mass entertainment and consumption that inevitably resulted from modernization. On the other end of the political spectrum, resistance to Yusin was frequently encoded in cultural forms, either in active dissident performances or scholarship addressing the experiences of the oppressed masses, or in a more passive manner as quietly subversive expressions of individual taste. But above all culture was the terrain of lived life and everyday practices whose messiness and irreducible heteronomy posed an ongoing challenge to the makers and enforcers of Yusin's policies, as well as their sharpest critics. It is this unruliness of culture that inspires the volume's diverse explorations. The plural form of the word in our title recognizes the richness and complexity of culture, even when it unfolded in a time of unprecedented insistence on political oppression and censorship.

Cultures of Yusin begins with Won Kim's essay on *Han'gukchŏk in kŏt*, variously translated here as "Koreanness" or "what is uniquely Korean." An abridged translation of a lengthier article originally published in Korean, the essay draws on South Korean scholarship of the last decade or so to provide a useful schema for understanding the major forces whose collision shaped the cultural topography of Yusin. The driver of one such force was, of course, the Park regime. Keenly aware of the power of a sense of shared past in mobilizing the masses toward state-defined goals, the regime adopted many of the cultural policies that were enacted in imperial Japan, especially in Manchukuo, as a means of creating "harmony and unity." National heroes were newly created out of old histories, and large-scale commemorative projects built memories deemed desirable around physical monuments and ceremonial events. While such statist uses of the past have become familiar to us since Eric Hobsbawm coined the phrase "the invention of tradition," Kim's essay highlights the use of a similar strategy by the progressive intellectuals of the dissident variety in their embrace of internal development theory in Korean history and literature. A means of pushing back against imperialist perspectives on Korean history that denied the possibility of an autonomously Korean path to modernization, the theory evolved into an orthodoxy among student dissidents on college campuses who decried the Park regime as collaborationist and comprador. Sharing an elitist orientation and an unchallenged faith in progress, both the Park regime and the student dissidents found aspects of contemporary popular youth culture distasteful and potentially threatening. In the youth culture of blue jeans, folk guitars, and draft beers or the melodramatic hostess films frequented by factory girls, Kim locates "traces" of irreverent pleasure that marked its distance from the wholesomeness prescribed by the fascist state or the ascetic solemnity of the dissident movement.

Hwisang Cho's chapter takes us to one of the national heroes catapulted into prominence during the Yusin era. T'oegye Yi Hwang, a sixteenth-century neo-Confucian scholar, became an iconic figure during Park Chung Hee's rule, selected as a representative of Korean cultural heritage to be celebrated on the face of every thousand-won note. T'oegye's legacy was refurbished and systematized: his scholarship was elevated to the status of an independent discipline called T'oegyehak, and the various physical remnants of his life were sacralized as traditions to be treasured. The ideological utility of T'oegye's brand of neo-Confucianism to the Yusin regime, as well as the regionalist dimensions of Park's support for T'oegye, are well known, but Cho cautions us against a too precipitate rush into the "invention of traditions" camp. While the Park regime's handprints on the demideification of T'oegye are everywhere visible, Cho gives us a much lengthier and nuanced history of T'oegye's reception through time, going back to the period immediately after the master's death and tracing the vicissitudes of these receptions as they move through the mid- to late Chosŏn period, and again through the Japanese colonial era, before arriving at the Park Chung Hee era. What Park brought about in reference to the old master was not his discovery per se but his iconization and a silencing of the master's voice, which had pulsated through the earlier receptions. Cho thus provides an important corrective to the common view that posits Park Chung Hee as the progenitor of T'oegyehak and highlights in the process an important dynamic that played out on the level of the visual and helped the Park regime consolidate its mass appeal.

Yusin's ideological constructions were hierarchical and gendered. In fact neo-Confucian philosophy proved such a great fit for the Park regime as a ruling discourse because of its aspirational prescriptions regarding virtuous behavior, which linked political loyalty, filial piety, and womanly chastity as three manifestations of the same essential principle of human relations. At the same time, the expanded role of women in the actual economy raises important questions regarding woman as a desiring subject, regardless of whether the pleasure she seeks is to be derived from sexual contact, the consumption of goods, or the accumulation of money. That question is explored through a specific social practice in Eunhee Park's chapter on the material culture of *kyebaram*. Although *kye* (rotating credit associations or RCAs) had been around since the Chosŏn period, it was during the 1960s and 1970s that their popularity reached a fever pitch. Both the managers of and participants in these RCAs, moreover, were primarily women. Examining the institutional and financial basis of this social phenomenon, Park analyzes how *kye* came to spread as a consequence of the tight credit market that the Park regime's planned economy created for individual families. As managers of their household economies, women began to create mutual credit networks and investment clubs. A form of microfinance, *kye* tutored these women on using credit, purchasing items on the installment plan, and other related economic activities, thereby supporting the capitalistic modernization of South Korea.

Han Sang Kim's exploration of private homeownership in Yusin Korea, if not as an actual reality to be enjoyed in the present then in the imagination as a vaguely attainable goal at some point in the future, reveals a moment of deep tension between state-led economic development and the ideals of liberalism and individualism that the Yusin regime sought aggressively to suppress. A private home, especially an apartment, is presented on the one hand as the embodiment par excellence of modernization and development. As a place of private—and often extramarital—desire, as well as a haven of individual taste among the trappings of modern domestic life, the apartment in Korean films and literary works of the 1970s is utopic for the women who dream of it as their "sweet home." For middle-class women, however, the modern apartment turns out to be a nightmarish space of compulsive consumption and stifling uniformity mediated by standardized commodities. Lower-class women suffer an even harsher fate as they are frequently ejected from the apartment space at the end of the narrative. Kim thus charts in this essay how the American way encapsulated in the discourse of "my sweet home" became resignified in the process of its vernacularization into a fetish object.

The gender-class nexus that Irhe Sohn examines in his chapter on action cinema is the one triangulated by urban working-class males, action films, and Techniscope technology. Nearly invisible in the existing discourse on action cinema of the 1970s, the urban working-class males that made up its spectatorship comprised the population whose potential for social unrest the Park Chung Hee regime appreciated keenly. The regime's labeling of the action film genre as violent and prone to leading young impressionable minds into the paths of juvenile delinquency was thus an attempt to preempt the legitimacy of any antigovernment actions that this demographic might take. In order to bring this erased group back into the field of vision and understand movie watching as a socially meaningful activity in the context of these men's lives, Sohn calls for "peripheral vision," a way of looking askance at the material to achieve a different level of focalization on the visual field. It is only by doing so that we can hope to understand, however fleetingly, the twinkling of something bright in the darkness of second-run theaters populated by tired male bodies seeking relief from their relentless mobilization in state-led industrialization by watching "violent and vulgar" films produced with cheap technology. Although the pleasures they produced have largely been forgotten, deemed unworthy of serious academic inquiry, Sohn reminds us that our understanding of the Yusin era will remain critically flawed without them.

Alternative truths enjoy the provenance of science fiction. Sunyoung Park's chapter on science fictional imagination in the 1970s discusses Ch'oe In-hun's *Typhoon* as a novel that belongs to the subgenre of alternate history, which narrates the present on the premise that World War II ended not in Japan's defeat but in its victory. The 1970s is largely dismissed in the existing scholarship on science fiction according to Park. Because it is so often taken for granted that the authoritarianism of the Yusin era was deeply inimical to certain flights of fancy, despite its emphasis on "scientific advancement," the decade has been overlooked in literary histories of the genre. Challenging this basic assumption, Park's chapter unearths fascinating utopian connections in the literature and film of the 1970s and works through the profoundly dissident visions that populate these texts. This revision of the existing history regarding the genre of science fiction then leads Park to a reconsideration of the decade's dissident culture more broadly, beyond its dismissal as a mere prelude to the more radical 1980s.

Focusing on the period just before the Yusin era, Se-Mi Oh's chapter unravels the tangled history of various urban planning efforts championed by different people that produced the transformation of an alluvial, shape-shifting island in the Han River into Yŏŭido, an "urban spectacle of Korea's insatiable appetite for development," by carefully attending not only to what ultimately came to be but also what failed to materialize. At the heart of this effort of recuperation is the architect Kim Swoo-geun's 1969 Master Plan for the development of Yŏŭido. The vision of modernist city that it contained clashed as well as collaborated with the administrative vision of Kim Hyun-ok (Kim Hyŏn-ok), then mayor of Seoul, known as "the bulldozer" for the massive urban-planning and construction projects he spearheaded. Both visions, however, were overridden by Park Chung Hee's penchant for anticommunist architecture and monumentality and the defense crisis he felt had arisen in the aftermath of a failed North Korean commando raid on the Blue House. In a manner that anticipates the violence of the Yusin years, the utopian dreams of 1969 Master Plan was paved over in concrete, but Oh's essay helps us to see why those dreams still matter, even if unrealized.

The possibility of resistance is at the heart of the last two contributions to the volume. Throughout the entire Park Chung Hee era, the dissident writer par excellence was Kim Chi-ha, whose satirical pen landed him in prison, and even on death row for a time, and turned him into an international icon of anti-authoritarian resistance. Beginning with Kim Chi-ha's play *The Gold-Crowned Jesus*, first staged in the same year as the October Yusin, Serk-Bae Suh's essay examines the figure of Jesus in several South Korean literary texts of the authoritarian era. This was the period of a progressive turn in South Korean Christianity, when the influence of Latin America's liberation theology, combined with the plight of the urban poor in the underbelly of the Park regime's relentless drive for development, led the traditionally conservative and anticommunist religion to embrace aspects of Marxism. Exploring soteriology in relation to political theories of emancipation, Suh notes that the representation of Christ in the period's literary works is characterized by an emphasis on his utter impotence and immanence in the material world. No longer the son of God whose self-sacrifice paves the way for humanity's redemption, Jesus in these works can do nothing but suffer along with the wretched of humanity. The reversal in these works of the relationship between God and man—"It is not God who will save us, it is we who will save God"—becomes the occasion for thinking about the limits and possibilities of the transformation of democracy into a gospel of salvation under the yoke of a prolonged military dictatorship in South Korea.

"Why performance in Yusin Korea?" asks Joan Kee provocatively in the final chapter in the volume. Against the backdrop of a totalitarian society run by a technocracy that worshiped efficiency and measurable performance, and in which movements of any kind not authorized by the state came under intense surveillance, Kee explores the aesthetic and political import of the performance art of Lee Kun-yong (Yi Kŏn-yong) and his colleagues. As "art centered on the process of executing a particular action or task," performance took on a special significance in light of the Yusin era's obsession with regulating the activities and movements of bodies both individual and collective. While they were not outright protests—Kee argues in fact that resistance as such would have been co-opted by the polarizing logic of the Yusin state—the "happenings," "events," and "incidents" that made up performance at the very height of Yusin opened up a space for recognizing how the state delimited not only what was desirable but also what was possible. The recognition would "reinstill faith" in other possibilities.

The conclusion of the volume explores Yusin's afterlife in the twenty-first century. The surprising return of Yusin under Park Geun-hye's presidency—what I have called "Yusin Redux"—ended spectacularly in the sequence of events that led to the historic impeachment of Park and a peaceful transition of power. The essay approaches the complicated legacy of the Yusin era through an analysis of a pair of satirical paintings by Hong Sung-dam (Hong Sŏng-dam). Uncannily presaging both the return and demise of Yusin, these paintings shed light on how a daughter's anachronistic attempt to rehabilitate her father's vision for the Korean nation resulted ironically in bringing to an end one of Yusin's most enduring legacies: the opposition between democracy and development.

In 1974 the Yusin government announced the First Five-Year Plan for

Revitalizing Culture and Arts. The initiative would carry out three main missions: establishing the proper perspective regarding national history, raising the cultural level of the populace, and promoting active international exchange in culture and the arts. The announcement revealed that, despite its keen appreciation of both the utility of culture and the threat it posed for the project of national mobilization, the Yusin regime essentially saw culture as an actionable realm no different from that of the economy. The five-year plans that had been so effective in developing the South Korean economy would be applied to culture as well; the level of culture, just like the gross domestic product, could be raised through concerted, coordinated government action. Just as the First Five-Year Plan for Economic Development had focused on building the infrastructure for economic development and securing the energy sources necessary for industrialization, the First Five-Year Plan for Revitalizing Culture and Arts would focus on building the cultural infrastructure, including cultural agencies, national museums, and honors such as the Anti-communist Literature Award. It would also fund cultural activities associated with the Saemaul movement. For the Park regime, culture was essentially the domain of national propaganda, whether directed at its own citizenry or at the international world. Its propaganda focused on the propagation of values seen as desirable by the state: diligence, cooperation, discipline, optimism, wholesomeness, and self-help. The ideal Koreans thus produced would engage in vigorous, purposive action without questioning the certainty of the purpose, even when that purpose was not of their own making. They would, in the end, cease to think.

The need for certainty, according to the psychoanalyst Christopher Bollas, is what drives the fascist state of mind. "Doubt, uncertainty, self-interrogation, are equivalent to weakness and must be expelled from the mind to maintain ideological certainty," he writes, and thus "the mind ceases to be complex, achieving a simplicity held together initially by bindings around the signs of the ideology. Political slogans, ideological maxims, oaths, material icons (such as the flag), fill the gap previously occupied by the polysemousness of the symbolic order." [23] And yet the power of culture lies in the very polysemousness of the symbolic order to which it attests. As the essays in this volume demonstrate so clearly, culture is inherently a field of doubt that multiplies with time and of uncertainty and self-interrogation that force us into meandering paths, even in a world of slogans, sirens, and straight lines.

NOTES

1. The cells were remodeled in 2000, and the tiled baths where water torture took place were removed, with the exception of Cell 509 where Pak Chong-chŏl died.

2. Kim Myŏng-sik, *Kŏnch'uk ŭn ap'ŭm ŭl ŏttŏke kiŏk hanŭnga* (Ttŭindol, 2007), 50.

3. "Chŏnmunga 100myŏngi ppobŭn 'Han'guk hyŏndae kŏnch'ungmul ch'oego wa ch'oeak," *Tong-a ilbo*, February 5, 2013. http://news.donga.com/3/all/20130205/52820 819/1

4. Jinyoung Lim and Seong Lyong Ryoo, *K-Architecture: Tradition Meets Modernity* (Korean Culture and Information Service, 2013), 90.

5. Cho Han, Seoul, *Kiŏk ŭi konggan, konggan ŭi kiŏk* (Seoul: Tolbegae, 2013), 220

6. Hyungmin Pai, "Dense Modernities: Kim Swoo Geun and the Architecture of Commitment," *Space*, July 6, 2011, http://www.vmspace.com/2008_re/eng/sub_emagazine_view.asp?category=architecture&idx=11344

7. The analogy is not merely analogical. The Dongdaemun Design Plaza, designed by the world-renowned architect Zaha Hadid, opened its doors in 2014 as a symbol of Seoul as a global city on the grounds where the Dongdaemun Stadium once stood, home to the many baseball tournaments that Park Chung Hee sponsored as president.

8. Pak Tae-gyun, "Segyesajŏk pop'yŏnssŏng kwa t'ŭkssusŏng ŭi ch'ŭngmyŏn esŏ pon Yusin ch'eje," *Yŏksa wa hyŏnsil* 88 (June 2013): 19.

9. Pae Kŭng-ch'an, "Nikssŭn tokt'ŭrin kwa Tong Asia kwŏnwijuŭi ch'eje ŭi tŭngjang," *Hanguk chŏngch'i hakhoebo* 22, no. 2 (1988): 321–338.

10. Tae Yang Kwak, "The Nixon Doctrine and the Yusin Reforms: American Foreign Policy, the Vietnam War, and the Rise of Authoritarianism in Korea, 1968–1973," *Journal of American–East Asian Relations* 12, nos. 1–2 (Spring–Summer 2003): 44.

11. Kim Chihyŏng, "Yusin ch'ejegi Pak Chŏng-hŭi ŭi nambuk kwangye kusang kwa silje," *Yŏksa wa hyŏnsil* 88 (June 2013): 72.

12. Kwak, "Nixon Doctrine," 54.

13. Taet'ongnyŏng pisŏsil, *Pak Chŏng-hŭi Taet'ongnyŏng yŏnsŏl munjip*, vol. 6 (Seoul: Taet'ongnyŏng pisŏsil, 1979), 34.

14. Yi Ch'ang-ŏn, "Yusin ch'eje ha hakssaeng undong ŭi chiphapchŏk chŏngch'esŏng kwa chŏhang ŭi kwangye," *Yŏksa yŏn'gu* 23 (December 2012): 13, 36.

15. Quoted in Hwang Pyŏng-ju, "Saemaŭl Undong ŭl t'onghan nongŏp saengsan kwajŏng ŭi pyŏnhwa wa nongmin p'osŏp," *Sahoe wa yŏksa* 90 (June 2011): 41.

16. Address delivered by Park Chung Hee at the First National Assembly of Saemaul Movement Leaders (November 21, 1973), quoted in Yi Yong-gi, "Yusin inyŏm ŭi silch'ŏn tojang, 1970-yŏndae Saemaŭl Undong," *Naeil ŭl yŏnŭn yŏksa* 48 (September 2012): 67.

17. Han Sŏk-chŏng, "Pak Chŏng-hŭi, hogŭn Manjugukp'an hai modŏnijŭm ŭi hwaksan," *Ilbon pip'yŏng* 3 (August 2010): 120–37.

18. Ibid., 128.

19. Yi Tong-jun, "Pak Chŏng-hŭi chŏnggwŏn, Ilbon nae Manju inmaek kwa kyŏlt'ak 'hŭngmak chŏngch'i,'" *Hanguk ilbo*, April 20, 2015.

20. Gregory J. Kasza, *The Conscription Society: Administered Mass Organizations* (New Haven, CT: Yale University Press, 1995), 1–6.

21. Janet Poole, *When the Future Disappears: The Modernist Imagination in Late Colonial Korea* (New York: Columbia University Press, 2014), 7.

22. Yu Sŏn-yŏng, "Tongwŏn chʼeje ŭi kwaminjokhwa pʼŭrojektʼŭ wa seksŭ yŏnghwa," *Ŏllon kwa sahoe* 15, no. 2 (2007): 5–6.

23. Christopher Bollas, *The Christopher Bollas Reader* (New York: Routledge, 2011), 83–84.

The Race to Appropriate "Koreanness"

National Restoration, Internal Development, and Traces of Popular Culture

Won Kim

Koreanness, Past and Present

An emphasis on "what is Korean" (*Han'gukchŏk in kŏt*) marks recent celebrations of the Korean wave, Korean tradition, and Korean culture, not only in the realm of creative industries, where these discussions have been most salient, but also in promotion of such concepts as national standing, national pride, and national consciousness.[1] This contemporary phenomenon is far from novel, however, rooted as it is in the consolidation of a national essence that took place in the 1960s and 1970s. The aim of this chapter is to chart the rise during these earlier decades of the discourse of "Koreanness" as a window onto the present social phenomenon of "discovering what is Korean." The chapter examines the active dissemination of the notion of Koreanness through government policies on culture and the arts, as well as the discourse's elaboration by critical intellectuals in the fields of history and literature. In addition, the chapter traces how the concept of Koreanness became manifest in popular culture and was appropriated by it in turn.

The late 1960s and 1970s witnessed the implementation of cultural policies, production of literary and historical knowledge, and execution of symbols and ceremonies surrounding Koreanness, all yoked to such concepts as national revitalization (*minjok chunghŭng*), national culture (*minjok munhwa*), and a "self-affirming view of national history" (*chagi kŭngjŏngchŏk minjoksa*).[2] But the discussion of Koreanness itself was slow to develop. The reason is that in the context of postliberation South Korea, where the legacy of pro-Japanese collaboration remained incompletely eradicated, the search for any kind Koreanness in the future tense was problematic from the start.[3] Given these developments, the discourse of "what is Korean" thus occupied a unique position during the period extending from the late 1960s through the 1970s. In the early days immediately following the military coup of May 16, 1960, the Park regime viewed Korean history negatively, even while maintaining a deep distrust of Western democracy and lifestyles.[4] And after the 1965 Normalization Treaty with Japan, the nationalist orientation that it had earlier sported under the motto "national democracy" (minjokchŏk minjujuŭi) became dormant, completely overshadowed by the regime's elevation of modernization as a categorical imperative. Then suddenly in the late 1960s the Park regime began emphasizing "that which is ours" (uri kŏt) across all aspects of society. The slogans were various—"overcoming national calamities" (kungnan kŭkpok) and "education with nationality" (kukchŏk innŭn kyoyuk), in addition to the aforementioned "national culture" and "national revitalization"—but they all aimed to recover Koreanness from specifically chosen facets of Korean history and tradition. Spiritual aspects were especially prized, as can be glimpsed in Park Chung Hee's (Pak Chŏng-hŭi) theory of the "Second Economy" or the Charter of National Education.[5] Such an emphasis on the spirit located something largely inaccessible to the Western way of thinking at the very pith of Korean national culture.

And the government was not alone in the endeavor to rearticulate Koreanness. With the 1967 establishment of the Association for Korean Historical Studies (Han'guksa Yŏn'guhoe) serving as an impetus, Korean historians mounted a concerted effort to overcome a colonial historiography that had long cast an oppressive pall over their field. In opposition to such theories as "stagnation" and "peninsularity," which had served as explanatory models for Korea's failure to modernize and thus a justification for its colonization, Korean historians began elaborating what came to be known as the "sprouts of capitalism" theory (chabonjuŭi maeng'aron).[6] As the theory became more refined, it began to affect other academic disciplines as well, most notably Korean literature, where it helped to spur the growth of a critically minded theory of national literature (minjok munhak). In other words, the postcolonial race to appropriate Koreanness had begun in earnest.

We can point to several historical factors as creating the backdrop for the massive proliferation of "all things Korean" at this time. The first was the widespread protests over the 1965 normalization talks with Japan. The brutal suppression of these protests hollowed out the regime's erstwhile slogan of national democracy.[7] At the same time, the prospect of resuming relations with Japan revived colonial memories and refueled the fear of colonization by Japan.[8] One manifestation of the inflamed fear was the search for a national identity and the perception that individuals must be absorbed into the collective identity of the national whole.[9]

The second context was the deepening sense of crisis that beset the Park regime when several security-related events erupted both internationally and at home. International events included the North Korean hijacking of USS *Pueblo*, East Asian détente, the reestablishment of Sino-US diplomatic relations, and the threat of US troop withdrawal from South Korea. At home the January 21 Incident and the discovery of armed North Korean guerrillas dispatched to the city of Ulchin and Samch'ŏk heightened the security crisis.[10] And, though less dramatic, the outbursts of growing discontent among the urban underclass raised an alarm in the Park regime. A rural exodus in the 1960s had given rise to a wide spectrum of urban masses. The rapid spread of mass media, mass production, and mass consumption that accompanied modernization and the attendant proliferation of social relations informed by capitalism heightened social volatility: "Though [capitalist] development had brought immediate victory to the Park Chung Hee regime, progress came without a guarantee of future success but accompanied instead by a threat of future defeat.... To the extent that they did not yet exist, the regime's enemies were ghostly, and to fight them, it needed weapons that were ghostly too and non-material, that is to say, spiritual."[11]

The Park regime's response to these "crises" was "total mobilization," which extended over the realm of culture. The regime redoubled its efforts on the one hand to censor and restrain the "undesirable" by-products of modernization, including the spread of popular culture and consumption of Western material goods. At the same time, it sought to control the Korean masses by means of a spiritual revolution that emphasized national identity and providing nation-affirming content that could easily be consumed by the public. Such content took concrete shape as acts of reinterpretation (of national history itself aimed at restoring a sense of national greatness) and rediscovery (of national heroes).[12]

Did this imposition of Koreanness from above actually enable the government to fully command hegemonic control over people's daily lives, structures of feelings, and practices of culture? I have my reservations. The government's exercise of censorship can in fact be seen as a sign of the very opposite, that is to say, the incompleteness and instability of the regime's hegemonic control over the populace. And the widespread censorship of popular and youth culture, as we will see, had the further unintended effect of triggering subconscious popular resistance that took shape within the blurred boundaries between decadence and subversion.

The Invention of Koreanness

The discourse on tradition (*chŏnt'ong*) has a long history in Korea that dates back to the colonial period. In the 1920s and 1930s, folklorists such as Ch'oe Nam-sŏn and Yi Nŭng-hwa took an interest in revitalizing tradition as the essence of the nation, seeking a corrective to the Japanese colonialist interpretation of Korean history and culture.[13] But, as is well known, tradition is far from a natural inheritance. Contrary to its dictionary definition as "historically transmitted material culture, thoughts, patterns of behavior, impressions of people or events, and various groups of symbols," it is something shaped and reinterpreted in the present. In Korea, *chŏnt'ong* is a Korean term that entered daily usage only in the twentieth century under Western influence as a translation of the English word *tradition*. As such, *chŏnt'ong* was defined by its inextricable relationship with modernization. For the advocates of Western-style modernization, *chŏnt'ong* was something to be negated and rejected and an inheritance to be transmitted for those espousing an autonomous route to modernization or opposed modernization altogether.

Koreanness, *tradition*, and *nationalism* were interchangeably used terms and component parts of an apparatus designed to elicit consent from the people by means of an appeal to their emotions and sentiments.[14] Precisely for this appeal, nationalism outside the context of anticommunism was often seen as a dangerous ideology in South Korea before the 1960s; the nationalist emphasis on tradition risked irrationality and particularism against which an underdeveloped nation striving for modernization should guard itself.[15] This view began to change, however, in the late 1960s and early 1970s. The Park government actively encouraged people to develop an emotional bond with and sense of political belonging to a national community. Nationalism became a way to combat two enemies simultaneously: communism and the West (or Western democracy).[16]

In this regard, the invention of "things Korean" in Park Chung Hee's Korea shared much with Taiwan under Chiang Kai-shek. In opposition to the brutal destruction of tradition that went on during China's Cultural Revolution, Taiwan's Cultural Revitalization movement was built on the equation of Westernization with communization and styled as a way to guard tradition.[17] In Korea, too, by invoking nationalism and inventing tradition, both the ruling power and the resistance movement sought to fill the void of national identity left by colonial rule, and each conferred a different set of meanings on knowledge systems that arose in relation to things Korean. In this regard, the late 1960s to the 1970s may be seen as the period when the battle over Korea's national subjectivity was waged in earnest.

The reason for stressing Koreanness in our discussion of Korea in the late 1960s and 1970s is that, contrary to previous discussions that equated tradition with existing conventions or long-established customs, the concept of Koreanness articulated during this period was orientated toward the future and became part of the broader discourse of self-reliant culture. To be sure, the concept was less than fully defined. The suffix -ness (-chŏk) in the term Koreanness suggests the coexistence of an imperfect awareness of what constitutes the Korean essence exactly, on the one hand, and a fervent yearning to discover and pursue Koreanness in spite of it all.[18] This search encoded the desire to create a new national character that would stand at the heart of a new national history, revive national greatness and its traditions, and rescue the past as a positive and self-affirming history.[19] To both the ruling power and the opposition, much of the 1960s had been an era of the "loss of self," a decade when the obsession to modernize had swallowed everything else. The 1970s, on the other hand, would be an era of "self-affirmation" marked by the recovery of that lost self.[20] On this positive recovery would also hinge the possibility of a different future.

The government was the first to lead the drive for what is Korean. Three government organs in particular—the Ministry of Culture and Public Information (Munhwa Kongbobu), the Bureau of Cultural Heritage Management (Munhwajae Kwalliguk), and the Korean Culture and Arts Foundation (Munye Chinhŭngwŏn)—implemented cultural policies and carried out vastly expanded censorship of and intervention in popular culture. As will be discussed in greater detail in the next section, the Park regime's cultural policies took three broad directions concerning the restoration of physical structures and historic sites: overcoming national crises, whose physical emblems were to be found in ancient sites associated with national crises such as Hyŏnch'ungsa, the memorial temple for Yi Sun-sin (1545–98) famed for defending Chosŏn from the Hideyoshi invasions in the sixteenth century; restoring structures of national cultural significance such as the old mansion of the renowned late Chosŏn painter and calligrapher Ch'usa Kim Chŏng-hŭi (1786–1856) in the historic city of Kyŏngju; and promoting the concept of loyalty and filial piety by restoring places like Ojukhŏn, the home of Sin Saimdang (1504–51), who perfectly embodied Chosŏn's feminine ideals, and her son, the Confucian master Yulgok Yi I (1537–84). The 1968 establishment of the Ministry of Culture and Public Information was especially significant. Through this organ, the government sought to unify and centralize the hitherto confused and unsystematic policies for culture and arts, thereby taking the primary role in the invention of Koreanness in the 1970s. At the same time, by serving as the coordinating organ for censorship, standardization, and outright prohibition of popular culture, it also engraved indelible memories of suppression in the minds of artists and cultural producers.

"Koreanness" According to the Government: Cultural Artifacts, Sculptures, and Heroes

Prominent within the topography surrounding what is Korean were state-led projects on rediscovering and restoring Korean culture. As was already visible in the rhetoric surrounding the theory of the Second Economy, the National Charter of Education, and the Social Purification movement, the Park regime placed a great emphasis on spiritual revolution not as a means toward an end called economic development but as that which must lead and guide "the material civilization." The modern spirit and material civilization imported from the West, Park argued, must be harmonized with the spiritual culture preserved within Korean tradition.[21] On the surface, it appeared that the regime was shifting its emphasis away from efficiency and toward the traditional spirit of cooperation; in actuality, however, the two overlapped. The emphasis on the spiritual culture was ultimately aimed at the cultivation of ethical subjects—ethical in the sense that they were efficiently productive and obedient—who would then become the agents of national revival.[22]

In order to stoke the primeval and deeply entrenched feelings for the fatherland, the government emphasized the excavation, cleanup, and consecration of cultural artifacts as core projects for national consciousness building. Following the establishment of the Ministry of Culture and Public Information, the efforts to systematize Korean culture proceeded apace. Buffeted by an enormous budget, manpower, and the president's own interest, numerous projects were launched to restore cultural properties, consecrate old battlefields and historically meaningful sites, and erect statues and sculptures. And with the creation of the National Institute for the Research of Cultural Properties (Kungnip Munhwajae Yŏn'guso) in 1975, the 1970s became the veritable "era of excavations." Seventy percent of the 48.5-billion-won endowment for the revival of culture and arts were funneled into the projects meant to fortify nationalist historiography. Through these large-scale projects, which rendered the history of overcoming national crises physically visible, the government sought to change the mass perception of Korean culture as withered and even autistic, a view that had taken hold in the 1960s. The projects enabled the government not only to position itself as the dominant actor in defining and regulating what constituted Koreanness but also to actively mobilize national sentiments and sensibilities toward a state-driven agenda by employing history and related natural objects.[23]

Let us examine in greater detail the policies concerning cultural properties first. In Korea the legal and institutional apparatus for such policies was established in 1961 with the founding of the Bureau of Cultural Heritage Management and in 1962 with passage of the Cultural Heritage Protection Law.[24] The "cultural heritage" covered by this law included (1) tangible and intangible cultural properties, historical monuments, and folkoric materials that make it possible to recall Korea's past; and (2) "natural monuments" and landscapes representative of Korea's physical environment. Such a definition of cultural heritage as encompassing both Korea's past and Korea's nature was built on the premise of an ethno-nation-state (*minjok kukka*) in which the nation and the state coincide. By making itself the arbiter and protector of cultural heritage, the state positioned itself as the medium for evoking all things Korean in the minds and hearts of the masses. The government made this explicit in its official publications by imbuing cultural heritage with particular significance: "Textbooks for enabling the creation of a new national culture, acquiring a vision of new development of the national territory and historical consciousness, and discovering the national self; a medium for national education that creates a new national history."[25]

Preservation and restoration of cultural properties thus focused on the refurbishment of people and places associated with national defense in the past and sought to achieve the educational effect of enlightening the Korean public regarding the greatness of the Korean nation and reinforcing self-affirmative history. Turning Yi Sun-sin's Hyŏnch'ungsa into consecrated ground, for example, was emphasized as an act more meaningful for the nation than building several hundred factories. Consecrated areas were to be located away from the more commercial districts, and Park Chung Hee himself harbored an almost professional interest in the matter, going so far as to give personal instructions for landscaping.[26]

In addition to consecration and preservation of cultural properties, the government embarked on a project of national hero making in an attempt to invent a new Korean character type. As had occurred in the West in late nineteenth and early twentieth centuries when large numbers of commemorative monuments were erected in an effort to construct a national identity and stimulate nationalist sentiments, bronze statues of notable figures from the Korean past were commissioned by the Committee for Erecting Statues of Patriotic Ancestors in Korea.[27] Statues were considered a particularly effective medium for creating nationalist sentiment among the public since they conveyed meaning visually without requiring the viewer to decipher a narrative, all the while generating a sense of awe. In 1968 the government erected a statue of Admiral Yi Sun-sin with a personal inscription by Park Chung Hee. Historical figures like King Sejong (r. 1418–50) and Admiral Yi were deemed especially meaningful in the 1970s when inter-Korean relations were particularly tense; the two men were presented as rare symbols of national prosperity and exemplary leaders the people could look up to within a history mottled with retrogression and stagnation. The 1970s was also likened to the time of the 1592 Japanese invasion of Korea when the national good was subsumed under the petty interests of individual groups, leaving the country vulnerable to an enemy attack. The historical parallel drawn between mid-Chosŏn under the Japanese and 1970s South Korea confronting the North Korean threat was intended to strengthen popular commitment to the defense of the homeland. In fact the emphasis on the 1592 Japanese invasion was such that we might even call it "the reinvention of 1592." Just as Chosŏn's civilian volunteers had organized themselves then as the Righteous Army (Ŭibyŏng) under Yi Sun-sin to defend Korea from the Japanese invaders, so the civilians under Park Chung Hee should now militarize themselves as the Hyangt'o Yebigun, the reserve army that Park resuscitated in 1968 after the foiled North Korean commando raid of January 1968 known as the Kim Sin-jo Incident. History was not merely excavated but commandeered to serve the needs of the present.[28]

The case of Yi Sun-sin is particularly instructive. His elevation as a hero who saved the people from a national crisis was accompanied by the establishment of a set of negative equations such as "North Koreans = Japanese invaders" and "the opposition party and activist students = factional strife." Apotheosized as national independence incarnate, Yi Sun-sin came to be viewed in terms of supreme patriotism and selfless devotion to the country. This was in fact the very image of "the new Korean character" that the Park Chung Hee regime sought to establish. This interpretation of Yi Sun-sin and his times borrowed heavily from the depiction of him by the novelist Yi Kwang-su (1892–1950).[29] Yi Kwang-su subscribed to colonial historiography and located the causes of the 1592 invasion not in the external factor of Japanese aggression but in internal factors such as an inept Korean monarch and factional strife between civil and military halves of the officialdom. The more glorified Yi Sun-sin appeared in this portrayal the more worthless the rest of the Koreans became by extension. The villainous officials, full of selfish ambitions and petty jealousies, were depicted as the prototype of the Korean character that needed to be reformed. The sanctification and commemoration of Yi Sun-sin thus functioned to reinforce the ideological justification for the government's active role in shaping the national character. Events like "The Great March of High School Students to Worship Sacred Places," which took place on Yi Sun-sin's birthday, put this project on full display. With the expressed goal of implementing the spirit of the patriot in everyday life, the event created the spectacle of hundreds of male high school students, decked out in military drill uniforms and equipped with rifles, reporting to the minister of education and the mayor of Seoul and then marching 124 kilometers from Seoul to Hyŏnch'ungsa on foot.[30]

We can now turn to the subject of policies concerning culture and the arts (*munye*). The Culture and Arts Promotion Act, promulgated in 1972, defined art as matters relating to literature, fine art, music, entertainment, and publishing, as well as theater and dance. While the legal apparatus for culture and the arts was already in place, what the new act provided for was further consolidation and integration of different administrative branches under a single entity. The biggest change was that the administration of culture and the arts, which had previously been assigned to the Ministry of Culture and Education, was absorbed into the Ministry of Culture and Public Information. With the establishment of the Korean Culture and Arts Foundation in 1973 following the passage of Culture and Arts Promotion Act the previous year, the Park Chung Hee government now had a central organ for overseeing its objectives of transmitting and developing national culture.

The Five-Year Plan for Revitalizing Culture and Arts, promulgated in 1973, brought the outline of the Park regime's cultural policies into particularly sharp relief. In its "Declaration of Revitalization for Culture and the Arts," the plan defined the contemporary era as a time of transition toward national restoration and emphasized the duty to inherit the orthodox legacy of the past in order to create a new culture, which could then be handed down to generations to come. Vulgar and decadent trends in thought were to be eliminated. Indulgence in nostalgia was cautioned against. The first phase of the plan invested 48.5 billion won over five years in four different categories: building infrastructure, establishing nationalist historiography (in relation to classical Korean literature, traditional arts, and cultural properties), promoting the arts (literature, fine art, music, theater, and dance), and developing popular culture (film and publishing). Of these establishing nationalist historiography received the lion's share of the funding at 70.2 percent, 63 percent of which was earmarked for the management of cultural properties.

Policies related to popular culture received the least amount of government funding during this period (8.9 percent). Popular culture was also the category that the government found the most difficult to control.[31] The government managed popular culture as "a process of eradicating the germs that gnaw at the nation," based on the determination that popular culture enabled the social evil of "degenerate" Western trends to spread and destroy Korea's "indigenous morality and beautiful customs" (mip'ung yangsok).[32] The targets of government censorship were various but belonged to three broad categories: the young generation called on to spearhead the social reforms demanded by the regime (the so-called new human type necessary for national revitalization); adolescents who had yet to develop their full personalities; and those classified as a danger to the normal operations of society, including morally corrupt women, sex traffickers, and unauthorized street vendors (the so-called subalterns).[33] The government cracked down on what it deemed the agents of moral corruption, including long hairstyles on men, acoustic guitars, marijuana, and gambling. In addition, it instituted late night curfews, penalizing individuals it considered inherently degenerate, and inspected the content of all movies, radio shows, dramas, recordings, and publications for violent, inflammatory, unethical, or vainglorious elements. To summarize, the Park Chung Hee regime maintained a solemn and abstemious stance toward popular culture, which it saw as undermining the nationally desirable traits of obedience and efficiency.[34]

Among the different genres of popular culture, film and television were the most conspicuous targets of censorship and control since they represented the most accessible media for consumers whose purchasing power had increased with modernization. A look at film policies reveals that the 1970s was a time of crisis for the film industry. On the one hand, the appearance of television as a new medium challenged the primacy of movies; on the other, censorship of antisocial (decadent) or antinational cultural content became a routine practice. "Censorship" at the time was an act of circumscribing the depicted and imagined reality of the masses, of determining the scope and content of the reality that the public wanted to believe was true. What's more, as it was practiced on popular culture, censorship was both everyday and arbitrary.[35] In place of the censored content, what the government promoted were "national policy movies" (kukch'aek yŏnghwa). Recognizing film's efficacy as a medium of propaganda, the government produced its own list of "national documentary films," as well as "cultural movies" that extolled the virtues of economic development, the will to achieve national restoration, and the accomplishments of patriots who had devoted themselves to national defense.

In addition to providing outright funding, the Park regime incentivized the production of wholesome (kŏnjŏn) and cheerful (myŏngnang) movies in less direct ways. Starting in 1976, in what has come to be known as the "screen quota system of 1976," the government granted the coveted import rights for foreign movies to those production companies that complied with the government's agenda. The Great Bell Award (Taejongsang), which honored the film industry's achievements, also became a part of government policy. The Korea Film Promotion Corporation, established in 1973, supervised the selection process for the Great Bell Award winners, and each year the government announced what it wanted of the movie industry under the heading "Movie Policies to Be Reinforced." In the 1970s, the government put forth no fewer than eighteen directives for selecting exemplary movies. They included elevation of national subjectivity, introduction of industrial warriors, overcoming national crises, contributing to rural development, welfare, and national harmony, increasing exports, promoting love of cultural assets, and observing good morals and beautiful customs.[36] Yielding to such interventions, the Great Bell Award degenerated into a mere pageant for enlightenment projects faithful to government directives, and production companies reached the point of internalizing these guidelines to such an extent that they would voluntarily produce "movies slated for the Great Bell Award."

The Evergreen (*Sangnoksu*), directed by Im Kwon-Taek (Im Kwŏnt'aek) in 1978, is a good example of such a film. The film was based on the popular novel of 1935, itself based on the true story of young, idealistic Narodniks who passionately devoted themselves to the cause of enlightening rural folk. The film, however, turned the energetic heroine of the novel, who epitomized the modern woman, into a passive character, emphasizing the female's role as the guardian of the hearth and savior of a male in crisis. The portrayal thus reproduced on screen "the Korean human type" promoted by the ruling discourse.[37] This kind of film, with one or two notable exceptions, was invariably met with cold indifference on the part of the audience. As such, these films serve as examples of how the Park Chung Hee regime's attempt to seed Koreanness in the medium of film failed to achieve emotional resonance with the viewing public. Rather than abandoning "the national policy movies," however, the government stepped up its censorship.[38] In addition, the government tried to control not just the thematic content of the movies but the manner of their screening. Starting in 1971, all movie showings had to be preceded by the national anthem, a news segment, and a cultural segment of "wholesome" nature. Thus the government's intentions intervened in even the masses' cultural practice of watching movies at the cinema.[39]

Television was another vehicle by which the government actively sought to extend its control over the people, setting the schedule for daily routines and regimenting the bodies of individual viewers by means of the television programming schedule.[40] In the 1970s, as the harmful effects of television watching came to the government's attention, censorship and regulation of programming intensified. Women, children, and teenagers were identified as being especially susceptible to the supposedly unproductive, immoral, and unethical nature of TV viewing.[41] In 1973 the government amended the broadcasting law to decrease the number and duration of commercials and instituted a system of monitoring television content in advance. Furthermore, the new programming guidelines required that stations cut back on daily serialized dramas and eliminate vulgar and decadent elements from variety and game shows while increasing the number of educational programs. The guidelines on purifying dramatic content, distributed by the Ethics Committee on Broadcasting, banned excessive depictions of amorous scenes between the sexes, as well as elements that could harm the institution of marriage and the sanctity of family life, fuel class or regional antagonisms, or upset the sensitive minds of children and adolescents.[42]

As with film, the prohibition of content perceived as harmful represented one axis of the government control of television, while the active promotion of content in line with the government agenda represented the other. Dramatizations of the national spirit and depictions of characters overcoming national crises appeared in large numbers on television. Already in the late 1960s, P'aldo kangsan (literally, "The Mountains and Rivers of the Eight Provinces," a proverbial reference to the southern half of the Korean Peninsula) had appeared in both films and television dramas, giving expression to the Cold War rivalry by reducing the territory of Korea to its southern half and then equating it to "the land of plenty." Through *P'aldo Son-in-Law* (1969), *P'aldo Maid* (1970), *P'aldo Daughter-in-Law* (1970), and *P'aldo Swordsman* (1970), movies and television dramas disseminated images of a cheerful and wholesome future for the southern half of the Korean Peninsula. Similarly, the genre of war dramas and action thrillers with an anticommunist message reinforced the government's agenda. Representing North Korean communists as belligerent and brutal and the North Korean ruling class as depraved and perverse, the genre married anticommunist ideology and prurient content in a formula that proved to be explosively popular. In the second half of the decade, government intervention in television programming became even more explicit with such measures as the Unified Guidelines for Programming (1976), Standards for Television Dramas (1977), and Measures to Refine Broadcasting Language (1977).

Koreanness According to Critical Intellectuals: The Sprouts of Capitalism Theory and the Theory of National Literature

As the government put in place a diverse array of cultural policies to promote national culture and national revitalization, the critical intellectual community, too, sought to synthesize Korean identity on its own terms. The late 1960s saw the rise of two influential theories that reoriented dominant discourses about Korea's development: the theory of "internal development" (*naejaejŏk kaebal*) within historical studies and the theory of "national literature" (*minjok munhak*) among literary critics.

In the field of historical studies, the theory of internal development was first proposed in 1967. It had been widely accepted until then that modernity in Korea arrived at the end of the nineteenth century, along with imperial aggression, but the internal development theory pushed back the beginning of Korea's modernity to the seventeenth century. It thus provided a critique of colonial historiography, which viewed Korean history in terms of stagnation, hidebound national character, heteronomy, and transplanted modernity. "Sprouts of capitalism" provided an alternative historical narrative and a basis for an autonomous national history.[43] The theory argued that sprouts of capitalism can be found in diversification among the peasantry and that the spread of independent handicraft industries in the late Chosŏn created new economic actors. In other words, the theory posited that autonomous social forces from below were capable of bringing about modernization in Korea. The Association for Korean Historical Studies, which spearheaded historical research in this vein, stated its mission as advancing the scientific nature of historical studies through positivistic methodology and locating Korean history within the universality of world history.[44]

Where might we look for the causes of this development? The most important factor was the intellectuals' understanding of recent history and the current state of affairs. For historians, the May 16 Coup of 1961, which installed Park Chung Hee's military regime, was a step back from the possibility of an autonomous historiography opened by the April 19 Revolution of 1960, when protests begun by students succeeded in unseating an authoritarian president. The view of the present as a state of retrogression became more acute with the subsequent formation of the Yusin system in 1972. But even if history was moving backward under Park, the past could still boast of a forward-moving historical development. By discovering such a history in the form of sprouts of capitalism, historians hoped to affirm the possibility of Korea's internal development and thereby part the thick pall of nihilism shrouding the nation.[45]

The theory of internal development exerted an influence on the field of Korean literature as well. The theory first gained visibility through the publication of Kim Hyŏn and Kim Yunsik's influential *History of Korean Literature* (*Han'guk munhaksa*, 1973), which located the first stirrings of modernity in Korean literature in King Yŏngjo's (r. 1724–76) and King Chŏngjo's (r. 1776–1800) era. The quarterly journal *Creation and Criticism* (*Ch'angjak kwa pip'yŏng*, hereafter *Ch'angbi*) then provided an important forum for the spread of this view, publishing several special issues on history that linked social and economic changes in the late Chosŏn period to the literary and artistic production of the Sirhak (Practical Learning) school.[46] For *Ch'angbi*, as we will see shortly, this represented a shift from its earlier position within the historical topography of progressive Korean journals concerning the subject of tradition. In the 1950s, that topography featured an opposition between the Oriental studies discourse and the Western liberal democratic position. Within this opposition, the journal *Sasanggye*, for example, rejected tradition and embraced the liberal-democratic project as the only way to escape from Japan and participate in the universality of world history, given the reorganization of the global order following World War II.[47] In the 1960s, the journals *Hanyang*, *Sanghwang*, and *Ch'ŏngmaek* debated how best to reappropriate Koreanness by means of tradition and how tradition might be employed to overcome national crises. Initially reserved about such attempts to recuperate tradition, *Ch'angbi* changed course toward the end of the 1960s and began to focus on the progressive nature of Sirhak's critique of feudalism. Just as the theory of internal development had located the sprouts of capitalism in seventeenth-century developments, *Ch'angbi* devoted its pages to combing through the thought of Sirhak philosophers such as Pak Chi-wŏn (1737–1805) for the sprouts of emancipatory modernity.

At the most immediate level, what accounted for the shift in *Ch'angbi's* position from the initial negation of literary tradition to active recuperation of Sirhak was the outlook of individual scholars such as Ku Chung-sŏ and Yŏm Mu-ung, who led the journal in the absence of Paik Nak-chung (Paek Nak-chŏng), its founder, who had left to study in the United States. But beyond that, the shift was also the outcome of intellectual solidarity that the editorial board of the journal forged with its historian counterparts, who advocated the internal development theory. Under the Yusin system, which it saw as a historical retrogression, *Ch'angbi* registered the work produced by historians in response to this system as a form of intellectual resistance. As much as *Ch'angbi's* survey of historical studies was guided by a sense of purpose, it was also a product of the state of political asphyxia at the time, which required a detour, a roundabout way to apprehend contemporary reality.[48]

But why was Sirhak the chosen vehicle for this detour? As the formation of the power elite around Park Chung Hee reached completion, a new species of intellectuals came into being for whom it was no longer possible to actualize their social selves except through writing. If the power elite banded together around the Park Chung Hee and became the ideologues of state-led modernization, the authority of critical intellectuals could only be attained through the critique of modernization.[49] Given this context, Sirhak helped mediate the prestige of critical intellectuals by providing an alternative genealogy for modernization, one that did not have to depend on wholesale denunciation of Korean traditions as backward and the subsequent resuscitation of selected nationalist icons. A school of thought identified as the native womb in which the seed of modern consciousness gestated in Korea, Sirhak was progressive and thus capable of reversing the previous notions of Korea's backward history. An interesting additional point to observe here is the similar place that the writer occupied in both Sirhak and the theory of national literature. Though historically progressive, Sirhak was in no way a literature of the people. Its scholars belonged to the learned class of literati and scholar-officials of the Chosŏn period. And yet, where it coincided with the internal development and national literature theories was in the progressiveness of the worldview of its practitioners. Proponents of the theory of national literature superimposed the role of the literati within Sirhak onto that of the critical intellectuals in the arena of national literature.[50]

Thus, in the literary field, the quest for Koreanness underwent a process of competitive construction surrounding the concept of national literature (*minjok munhak*). The mainstream writers of the literary establishment, with the support of the Korean Culture and Arts Foundation, sought to graft the state-led agenda of national revitalization directly onto literature. National literature in this regard was equated with works that extol the historical greatness of the Korean people, highlight the achievements of economic development and the Saemaul movement, and otherwise help make manifest the new "national character" prescribed by the Park regime.[51] Attempts to define national literature also led to a kind of traditionalism implied in the view of the Korean nation as a community of blood with little relation to Western modernity. Just as the Park regime had culled the Korean past for usable icons, the sources of national literature were to be located in premodern genres, including legends, myths, and verse (*kasa*), and distinct archetypes drawn from Korea's native traditions such as shamanism. In both respects, Kim Tong-ni (1913–95), a leading figure of the literary establishment whose best-known works of fiction included *The Portrait of a Shaman* (*Munyŏdo*) and *The Legend of Yellow Earth* (*Hwangt'ogi*), was singled out as the most representative writer of Korean national literature. In this manner, the conservative mainstream writers elevated *minjok* to an everlasting entity and a value of noble purity. To disparage Korea from an excessively Westernized vantage point even before Koreanness could be adequately defined on its own terms, they argued, was to lack national consciousness altogether.[52]

It was within this topography, where tradition was overdetermined by both the state and the pro-state literary establishment, that the two major literary quarterlies of the 1970s, *Literature and Intellect* (*Munhak kwa chisŏng*, hereafter *Munji*) and *Ch'angbi* positioned themselves. *Munji* was unequivocal in its criticism of national literature. Kim Hyŏn, the journal's editor in chief, opted to use the term *Han'guk munhak* rather than *minjok munhak* and heaped on the latter a pile of unflattering adjectives: right-wing, conservative, retro, and pro-enlightenment. The critique revealed the journal's full embrace of liberalism and its bias toward Western universality, a position from which it would be impossible to think through the question of Koreanness. *Munji*'s identity was a form of "resistance" against the fact that the discursive structures established by the immediate postwar generation were still exercising influence at a time when the possibility of a citizens' revolution suggested by the April 19 Revolution of 1960 had been closed off by the harsh reality of Yusin. It was also an attempt to redefine literature by reappropriating the sociopolitical meaning of April 19 and shift the bearer of that meaning from "citizens" (*simin*) to "individuals" (*kaein*). Put differently, by emphasizing the individuality of intellect and calling attention to the role of the intellectual, *Munji* reframed the basic social struggle as one between individuals endowed with a critical consciousness and the society that oppresses them. Such framing of the relationship between the intellectual and society, however, depoliticized literary interpretations of society by making the act of critique dependent on the given individual's self-awareness and acute sensibility.[53]

Ch'angbi, launched in 1966, also adopted a position critical of tradition in its early days. "We must first recognize," wrote Paik Nak-chung in the inaugural issue, "that there is absolutely no literary tradition that we have inherited as we would flesh and blood from our parents."[54] *Ch'angbi*'s point of departure was a sense of difference from the tradition of Korean literature. Such an orientation can be glimpsed, albeit vaguely, in the journal's high estimation of Kim Su-yŏng (1921–68) as a modernist poet and its early serialization of Arnold Hauser's *Social History of Art and Literature*, which espoused the new leftist tendencies of the Frankfurt school.[55] Yŏm Mu-ung, the editor of *Ch'angbi* in the early 1970s, recalled that, despite the fact that the journal did take some interest in national culture through its earlier special features on Sirhak, it was only after 1970 that *Ch'angbi* was able to shake off its pro-Western tendencies.[56] It was under the leadership of Yŏm Mu-ung as editor in chief that *Ch'angbi* began to criticize the limits of its own liberal orientation and to place greater importance on national subjectivity and national tradition, with the belief that "indigenousness" constituted the last foothold of the spirit of national resistance.

As summarized earlier, "national crises" constituted the government's justification for establishing the National Charter for Education, enforcing the use of government textbooks, implementing "education with nationality," and even adopting the Yusin system. A sense of crisis shaped the theories of internal development and national literature as well. Of course, we cannot simply equate the Koreanness of the national literature theory with the Koreanness of the "democracy Korean style" that the Park regime advocated. But the attempt to define *Koreanness* was itself rooted in the idea of overcoming the national crises of the present by utilizing the history of the past. For sure the Koreanness pursued here was not a single idea but two, appropriated and interpreted to different ends both at the time of their articulation and in the years that followed. However, the shared ideas that both the Park regime and critical intellectuals drew on in order to consolidate "what is Korean" as a response to a perceived crisis in the national community provide a key to understanding the decade of 1970s.

Traces of the Popular: Between Censorship and Deviation

The 1970s pitted two different attempts to politicize "what is Korean" against each other. On the one hand, there was the state's sponsorship of the rediscovery of all things Korean, accompanied by political suppression ranging from arbitrary censorship to surveillance and control. On the other, there was the national cultural movement led by students and intellectuals, who re-created traditional performance arts as a vehicle for dissidence. But the struggle for Koreanness in the 1970s reveals a degree of complexity that resists its simplification as a contest between the oppressive government and the resistant and critical intellectuals. In diverse realms of youth culture, popular music, melodramas, and so on, there existed "subconscious practices" that both overlapped and deviated from the kind of Koreanness that the government sought to impose. What deserves our closer attention is the ambiguity and fragmentation that pertain to the opposition between the dominant and the dominated in popular culture. The dominated are not unilaterally subordinated to the ruling class's desire for modernization but exist heterogeneously within cracks and between boundaries. From this perspective, the popular culture of the times cannot be reduced to the self-identity of terms such as *censorship, oppression, subordination,* and *domination.* Poised between subversion and decadence, and often crossing the boundary between the two, popular culture of the period richly reveals the numerous fissures in the seemingly uniform surface of Yusin rule.[57]

It should also be noted that in the 1970s, cultural policies highlighting Koreanness or emphasizing the overcoming of national crises penetrated the everyday lives of the people and even entered the rhythm of their bodies. At such a time, as the Park Chung Hee government was fully aware, the consumption of popular culture could become an expression of individual desires, identities, and tastes distinct from the prescriptions of the nation. Acts of consumption could also lead to contemplations of the gloomy reality under the Yusin Constitution. Indulging in the familiar sensationalism of "hostess movies," so-called on account of the prostitutes and otherwise "fallen women" who served as the genre's heroines, the self-consciously Western proclivities of youth culture, and various styles of deviation from social norms, individuals were able to postpone, albeit temporarily, the encroachment of the world as it was hierarchically ordered by the dominant culture. However, as Yu Sŏn-yŏng has argued, the line between domination and deviation was blurry at best.[58] Popular culture of the Yusin era pulled people into the magnetic field of its cultural politics in ways that were both ambivalent and fragmented.

We might call this phenomenon "traces of popular culture." Here what I mean by "traces" is the ways in which people found themselves, in the process of consuming youth culture, hostess melodramas, and other forms of popular culture, subconsciously at "odds" with the government protocol of ethics, norms, and cultures designed to produce new national character types, which would then serve as the agents of national revival.[59] What deserves our attention here is the fact that, while both the government and critical intellectuals delivered solemnly rigid and normative judgments against popular culture, people consumed popular culture in different ways within their individual spheres and tried to construct a sense of their unique identity and desires through these actions. Youth culture and hostess melodramas (as well as their audiences) constitute such "traces." Neither conformed to the Korean national character desired by the state. The college students who might have accepted docilely the government's claim that democratization had to be postponed for the sake of economic development fell out of line with the government's standardized view of the desirable Korean character when it came to questions of style. Female factory workers as well, though hailed as "industrial warriors," did not agree with the government's pronouncement that the melo-dramatic films they enjoyed were vulgar and hardly fit for buttressing their moral fiber as industrial warriors. (These movies, after all, provided an outlet for their suppressed and unfulfilled desire to be like college girls.) Though unavowed, the Koreanness pursued by the government and the critical elites bore innumerable traces of these nameless masses.

Traces of Youth Culture

One of the most interesting debates concerning popular culture in South Korea in the 1970s concerned the so-called youth culture (*chŏngnyŏn munhwa*). The arguments in this debate revealed the heteromorphic ho-mogeneity between the Park regime and the dissident college students. A full-scale debate on the topic of youth culture was sparked by the 1974 publication of Ch'oe In-ho's novel *The Hometown of the Stars* (*Pyŏldŭl ŭi kohyang*). Along with Ch'oe In-ho, the folk singers Yi Chang-hŭi, Yang Hŭi-ŭn, and Kim Min-gi and the professional *paduk* player Sŏ Pong-su, an autodidact who challenged the conservative orthodoxy of the *paduk* world, rose to stardom as the "youthful idols of the new era" and represen-tatives of the decade's youth culture. The debate was also intensified by the popularity of the so-called Pyŏng-t'ae and Yŏng-ja style, named for the protagonists of Ha Kil-jong's 1975 film *March of Fools* (*Pabodŭl ŭi haengjin*), which unwittingly muddled the line between male and female in a culture that insisted on clear gender roles, and episodes of streaking that took place around the country in 1974 that shocked many with the sight of na-ked bodies running through a public place.[60]

The youth culture at the time belonged to the so-called postwar baby boom, or Hangŭl Generation, born between 1954 and 1961. In contrast to their parents, who had grown up under Japanese colonial rule, this gen-eration had received a Korean-language education. They had benefited from rapid economic growth and increases in per capita income and en-tered their twenties with the ability to consume a far greater range of pop-ular culture than the previous generation had. In the 1970s, the middle-and even low-income classes became capable of a certain level of cultural consumption. Furthermore, the construction of a host of new universities in the early 1970s in Seoul brought a large number of college students to the city. Despite the dramatic increase in their numbers, however, college students still constituted a small minority within the general population; they were recognized by themselves and others as a privileged class.[61]

These college students indulged in the hippie culture, sported mini-skirts and long hair, frequented go-go dance clubs and music listening halls, and listened to folk music. In March 1974, they shocked the nation by carrying out streaking events in succession in Ch'ungmu, Yongsan, P'aju, and Yangju and rattling the society, which treated nudity and even the use of the body to express emotions as taboo. On the surface, streaking was "a form of self-expression," but it was also deeply imitative of the West.[62] American influence was ubiquitous, in fact, among college youths. The blue jeans they wore, the songs they enjoyed, the guitar techniques they learned—in all these and more, they looked to the United States and the West as a model. In this regard, they were "children of the city" already Westernized. In imitating the style of Western youths, they found a temporary escape from the constraints of a state and society that emphasized their duty toward national revival even in an era of mass production and consumption. They discovered a way to encode their status and co-own it. As elites and members of a group bound by a shared cultural mode, they possessed a sense of entitlement.[63]

Variously labeled an anticulture, subculture, and decadent culture, youth culture generated many arguments both pro and con; what remains indisputable is the fact that, at least as of 1974, youth culture was emergent, not dominant. The Park regime's response was to step up censorship. In 1974 the government officially announced that it would support the transmission of national culture while prohibiting and/or controlling those programs or media with the potential to disturb the social order and suppressing the indiscriminate importation of foreign culture. These declarations were reinforced by the ban in 1975 of songs deemed harmful to public morality. The Koreanization of sports terms followed in 1976. The process branded consumers of Western/American culture as unethical "criminals" who corrupted the social order and posed a threat to the wholesome national spirit. In other words, they were seen as anti-Korean and thus deficient in the proper attitude necessary for national restoration.

Interestingly, the producers of (dissident) college culture also denounced youth culture as "radish kim-chi coated with butter," a practice lacking all critical spirit and merely imitative of lowbrow Western culture and thus estranged from any sense of natural culture. What catches our attention here is the degree to which the logic employed by these dissident students in polemicizing youth culture mirrors the government's. According to these producers of college culture, youth culture was lacking a nationality. College culture could gain legitimacy only by participating in the restructuring of traditional culture and invigorating national culture.[64] In "Fashion or Rebellion?" a debate published in the July 1974 issue of *Sin tonga*, No Chae-bong argued that the youth culture's roots in nightclubs and similar venues might make it a trendy form of entertainment, but since the music favored in such venues was essentially escapist and palliative, popularizing it would ultimately help prolong the rule of the dictatorial regime.[65] The hostility of student dissidents toward youth culture was understandable to an extent in the context of the National Democratic Federation of Youths and Students (Minchŏng Hangnyŏn, or NFDYS) incident and the promulgation of Emergency Decree No. 4 in 1974.[66] At such an oppressive time, dissident students looked to aspects of Korean tradition, especially the vitality and humor of *minjung* nationalism and oral literature, as their intellectual inspiration.[67] Their interest in tradition was expressed as a movement for cultural struggle and the rejection of commercialized popular culture, as well as the traditional culture regulated by the government. It took further shape as a movement for the revival of mask dance and theater in the early and mid-1970s in various universities. These student groups spearheaded a *madanggŭk* movement, adapting traditional Korean performance arts to a theater of resistance relevant in contemporary times.

Equated with Western culture, which was in turn condemned as decadent and vulgar, youth culture was denounced by the government and dissident circles alike; and its negative image owed in large part to its association with the American GI culture in Korea. America was seen as an economic powerhouse, on the one hand, but on the other a producer of vulgar culture. The inevitable need for modernization had to be acknowledged, but it was also vital that Korea guard itself against the vulgar popular culture flowing in from America—the sound of chewing gum reverberating everywhere on the streets and buses and in theaters and cafes.[68] Without a doubt, youth culture aspired to be Western in style and its pattern of consumption. As earlier noted, this was made possible by the elevated levels of consumption, increased access to popular media, and the expansion of popular culture—such as the direct importation and broadcast of foreign dramas and programs and the proliferation of foreign monthly magazines and publications—that accompanied modernization.[69]

The misalignment between the dominant culture and youth/popular culture arose from the fact that the Korean character type idealized by the government did not fit the lifestyle to which youths aspired. Those who felt a sense of kinship with Western youth culture, its styles, and its manner of conduct nurtured a desire to escape the gloom and sorrow of Korean society, where armored vehicles and riot police patrolled college campuses, armed soldiers invaded libraries, cops carrying hair trimmers scoured the streets, and students were required to participate in military drills and join the Student National Defense Corps.[70] "Whale Hunting" (Korae sanyang), a song by the popular folksinger Song Ch'angsik, captured the despair and sorrow of the times: "Try as I might, drinking, singing, dancing / I feel nothing but sadness in my heart / Try as I might, looking around to find something to do / I see nothing but backs turned against me." The negative sentiments expressed in this song had no place in the spiritual reform program championed by the state that would generate the Korean national character.

Branding youth and popular culture as decadent, prurient, and vulgar only increased their popularity. In response to the criticism of "t'ong-pŭlsaeng" (short for "acoustic guitar, blue jeans, and draft beer") as lowbrow culture, the writer Ch'oe In-ho argued that the diminishing gap between highbrow and lowbrow culture was in fact one notable characteristic of the youth culture. This did not mean, however, that the youth culture was broadly inclusive. College students in the cities excluded from their youth culture urban laborers who belonged to the same age group but came from very different socioeconomic backgrounds. The college badges they wore and their taste for folk songs as opposed to "trot" music underscored the difference between the two groups.[71] While college students tended to frequent foreign movies newly released in theaters, urban laborers who settled on the periphery of Seoul starting in the 1960s constituted the main audience for Korean movies. Because of the low admission price, these laborers preferred re-release theaters where they could watch two movies at a time, and these theaters in turn became their main cultural space.[72] Re-release theaters were perceived as hotbeds of crime and low-class decadent culture. First-and second-run theaters were seen as distinct spaces frequented by different classes of audience.

In the end, both youth culture, branded as decadent, and the dissident national culture of student resistance, suppressed for being subversive, were indifferent to each another. Within the fissures of the dominant culture, which promoted an efficient and productive Korean national character, youth culture became a new emergent culture. While it would be unfair to evaluate this culture, which arose from the desire of a particular group of youths to use popular culture to differentiate themselves from other groups of young people, in political or ethnonational terms, it would be equally mistaken to deny the political impact of the culture's repeated association with deviance during the Yusin era. As the public watched all aspects of this youth culture—the songs, the fashion, the spaces where they could express their desires—branded time and again decadent, the standards by which "decadence" was determined themselves came into question. The unintended effect may in fact have been the growth of skepticism.[73]

Misaligned Trajectories: Low-Class Women, Melodrama Films, and National Restoration

The 1970s, as noted earlier, is widely considered a decade of low-quality movies. The statement begs the question of what constitutes "low-quality."[74] Setting aside the question for the moment, we should also note that, despite the much-criticized shoddiness of the genre, melodramas consistently topped the box office charts during the decade. In particular, the hostess melodramas achieved commercial success year after year, striking a chord with the urban lower-class audiences that frequented second-run theaters.[75]

Hostess melodramas featured "hostesses," generally a euphemism for prostitutes and other women of pleasure. Straying from the typical plot of the "family melodrama," which featured a woman's struggle and sacrifice to preserve her family, emphasized at the time as the basic unit of the nation, the genre's depiction of the strength of women who successfully broke away from the family was itself an aesthetic criticism directed at the family-centered ideology and the contradictions inherent in the family system. At the same time, because the hostesses onscreen frequently hailed from lower-class backgrounds and suffered both material hardship and disappointments in love, they enabled identification on the part of female audiences.[76]

Hostess melodramas thus represented the reality of the lower class. But the genre also accommodated the nationalist agenda by filling the screen with images of pure women—pure of heart if not of body—who saved men in crisis and restored their threatened manhood. For example, the low-class male protagonist of *Yŏng-ja's Heyday* identifies a low-class woman, a prostitute in fact, as a figure of compensation for his threatened masculinity. Someone against whom he can express his gender superiority, she helps him manage the sense of inferiority he feels on account of his class and provides him with endless comfort.[77] Yet another way in which hostess melodramas evinced an affinity with the ruling ideology of the time concerned how the characters handled adversity. Embedded even in the portrayal of women's suffering in hostess movies was a strong, ends-oriented stance that valorized the will to overcome adversity as ethical in and of itself. Such a narrative forged a homological relationship with the narrative of overcoming national crises that the Park regime so heavily emphasized, as we have seen time and again in this chapter. And therein lies the complexity of the 1970s' popular culture: the hostess films, produced by directors who were influenced by youth culture, manifested antiauthorial and antisystemic characteristics, but while they opposed forms of political oppression such as censorship, they also collaborated with other dominant values upheld by the system, including patriarchy and the restoration of masculinity.[78]

Given the limitations of the genre, how did it command such explosive popularity among urban lower-class audiences? We can identify several factors. First, the hostess melodrama movies produced in the 1970s took an indirect approach to depicting the contemporary reality. Directors of the Yŏngsang sidae (Age of Screen) coterie, including Ha Kil-jong, Yi Chang-ho, and Kim Ho-sŏn, were all avid consumers of youth culture and utilized filmmaking conventions seen in movies like *The Graduate* (dir. Michael Nichols, 1967) in their depictions of youthful vitality, innocence of the female protagonist and her loss of virginity, and scenes set in a red light district. At the same time, they incorporated a quintessential feature of melodrama—the sexual objectification of women. As portrayed by the actress Yŏm Pok-sun, Yŏng-ja in *Yŏng-ja's Heyday* embodies the visual sexual codes associated with a dumb bimbo in her looks. However, the film highlights the woman's independent subjectivity even while objectifying her body. Another cinematic Yŏng-ja, the heroine of *A March of Fools*, is described in following terms by Song Ŭn-yŏng: "Dressed in a raggedy blouse that nevertheless hugs her backside tightly, she wears her long straight hair down, parted in the middle. She is always seen in sneakers with the back folded down. . . . The long straight hair represents women's liberation and freedom from artificial ornamentation, and the tight jeans reveal her as a women of activity, unfettered by the femininity of skirts."[79] Yŏng-ja's style is marked by a self-conscious misalignment with the normative Koreanness that the dominant culture, either of the state or of the dissident elite, sought to imprint on the collective unconscious.

Against the extreme and indiscriminate suppression of popular culture carried out during the Park Chung Hee era, college students, female factory workers, and the urban lower class continued to consume popular and youth culture. With that act, they expressed their subconscious desire to free themselves from the solemnity of values, norms, and ethics forced on them in the name of the new national character, the revival of national culture, and glorification of "all things Korean," which depended on censorship and the expulsion of "all things decadent" (read "foreign").[80]

Conclusion

Starting in the late 1960s, a concern with "what is Korean" spread into all areas of cultural policy and popular culture as well. Among intellectuals, the issue was at the heart of many heated discussions: the theory of internal development and the call for education with nationality in the field of history, the problem of locating a national identity to inherit in face of a severed tradition in Korean literature and history, and the articulation of a national literature as a counterhegmonic discourse.

The trend deepened as the state sought to mobilize the structures of feeling by regimenting and disciplining how it would approach the significantly expanded arena of culture. The narration of Korean history as a history of overcoming national crises, adoption of government textbooks, excavation of cultural properties, consecration of historical sites for purposes of both commemoration and education, institution of ceremonies at these sites, monumentalization and memorabilization of national heroes, and the production of national policy films and television dramas were some of the salient initiatives. The invention of Koreanness took place in the late 1960s and early 1970s as a measure intended to stabilize the regime under a perception of crisis by securing the emotional and sentimental consent of the masses. But the bombardment of Koreanness and nationalism that was intended to draw out a sense of emotional rootedness and political belongingness brought about everyday practices of deviation, which in turn registered as "traces" in the lives of the people. The traces denote instances of unintended and even subconscious disjointedness that occurred among the ethics, norms, and culture of the new Korean national character espoused by the government as an agent of national revival and the consumption and practice of youth and popular culture such as hostess melodramas by the public. In this essay, we were able to discover those traces through youth culture and hostess films. The relationship between the dominant and the dominated in the

1970s was not a simple one of dichotomy defined only by control and subordination at the political level. The dominated were not unilaterally subordinated to the hegemonic but continued to repeat a cycle of subordination and escape, subversion, decadence, and deviation, taking advantage of the heterogeneity that clung to those fissures between the dominant and the dominated.

Youth and popular culture maintained an uneasy coexistence with the Koreanness created by the dominant culture, the literature, history, and art defined and enforced as essentially Korean by the government. We can find in the popular cultures of the Yusin era no intention or deliberate design to dismantle the hegemonic culture, and we even see a curious kind of compliance with or endorsement of the government-espoused values other than political oppression and censorship. At the same time, though unintended, it left behind traces of Westernization and individualism that maintain tension with the perceived Koreanness. In this regard, attempting to answer the question "Who represents the true national subject?" will not constitute a productive discussion concerning the daily lives and culture of the masses during the Yusin period. A more meaningful task would be to examine the rise, coexistence, and extinction of various elements—Korean/Western, spiritual/materialistic, decadent/lewd—under the condition of persecution, censorship, and outright prohibition.

During the Park Chung Hee era, the West was synonymous with modernization but also with decadence, moral corruption, and individualism and as such something to be criticized and eliminated. Censorship and control in the 1970s, carried out in an arbitrary and brutal fashion, demanded that popular desires and feelings be replaced with what is Korean and national even in the domains of youth culture, hostess movies, and TV dramas. The invention of Koreanness, a concerted attempt by the Park Chung Hee regime to ride out political crises and achieve normalcy by requiring emotional bonding and political attachment to the nation and the state was only half successful. People consumed popular culture in their own ways and walks of life, turning to it as a resource for constituting identity and expressing desires against the grain of the government's solemn, ethical, and normative dictation of Koreanness. Various lives—of female factory workers, the urban poor, maids, teenagers—continued to exist beyond the pale of norms prescribed as part of the national character. In much the same way, the recent emergence of a new version of Koreanness, which emphasizes anew national identity, national pride, national excellence, and tradition, along with the debates and policies it has occasioned, may be presenting to us a symptom of a "new internal crisis."[81]

NOTES

1. *Hangukchŏk in kŏt* is translated variously in this essay as "what is Korean," "(all) things Korean," "Koreanness," and "Korean essence." (Abridged and translated by AL-TEA from Kim Wŏn, " 'Hangukchŏk in kŏt' ŭi chŏnyu rŭl tullŏssan kyŏngjaeng," *Sahoe wa yŏksa* 93 (2012): 185–235.)

2. *Minjok*, which combines the graphs for "people" and "tribe," is a term that renders the nation as a community of blood. For this reason, the term is sometimes rendered as "ethnonation," although it is translated simply as "nation" here for the sake of readability. (Trans.)

3. Kim Chu-hyŏn, "1960-yŏndae Han'gukchŏk in kŏt," 380.

4. Hwang, "Park Chŏng-hŭi ch'eje ŭi chibae tamnon."

5. *Second Economy* is a term that Park Chung Hee began to use in 1968 to refer to the "spiritual dimension" of economic development, and to the proper philosophy and attitudes that the Korean people must adopt in order to pursue modernization of the homeland. If *First Economy* focused on the external factors of "production, export, and construction," *Second Economy* would focus on the internal. Promulgated also in 1968, the National Charter of Education was a pledge emphasizing the ideology of patriotism and anticommunism that all schoolchildren were required to memorize. It began with the famous line "Unto this land we were born with the historical mission of national revitalization *(chunghŭng)*." The mandatory memorization of the pledge was abolished in 1994. See Pak T'ae-gyun, "1960-yŏndae chungban anbo wigi wa che 2 kyŏngjeron," *Yŏksa pip'yŏng* 72 (2005): 265–69. (Trans.)

6. Kim Won, "1960-yŏndae naengjŏn ŭi si'gan kwa tŭit'ŭllin chuch'e."

7. Public sentiments in South Korea were very much stacked against what was seen as the humiliating terms of the Normalization Treaty with Korea's former colonizer. Park Chung Hee's regime pushed it through anyway and suppressed antinormalization protests with force. (Trans.)

8. Critical intellectuals of the mid- to late 1960s frequently voiced their concerns about the possibility of Korea's recolonization due to Japan's economic invasion. See Ri Yŏng-hŭi and Im Hŏn-yŏng, *Taehwa*, 327–32.

9. See Kim Chu-hyŏn, "1960-yŏndae Han'gukchŏk in kŏt," 396.

10. See the "Introduction" for a more detailed discussion of the major historical events of the mid- to late 1960s. (Trans.)

11. Hwang, "Pak Chŏng-hŭi ch'eje ŭi chibae tamnon," 137.

12. *Chunghŭng* (translated variously as "reconstruction," "restoration," and "revival" in the original essay [trans.]) suggests the act of resurrecting and reactivating what has been lost. It can mean "to restore the original form" but also "to reinvent and reformulate the past according to the needs of the present."

13. Moon, "Begetting the Nation," 36.

14. In the mobilization of emotions and the politics of pathos, "emotions" signify the basis of passionate feelings that can seal off logical and rational thoughts capable of casting doubt on the legitimacy of the ruling system.

15. Kim Chu-hyŏn, "1960-yŏndae Han'gukchŏk in kŏt," 392.

16. Yu, "Tongwŏn ch'eje ŭi kwaminjokhwa p'ŭrojekt'ŭ," 3–4; Yun, "Naengjŏn'gi kungminhwa p'ŭrojekt'ŭ," 244.

17. Yun, "Naengjŏn'gi kungminhwa p'ŭrojekt'ŭ," 225–27.

18. Kim Chu-hyŏn, "1960-yŏndae Han'gukchŏk in kŏt," 380.

19. As Partha Chatterjee has argued, nationalists under the experience of colonial modernity emphasized the spiritual domain as that which remained intact despite their defeat and subordination in the material realm. This emphasis was a means of maintaining an independent national identity while selectively incorporating aspects of Western modernity. See Chatterjee, *The Nation and Its Fragments*.

20. See Ŭn, "Pak Chŏng-hŭi sidae sŏng'yŏkhwa saŏp."

21. Pak Chŏng-hŭi, *Minjok chunghŭng ŭi kil*.

22. Hwang, "Pak Chŏng-hŭi ch'eje ŭi chibae tamnon," 143.

23. O, "1960–70-yŏndae ŭi munhwa chŏngch'aek," 122–23.

24. The Cultural Heritage Protection Law identified tangible and intangible cultural properties, geographic spaces, and nature, including flora and fauna, as the nation's cultural heritage and provided for state intervention to preserve and manage them. In other words, the law applied the concept of public property to cultural heritage and restricted the rights of private property. See O, "1960–70-yŏndae ŭi munhwa chŏngch'aek," 125; and Munhwa kongbobu, *Munhwa Kongbo 30 nyŏn*.

25. Munhwa kongbobu, *Hoguk sŏnhyŏn ŭi yujŏk*; Munhwajae Kwalliguk, *Uri nara ŭi munhwajae*.

26. Afforestation was at the core of Park Chung Hee's early landscaping projects. Park saw deforested mountains as a sign of poverty and reforestation as a standard by which Korea's development could be judged, and he even went so far as to declare, immediately after visiting Germany in 1964, that he would not set foot in Europe again until the Korean mountains had turned green once again. Two or three times a month Park gave the secretaries at the Ministry of Construction/Landscaping detailed and specific orders concerning the development of hillocks, lumbering methods, and landscaping along highways. In particular, he spared no effort and passion in furthering the Hyŏnch'ungsa consecration project. It was during this time that the word *chogyŏng* (landscaping) began to be used officially. The Department of Landscaping at Seoul National University's Graduate School of Environment was established in 1973 by a special order of Park Chung Hee, in part motivated by his interest in landslides and aesthetic restoration of the mountains bisected by new highway construction or damaged in the process of restoring historical sites commemorating national crises overcome such as Hyŏnch'ung-sa. As a result, Park-style construction and landscaping projects, ordered on site by Park himself, could be found all over the country. Landscaping at the time was intimately tied to economic development and the consecration policies. See Pae, "Pak Chŏng-hŭi ŭi chogyŏnggwan," 15–17.

27. Chŏng Ho-gi, "Park Chung Hee sidae ŭi 'tongsang kŏllip undong' kwa aeguk chuŭi."

28. Ŭn, "Pak Chŏng-hŭi sidae sŏng'yŏkhwa saŏp."

29. Yi Kwang-su, the proverbial "father of modern Korean literature" and author of

the first modern Korean novel, began his public life as the drafter of the February 8, 1919, Declaration of Independence and ended it in ignominy as one of the most famous and controversial of Korea's pro-Japanese collaborators. Yi Kwang-su serialized a biography of Yi Sun-sin in *Tong-a ilbo* from 1931 to 1932, which effectively rewrote the history of the 1592 Japanese invasion from one of international struggle to one of internal strife by highlighting factionalism as an inherent Korean trait.

30. Ŭn, "Pak Chŏng-hŭi sidae sŏng'yŏkhwa saŏp," 254–55, 262; Pak Kye-ri, "Ch'ungmugong tongsang kwa kukka ideollogi," 169.

31. O, "1960–70-yŏndae ŭi munhwa chŏngch'aek," 134.

32. Yi Sang-nok, "1960–70-yŏndae pip'anjŏk chisigindŭl ŭi kŭndaehwa insik," 339.

33. Ibid., 339, 352.

34. O, "1960–70-yŏndae ŭi munhwa chŏngch'aek," 142.

35. Yu, "Tongwŏn ch'eje ŭi kwaminjokhwa p'ŭrojekt'ŭ," 26.

36. The "Eighteen Points for the Selection of Exemplary Movies" were (1) content embodying October Yusin; (2) content that serves to establish an independent national spirit and stimulate patriotism and love of *minjok; (*3) content that serves to nurture a progressive national mind-set filled with motivation and faith; (4) content that encourages active participation in the Saemaul movement; (5) content that emphasizes cooperation and unity and takes as its subject matter the "human evergreens" who possess both wisdom and motivation; (6) content that gives farmers hope and faith and enables them to participate in the development of local, indigenous culture; (7) content that portrays people who are thrifty, earnest, and industrious; (8) content that focuses on industrial warriors, the workers who devote themselves to modernization of the fatherland; (9) content that treats the subject of the history of overcoming national crises; (10) content that depicts national consensus and unity as the road to overcoming national crises; (11) content that calls for the awakening of the masses in light of national crises; (12) content that treats the subject of increasing exports; (13) content that accentuates the image of civil servants devoted to the cause of the nation and the people; (14) content that contributes to the purification of people's emotional state and established social morals and good manners; (15) content that promotes a cheerful life through wholesome entertainment; (16) content that fosters love of cultural assets; (17) content that exalts national arts and a unique national culture; and (18) content that elevates pure art. See Pak Sŭng-hyŏn, "Taejung maech'e ŭi chŏngch'ijŏk kijehwa," 49–55.

37. Pak Yŏng-u, Kim Ŭn-ha, and Yi Tae-yŏn, "Kukka chaegŏn ŭi sidae."

38. Yu, "Tongwŏn ch'eje ŭi kwaminjokhwa p'ŭrojekt'ŭ," 10.

39. Yi Kil-sŏng, et al. *1970-yŏndae Seoul ŭi kŭkchang sanŏp*, 49.

40. The introduction of television broadcasting was advertised as a Christmas present from the revolutionary government to the people, as well as a shining achievement of its cultural policies.

41. Song, Ŭn-yŏng, "1960–70-yŏndae Han'guk ŭi taejung saehoehwa," 196–99.

42. O, "1960–70-yŏndae ŭi munhwa chŏngch'aek," 144.

43. For an English-language overview of the sprouts of capitalism theory, see Gi-Wook Shin, "Neither 'Sprouts' nor 'Offspring: The Agrarian Roots of Korean Capital-

ism,'" in *Transformations in Twentieth Century Korea*, ed. Yun-shik Chang and Steven Hugh Lee (New York: Routledge, 2006), 33–63. (Trans.)

44. Yi Kyŏng-nan, "1950–70-yŏndae yŏksahakkye yŏksa yŏn'gu," 357–58, 360.

45. Lee, "Time of Capital, Time of a Nation."

46. Yi Kyŏng-nan, "1950–70-yŏndae yŏksahakkye yŏksa yŏn'gu," 374.

47. Kim Chu-hyŏn, "1960-yŏndae 'Han'gukchŏk in kŏt," 381.

48. Lee, "Time of Capital, Time of a Nation," 84, 100.

49. Ibid.

50. Kim Chu-hyŏn, "Sirhak suyong," 335–36.

51. O, "1960–70-yŏndae ŭi munhwa chŏngch'aek," 136.

52. Chŏn, "1960–70-yŏndae munhak pip'yŏng tamnon."

53. Yi Hyŏn-sŏk, "419 hyŏngmyŏng kwa 6onyŏndae mal munhak tamnon," 230–31.

54. Paik, "Saeroun ch'angjak kwa pip'yŏng ŭi chase."

55. Paik Nak-chung touted Kim Su-yŏng at the time as the writer whose works confirmed the value of civic literature and provided outstanding poetic visualizations of the criticism of and resistance to the reality that spurred the transformation into petit bourgeois. See Yi Hyŏn-sŏk, "419 hyŏngmyŏng kwa 6onyŏndae mal munhak tamnon," 235.

56. Kang Chin-ho, *Chŭngŏn ŭrosŏŭi munhaksa*, 296, 419.

57. Kim Han Sang, "Pak Chŏng-hŭi chŏnggwŏn'gi kajok sŏsa."

58. Yu, "Tongwŏn ch'eje ŭi kwaminjokhwa p'ŭrojekt'ŭ," 43.

59. Song Ŭn-yŏng, "Taejung munhwa hyŏnsang," 192.

60. Chu, "1970-yŏndae chŏngnyŏn munhwa," 87–88.

61. Yi Hye-rim, "1970-yŏndae chŏngnyŏn munhwa," 18; No Chi-sŭng, "'Yŏng-ja ŭi chŏnsŏng sidae,'" 184.

62. Chu, "1970-yŏndae chŏngnyŏn munhwa."

63. Yi Hye-rim, "1970-yŏndae chŏngnyŏn munhwa"; Yi Yŏng-mi, *Kwanghwamun yŏn'ga*, 157–58.

64. Later, in a 1976 colloquium titled 10 Years, they once again inveighed against fiction writers—writers of popular fiction like Ch'oe In-ho in particular—who did not place themselves within the framework of national and mass consciousness, claiming that vulgar consumerism and commercialism were rampant, with literature serving as their fawning accomplice, and that they even stimulated authoritarianism.

65. Chu, "1970-yŏndae chŏngnyŏn munhwa," 90; Sin Hyŏn-jun, "Yi Chang-hŭi wa 1970-yŏndae," 65; No Chae-bong, "Chwadam—yuhaeng inya panhang inya."

66. Emergency Decree No. 4 made it illegal to join the NFDYS. According to Namhee Lee, "A total of 1024 university students, religious leaders, politicians, writers, and academics were implicated in the NFDYS incident, and seven received death sentences. NFDYS was not an organization based on any set of interests or principles nor was it a Leninist vanguard organization; it was essentially a mobilization of all relationships forged through ties of personal, regional, school, and university circles." Namhee Lee, *The Making of Minjung: Democracy and the Politics of Representation in South Korea* (Ithaca, NY: Cornell University Press, 2007), 170. (Trans.)

67. Here, satire and comedy were not merely seen as literary methods to inherit but

as the very essence of narrative art, and they regarded the period marked by the development of satirical fiction as the period when transmission of values and social relations became radicalized and considered the works that restored oral tradition such as Kim Chi-ha's ballad "Five Bandits" and Pak T'ae-sun's "Collaborative Work on Oech'on District"—as representative works from this period. See Sin Hyŏn-jun, "Yi Chang-hŭi wa 1970-yŏndae"; Kim Chu-hyŏn, "1960-yŏndae 'Han'gukchŏk in kŏt," 350.

68. Kim Chu-hyŏn, "1960-yŏndae 'Han'gukchŏk in kŏt," 402.

69. Yi Hye-rim, "1970-yŏndae chŏngnyŏn munhwa," 24.

70. Yi Yŏng-mi, *Kwanghwamun yŏn'ga,* 183.

71. Yi Sang-nok, "1960–70-yŏndae pip'anjŏk chisigindŭl ŭi kŭndaehwa insik," 362; Song Ŭn-yŏng, "1960–70-yŏndae Han'guk ŭi taejung saehoehwa," 433, 440. The attitude toward TV and magazines exhibited a similar tendency. The harmful effects of TV viewing were blamed on the fact that its main viewership consisted of housewives, maids, and members of the lower class; in the same way, the sensationalism found in magazines was blamed on lower-class women and the uneducated and poor, who, it was asserted, constituted the main body of the readership. These discussions were a reaction to the ethical and moral crises accompanying the expansion of popular culture. In reality, middle-class men were the main consumers of pop culture, but instead of sharing the responsibility they dodged and hid it by transferring the blame to the urban lower class and women workers. A similar trend can also be found in the attempt to blame housemaids and housekeepers for the instability of the middle-class family. See Kim Won, *Yŏgong 1970,* chap. 2.

72. No Chi-sŭng, "'Yŏng-ja ŭi chŏnsŏng sidae,'" 185; Yi Kil-sŏng et al., *1970-yŏndae Seoul ŭi kŭkchang sanŏp,* 86–89.

73. Yi Hye-rim, "1970-yŏndae chŏngnyŏn munhwa," 35; Yu, "Tongwŏn ch'eje ŭi kwaminjokhwa p'ŭrojekt'ŭ," 44.

74. The 1970s is often considered a depressed period for Korean movies, but this deserves a closer look. "Depressed" was an evaluation based on first-release movie theaters; re-release theaters, in fact, showed the opposite, reaching their highest box office sales between 1972 and 1974. Urban planning and redevelopment of city centers led to satellization and population increase in the outer regions of Seoul. This in turn led to an increase in the number of re-release theaters on the periphery of the city, reflecting the expanding audience base in those areas.

75. The most popular films included *Separation* (1974, 140,000 viewers), *The Hometown of the Stars* (1974, 460,000), *Yŏng-ja's Heyday* (1975, 390,000), *Streets Where Only Women Live* (1976, 87,000), *Susanna My Love* (1976, 170,000), *The Winter Woman* (1977, 580,000), *The Woman I Abandoned* (1978, 370,000), and *The Hometown of the Stars, the Sequel* (1979, 300,000). See Chu, "1975-yŏn chŏnhu Han'guk tangdae munhwa," 13; Yu, "Tongwŏn ch'eje ŭi kwaminjokhwa p'ŭrojekt'ŭ," 13.

76. Yi Ho-gŏl, "1970-yŏndae Han'guk yŏnghwa"; No Chi-sŭng, "'Yŏng-ja ŭi chŏnsŏng sidae,'" 193.

77. No Chi-sŭng, "'Yŏng-ja ŭi chŏnsŏng sidae,'" 189.

78. Not all melodramas espoused patriarchal values. Kim Su-hyŏn's melodramas, for

example, often started with a tragedy in a woman's life, but instead of leading to rein-
forcement of family values through reconciliation, they often highlighted a fractured
family structure with no room for forgiveness, which was not permitted under patriarchy. See "Pak Chŏng-hŭi chŏnggwŏn'gi kajok sŏsa ŭi kunyŏl kwa chŏhang," 283 (Kim
Han Sang 2009).
79. Song Ŭn-yŏng, "1960–70-yŏndae Han'guk ŭi taejung saehoehwa," 430.
80. Ibid., 440.
81. See O, "1960–70-yŏndae ŭi munhwa chŏngch'aek," 145–46.

BIBLIOGRAPHY

Ch'a Hye-yŏng. "Sŏngjang sosŏl kwa palchŏn ideollogi." *Sanghŏ hakpo* 12 (February
2004): 129–63.

Chang Mun-sŏk. "Sŏp'yŏng: P'asijŭm ŭi ch'oesoch'i wa ch'oedaech'i sai esŏ Robŏt'ŭ
P'aeksŭt'ŏn, P'asijŭm: Yŏlchŏng kwa kwangki ŭi chŏngch'i hyŏngmyŏng."
Sŏyangsaron 84 (2005): 331–41.

Chang Yŏng-min. "Pak Chŏng-hŭi chŏnggwŏn ŭi kuksa kyoyuk kanghwa chŏngch'aek e
kwanhan yŏn'gu." *Inmunhak yŏngu* 34, no. 2 (2007): 447–89.

Chatterjee, Partha. *The Nation and Its Fragments: Colonial and Postcolonial Histories.*
Princeton, NJ: Princeton University Press, 1993.

Cho Tong-il. "Chosŏn hugi kamyŏn'gŭk kwa minjung ŭisik ŭi sŏngjang." *Ch'angjak kwa
pip'yŏng* 7, no. 2 (1972): 232–68.

Chŏn Sŭng-ju. "1960–70-yŏndae munhak pip'yŏng tamnon sok ŭi 'minjok(juŭi)' inyŏm
ŭi tu yangsang." *Minjok munhaksa yŏn'gu* 34 (2004): 32–67.

Chŏng Chi-yŏng. "1970-yŏndae 'Yijo yŏin' ŭi t'ansaeng: 'Choguk kŭndaehwa' wa 'minjok chuch'esŏng' ŭi t'ajadŭl." *Yŏsŏnghak nonjip* 24, no. 2 (2007): 41–78.

Chŏng Ho-gi. "Pak Chŏng-hŭi sidae ŭi 'tongsang kŏllip undong' kwa aeguk chuŭi: 'aeguk sŏnyŏl chosang kŏllip wiwŏnhoe' ŭi hwaltong ŭl chungsim ŭro." *Chŏngsin munhwa yŏn'gu* 30, no. 1 (2007): 335–63.

Chŏng Pyŏng-uk. "Yijo hugi siga ŭi pyŏni kwajŏng kŏ." *Changjak kwa pip'y*ŏng 9, no. 1
(1974).

Chu Ch'ang-yun. "1970-yŏndae chŏngnyŏn munhwa sedae tamnon ŭi chŏngch'ihak."
Ŏllon kwa sahoe 14, no. 3 (2006): 73–105.

Chu Ch'ang-yun. "1975-yŏn chŏnhu Han'guk tangdae munhwa ŭi chihyŏng kwa
hyŏngsŏng kwajŏng." *Han'guk ŏllon hakpo* 51, no. 4 (2007): 5–31.

Han'guk Munhwa Yesul Chinhŭngwŏn. *Han'guk ŭi munhwa chŏngch'aek.* Munhwa
Palchŏn Yŏn'guso, 1992.

Hong Kyŏng-p'yo. "Yi Mun-gu ŭi *Uri tongne* yŏnjakp'um yŏn'gu." *Hyŏndae sosŏl yŏn'gu*
20 (December 2003): 31–53.

Hwang Pyŏng-ju. "Pak Chŏng-hŭi ch'eje ŭi chibae tamnon: Kŭndaehwa tamnon ŭl
chungsim ŭro." PhD diss., Hanyang taehakkyo, 2008.

Im Chong-su. "1960–70-yŏndae t'ellebijŏn pum hyŏnsang kwa t'ellebijŏn toip ŭi maengnak." *Han'guk ŏllon hakpo* 48, no. 2 (2004): 79–107.

Im Hŏn-yŏng. "Kŭndae munhaksa non'go." *Ch'angjak kwa pip'ŏng* 10, no. 1 (1975): 69–84.

Kang Chin-ho, ed. *Chŭngŏn ŭrosŏŭi munhaksa*. Kip'ŭnsaem, 2003.

Kang Chŏng-gu. "1970-yŏndae minjung-minjok munhak ŭi chŏhangsŏng chaego." *Kukche ŏmun* 46 (August 2009): 45–68.

Kang Man-gil. "'Minjok sahak' non ŭi pansŏng." *Ch'angjak kwa pipyŏng* 11, no. 1 (1976): 317–27.

Kang Man-gil. "Sagwan: Sŏsul ch'ejae ŭi kŏmt'o." *Ch'angjak kwa pipyŏng* 9, no. 2 (1974): 413–45.

Kang Man-gil. *Yŏksaga ŭi sigan: Kang Man-gil chasŏjŏn*. Ch'angbi, 2010.

Kang Sŏng-nyul. "Yŏnghwa ro ponŭn uri yŏksa 1: 'Pabodŭl ŭi haengjin' kwa Yusin sidae—igil su ŏpnŭn sidae e chŏhanghan tu chŏlmŭm." *Naeil ŭl yŏnŭn yŏksa* 19 (March 2005): 234–40.

Kim Chŏng-bae. "Sanggosa e taehan kŏmt'o." *Ch'angjak kwa pip'yŏng* 9, no. 2 (1974): 425–29.

Kim Chu-hyŏn. "1960-yŏndae 'Han'gukchŏk in kŏt ŭi tamnon chihyŏng kwa sinsedae ŭisik." *Sanghŏ hakpo* 16 (February 2006): 379–410.

Kim Chu-hyŏn. "Sirhak suyong kwa 1960-yŏndae minjok munhangnon ŭi chŏn'gae." *Ŏmun yŏn'gu* 34, no. 4 (2006): 331–53.

Kim Han Sang (Kim Han-sang). *Choguk kŭndaehwa rŭl yuram hagi: Pak Chŏng-hŭi Pak Chung Hee chŏnggwŏn hongbo tŭraibŭ, P'aldo kangsan 10-yŏn*. Hanguk yŏngsang charywŏn, 2008.

Kim Han Sang (Kim Han-sang). "Pak Chŏng-hŭi chŏnggwŏn'gi kajok sŏsa ŭi kunyŏl kwa chŏhang." *Taejung sŏsa yŏn'gu* 15, no. 2 (2009): 283–313.

Kim Hunggyu (Kim Hŭng-gyu). "P'ansori ŭi iwŏnsŏng kwa sahoesajŏk paegyŏng." *Ch'angjak kwa pip'yŏng* 9, no. 1 (1974): 69–100.

Kim P'an-su. "'Kukka' e ŭihan sangjing esŏ 'kungmin' ŭl wihan sangjing ŭro: Han'guk sin'kwŏn hwap'ye 'toan' sŏnjŏng ŭl tullŏssan chŏngch'ijŏk kaltŭng ŭl chungsim ŭro." *2007 chŏn'gi sahoehak taehoe Han'guk sahoehak 50-yŏn chŏngni wa chŏnmang*. Han'guk Sahoehakhoe, 2007: 35–51.

Kim Su-jin. "Chŏnt'ong ch'ang'an kwa yŏsŏng ŭi kungminhwa." *Sahoe wa yŏksa* 80 (2008): 215–55.

Kim Su-jin. "Yŏsŏng ŭibok ŭi pyŏnch'ŏn ŭl t'onghae pon chŏnt'ong kwa kŭndae ŭi chendŏ chŏngch'i." *P'eminijŭm yŏn'gu* 7, no. 2 (2007): 281–320.

Kim Won (Kim Wŏn). "1960-yŏndae naengjŏn ŭi sigan kwa t'ŭit'ŭllin chuch'e: Simin ŭi sigan kwa minjok ŭi sigan." *Sŏgang inmun nonch'ong* 38 (December 2013): 119–57.

Kim Won (Kim Wŏn). "Palgul ŭi sidae: Kyŏngju palgul, kaebal kŭrigo munhwa kongdongch'e." *Sahak yŏn'gu* 116 (2014): 479–542.

Kim Won (Kim Wŏn). *Yŏgong 1970, kŭnyŏdŭl ŭi panyŏksa*. Imaejin, 2006.

Kim Ye-rim. "1960-yŏndae chunghuban kaebal naesyŏnŏllijŭm kwa chungsanch'ŭng kajŏng p'ant'aji ŭi munhwa chŏngch'ihak." *Hyŏndae muhak ŭi yŏn'gu* 32 (2007): 339–75.

Kong Che-uk. "Kukka tongwŏn ch'eje sigi 'honbunsik changnyŏ undong' kwa siksaeng-hwal ŭi pyŏnhwa." *Kyŏngje wa sahoe* 77 (March 2008): 107–38.

Lee, Hye Ryoung. "Time of Capital, Time of a Nation: Changes in Korean Intellectual Media in the 1960s–1970s." *Korea Journal* 51, no. 3 (2011): 77–103.

Moon, Seung-sook. "Begetting the Nation: The Androcentric Discourse of National History and Tradition in South Korea." In *Dangerous Women: Gender and Korean Nationalism*, edited by Elaine H. Kim and Chungmoo Choi. New York: Routledge, 1998.

Munhwa Kongbobu. *Hoguk sŏnhyŏn ŭi yujŏk*. Seoul: Munhwa Kongbobu, 1978.

Munhwa Kongbobu. *Munhwa kongbo 30 nyŏn*. Seoul: Munhwa Kongbobu,1979.

Munhwajae Kwalliguk. *Uri nara ŭi munhwajae*. Seoul: Munhwajae Kwalliguk, 1970.

Nam Kŭn-u. "Cho Chi-hun ŭi minjok munhwahak." *Han'guk munhak yŏn'gu* 18 (December 1996): 121–37.

No Chae-bong. "Chwadam—yuhaeng inya panhang inya: Han'guk ŭi chŏngnyŏn mun-hwa." *Sin tong'a*, July 1974.

No Chi-sŭng. "'Yŏng-ja ŭi chŏnsŏng sidae' e nat'anan hach'ŭngmin yŏsŏng ŭi kwaerak: Kyech'ŭng kwa chendŏ ŭi munhwasa rŭl wihan siron." *Han'guk hyŏndae munhak yŏn'gu* 24 (April 2008): 413–44.

O Myŏng-sŏk. "1960–70-yŏndae ŭi munhwa chŏngch'aek kwa minjok munhwa tam-non." *Pigyo munhwa yŏn'gu* 4 (December 1998): 121–52.

Pae Chŏng-han. "Pak Chŏng-hŭi ŭi chogyŏnggwan." *Han'guk chogyŏng hakhoeji* 31, no. 4 (2003): 13–25.

Paik Nak-chung (Paek Nak-chŏng). "Minjok munhak ŭi hyŏn tan'gye." *Ch'angjak kwa pip'yŏng* 10, no. 1 (1975): 35–68.

Paik Nak-chung (Paek Nak-chŏng). "Saeroun ch'angjak kwa pip'yŏng ŭi chase." *Ch'angjak kwa pip'yŏng* 1, no. 1 (1966): 5–38.

Paik Nak-chung (Paek, Nak-chŏng). "Yŏksajŏk in'gan kwa sijŏk in'gan." *Ch'angjak kwa pip'yŏng* 12, no. 2 (1977): 579–607.

Pak Chung Hee (Pak Chŏng-hŭi). *Minjok chunghŭng ŭi kil*. Kwangmyŏng Ch'ulp'ansa, 1978.

Pak Kye-ri. "Ch'ungmugong tongsang kwa kukka ideollogi." *Han'guk kŭnhyŏndae misul-sahak* 12 (August 2004): 139–75.

Pak Süng-hyŏn. "Taejung maech'e ŭi chŏngch'ijŏk kijehwa Han'guk yŏnghwa wa kŏnjŏnsŏng koyang (1966–1979)." *Öllon kwa sahoe* 13, no. 1 (2005): 46–74.

Pak Yŏng-u, Kim Ün-ha, and Yi Tae-yŏn. "Kukka chaegŏn ŭi sidae wa kŭndaejŏk yŏsŏng chuch'esŏng ŭi kusŏng." *Han'guk munhak iron kwa pip'yŏng* 13, no. 2 (2009): 485–512.

Ri Yŏng-hŭi, and Im Hŏn-yŏng. *Taehwa*. Han'gilsa, 2005.

Shin Hyunjoon (Sin Hyŏn-jun). "Yi Chang-hŭi wa 1970-yŏndae: Silchongdoen 1970-yŏndae, t'oep'ye hogŭn puron?" *Tangdae pip'yŏng* 28 (December 2004): 49–68.

Shin Hyunjoon, and Viriya Sawangchot. "Ŭmakchŏk konggong konggan kwa 'sunsu/t'oep'ye' ŭi munhwa chŏngch'i(hak): 1970-yŏndae naengjŏn'gi Han'guk kwa T'aeguk esŏ chŏngnyŏn munhwa ŭi ch'uryŏn kwa chongŏn." In *Naengjŏn Asia ŭi munhwa p'unggyŏng: 1960–1970-yŏndae*, edited by Sŏnggonghoedae Tong Asia Yŏn'guso, vol. 2. Hyŏnsil Munhwa Yŏn'gu, 2009.

Sin Tong-mun, Yi Ho-chŏl, Sin Kyŏng-nim, Yŏm Mu-ung, and Paek Nak-chŏng. "Ch'angbi 10 nyŏn: hoego wa pansŏng." *Ch'angjak kwa pip'yŏng* 11, no. 1 (1976): 4–32.

Sin Tong-uk. "Sunggomi wa kolgyemi ŭi yangsang." *Ch'angjak kwa pip'yŏng* 6, no. 3 (1971): 732–45.

Song Ch'an-sik. "Chosŏn hugi." *Ch'angjak kwa pip'yŏng* 9, no. 2 (1974): 446–56.

Song Ŭn-yŏng. "1960–70-yŏndae Han'guk ŭi taejung saehoehwa wa taejung munhwa ŭi chŏngch'ijŏk ŭimi." *Sanghŏ hakpo* 32 (June 2011): 187–226.

Song Ŭn-yŏng. "Taejung munhwa hyŏnsang ŭrosŏŭi Ch'oe In-ho sosŏl." *Sanghŏ hakpo* 15 (August 2005): 419–45.

Ŭn Chŏng-t'ae. "Pak Chŏng-hŭi sidae sŏngyŏkhwa saŏp ŭi ch'ui wa sŏngkyŏk." *Yŏksa munje yŏn'gu* 15 (December 2005): 241–77.

Wi Kyŏng-hye. "Han'guk chŏnjaeng ihu 1960-yŏndae pidosi chiyŏk sunhoe yŏnghwa sangyŏng." *Chibangsa wa chibang munhwa* 11, no. 2 (2008): 267–305.

Yi Chong-nim. "1960–70-yŏndae t'elebijŏn t'ŭrama rŭl t'onghan 'konggong' ideollogi hyŏngsŏng e kwanhan yŏn'gu: Han'guk Ilbon ŭl chungsim ŭro." In *Naengjŏn Asia ŭi munhwa p'unggyŏng: 1960–1970-yŏndae*, edited by Sŏnggonghoedae Tong Asia Yŏn'guso, vol. 2. Hyŏnsil Munhwa Yŏn'gu, 2009.

Yi Ho-gŏl. "1970-yŏndae Han'guk yŏnghwa." In *Han'guk yŏnghwasa kongbu: 1960–1979*, edited by Yi Hyo-in et al. Ich'ae, 2004.

Yi Hye-rim. "1970-yŏndae chŏngnyŏn munhwa kusŏngch'e ŭi yŏksajŏk hyŏngsŏng kwajŏng: Taejung ŭmak ŭi sobi yangsang ŭl chungsim ŭro." *Sahoe yŏn'gu* 10 (2005): 7–40.

Yi Hyŏn-sŏk. "419 hyŏngmyŏng kwa 60-yŏndae mal munhak tamnon e na'tanan pichŏngch'i ŭi kamgak kwa nolli." *Han'guk hyŏndae munhak yŏn'gu* 35 (December 2011): 223–54.

Yi Kil-sŏng et al. *1970-yŏndae Seoul ŭi kŭkchang sanŏp mit kŭkchang munhwa yŏn'gu.* Yŏnghwa chinhŭng wiwŏnhoe, 2004.

Yi Kyŏng-nan. "1950–70-yŏndae yŏksahakkye yŏksa yŏn'gu ŭi sahoe tamnonhwa." *Tongbang hakchi* 152 (2010): 339–83.

Yi Sang-nok. "1960–70-yŏndae pip'anjŏk chisigindŭl ŭi kŭndaehwa insik." *Yŏksa munje yŏn'gu* 18 (October 2007): 215–51.

Yi Tong-yŏn. "Chubyŏnbu sŭp'och'ŭ ibent'ŭ t'ansaeng kwa kukka narŭsisijŭm: 1970-yŏndae Asia kukche ch'ukku taehoe ŭi kŭndae p'yosang." In *Naengjŏn Asia ŭi munhwa p'unggyŏng: 1960–1970-yŏndae*, edited by Sŏnggonghoedae Tong Asia Yŏn'guso, vol. 2. Hyŏnsil Munhwa Yŏn'gu, 2009.

Yi U-sŏng. "Chosŏn chŏn'gi." *Ch'angjak kwa pip'yŏng* 9, no. 2 (1974): 435–45.

Yi U-sŏng. "Koryŏ sidae." *Ch'angjak kwa pip'yŏng* 9, no. 2 (1974): 430–34.

Yi Yŏng-mi. *Kwanghwamun yŏn'ga.* Yedam, 2008.

Yŏm Ch'an-hŭi. "1960-yŏndae tasi ilki: Pan'gong kwa palchŏn nolli rŭl chungsim ŭro." In *Naengjŏn Asia ŭi munhwa p'unggyŏng: 1960–1970-yŏndae*, edited by Sŏnggonghoedae Tong Asia yŏn'guso, vol. 2. Hyŏnsil munhwa yŏn'gu, 2009.

Yu Sŏn-yŏng. "Tongwŏn ch'eje ŭi kwaminjokhwa p'ŭrojekt'ŭ wa seksŭ yŏnghwa." *Ŏllon kwa sahoe* 15, no. 2 (2007): 2–56.

Yun Yŏng-do. "Naengjŏn'gi kungminhwa p'ŭrojekt'ŭ wa 'chŏnt'ong munhwa' tamnon: Han'guk T'aiwan ŭi sarye rŭl chungsim ŭro." In *Naengjŏn Asia ŭi munhwa p'unggyŏng: 1960–1970-yŏndae*, edited by Sŏnggonghoedae Tong Asia Yŏn'guso, vol. 2. Hyŏnsil Munhwa Yŏn'gu, 2009.

[De]Popularizing a Confucian Master

Yusin and the Birth of T'oegye Studies

Hwisang Cho

> A story is the shortest distance between people.
> —Pat Speight (Irish storyteller)

Gaunt and stern in the simple *simŭi* robe favored by Confucian scholars, the image of T'oegye Yi Hwang (1501–70) has been a familiar fixture on the Korean thousand-won note since 1975. There may be no better way to turn a historical personage into a popular icon than to paste his or her image on a piece of currency roughly equivalent in value to a dollar bill, and if today T'oegye is the single most prominent Confucian master of Korea, it was during Park Chung Hee's rule, especially the Yusin years, that many aspects of his image were shaped. From the late 1960s to the early 1970s, the Korean government comprehensively and systematically popularized T'oegye's legacy, beginning with the translation of his writings from classical Chinese into vernacular Korean in 1968. In 1969, Park commanded and directed the restoration of the Tosan Academy, the seat of T'oegye's intellectual heritage. In 1970, T'oegye's statue was erected in front of Namsan Library in Seoul and unveiled by Park himself, and a tour of government-sponsored public lectures on T'oegye's life and scholarship took place in major cities, including Seoul, Andong, Taegu, Kwangju, and Pusan. In December of that year, while attending the ceremony celebrating the completion of the restoration of the Tosan Academy, Park Chung Hee expressed a wish to see in print the papers presented at the event and to have a research institute established that would be dedicated solely to illuminating T'oegye's scholarship. Thus was born the *Journal of T'oegye Studies*, whose publication began in 1973 and continues to this day.

For the Park regime, the flurry of government initiatives devoted to T'oegye was to be rationalized as a way to promote the "national spirit," which had been forgotten and denigrated during the rapid modernization of Korean society. Emphasizing the need for the government to honor national heroes, Park asserted, "The traditional culture is a productive force in and of itself in the process of modernization, contrary to what was generally believed in the past."[1]

The efforts certainly succeeded in elevating popular awareness of T'oegye beyond what he enjoyed in his own lifetime or the centuries thereafter. That fact has led scholars to argue that T'oegye's fame was actually invented during the Park Chung Hee era.[2] Such scholarship harkens back to Eric Hobsbawm's much-traveled notion of "invented tradition"— "'traditions' which appear or claim to be old are often quite recent in origin and sometimes invented"—and yet the claim requires us to also take into account Hobsbawm's warning about the all too common oversight in understanding the relationship between invented traditions and their historical antecedents.[3] Invented traditions do not arise because "old ways are no longer available or viable" but because they are deliberately discarded.[4]

Challenging the increasingly fashionable view of T'oegye's image as a wholesale modern invention, a view that occludes the variety of specific cultural and political dynamics that were at play at different historical moments, this chapter examines the evolution of T'oegye's charismatic authority since the late sixteenth century. Central to the argument of this chapter is the notable fact that T'oegye is the only Confucian master for whom the authentic written records of his words and deeds (*ŏnhaengnok*) were compiled and published in Korea before the twentieth century. I argue that these texts inscribing T'oegye's spoken words functioned as the locus of his charismatic authority in the late Chosŏn period, which continued to affect the making of national heroes in the early twentieth century.

This is not to deny the active role the Park regime played in popularizing the image of T'oegye that is pervasive in Korea today. In fact the regime manipulated T'oegye and Confucian values as an alternative to the resistant and subversive urban popular culture. Criticizing the indiscriminate acceptance of Western democracy as the cause of social unrest and spiritual anomie, Park put forth the Confucian tradition deeply rooted in the rural areas as the cure. The process of honoring T'oegye implemented in this context bore a striking resemblance to the Japanese imperialists' appropriation of T'oegye during the late colonial period to justify their assimilation policy. Japanese scholars had focused on T'oegye's neo-Confucian theories to show his putative connection to the Tokugawa scholarly tradition. In a manner parallel to what Stephen Vlastos has argued about the political manipulation of tradition in modern Japan, both Japanese scholars during the late colonial period and elites in authoritarian South Korea appropriated T'oegye to tighten social control.[5]

The colonial pattern of elevating T'oegye as a great philosopher, however, had the effect of dehumanizing him and turning his image into something lofty and idealized and, by that very definition, more distant from the general public. Wiped out in this process of glorification was the practice of telling and retelling stories about T'oegye's everyday life based on the records of his words and deeds. In the late Chosŏn period, such storytelling had served as the main mechanism for building T'oegye's charisma. While the Park regime did differ from the Japanese colonialists in making the visual image of T'oegye readily available, this image inserted into people's everyday lives was not accompanied by any story through which they could connect themselves to T'oegye. Thus, the development of T'oegye studies as an academic discipline and the dissemination of T'oegye's image as an icon, though intended to popularize him, undermined the popular basis of his legacy. The double enshrinement of T'oegye by the Park regime, a practice inherited in large part from the Japanese imperial appropriation of T'oegye and deployed toward the political goal of reconstructing the "national spirit," turned the Confucian master into a universally recognizable figure about whom no stories can be told, thus confining the discourse about him to a narrow academic field dominated by a few intellectuals.

We can thus identify at least four distinct moments in the long history of T'oegye's reception, beginning with the Chosŏn period when his spoken words were written down, published, and circulated as a source of academic authority. Korean nationalists in the early twentieth century appropriated this heritage to create national heroes in modern print media. During the colonial period, Japanese scholars minimized or eliminated these oral components of T'oegye's legacy while using T'oegye to justify their assimilation policy. It was this colonial approach that the Park Chung Hee regime largely inherited and utilized to suppress the defiant urban popular culture.

T'oegye as *the* Confucian Master in the Late Chosŏn Period

During his lifetime, T'oegye had several different images—as a court minister, scholar, and teacher. The consolidation of his image as an esteemed Confucian master, which emphasized his role as a scholar respected by many pupils, did not begin until after his death in 1570. The work of constructing this venerated image was taken up by his students, who produced diverse texts about their teacher. In the Confucian tradition, it was a common practice to collect the writings of prominent scholars and posthumously publish them as books, but those scholars who were especially esteemed also had their speeches and deeds recollected, recorded, and transmitted as a way of being honored and remembered by a younger generation of scholars. The *Analects of Confucius* provided a solid precedent in this tradition. Very few Confucian masters enjoyed this level of honor in Korea.

Although the practice of writing about the dead for ritual purposes was common enough in the Confucian tradition, T'oegye's case stands out for the way his self-representation in the writings he left behind was incorporated into these more conventional pieces. In his own tomb inscription, drafted three days before his death, for example, T'oegye detailed how he wanted to be perceived. Emphasizing his devotion to Confucian learning while implying ambivalence about the compatibility between his service in officialdom and his desire for Confucian scholarship, T'oegye's tomb inscription ordained his posthumous representation as a scholar rather than a court minister.

Scholars in T'oegye's circle picked up and further developed this representation. Writing in response to Yi An-do's (1541–84) request for textual accounts of "what they heard and saw in daily practices (*chŏ p'yŏng'il mun'gyŏn)*" with his grandfather,[6] T'oegye's pupils employed diverse narrative strategies toward the common goal of proving that T'oegye was the reincarnation of Zhu Xi (1130–1200), interpreting their teacher's words and conduct in ways that would place him within the scholarly lineage (*tot'ong*) of the prominent neo-Confucian master of Song dynasty (960–1279) China and the Way in Confucian civilization. Ku Pong-nyŏng (1526–86), for instance, claimed that the origin of the Confucian Way had not been illuminated in China until Zhu Xi disseminated neo-Confucian learning and that in the Korean context only T'oegye had achieved the proper understanding of the Confucian Way by virtue of mastering Zhu's neo-Confucian theories.[7] Yi Tŏk-hong (1541–96) made a similar claim that T'oegye stood at the very acme of the Confucian scholarship of his time and should be revered for one hundred generations as "the reincarnation of Zhu Xi" (*Kojŏng kwirae*).[8]

This lineage, moreover, excluded all other Korean scholars. T'oegye's disciples repeatedly and unanimously emphasized that their teacher was an autodidact in his mastery of neo-Confucianism (*pullyu sasŭng* or *pullyu sajŏn*). Ku Pongnyŏng claimed that T'oegye was able to resuscitate Zhu Xi's neo-Confucianism in Korea through his innate intelligence and benevolence, as well as the firmness of will required to embody this learning in his life, without recourse to any tutelage from teachers. These narratives sequester T'oegye from the academic tradition of his time and erase his immediate predecessors in order to connect him directly to a more ancient past. This strategy enabled T'oegye's disciples to bypass the existing hegemonic scholarly culture, reducing it to an inferior or obsolete legacy, and thus to uphold their own academic and moral authority.

All these testimonials about T'oegye transformed individual memories of disciples, which were unstable and unsystematic, into authentic references based on the reliability of collectively verified accounts. Pupils could elevate their own position by inscribing previously unknown scenes of daily life in this newly created textual space. The transformation of individual memories into collective stories of their master provided the mechanism for inextricably weaving the master, the disciples, and the texts together. In other words, the textual transmission of stories about the master allowed the pupils of T'oegye not only to venerate him but also to create and reinforce his image as a moral exemplar, and thereby to claim, as T'oegye's intellectual heirs, the academic and political authority that emanated from this representation.[9]

According to Brinkley Messick in his analysis of the importance of textual practices in Muslim societies, "Writing rescued words from perishing, but only at the cost of another death, that of the original meaning conveyed by speech. In its written form speech was absent, altered, and open to a potentially infinite number of interpretive readings."[10] Writing down oral interactions, Messick argues, paradoxically frees them from constraints associated with the initial context of utterance. The possibility of reactivating the original utterance in a different time and space opens up diverse practices of reading, which in turn produces an infinite number of meanings.

The decontextualization that accompanies the process of textualization became the basis of intergenerational communication in T'oegye's case as well, especially when the master's oral discussions, as inscribed by his pupils, became reading materials for later generations. The emphasis on transforming oral communication into written forms did not down-play the value of orality, however. What gave the written speech value was precisely the readers' assumption that their reading practices could re-cover or reenact the original contexts of that speech. The record of the conversation between master and disciples thus gave rise to a new mode of textual interpretation in which the oral and the written are interspersed rather than the oral components being silenced in favor of the written.[11] The case of T'oegye was representative in Korea, where, because everyday practices were deemed the origin of cultural and political authority, the written records of spoken words were significant in buttressing the cha-risma of historical figures. Thus, despite the inevitable loss of original meanings of speech in written form, the readers' belief that the original contexts would be resurrected from these texts fed the charismatic au-thority of interlocutors.

We can see in detail how the academic authority of T'oegye's spoken words was consolidated in the process of written transmission by examin-ing the layers of textual practice surrounding specific cases of inscription. Although the writing of testimonials about T'oegye began almost immedi-ately after his death, it was in the late seventeenth century that narratives about his words and deeds began to be collected in anthologies for neo-Confucian studies rather than merely circulated in a more individual and. scattered fashion for commemoration of the master. The anthologization of these narratives appropriated "everydayness" and underscored it as the focal point of Confucian scholarship, transforming seemingly trivial ele-ments of daily practices into a mainstream academic subject. The editors of these anthologies also clearly tried to preserve the interaction between orality and literacy in the transmission of T'oegye's legacy. The layering of texts, the tradition of building on earlier scholars' testimonials, further facilitated intergenerational communication.

The oldest extant anthology, allegedly published sometime after 1679, is Im Yŏng's (1649–96) *Record of T'oegye's Words* (*T'oegye ŏrok*). Nam Ku-man's (1629–1711) preface makes an intriguing point about the relation-ship between speech and its transcription: "It is generally said that the production of texts (*mun*) in the past meant recording speech (*ŏn*). Just as the opening of mouths constitutes speech, writing [it] down forms texts. *Both speech and text stem from the same [thoughts or intentions] but are called by different names. The texts record speech, which is how [oral] speech is put to use and passed down to posterity.*"[12] Nam implied that writing down spoken words carries them over to future generations; furthermore, this textual practice generalizes the relationship between the word and its referent so that spatiotemporal limitations of oral culture may ultimately be transcended. Foreshadowing what Jack Goody and Ian Watt would argue about the effects of literacy, Nam's statement reveals that writing down oral speech requires the author to be sensitive to the conception and potential immediacy of the past in different temporal and spatial contexts.[13] Nam nevertheless made it clear that spoken words are the provenance of this type of textual production. Although writing enabled both editors and readers to make what had been dubious more explicit and systematic, there always remained room for oral cultures to complement the written. The editors thus underscored that mastering T'oegye's scholarship was possible through reading both his own written works and the records of his words and deeds, as the latter exhibit how the former were put into practice.

About three decades later Kwŏn Tu-gyŏng (1654–1725) echoed Im's idea about the pedagogic advantage of eyewitness testimonials and went on to compile them as *Complete Record of the Words and Deeds of T'oegye* (*T'oegye Sŏnsaeng ŏnhaeng t'ongnok*) in 1707.[14] Kwŏn's work was much more comprehensive and referenced all thirty-three available records. Just as Im Yŏng did, Kwŏn elaborated on the pedagogic function of this narrative genre in concert with the scholarly works produced by the master himself.[15] Scholars were expected to learn the master's Confucian theories from his own writings and then grapple with concrete ideas about how to put these abstract concepts into practice by reading the records delineating the master's everyday life as the embodiment of learning. In this regard, the master's writing collection and his pupils' eyewitness testimonials formed a dovetailed set of readings in Confucian studies. Compiling and publishing the narratives written by T'oegye's disciples, therefore, did not simply preserve scattered records on T'oegye. It marked an important addition of a textual corpus that fundamentally changed the way T'oegye would be studied and understood in the Chosŏn scholarly scene.

Kwŏn also emphasized the historical significance of the eyewitness testimonials in the formation of Confucian civilization. He claimed that it would not be possible to study the scholarship of past Confucian masters unless their pupils had recorded their experiences and observations. Kwŏn's own preface articulates the significance of the *Analects of Confu-*

cius in propagating the master's scholarship, then underscores that Zhu Xi's disciples recorded their master's words and deeds in addition to compiling the annotated collection of his writings. Kwŏn specifically states, "The practice of recording tremendously contributed to the transmission of the Confucian Way to the future generations."[16] He recognized that the greatness of Confucian scholarship expressed in daily conversations is always at risk of slipping away unless someone who hears them writes them down. The oral and written components complemented each other in the formation of Confucian scholarly authenticity, so one should not be emphasized at the expense of the other.

Although some criticized Kwŏn's work for biased editing,[17] it was generally well received by most scholars, including Yi Ik (1681–1763),[18] who published another compilation of records about T'oegye two decades later. Yi Ik's *Essential Words of Master Yi [T'oegye]* (*Yija suŏ*) was distinctive because it included excerpts from both T'oegye's own writings and his disciples' records of his life in a single work. As discussed, both Im Yŏng and Kwŏn Tugyŏng underlined the importance of reading the records of T'oegye's daily life along with his writings. Although neo-Confucian theories and their application to daily practices were mutually beneficial, it was believed that the theoretical discourse delivered in written language and its application to daily practice through speech actions had to be located in separate textual spaces. Yi Ik, however, integrated written works and recorded speeches into the same text when their messages dealt with the same Confucian concepts. He showed that just as everydayness does not form several different conceptual domains, these two discursive levels could be intermingled.

The postscript to this work, which Yun Tong-gyu (1695–1773) wrote in 1754, accentuates the connection between T'oegye and Zhu Xi in terms of neo-Confucian pedagogy.[19] Yun's argument is innovative in its attention to the sequence of learning and the place of Yi's text in it as the prerequisite for mastering Zhu Xi's scholarship. This created a novel textual map that would guide the learning process of Confucian scholars. An Chŏngbok (1712–91) also recommended that scholars study T'oegye before studying Zhu Xi.[20] In this sense, T'oegye was connected to past Confucian sages not only through rhetorical claims but also through his textual contribution to the Confucian classical tradition. The process also allowed Korean scholars to see their role as that of major contributors to the Confucian civilization rather than mere recipients of the theories of Chinese Confucian masters. The publication of T'oegye's words and deeds inducted a new era in the Korean Confucian tradition, as scholars now had their own Confucian master on par with foreign teachers of the past.

Other Masters' Words

Why were the records of T'oegye so distinctive in creating charismatic academic authority in Chosŏn Korea? After all, he was not alone among Confucian scholars in leaving behind written records of their spoken words. The collection of writings by Yi I (1536–83), for example, includes a two-volume record of his words (Ŏrok), and the collection of writings by Song Si-yŏl (1607–1689), one of the strongest personalities of Chosŏn Confucianism, also includes the record of his words and deeds (Ŏnhaengnok). But neither commanded the kind of authority that T'oegye did. In the case of Yi I, the two-chapter accounts about the master, compiled respectively by his two disciples, Kim Chin-gang (d.u.) and Pak Yŏ-ryong (1541–1611), provoked much criticism, even among Yi I's academic offspring, for deviating from the master's original ideas.[21] The second chapter, containing accounts of Yi I extracted exclusively from Kim U-ong's (1540–1603) Lectures at the Royal Classic Mat (Kyŏngyŏn kang'ŭi),[22] lacked comprehensiveness. The reverse direction, that of extracting the oral teachings from the written records, could not generate the everydayness that was the prime source of charismatic authority. In the publication of eyewitness testimonials about T'oegye, oral components that the master could not record himself comprise the core of everydayness. Thus, the successful capture of the master's speeches hinged on his pupils' extraordinary attention to ephemeral conversations and their determination to write them down. The master's charisma could not be resuscitated from other texts, where oral components were obfuscated and thus undetectable.

In contrast, Song Si-yŏl's record imported various accounts only from the collection of his writings, the Great Compendium of Master Song (Songja taejŏn). This volume purportedly offers written references for all records, excluding the orally transmitted memories or anecdotes about Song that circulated among his family members or disciples.[23] The exclusive dependence on written works and the resulting emphasis on the written over the oral starkly contrasted with the records about T'oegye, which prioritized firsthand experiences and observations as the basis for faithful representation.

These examples seem to resonate with Jacques Derrida's criticism of logocentrism in the Western intellectual tradition, which set up the binary opposition between speech and writing and privileged the former. Despite the importance of writing in Western civilization as the main indicator of human progress and cultural achievement, Derrida demonstrates that speech reigns supreme in the key academic breakthroughs from Plato to Rousseau and all the way down to Lévi-Strauss.[24] The Chosŏn Confucian tradition also prized speech over writing as the source of charismatic authority. However, the relationship between speech and writing in Korea reveals more intricate interactions. In Derrida's critique of logocentrism, writing inherently lacks semantic value because it only contains "traces" of speeches rather than the whole meaning. The written records of masters' speeches in Korea, however, created authenticity based on the assumption that the original contexts could be reactivated by reading them. To put it differently, writing was believed to preserve the key characteristics of oral speeches in Korea, which readers could retrieve. But this held true only when writers were conscious of the subtle interaction between the oral and the written. As in the cases of Yi I and Song Si-yŏl, the masters' spoken words could not be exhumed from their own writings.

By failing to meet the academic demand for records of the masters' spoken words that could serve as authentic companions to the masters' own works, the records about Yi I and Song Si-yŏl ironically reveal the mechanism by which academic charisma was consolidated in the late Chosŏn: the decontextualization of the oral on its textual inscription, which then sets in motion the inexhaustible activity of interpretation, that is to say, the recovery of the original contexts through reading and rereading of the written records. These readings, in turn, would generate additional textual practices as scholars shared their analyses with one another in writing. The result was an intricate intergenerational network mediated by written texts that perpetually sought to recover the original contexts of the master's spoken words. This partly explains why the records about Yi and Song did not appeal to nationalist intellectuals in the twentieth century the way T'oegye's did.

Making National Heroes in the Early Twentieth Century

The elaborate and rich academic traditions of Chosŏn's literati culture took on a completely different cast in the early twentieth century when both Japanese colonialists and Korean nationalists began to criticize the

Confucian tradition, though to opposite political ends, as the cause of Chosŏn's failure to reform itself into a strong and modernized nation-state. For the Japanese colonialists, the negative pronouncements about Chosŏn's hidebound culture functioned to justify the need for colonization. For the Korean nationalists, such critique served as a rallying cry for the unification of the Korean people in a new modern nation.

Unlike the Japanese, who denounced the tradition wholesale, Korean nationalist intellectuals had to treat Chosŏn's Confucian culture in ways at once more nuanced and more ambivalent. The social structure of the recent past needed to be criticized for failing to modernize Korea and enlighten the people, but this same past had to serve as a source of national identity from which positive images could be extracted to oppose Japanese colonization. As a result, the nationalists developed a bifurcated discourse about the Confucian tradition and Confucian worthies. In a diatribe against contemporary Confucians published in 1921 in the nationalist journal *Kaebyŏk*, Kim Yun-sik (1835–1922) criticized as anachronistic various activities promoted by newly formed Confucian organizations, singling out the discourse on human nature and Confucian principles (*sŏngni*) as useless and impractical.[25] Kim's critical stance toward the Confucian past of Chosŏn Korea was shared by the editors of *Kaebyŏk*, but the journal also made use of historical figures to raise national consciousness. In the same year that it published Kim Yun-sik's piece, the journal surveyed its readers about who they thought were the ten greatest historical figures of Korea and carried an anonymous article on T'oegye called "T'oegye, the Progenitor of Korean Confucianism."[26] On display in this article is the strategy by which Korean nationalists managed to rescue T'oegye from the supposed "backwardness" of the Korean Confucian tradition.

According to the article, the negative effects of Confucianism that hindered Chosŏn's progress for four hundred years with its empty doctrines and factional strife were the fault of T'oegye's disciples and intellectual heirs rather than T'oegye himself. It was their blind and excessive veneration of the master that sidetracked them into political partisanship that crippled the government and into debates on metaphysical issues that were completely impractical.[27] This isolation of Confucian worthies from the purported social harm caused by of Neo-Confucian discourse facilitated the nationalists' strategy of condemning the recent past while using it as the basis for a newly emerging national consciousness. The article then reconstructs T'oegye as a national hero on the basis of the records of his words and deeds. These records, it argues, provide the ideal guidance for self-cultivation by people of all ages since they contain the most truthful account of T'oegye's personality.[28] Several eyewitness accounts recorded by T'oegye's pupils are then cited. One recounts how T'oegye interacted with mediocre scholars in discussing academic issues. Rather than making his argument directly, T'oegye always tried to embrace all perspectives. And even in the heat of the debate T'oegye would wait patiently until his counterpart had completed his argument, expressing his own ideas only afterward.[29] The revelation of T'oegye's human qualities in these accounts, set against the pedantic and impractical formalism that nationalists denounced in the doctrinalism of the Chosŏn Confucian literati, highlights the contrast between the virtue registered in the everyday speeches of the master and the Confucian discourse associated with the written texts, privileging the former as the basis of T'oegye's representation as a moral paragon. Precisely in its capacity to transmit spoken words, the premodern textual tradition crept into the modern print media, which enabled the nationalists to cast Korean culture as something relevant to the modern society. The moral force of Confucian tradition thus lent itself to building nationalism in colonial Korea.

The Confucian literati of this period also valued "unofficial" histories as the authentic representations of the Korean self. For instance, Kang Hyo-sŏk (d.u.) collected anecdotes and stories about notable historical figures under the title *Strange Hearsays in Korea* (*Taedong kimun*) in 1926. In the preface, Kim Yŏng-han (1878–1950) claimed that Korean people neglect things close to home and admire whatever is new and mysterious and foreign in origin. People tend to know about the affairs of foreign countries yet remain ignorant of "the words and deeds" of their fathers and grandfathers.[30] This statement implies the overwhelming impact of foreign cultures, which sparked intellectuals' scrutiny of Korean self-identity. It also shows that Confucian literati of this period tried to find "Koreanness" in the everyday interactions discovered in the eyewitness testimonials. In other words, the testimonials produced in unofficial sectors were the literary genre that most effectively shielded Korean identity from the encroachment of foreign influences.

As short vignettes, stories about T'oegye derived from the oral tradition also populated the pages of newspapers in the early twentieth century. Readily accessible to the general public, these stories seem to have been well suited for the readers of the modern mass media, who were very familiar with traditional storytelling. As Japan's annexation of Korea loomed, anecdotes about T'oegye as a moral exemplar—like the famous episode in which T'oegye returned a plum from the neighbor's tree that had fallen into his yard—were tied to didactic purposes.[31] The intertextual reading practice engendered by the print medium of the modern newspaper further amplified the nationalist relevance of the anecdote. This story about T'oegye's high moral standards was placed immediately after an editorial criticizing a pro-Japanese organization, Ilchinhoe. The drastic turn of topic and tone between the two newspaper articles delivered the editor's perception about the function of the Confucian past amid the imminent Japanese colonization of Chosŏn. The Confucian past was to be the moral guideline when collaborators such as members of Ilchinhoe easily abandoned the nation. This moral function of stories about Confucian worthies continued even after 1910. Another article in the newspaper *Kwŏnŏp sinmun* introduces an anecdote that is claimed not to be found in the *Record of Words and Deeds of Master T'oegye* (*T'oedo ŏnhaengnok*) while arguing that T'oegye's moral virtues should be learned even if the times change.[32] It states that, although T'oegye's clothing (alluding to his neo-Confucian theories) does not fit the bodies of contemporary people due to the temporal distance between them, his devotion to moral values is always fitting.[33] This radical editorial policy of including historically inauthentic stories demonstrates the effectiveness of using Confucian masters to raise people's national consciousness and inspire them to become members of an "imagined community."[34] The Korean case, however, demonstrates a more complicated deployment of what Benedict Anderson calls the "temporal coincidence" that made newspapers "one-day best-sellers" through the mass ceremony of simultaneously consuming sociopolitical information.[35] In Korea reading newspaper articles about Confucian masters led readers to retell, relay, and comment on these stories spontaneously and communally. The remnants of premodern storytelling in modern newspapers could tie Korean people into a community sharing both diachronic ethical values and synchronic political urgency.[36]

Such newspaper accounts about T'oegye did not supplant the more traditional works but existed alongside them. Indeed, the successful reincarnation of T'oegye as the moral paragon representative of the Korean nation in this period can partly be ascribed to the active publication of traditional works about him. Local Confucian scholars continued to produce the collections of T'oegye's words and deeds, and these maintained multilayered discourses with the new narratives about T'oegye in the modern media. The *Record of T'oegye's Words and Deeds* (*T'oegye Sŏnsaeng ŏnhaengnok*) was published in 1905 by Tosan Academy and reprinted in 1923 by Yi Ch'ung-ho (d.u.), T'oegye's thirteenth-generation descendant. Yi Ch'ung-ho also oversaw the first publication of Yi Ik's *Essential Words of Master Yi* [*T'oegye*] in 1920 by Chagye Academy of Andong.

If T'oegye prevailed in the modern nationalist discourse by the virtue of his image as a moral scholar, it was not his own writings on Confucian metaphysics but the records of his spoken words and daily practices from which his moral superiority was recuperated. In relating to T'oegye, Korean readers of magazines and newspapers in the early twentieth century did not have to understand, or even care about, the difficult and arcane discourse of Confucian philosophy. T'oegye became a Confucian master in a modern sense through nonacademic and anecdotal storytelling. But since psychosocial proximity to T'oegye constituted the core of his charismatic appeal, the loss of the kinds of narratives that humanized him radically changed his image in subsequent decades.

Japanese Appropriation of T'oegye in the Late Colonial Period

In the early colonial period, the Japanese government commissioned Takahashi Tōru (1878–1967) to conduct research on Chosŏn Confucian culture as part of its attempt to justify the colonization of Korea historically. Takahashi delved into T'oegye's scholarship and came up with a means of categorizing Chosŏn Confucian discourses in two distinct schools, one emphasizing *i* (Confucian principles) and the other *ki* (material force). The two schools attested to the intellectual heritage of T'oegye and Yulgok respectively. Takahashi further argued that of all the Confucian scholars who were active during Chosŏn, only these two men had contributed to the development of Chosŏn Confucian culture. However, he discounted their scholarship as being completely derivative of Zhu Xi's, often going so far as to merely parrot Zhu Xi's theory verbatim.[37] In Takahashi's eyes, T'oegye and Yulgok thus became testaments to the absence of creativity in Korean tradition, which copied Chinese culture. Although Takahashi's scholarship aimed to justify Japanese colonial rule by denigrating the Korean past, his binary approach to Chosŏn Confucianism paradoxically developed into one of the main approaches to Korean intellectual history in postcolonial South Korea.[38] More significant, his interpretation marked the dramatic turn from the oral to the written in modern adaptations of Korean Confucianism.

The Japanese treatment of Korean Confucianism changed toward the end of the colonial period, particularly during the Japanese engagement in World War II when the commonality and connection between Korea and Japan had to be emphasized in order to encourage Koreans to willingly join the war mobilization.[39] As the imperial policy in the colony shifted toward assimilation, so did the dominant approach to T'oegye. Rather than criticizing his scholarship as a mere copy of the Chinese original, the colonizers attempted to incorporate T'oegye into the Japanese classical tradition. For example, a lecture series on Japanese classics sponsored by the colonial government in 1943 had the expressed goal of invigorating the imperial spirit for victory in the war. At this event, Abe Yoshio (1905–?) lectured on T'oegye's influence on Yamazaki Ansai's (1619–82) theory of the national body (*kokutai*).[40] Japanese scholars handpicked T'oegye as the key link connecting the intellectual cultures of Korea and Japan and made use of this idea in their contemporary political schemes. Interestingly, Korean nationalist intellectuals echoed the Japanese discourse to increase national pride, interpreting it against the grain of the imperial agenda. For them the fact that T'oegye's Confucian theory had shaped Japanese scholarly culture indicated the superiority of Korea to Japan.

What Takahashi's and Abe's approaches to T'oegye had in common, despite their divergent political purposes, was a persistent focus on the theoretical aspects of T'oegye's scholarship. At the same time, this distanced T'oegye from the general public, which could not be expected to appreciate the highly technical and abstract theoretical discussions surrounding neo-Confucian metaphysics. Because ordinary readers could no longer reproduce stories about T'oegye, scholars dominated the discourse, not in newspapers or magazines but in academic publications. The academic exchange depended mainly on T'oegye's written works; thus, the dynamic between the oral and the written that had shaped Korean Confucian tradition was significantly attenuated. The displacement of storytelling about T'oegye kept him out of the popular discourse. He was honored as a great master but narrowly enshrined in an ivory tower, the relevance of his greatness limited to only a few scholars with in-depth knowledge about neo-Confucianism. This colonial legacy influenced both intellectual history and popular discourse in postcolonial South Korea, particularly during the Park Chung Hee period.

Constructing a National Tradition as the Antidote to Democracy

Park Chung Hee's perspective about the past was influenced by the historical inquiries of the 1950s and 1960s, during which South Korean historians attempted to find the indigenous origins of modernization as part of downplaying the effects of the colonial experience. These postliberation historians reduced Chosŏn Confucian culture to impractical and empty intellectualism as they looked to recuperate an alternative legacy from less orthodox movements.[41] In order to justify the coup that overthrew the Korean Second Republic in 1961, the Park regime had to improve actual economic conditions while rhetorically inculcating its superiority to past political systems. From the beginning of his presidency, therefore, Park promoted economic development and anticommunism as the prerequisites for democracy.[42] On many occasions he overtly denounced the Chosŏn tradition as a deterrent to economic momentum. As early as 1962, he claimed that Chosŏn's legacy abetted national disunity by ingraining subservience, factionalism, exclusionism, and a sense of special privilege in the Korean people.[43] He criticized Confucian ideology for its extreme formalism and dogmatism, manifested in the lack of tolerance for other schools of thought and learning,[44] and elaborated on Chosŏn's negative economic legacy especially. In the Chosŏn, he opined, economy and politics were not sufficiently differentiated; the politicians pursued surplus value only in terms of political power, and private merchants were reluctant to undertake independent enterprises without the backing of bureaucrats.[45] This history was incompatible with Park's political blueprint for state-led economic development. In evaluating his eighteen-year presidency in 1979, Park proudly claimed that modern Korea had managed to achieve miraculous economic development by wiping out "premodern elements."[46]

In another publication written in 1971, Park emphatically discounted the scholarship of T'oegye and Yulgok as empty words, highly speculative and aloof from reality. Park praised instead the Sirhak (Practical "Science") school, which, he argued, had initiated national modernization by admitting scientific knowledge imported from China and Europe into the field of scholarly inquiry.[47] This approach to the Chosŏn led some later scholars to argue that Park set up a dichotomous relationship between "Korean" and "modern."[48] However, the past remained bittersweet. As it had been for the early-twentieth-century nationalists, the past was something that had to be decimated and overcome in order to achieve the promise of a better national future. But it also provided a crucial political means of uniting and rallying the people. Carrying these contradictory sociocultural connotations, Park's treatment of Chosŏn Confucian tradition changed repeatedly under different political circumstances brought on by rapid urbanization during his presidency.

State-led economic development under the Park regime accelerated the urbanization of Korean society. The government promoted the concentration of people in industrial centers in order to foster growth in the manufacturing sector. Urbanization, however, also substantially undermined the political base of Park Chung Hee. Young laborers, gathered in the emerging industrial centers, formed a significant portion of the urban population and developed into new social groups. Their social consciousness raised as a result of mistreatment and exploitation in the workplace, these young people were susceptible to new ideas about society and politics. Their radicalization was also spurred by interactions with dissident university students, many of whom infiltrated the manufacturing sector through night school, where they taught young workers about such ideas as class struggle, labor relations, and social inequality. Many young workers grew into political dissidents through these experiences. Even though Park, from the very early years of his presidency, attempted to infuse the ideologies of nationalism and developmentalism into the working population to make them accept state policies,[49] voters in urban areas turned against him in ever greater numbers. The regime therefore depended disproportionately on electoral support from the rural sectors.[50] Although economic development was vital if Park Chung Hee was to hold on to political authority, the urbanization accompanying industrialization caused the rapid erosion of his political base. The regime fell into a predicament that required it to constantly mobilize urban workers economically as the key element of production while demobilizing them politically as a threat to national security.[51]

The regime was particularly hostile to urban popular culture, which was dominated by the young generation. People in their early twenties in the late 1960s and early 1970s had been born after the end of Japanese colonial rule and the beginning of American military power in Korea and thus were influenced more by American than Japanese culture. Although they did not experience democracy, they were taught its values through the postcolonial educational system.[52] Therefore, many would not willingly accept the legitimacy of the military authority and engaged in cultural forms that functioned as channels for political expression. The more radical among them even admired the hippie culture introduced through American pop culture, which imbued them with anarchistic ideas.[53]

The government summarily labeled these cultural backlashes against authoritarianism as the degradation of social morale caused by rapid industrialization. Park Chung Hee claimed that a highly industrialized society put human beings into unhappy and fettered situations, making men the slaves of machines and materialism. In a mass society, he continued, fraternity and compassion disappear, and man finds himself in a state of increasing alienation and loneliness.[54] Identifying a "spiritual vacuum" and "excessive materialism" as the most heinous outcomes of rapid urbanization, Park claimed that beautiful native customs and lifestyles had been eclipsed while fads and fashions made people blind to the reality of Korean society.[55] He singled out the young generation as being especially susceptible to these social ills, "turning to decadence and growing their hair long" in an attempt to fill the spiritual vacuum.[56] Taking the president's diagnosis as a prescription for action, the government began to regulate men's hair and women's skirt length.[57] The government also banned 225 popular songs and arrested 27 singers, instead giving the youngsters several hundred "morally sound popular songs" to sing.[58] Further, it subjected them to military training as part of the regular curriculum in high schools and universities starting in 1968.[59] Regarding urban popular culture as a threat and attempting to eradicate it, the Park regime needed some alternative to suppress the young urban trends and consolidate people around the state by raising their group consciousness.

Park also argued that the moral decadence of Korean society was closely related to the people's hasty demand for democracy. Koreans' thoughtless imitation of foreign political systems had brought on disorder and confusion, which were followed by continued poverty and instability.[60] The developing countries with historical experience of colonialism or semicolonialism, he opined, had ended up inviting antisocial groups to voice their political demands all at once when Western-style democracy was too precipitately introduced.[61] Moreover, he asserted that the indiscriminate importation of individualism and democracy from the West after 1945 had turned people against their own culture, thereby causing inferior elements of Western culture to ruin the glorious Korean tradition.[62] Park asserted that Western democracy was not compatible with the historical and social conditions of South Korea, and, more significant, he condemned democracy as the origin of sociopolitical problems.

His diatribe against "Western-style democracy" foregrounded the national spirit as the driving force for development that would form the core of national identity and regenerate the Korean nation.[63] The president's call for the creation of a new national culture was accompanied by a look back at the moral thought of traditional Korean philosophers in the search for "the foundation of subjective spirit" (*chuch'ejŏk chŏngsin kiban*).[64] The resurrection of T'oegye under the Park presidency took place in this context. Neglected and belittled as Koreans slavishly accepted Western democracy, historical figures, such as T'oegye, who were associated with Korea's Confucian past were rediscovered and resuscitated by order of the state.

For the Park regime, such a Confucian revival had yet another benefit. The seat of authority for historical figures like T'oegye was often located in rural areas. T'oegye's legacy, for example, was in Yean, the site of his academy, which Park ordered restored in 1969. In emphasizing T'oegye's importance, Park paid tremendous attention to rural society as an alternative cultural base while elaborating on the "national spirit" as the antidote to defiant urban culture. He proclaimed that it was in the countryside that such "pristine" Korean sentiments as compassion and fraternity could be found and revived. In this vein, he put forth the spiritual values of Confucian culture, which had been buried in the rural society, as the alternative lifestyle in modern Korea. However, the ways in which he honored Confucian tradition actually made it inaccessible and arcane for the general public.

Visualizing the Master, Silencing His Voice

T'oegye was only one of several historical figures that Park resurrected. In 1966 the regime renovated Hyŏnch'ungsa, the shrine dedicated to the legendary admiral of the Imjin War, Yi Sun-sin (1545–98). There followed construction of a memorial hall for King Sejong (r. 1418–50), arguably the greatest monarch of Chosŏn, in 1967. Yi became the symbol of patriotism, sacrifice for the state, and martial prowess—the values that the military government propagated among its citizens. Meanwhile, King Sejong stood for creativity and practicality, as exemplified in the invention of the Korean alphabet and various scientific instruments. Honoring national heroes entailed erecting their statues, and between 1968 and 1972 the government commissioned no fewer than fifteen statues of historical figures, starting with Yi Sun-sin and Sejong.[65] Although the Park regime claimed that these activities were designed to infuse South Korean minds with national consciousness, they deliver much more complex connotations in the sociopolitical context of Park's dictatorship. Unlike the traditional ways of honoring the past, which focused on storytelling about historical figures, the regime created monumental spectacles—architectural edifices and sculptures that awed viewers into a consensus. Their shared role as spectators and their distance from the magnificent images of historical figures made the public a deferential community. The veneration of national heroes thus worked to unite all citizens through a shared past regardless of their political stances. Examining the government's process of honoring Yi Sun-sin, Saeyoung Park rightly explicates its political effects: "Spectacles succeed through obfuscation, by concealing the brute immediacy of power underneath an 'uninterrupted monologue of self-praise.'"[66]

T'oegye's statue was erected in front of the Namsan Municipal Library in the heart of Seoul in 1970 and unveiled by Park Chung Hee himself. According to Chŏng Ho-gi, the Park regime's simultaneous and systematic installation of statues in everyday spaces was unprecedented; the statues mainly targeted Seoul residents rather than the whole population.[67] Because the "national spirit" constructed through such heroes was aimed at discrediting defiant urban pop culture influenced by Western democracy, these historical figures representing pristine Korean tradition needed to be in the city center. The government explicated their significance with such current political terms as *modernization, anticommunism,* and *economic development.* T'oegye was packaged as the symbol of diligence and frugality.

Even if we take into account the political effectiveness of monumental installations, Park's reemphasis of the Confucian tradition is quite shocking given that he had denounced the Chosŏn Confucian heritage as a deterrent to modernization and economic development. However, he later asserted that the nation could achieve greater development by reawakening the strength of Korea's long tradition.[68] Park had been ambivalent about the past, and he eclectically appropriated parts of it under discrete sociopolitical circumstances. T'oegye's monumentalization was accompanied by the institutionalization of his legacy in a couple of additional ways. One was the restoration of Tosan Academy. The record of the restoration published by the Ministry of Culture and Public Information reveals clearly how the government sought to represent T'oegye within the modernization discourse and, by extension, how the Park regime intended to position itself in the long history of Korea. The record traces the origin of modernization in Korea back to the enlightenment movement at the beginning of the twentieth century, explains this movement as an offshoot of the Practical Learning school of Confucianism, and finally claims that Practical Learning was influenced by T'oegye's scholarship. In sum the narrative credits T'oegye's studies of human nature and Confucian principles with opening the way to modernization in an exact reversal of Park's earlier criticism of T'oegye.[69] This revision of the status of Confucianism made a strong case that modernization did not necessarily have to be Westernization.[70]

This account also argues that T'oegye embodied diligence and frugality throughout his life by rejecting formalistic and extravagant pretenses, and thus provided a model that Korean people in the modern period could follow.[71] It is striking that T'oegye became the symbol of rational economic activities, because we have no concrete historical record supporting this interpretation. Instead of providing the general public with anecdotes or scenes of everyday life to share and reproduce, the Park regime arbitrarily created a new image of T'oegye for its own purposes.

In thus honoring T'oegye, the Park regime made his own scholarship available to the public rather than circulating stories drawn from secondary records of his words. As I pointed out, the collection of his writings was first translated into *han'gŭl* in 1968. Park ordered a complete translation of T'oegye's writings again in 1970 and authorized a lecture series about T'oegye's scholarship to be held in several major cities that same year. The following year, while visiting Tosan Academy, Park ordered the publication of the papers presented in this series; they appeared in 1972 under the title *Research on T'oegye Studies* (*T'oegyehak yŏn'gu*). He also ordered that a research institute dedicated to T'oegye be established adjacent to the academy. In this way, the regime sanctified Tosan Academy as the birthplace of the national spirit.

The contents of *Research on T'oegye Studies* show that the government-sponsored scholars mainly focused on philosophical and metaphysical aspects of T'oegye's scholarship.[72] The term *T'oegye studies* was first used in this publication; it later took root as a bona fide subject of Korean philosophy and some related disciplines. The emphasis on his academic feats made T'oegye's own writings the essential source legitimating this process of national anointing. As in the late colonial period, academic journals replaced the mass media as the discursive space in which to address T'oegye. Publication of the *Journal of T'oegye Studies* (*T'oegye hakpo*) began in 1973; it remains today the main academic channel for scholarly discussions about T'oegye. The nature of the discourse and the forms of media that delivered it substantially reduced the exposure of T'oegye to the public. Even though his writings were translated into Korean, the arcane, metaphysical issues he discussed could hardly attract general readers' attention. The development of T'oegye studies in modern scholarship was dominated by the very few academics who could command the language of Confucian metaphysics. To the public, therefore, T'oegye became at once a great man and an incomprehensible one. This development of T'oegye studies as an elite enterprise contrasted with the rise of urban popular culture favored by ordinary young people, which the Park regime wanted to repress.

The emphasis on academism bears a striking resemblance to how Japanese scholars portrayed T'oegye as part of their assimilation policy in the late colonial period. Both the Japanese colonial government and the Park regime eulogized T'oegye as *the* Confucian master; however, their focus on esoteric philosophical issues distanced him from the public. This pattern made the position of the state authority explicit, because the state systematically excluded the general public from honoring historical figures, and reinforced this power relationship. People had no choice but to legitimate the state project due to its monopoly over and construction of a shared history to which all social actors were supposed to belong. Unlike the traditional mode of honoring T'oegye, which invited all readers to interpret and reproduce the stories about him in a spontaneous and organic fashion, the mechanism installed by modern governments, be it colonial or authoritarian, aimed to create a rigid and monolithic narrative that could be studied and accepted but not embodied or hybridized.

Instead of disqualifying the general public from their storytelling roles, the Park regime inserted visual images of T'oegye into everyday life. The lack of correlation between the historical contexts in which these figures lived and the modern political rhetoric, however, was not appealing.[73] Although the image of T'oegye had become as mundane and ubiquitous as the thousand-won banknote by 1975, the visual familiarity created by this national circulation did not develop into the charismatic attraction that he had in the late Chosŏn and early modern periods. Without stories to reproduce and appropriate, people could not easily engage with T'oegye.

Still, the tradition of storytelling lingered even as a new mechanism of charisma focusing on the visual reached all the way down to elementary schools. Across the country, statues of historical figures were erected on school grounds to serve as embodiments of the didactic lessons that the state sought to instill in young minds. These new visual installations at the local level, however, became clusters of new practices of storytelling unsanctioned by the state as people began to create a variety of spooky stories about the statues coming alive.[74] Their reactions epitomize how badly the general public needed stories in order to relate to historical figures. It also demonstrates that the verbal embodiment of historical figures was what generated their charismatic authority.

The written reproductions of the oral tradition and the visual installations honor T'oegye in vastly different ways. Whereas the former invite virtually anyone to join the process of revising, reinterpreting, and reproducing the stories, the latter are simply given to the people without any possibility that they can add to them. Notably, both the visual and the written constrained members of the general public from contributing their interpretations of or objections to the representations of the past granted by the state. Here Jack Goody's analysis of the difference between the oral and the written applies and can be extended to embrace the visual. While continual creation characterizes the oral tradition, the written only encourages readers to repeat and internalize established texts.[75] This passive role reflects the political status of South Korean citizens during the Yusin period. The state monopolized and locked in the meanings of the past in the written and visual domains, confining social actors to the role of mere docile recipients. The "national spirit" originating in the historical past again reinforced the citizens' passive role, as they could not deny the sublimity of the nation. The shift in the pattern of honoring T'oegye from the oral to the written and the visual exemplifies the intensification of control over the society by the Park regime during the Yusin era.

Conclusion

By honoring T'oegye, the Park Chung Hee regime intended to present an alternative to the urban pop culture that defied authoritarianism. The values that the state brought forth promoted using T'oegye were explicitly antithetical to the voices opposing the regime: rural areas as the origin of Korean identity against the cities, the established generation against youngsters, elites against the general public, frugality against consumerism, and, most important, Korean-style political institutions against democracy. However, the honoring of T'oegye did not appeal to the people in the way Park Chung Hee intended. The Park regime focused on creating the image of T'oegye by establishing his scholarly excellence through his written works and his personal awesomeness through diverse visual images. This process defied the way T'oegye had been eulogized as *the* Confucian master of Chosŏn through eyewitness testimonials about his life, which invited future generations to join the constant, open storytelling about him. Although the visual image of T'oegye on the banknote and in statues made him part of citizens' daily lives, the arcane neo-Confucian theories in his writings made him inaccessible. The field of T'oegye studies, developed in the Yusin period, excluded the general public from the process of creating T'oegye's image. This elite enterprise mainly delved into the meanings of T'oegye's own scholarly treatises rather than organically bringing him into the contemporary context by embodying the stories about him. This shift from the oral to the written and the visual demonstrates the ways the Yusin regime displaced the relationship between the historical past and the people in contemporary Korean society.

Epilogue

The many afterlives of T'oegye's words that this chapter has traced reveal the relationship between orality and literacy in the establishment and transmission of charismatic authority. T'oegye's case is not unique, of course. The records of spoken words, including the Bible, the Qur'an, and Buddhist sutras, have established diverse charismatic religious figures in world history. From Confucius's *Analects* to Plato's *Socrates*, great scholars of all periods have depended for their recognition on the written records of their speech produced by their disciples. The global history of charisma attests to the fact that members of the general public have always wanted to connect themselves directly to great minds. The records of spoken words also allowed them access to the specific contexts of historical moments in order to manipulate them for their diverse causes. This interface between the oral and the written continues to empower historical figures to attain and perpetuate charismatic authority.

For more recent examples from East Asia, we might turn to Mao Zedong's *The Little Red Book*, so instrumental in mobilizing teenagers as the vanguard in shattering the existing power structure in China during the Cultural Revolution. Kim Il Sung (Kim Il-sŏng) also made his speeches available in written form in diverse publications and went a step further by declaring his idiolect the lexical norm of the reformed "cultural language" (*munhwaŏ*) that would not favor any one geographic area at the expense of others in the formalization of the standard national language.[76]

Park Chung Hee, too, may have been keenly aware of the importance of the textualization of the verbal. While depriving T'oegye of this same mechanism, the regime meticulously recorded Park's speeches and conversations, publishing his speeches starting in 1965. Some were compiled into separate volumes on special topics.[77] But even more influential in creating Park's popular image were newspaper serials published after his death. For example, Kim Chŏng-nyŏm, who was Park's chief of staff from 1969 to 1978, serialized a memoir in *JoongAng Daily (Chungang ilbo)* in 1997. His eyewitness testimony delivered anecdotes showing that Park was obsessed with his mission to make the country wealthy yet gave up his personal comfort and luxuries. This memoir, published as a monograph in 1998, spread the well-known stories about Park, such as his preference for inexpensive, unfiltered Korean rice wine rather than Western liquors. In the late 1990s, Cho Kap-che, a journalist who publicly eulogized Park as the most prominent and charismatic leader of Korea, serialized a similar memoir in *Chosun Daily (Chosŏn ilbo)*.[78] In 2005 the *JoongAng Daily* serialized a memoir by Kim Sŏng-jin, who had worked for the Ministry of Culture and Public Information during the Yusin period.[79] Reflecting on the rapid economic development during the Park regime in the wake of the Asian financial crisis, the populist rhetoric called for another strong leader to lift the country from its gloomy economic situation.[80] Just as glimpses into T'oegye's daily life attracted newspaper readers in the early twentieth century, the exposure of Park's human aspects changed the public perception of him. These ex-bureaucrats and journalists did the same job that T'oegye's disciples had done to honor their master. The psychological proximity constructed in the newspaper serials was remarkably useful in creating emotional portrayals of Park. The general public could manipulate the stories about him as well as process the history of the Park regime in their own terms. This distinguished Park Chung Hee from other historical figures of modern Korea and became the basis of his popular support.

NOTES

1. Park, Chung Hee (Pak Chŏng-hŭi), *To Build a Nation* (Washington, DC: Acropolis, 1971), 193.

2. Kim Chong-sŏng, *Han'guksa inmul t'ongch'al: P'yŏmha wa ch'ansa ro twibakkwin 18-in ŭi tu ŏlgul* (Kyŏnggi-do, Koyang-si: Yŏksa ŭi Ach'im, 2010), 174–75.

3. Eric Hobsbawm, "Introduction: Inventing Traditions," in *The Invention of Tradition*, edited by Eric Hobsbawm and Terence Ranger (Cambridge: Cambridge University Press, 1983),1.

4. Ibid., 8.

5. Stephen Vlastos, "Tradition: Past/Present Culture and Modern Japanese History," in *Mirror of Modernity: Invented Traditions of Modern Japan*, edited by Stephen Vlastos (Berkeley: University of California Press, 1998), 8.

6. *Mongjae chŏnsŏ*, 1:11a–13b.

7. *T'oegye Sŏnsaeng yŏnbo*, 3: 24a.

8. *Kanjae Sŏnsaeng munjip*, 7: 20a–21b. Kojŏng (Ch. Kaoting) is an alias of Zhu Xi. This name originated from the fact that Zhu Xi studied and taught students at Kaoting in the Jianyang area.

9. For more discussion about the triangular connection among the master, his disciples, and the texts, see Mark Edward Lewis, *Writing and Authority in Early China* (Albany: State University of New York Press, 1999), 58.

10. Brinkley Messick, *The Calligraphic State: Textual Domination and History in a Muslim Society* (Berkeley: University of California Press, 1996 [1993]), 252.

11. For the interconnected relationship between the oral and the written, see Jack Goody, *The Interface between the Written and the Oral* (Cambridge: Cambridge University Press, 1987), xii; Walter J. Ong, *Orality and Literacy: The Technologizing of the Word* (London: Routledge, 1982), 9.

12. *Ch'anggye chip sŏ*, 1a, emphasis added. Note that both a preface written by Kim Ch'ang-hyŏp is also called *Ch'anggye chip sŏ*.

13. Jack Goody and Ian Watt, "The Consequences of Literacy," in *Literacy in Traditional Societies*, ed. Jack Goody (Cambridge: Cambridge University Press, 1968), 27–68.

14. *Ch'angsŏl Sŏnsaeng munjip*, 8: 26a–b.

15. Ibid., 1: 1b.

16. *T'oegye Sŏnsaeng ŏnhaengnok*, 1: 1a.

17. Most notably, Yi Su-yŏn (1693–1748), a sixth-generation descendant of T'oegye, published another such compilation in 1722 by revising Kwŏn's work, which had been published one year earlier. Yi criticized Kwŏn by arguing that his work displays many discrepancies with disciples' original records. Considering that Kwŏn's work was well received by other scholars, Yi's immediate reaction can be understood as stemming from anxiety about his loss of dominance over T'oegye's heritage. For more details, see Hwisang Cho, "The Community of Letters: The T'oegye School and the Political Culture of Chosŏn Korea, 1545–1800" (PhD diss., Columbia University, 2010), 299–306.

18. *Sŏngho Sŏnsaeng chŏnjip*, 24: 28a–29b.

19. *Yija suŏ pal*.

20. *Sunam chip haengjang*, 9b–10a.

21. *Yulgok chŏnsŏ kwŏn samsibil mongnok*, 1a. This comment from *Yulgok chŏnsŏ* does not specify who criticized the authenticity of Pak's record. However, according to the Korean translation Song Si-yŏl made this criticism. I have not figured out how the

scholars who translated it concluded that it was Song who expressed skepticism about Pak's record. See *Kugyŏk Yulgok chip I* (Seoul: Minjok Munhwa Ch'ujin Wiwŏnhoe, 1968), 446.

22. *Yulgok chŏnsŏ kwŏn samsibil mongnok*, 1a.

23. *Uam Sŏnsaeng ŏnhaengnok pŏmnye*, 1a.

24. Jacques Derrida, *Of Grammatology*, trans. Gayatri Chakravorty Spivak (Baltimore: Johns Hopkins University Press, 1976).

25. Kim Yun-sik, "Yurimgye rŭl wihaya," *Kaebyŏk* 7 (January 1921): 16. The Confucian organizations mentioned here include Yudo Chinhŭnghoe, Taedong Samunhoe, and T'aegŭkhoe.

26. The journal categorized the ten great figures in ten fields: Yi Hwang for philosophy, Ch'oe Che-u (1824–64) for religion, Yi I (1536–84) for politics, Sŏ Kyŏng-dŏk (1489–1546) for science, Yi Sun-sin (1545–98) for military affairs, Mun Ik-chŏm (1329–98) for industry, Ch'oe Ch'i-wŏn (857–?) for literature, Solgŏ (d.u.) for arts, Ch'oe Ch'ung (984–1068) for education, and Yu Kil-chun (1856–1914) for social reform. See "Wiin t'up'yo palp'yo," *Kaebyŏk* 13 (July 1921): 148.

27. "Tongbang ihak ŭi chongjo in Yi T'oegye Sŏnsaeng, Chosŏn siptae wiin sogae ŭi ki i," *Kaebyŏk* 15 (September 1921): 73–85.

28. Ibid., 75, 84.

29. Ibid., 78.

30. Kim Yŏng-han, "Sŏ Taedong kimun," in *Taedong kimun*, ed. Kang Min-sŏk (Kyŏngsŏng: Hanyang Sŏwŏn, 1926), n.p.

31. "Chaptongsani," *Taehan maeil sinbo*, November 30, 1909. This record also appears in *Hearsay in Korea*, compiled in 1926, which the editor quoted from Kwŏn Mun-hae's (1534–91) *Encyclopedia of Korea Sorted Out by Rhymes* (*Taedong unok*), completed in 1589.

32. *Kwŏnŏp sinmun*, February 9, 1913.

33. "Mobŏmhal manhan inmul ŭi mobŏmhal manhan illo T'oegye Sŏnsaeng ŭi haengjŏk ŭl tŭnora," ibid.

34. Benedict Anderson, *Imagined Communities: Reflections on the Origin and Spread of Nationalism* (London: Verso, 1991).

35. Ibid., 24, 35.

36. For more examples of the historical traces that reside in new media forms, see Charles R. Acland, ed., *Residual Media* (Minneapolis: University of Minnesota Press, 2007).

37. Tak'ahasi Tooru, *Chosŏn ŭi yuhak*, trans. Cho Nam-ho (Seoul: Chohap Kongdongch'e Sonamu, 1999), 213–27.

38. Cho Nam-ho, "Yŏkchuja haesŏl," in Tak'ahasi, *Chosŏn ŭi yuhak*, 8–19; also see Cho Nam-ho, "Churi chugi nonjaeng: Chosŏn esŏ chugi ch'ŏrhak ŭn kanŭnghan'ga," in *Nonjaeng ŭro ponŭn Han'guk ch'ŏrhak*, ed. Han'guk Ch'ŏrhak Sasang Yŏn'guhoe (Seoul: Yemun Sŏwŏn, 1995), 129–31.

39. See Gi-Wook Shin, *Ethnic Nationalism in Korea: Genealogy, Politics, and Legacy* (Stanford, CA: Stanford University Press, 2006), 41–57.

40. *Maeil sinbo*, October 16, 1943.

41. Ko Yŏng-jin, *Chosŏn sidae sasangsa rŭl ŏttŏke pol kŏsin'ga* (Seoul: P'ulpit, 1999), 411–15.

42. Hyung-A Kim and Clark W. Sorensen, eds., *Reassessing the Park Chung Hee Era, 1961–1979: Development, Political Thought, Democracy, and Cultural Influence* (Seattle: University of Washington Press, 2011), 5.

43. Park Chung Hee (Pak Chŏng-hŭi), *Our Nation's Path: Ideology of Social Reconstruction* (Seoul: Dong-a Pub. Co., 1962), 13.

44. Ibid., 41–42.

45. Ibid., 57.

46. Park Chung Hee (Pak Chŏng-hŭi), *Korea Reborn: A Model for Development* (Englewood Cliffs, NJ: Prentice-Hall, 1979), 142.

47. Park translated the term *sirhak* as "practical science" instead of the more conventional "practical learning." This demonstrates that practicality for Park meant only scientific knowledge and technological advancement. This approach excludes other characteristics of practical learning such as social and administrative reforms. See Park, *To Build a Nation*, 38.

48. Saeyoung Park, "National Heroes and Monuments in South Korea: Patriotism, Modernization, and Park Chung Hee's Remaking of Yi Sunsin's Shrine," *Asia-Pacific Journal* 24 no. 3 (2010) n.p.

49. Namhee Lee, *The Making of Minjung: Democracy and the Politics of Representation in South Korea* (Ithaca, NY: Cornell University Press, 2007), 213–39; Hagen Koo, "The State, Minjung, and the Working Class in South Korea," in *State and Society in Contemporary Korea*, edited by Hagen Koo (Ithaca, NY: Cornell University Press, 1993), 137–42.

50. Clark W. Sorensen, "Rural Modernization under the Park Regime in the 1960s," in *Reassessing the Park Chung Hee Era, 1961–1979: Development, Political Thought, Democracy, and Cultural Influence*, edited by Hyung-A Kim and Clark W. Sorensen (Seattle: University of Washington Press, 2011), 146.

51. Ibid., 128.

52. Han Hong-gu, *Yusin: Ojik han saram ŭl wihan sidae* (Seoul: Han'gyŏre Ch'ulp'an, 2014), 160–61.

53. Kong Che-uk, "Sŏron: Pak Chŏng-hŭi sidae ilsang saenghwal yŏn'gu ŭi ŭimi," in *Kukka wa ilsang: Pak Chŏng-hŭi sidae*, ed. Kong Che-uk (Kyŏnggi-do P'aju-si: Tosŏ ch'ulp'an Hanul, 2008), 18–19.

54. Park, *Korea Reborn*, 105.

55. Ibid., 108.

56. Ibid., 107.

57. Kong Che-uk, "Sŏron," 18–19.

58. Han Hong-gu, *Yusin*, 155.

59. Ibid., 160–62.

60. Park, *Korea Reborn*, 13.

61. Ibid., 42.

62. Ibid., 191.

63. Ibid., 20–21.

64. Yi Tong-jun, "T'oegye Sŏnsaeng sabaek chugi kinyŏm saŏp pogo," *T'oegye hakpo* 1 (1973): 42.

65. Other historical figures include Samyŏngdang (1544–1610), Yi I, Wŏnhyo (617–86), Kim Yu-sin (595–673), Ŭlchi Mundŏk (d.u.), Yu Kwan-sun (1902–20), Sin Saimdang (1504–51), Chŏng Mong-ju (1337–92), Chŏng Yak-yong (1762–1836), Yi Hwang, Kang Kam-ch'an (948–1031), Kim Tae-gŏn (1821–46), and Yun Pong-gil (1908–32). See Chŏng Ho-gi, "Ilsang konggan sogŭi yŏng'ung kwa aeguk chuŭi," in *Kukka wa Ilsang: Pak Chŏnghŭi sidae*, edited by Kong Che-uk (Kyŏnggi-do P'aju-si: Tosŏ ch'ulp'an Hanul, 2008), 470–508.

66. Saeyoung Park, "National Heroes and Monuments in South Korea."

67. Chŏng, "Ilsang konggan sogŭi yŏng'ung kwa aeguk chuŭi," 470, 497.

68. Park, *Korea Reborn*, 142.

69. Munhwa Kongbobu, ed., *Tosan Sŏwŏn chungsuji* (Munhwa Kongbobu, 1970), 9.

70. Park, *Korea Reborn*, 30; Park, *To Build a Nation*, 193.

71. Munhwa Kongbobu, *Tosan Sŏwŏn chungsuji*, 9–10.

72. See T'oegye Sŏnsaeng Sabaek Chugi Kinyŏm Saŏphoe, ed., *T'oegyehak Yŏn'gu* (Seoul: Seoul Taehakkyo Ch'ulp'anbu, 1972).

73. Ibid., 496, 500.

74. Ibid., 502–3. Also see Kim Chong-dae, *Han'guk ŭi hakkyo kwaedam* (Seoul: Tarŭn Sesang, 2002), 31–37. In June 2014, this theme was also staged in a play titled *A Spooky Story of a School: The Curse of the Statue*.

75. Goody, *Interface between the Written and the Oral*, 85.

76. Ross King, "North and South Korea," in *Language and National Identity in Asia*, edited by Andrew Simpson, (Oxford: Oxford University Press, 2007), 213–14; Akiyasu Kumatani, "Language Policies in North Korea," *International Journal of the Sociology of Language* 82 (1990): 87–108.

77. See, for example, Park Chung Hee (Pak Chŏng-hŭi), *Pak Chŏng-hŭi Taet'ongnyŏng yŏnsŏlmun chip* (Seoul: Taet'ongnyŏng Kongbo Pisŏgwansil, 1965–; Shin Bum Shik, ed., *Major Speeches by Korea's Park Chung Hee* (Seoul: Hollym, [1970]); Park Chung Hee (Pak Chŏng-hŭi), *Charip e ŭi ŭiji: Pak Chŏng-hŭi Taet'ongnyŏng ŏrok* (Seoul: Hallim Ch'ulp'ansa, [1972]); Park Chung Hee (Pak Chŏng-hŭi), *Toward Peaceful Unification: Selected Speeches* (Seoul: Kwangmyong, 1976); Park Chung Hee (Pak Chŏng-hŭi), *Saemaul: Korea's New Community Movement* (Seoul: Korea Textbook, 1979).

78. Cho Kap-che frequently quoted the records of Park's speeches in his articles. The website of the Park Chung Hee Presidential Library and Museum has a category devoted to the records of Park's spoken words (Ŏrok). See http://www.chogabje.

com/board/subcon/list.asp?c_cc=F1081 and http://www.516.co.kr/, accessed September 15, 2014.

79. Seungsook Moon, "Cultural Politics of Remembering Park Chung Hee," *Harvard Asia Quarterly* 9 (2008): 29.

80. Won-Taek Kang, "Missing the Dictator in a New Democracy: Analyzing the 'Park Chung Hee Syndrome' in South Korea," *Journal of Political and Military Sociology* 38, no. 1 (2010): 1–25.

Kyebaram

The Culture of Money and Investment in South Korea during the 1970s

Eunhee Park

> I regret to acknowledge that kye and private loans are detrimental activities based in underdeveloped financial systems . . . so we are trying to bring kye money into the public banking system.
> —Nam Tŏk-u, Minister of Finance, May 1970

> My family benefited greatly from kye. The money our mother borrowed went toward purchasing our home and sending me and my siblings to college.
> —Middle-class retiree in Seoul, April 2014

The Korean word *param*, whose literal meaning is "wind," frequently appears as part of a compound word to designate a notable social trend or phenomenon. The expression *ch'umparam*, for example, dotted newspapers in the 1960s and 1970s to serve as a warning against the craze over social ballroom dancing that was purportedly sweeping up lonely housewives and leading them into dark paths while their husbands were off fighting in the Vietnam War or slaving away in the deserts of Middle East on construction projects to send money home. The word *ch'imatparam*—literally "the wind raised when a skirt swishes"—was a popular expression referring to the feverish zeal that afflicted school mothers in their quest for the best educational opportunities for their children. Loaded with gender biases, such terms were used to satirize activities engaged in by women, especially middle-class women. Pervasive sexist attitudes envisioned middle-class housewives as highly emotional beings who were prone to suffering fevers as they indulged themselves to the point of hysterical obsession. It is in this context that we can understand the entry of a new compound word featuring *param* into common parlance during the Park Chung Hee (Pak Chŏng-hŭi) era: *kyebaram*.

Kye is a type of microfinance called rotating credit association (RCA). Although *kye* had been in existence in Korea since the premodern era, it was during the 1960s and 1970s that they became a major social phenomenon, popular with and dominated by women. As is well known, the period witnessed rapid industrialization of South Korean society. Still reeling from years of conflict, hardship, and deprivation, postwar South Korea in the 1950s struggled to regain its economic footing. State-led stimulus programs spurred some growth in the latter part of the decade, but progress was slow until the state adopted much more aggressive economic measures in the 1960s and 1970s, which created dramatic, even explosive growth. While the ultimate success of these efforts secured South Korea its recognition around the world as a "tiger economy," not everyone shared equally in that prosperity: many in the working class struggled to make ends meet, and those who had managed to rise to the much coveted ranks of the middle class could not afford all the luxuries and modern consumer goods that signified membership in that vaunted class. Wages remained relatively low and credit was tight. The state-controlled public sector banking system preferentially lent to big business and heavy industry, as they were considered vital to the nation's economic well-being. Most private citizens had few options to improve their finances or seek credit because public-sector banks rarely agreed to lend them money, focusing their resources instead on business and industry. Men toiled ever longer hours to increase their take-home pay, while wives sought innovative ways to supplement their families' income and gain access to much-needed credit.

Many of these women turned to *kye*. Rotating credit associations occur throughout the world, especially in the global south, where they function as a way for poor and low-income individuals to secure loans and other financial assistance.[1] Networks of friends, neighbors, relatives, and others pool their resources, and each in turn borrows a lump sum to finance whatever is needed. The money is later paid back so that other members can take out loans and repeat the process. Women are commonly the driving force within RCAs, and *kye* of the 1960s and 1970s in South Korea were no exception for most of their leaders and members consisted of women. But *kye* can be distinguished from RCAs in other parts of the world in one key aspect: most

RCAs are a vital tool employed by poor and low-income people to improve their financial well-being, whereas *kye* served both low- and middle-income families in South Korea. Working-class women *and* reasonably affluent middle-class women eagerly joined *kye* in the 1960s and 1970s.

In premodern Korea, *kye* tended to bolster the economic well-being of communities and drew members together through bonds of kinship and friendship. After the colonial period, *kye*'s social function diminished while their financial function grew, and that trend has continued. The economic hardships experienced in postwar South Korea naturally spurred participation in *kye* because the banking system was woefully underdeveloped at that time; only a few state-controlled public-sector banks existed, and they catered to business and industry. Considering the continuous expansion of the public-sector banking system since the late 1950s, *kye* membership should have gradually declined over the next few decades, but that expectation was foiled when *kye* became increasingly popular, until *kyebaram* swept the nation in the 1970s. In 1970, alarmed at the serious competition it faced from *kye*, the Bank of Korea surveyed 4,500 households nationwide and reported that 72.3 percent participated in *kye*.[2] That surge in *kye* membership placed it in direct competition with public-sector banks by siphoning off potential customers and considerable financial resources. Not surprisingly, *kyebaram* was an affront to the government's authority and its efforts to exert complete control over all economic activities during the Yusin period (1972–79). The very fact that these unofficial financial activities, which subversively evaded state control, contributed far more to the success of national savings campaigns in the 1960s and 1970s than did the activities of state-sanctioned banks incensed government officials (Kim 1981, 337). For many families that needed money urgently, *kye* replaced bank loans; for others *kye* served as a way to earn a bit of extra income. Some *kye* even mimicked their premodern antecedents by having not only a financial function but a social one as well, which maintained bonds of friendship among high school alumni, relatives, and neighbors rather than simply serving as a way to make money.

The social function of these friendship-oriented *kye* has roots in Korea's past. In premodern Korea, *kye* fostered cooperation among people within a given community. Various types of *kye* operated in specific ways to meet each community's needs, but financially oriented *kye* played an essential role in making communities autonomous and stable.[3] *Kye* were initially the purview of men, as women were forbidden to join until near the end of the Chosŏn dynasty (1392–1897). During the colonial period, when all strictures on women's participation in *kye* were removed, their membership naturally increased, and some *kye* catered specifically to women such as *chakppak kye* (a form of bidding *kye* that used ginkgo tree nuts as "dice" to determine who would receive the next loan) and *tongch'al kye* (a religiously oriented *kye*). Members of the latter donated their *kye* monies to Buddhist temples, though in their husbands' names rather than their own. Interestingly, these women felt that it was inappropriate to publicly reveal their participation in *kye*, perhaps due to a pious belief in Buddhist selflessness or because they acquiesced to sexist attitudes of the day, which expected a woman to demurely bolster her husband's reputation by giving him credit for her own actions. After the colonial period, the social and communal aspects of *kye* diminished while the financial function strengthened as *kye* became firmly established as a source of loans or supplemental income.[4] By the 1960s, however, the number of middle-class housewives participating in *kye* had risen sharply and women now dominated them. This reversal of the gender composition had much to do with the Korean War. Since most men were conscripted to fight in that war and were absent from home for years, if they returned at all, many housewives became the breadwinners of their families and took on the responsibility of managing household budgets. The dramatic increase in married women's participation transformed *kye* into a leading grassroots credit system in postwar South Korea.

This chapter examines the popularity of *kye*, which reached a fever pitch from the late 1960s through the 1970s in South Korea, through the lens of gender and discusses modern-day *kye* as a comprehensive social, economic, and political phenomenon. Why were *kye* so popular at the peak of the drive toward modern capitalism during the Yusin period? Were *kye* a sign that the government's capitalist policies had overlooked the limited finances of most South Korean families? Why did a majority of South Korean families practice *kye* despite governmental resistance to them and what can *kyebaram* reveal about the little studied and often undervalued topic of women's role in managing household finances during South Korea's modernization drive?[5] In addressing these questions, we will see how *kyebaram* emerged as a uniquely South Korean phenomenon that taught ordinary people, especially housewives, valuable financial skills and empowered them to take on leadership roles within their own communities and beyond.

Mixed Reception for *Kye*

The dramatic increase in women's membership in *kye* in the postwar period drew attention to the practice and changed what had been a peripheral financial entity into an important economic force within South Korean society. The change elicited a mixed reception: positive encouragement from some quarters and disparaging sexist criticism from others. Urban families that had benefited financially from *kye* considered them a godsend. Spurred on by such positive reactions, some *kye* expanded their function from casually lending money to neighbors to participation in small-scale private bond businesses. Simultaneously, the number of speculative *kye* grew dramatically, which was met with widespread disapproval. Due to their increased visibility, more people were now aware of *kye*, and some objected to women's new prominence and the prevalence of financially risky *kye*. Those objections grew stronger when interest in *kye* peaked in the 1970s and women began to exert real economic clout. Women's newfound prominence and financial power challenged age-old patriarchal attitudes that saw women as the "weaker" sex incapable of wielding crucial economic power in their own communities and beyond.

Citizens and government officials alike looked askance at *kye*, despite the significant economic benefits reaped through them by individual families and the national economy. Even as it begrudgingly acknowledged the economic stimulus provided by *kye*, the Park Chung Hee regime distrusted *kye* because these women-led grassroots community organizations eluded the iron grip of state control and were thought to foster risky speculative economic practices that could have a potentially destabilizing effect. As indicated by Park's financial minister, Nam Tŏk-u (quoted in the epigraph that opens this chapter), investing in *kye* was considered a harmful activity that siphoned resources from state-controlled banks, creating a subversive underground economy.[6] Yet the government's adversarial stance dissuaded few South Koreans from participating in *kye* because they were often so lucrative, benefiting participants both economically and socially, and gave individuals and their families real autonomy in their financial decisions within a society otherwise tightly regulated by the state. Meanwhile, the widespread participation of middle-class women, which was a defining characteristic of these *kye*, fueled the ire of some within the general public. Virulent sexism was pervasive throughout South Korean society during that time. Many likely objected to *kye* simply because they were dominated by women, irrespective of which class affiliation those women had. All South Korean women suffered the sting of sexist criticism, but middle-class women were especially targeted. Most middle-class women were stay-at-home housewives who were expected to care for hearth, home, and husband. Relegated to the private domestic sphere, they were supposed to have little impact, if any, in the public realm and certainly were not to become leaders within their communities. Many people, especially men, overlooked the considerable effort and hard work that taking care of a home and family entailed, so middle-class women were often characterized as pampered, vain, and too delicate to withstand the travails of public life. Middle-class housewives were expected to be modern and rational, yet many perceived them to be ruled by their emotions. That gender bias informed public opinion regarding many of the activities that middle-class women pursued. The pejorative label "fever"—with its negative connotations of obsessive behavior, intense emotion (if not hysteria), and malady—was quickly attached to various activities engaged in primarily by middle-class women from the 1950s through the 1970s. As mentioned earlier, the popularity of social dancing was called *ch'umparam* (social dance fever); many women took a keen interest in their children's education, which was labeled *ch'imatparam* (school mother fever). It is within this gender-charged context that the intense popularity of *kye*, which peaked during the 1970s, should be seen. Like these other social phenomena, it received the moniker "fever" as the newly minted term *kyebaram* began to circulate widely. Of course, all three febrile terms were used to satirize middle-class women's involvement in social activities, which many maligned as excessive, but the prevalence of those terms also suggests that people had become more aware of the significant impact women now had on South Korean society, which was celebrated by some even as it caused unease in others.

Women's enhanced economic clout, as evidenced by their participation in *kye*, further irritated the government because their actions appeared to contradict the notion of "good citizenship" espoused by the Yusin regime. Government slogans such as *choguk kŭndaehwa* (modernization of the fatherland) and *sŏnjinguk* (advanced nation) were intentionally nationalistic and demanded that individual citizens make huge sacrifices to support the economic well-being of the whole nation. As the Park regime attempted to stimulate the national economy, *kye* were deemed problematic and undesirable because they bypassed official channels, siphoned off resources and profits from state-controlled banks, and put that money directly into the hands of individual women. Naturally, those women spent that money in their communities, which put those funds back into circulation and thereby stimulated the national economy. That should have recuperated those women as "good citizens," but the unofficial nature of their activities forever tainted them in the eyes of the government. The strong association of women with the domestic sphere also deemed their actions private and inherently self-interested, even materialistic and greedy, making them all the more subversive from the government's point of view. And the individual pursuit of affluence that *kye* fostered was at odds with the collectivist national approach that the government espoused for its "good citizens."

Despite the mixed reception, *kye* continued to attract new members, especially during the *kyebaram* era, due to the companionship and profitability it offered in addition to ready access to capital. The access to much-needed funds that *kye* provided was one of the few avenues through which working-class, and even many middle-class, families could ever hope to afford their own homes. For example, how could an urban working-class family with a monthly income of less than five hundred dollars in the late 1970s purchase a home worth fifteen thousand or more without the help of a loan?[7] Even though the public sector banking system had grown considerably by the 1970s, its stringent loan requirements precluded access to bank funds for the average person; instead, people turned increasingly to *kye* for the necessary funds to purchase homes and other goods.

Kyebaram and Loan Problems

The explosive popularity of *kye* in the 1970s had much to do with the biased economic policies of the Park Chung Hee regime, which privileged the financial needs of big business and industry over those of individual citizens. Under the state-led, export-driven development policies of the mid-1960s, the role of the state-controlled banking system was to support large companies and clear financial obstacles that might limit exports (Kim and Kim 2014, 15). In the late 1960s, the government directed nearly 50 percent of public-sector bank loans to large companies for purchasing expensive equipment (Kim 1993, 336). This role of banks as "credit-rationing outlets for the government" intensified as the transition from light to heavy industries that began in 1973 necessitated costly national projects (Lee 1992, 190).[8] A key component of Park's modernization efforts, heavy industry drained vast sums from the national budget, increasing South Korea's dependence on foreign loans. To help offset the high cost of jump-starting heavy industry, the Kungmin T'uja Kigŭm (National Investment Fund) was sold through special bonds to individuals (Yi 2009, 97). In the 1970s, much of the money coming in from foreign loans, in addition to more than half of all national bank loans, was channeled to heavy industries (Kim 1993, 262–63). Meanwhile, individuals and small businesses had difficulty borrowing money from banks because strict loan conditions required valid collateral and a guarantor. Banks charged higher interest rates for loans and paid lower interest rates for savings than did *kye* (Yi 2004, 383). This situation tarnished banks in the eyes of many South Koreans and encouraged them to look elsewhere for loans. Compared to the banks, *kye* provided friendly, individualized, and ready access to capital, so South Koreans increasingly looked to *kye* to help solve their financial problems.

As industrialization and concomitant urbanization accelerated, many people migrated from rural areas to the cities in search of work. Urban populations swelled, which put a severe strain on existing housing stock and drove up the cost of living due to greater demand for limited resources. This created considerable financial hardship for many families. By the 1970s, housing shortages and recurrent inflation had reached critical levels as the population density of South Korea grew to become the third highest in the world in 1973.[9] Despite the state's aggressive drive to construct more housing projects, the shortage rate did not fall below 40 to 50 percent throughout the 1970s.[10] *Kyŏnghyang sinmun*, a major newspaper, reported in January 1978 that housing prices in Seoul had increased more than two-hundred fold in 14 years from 1963 to 1978. Rents also skyrocketed and added to the financial burdens of many tenants. As real income declined due to inflation and rising housing costs, the financial situation for most urban dwellers deteriorated. This almost inevitably put many urban families into serious debt because they could not afford to set aside sufficient funds for major expenses such as medical fees for serious illnesses and tuition for their children's education after paying exorbitant housing costs. According to a survey conducted by the Seoul Chamber of Commerce, nearly 67 percent of Seoul's households headed by a salaried worker routinely found themselves in the red at the end of the month, with 39 percent reporting chronic deficits.[11] By mid-1972, the estimated amount of household debt had reached the equivalent of more than four billion dollars, which was equal to one-fourth of the debenture of all South Korean companies combined.[12]

Many urban families had no relief from the worry and stress caused by their financial struggles.

To examine how people managed their household finances and whether or not they sought help from *kye*, I conducted ethnographic interviews in Seoul from August 2013 to July 2014. These interviews offer a glimpse into perceptions about *kye* and how they actually functioned to alleviate the financial struggles of urban families. Interview subjects were senior citizens who had been married and lived in urban areas from the 1960s through the 1980s.[13] Most interviewees' answers reflected a deeply rooted aversion to bank loans because their stringent rules usually limited access to much-needed funds. Only two out of thirteen in-person interviewees said that they had taken out loans from banks. One subject (male) said that he paid off his bank loan within six months by reselling his apartment within that same period. Due to the rapid rise in real estate prices, he was able to repay his loan and make a large profit. The other subject (female) financed her home purchase by taking out only a small bank loan and relying on her in-laws for the rest. Although she did not explain how her in-laws were able to lend her a large sum of money, it is possible that they had accumulated those funds through participation in *kye*. Except for these two respondents, the rest of the in-person interviewees described bank loans as "almost impossible" to obtain, "too strict" in their regulations, and requiring a "high threshold." Banks did little to counteract the widespread aversion to their loan policies and even failed to market their loan services adequately. Articles in women's magazines, which clearly espoused the government's view, promoted the relative merits of bank loans and installment savings compared to *kye*, yet few people found the message persuasive.[14] All this led many working- and middle-class urban families to prefer other financial strategies over reliance on public-sector banks.

It seems clear, then, that what first attracted many urban families to *kye* was the relative unavailability of bank credit. But it was also the flexible nature of most *kye* that made joining one appealing in its own right, as this allowed members to tailor *kye* rules and activities to their specific needs. Members themselves decided on every aspect of a *kye* at the time of its formation, including its purpose, payment period, number of members, interest rates, order of rotation, and so on. One exemplary *kye*, operated by middle-class women employed as middle school teachers in the 1970s, demonstrates the flexibility of *kye* admirably. The *kye* was described in detail to me by one of its members, a middle school teacher in Seoul who formed the credit association with close colleagues at her school.[15] This particular *kye* was structured as a *nakch'al kye* (bidding *kye*). The eldest member took the *kyeju* (*kye* manager) role, not because of her age but because she was already experienced at managing *kye*. Since public school teachers were transferred to a new post every four years, they decided on a two-year term for each loan, twelve members, and a thousand-dollar lump sum per loan. The order of receipt was determined by bidding, with each member allotted two bidding spots. Members could keep both spots or sell one. Since a bidding *kye* ran less smoothly if some bidding spots remained vacant, the skillful *kyeju* in charge here made sure that all the spots were filled. In general, *kyeju* was also required to have sufficient funds themselves in order to help keep the *kye* solvent in case some members delayed their payments or failed to make all of them. Some *kye* lasted less than two years, but this *kye* ran well for four years with the same members without being dissolved. Many other *kye* were just as successful, some because they offered members the chance to engage in other financial activities such as collective purchasing, savings, and investment, in addition to receiving loans. Above all, participation in *kye* allowed members to save face by avoiding the almost certain humiliation and rejection they would have had to endure had they sought a loan either from a bank or from friends and family.

Many people benefited from participation in *kye,* which helped fuel *kye* fever during the 1970s, but not everyone wanted to be a *kye* member. As *kye* grew more popular, criminal activity associated with them increased, which dissuaded many from joining. Fraud cases linked to *kye* increased in number as some managers absconded with all the installment payments they had collected. And there were few legal resources that members could turn to if someone could not pay or abruptly dissolved her membership. Such problems with *kye* were considered more salacious because the lapses were committed by women, so in newspapers throughout the 1970s they were prominently featured in the society columns rather than the financial sections. Besides fraud, newspapers singled out two other types of *kye* for special criticism—*sagyo kye* (friendship *kye*) for their members' purported vanity and *singni kye* (high-interest *kye*) for their risky activities and potential for speculation. And yet these newspaper accounts did little to curb enthusiasm for *kye* among the general public, perhaps because such negative images of *kye* were not new, with many dating all the way back to the colonial period. Those who were already active in *kye* were also not influenced by such negative accounts in newspapers. In my interviews, I found that the negative press functioned mostly to reinforce peoples' natural inclinations rather than serving as a deterrent to those interested in participating in *kye*. Interviewees who joined *kye* said that the stories of fraud did not worry them because they knew that once trust had been established among members of their own *kye* the association would remain strong and there would be little risk that it would disband.[16] Even those who had had a negative experience with *kye* sometimes participated in them again.[17] People who had never joined *kye* were the most likely to be dissuaded from participation due to the news reports about fraud cases, which made them concerned about the security of *kye*. Generally speaking, those who had not already participated in a *kye* refrained from doing so, but those who had already benefited from participation in a *kye* continued with it.[18] These contrasting attitudes about *kye* sometimes caused conflicts of opinion between family members or close friends when some participated in *kye* and others did not. As a result, many participants in *kye* preferred to keep their membership a secret.

Even though some people felt the need to conceal their affiliation with *kye*, most did not. *Kye* continued to flourish as grassroots financial institutions that garnered increasing support within the general populace. Driven by its antipathy toward *kye* and other unofficial activities, the authoritarian South Korean government tried to exert heavy-handed control over the financial decisions of its citizens in an effort to transfer their loyalty from *kye* to state-sanctioned financial institutions. Financially strapped urban families, already buffeted by skyrocketing housing prices and suppressed wages, and frequently denied bank loans, were coerced by their government to save beyond what they could comfortably put away and favor public-sector banks. South Koreans resented the government's attempts to stifle their financial agency, which drew many to *kye*, for *kye* offered a flexible, individualized approach to finance that was the very antithesis of strict governmental control. *Kye* gave their members ready access to much needed capital without the insurmountable barriers imposed by banks and empowered them, especially women, to hone their financial and managerial skills to ensure that they made smart financial decisions appropriate to their own family's needs; some managers built on those skills to become highly successful businesswomen. Ironically, the Park regime's efforts to impose strict socioeconomic control backfired and led many urban working-class and middle-class women to join *kye*, where they reveled in the individualized women-centric financial agency that typified membership in *kye*.

Vying for Cash: Alternatives to *Kye*?

The Yusin period began amid grim economic prospects.[19] The global economy was entering a period of slow growth. As the value of the dollar dropped and the volume of South Korean exports diminished, the continued reliance on cheap labor could not make up for the income lost to South Korean industries due to the unfavorable conditions in the international market. However, the Park regime was determined not to allow these difficult circumstances to interfere with its drive to complete the state-led Five-Year Plan, the economic blueprint for stimulating the national economy, especially the industrial sector.

The Park government was so preoccupied with rescuing the industrial sector from ruin that it had neither the economic capacity nor the political motivation to try to ameliorate the everyday financial hardships faced by most working- and middle-class families. So the pressing matter of improving living conditions for ordinary South Koreans took a backseat to national economic projects. Even though the Park government initiated the establishment of a pension system in 1973 (No 2013, 19) and a national health insurance system in 1977 (Wang 2013, 79), its "economic development first" agenda delayed full implementation of the welfare system until the late 1980s. Unable to rely on the government for much financial assistance, more and more people turned to *kye* as the best way to improve their situation. Ironically, then, it was the very same government that so mistrusted and despised *kye* that helped fuel *kye* fever with its decision to favor national economic development over improving living conditions for its citizens. For the authoritarian Park regime, the *kye's* evasion of state control and its operation in the unofficial market economy made it all the more unsavory, despite the fact that the intensity of *kyebaram* was an inadvertent result of state-sponsored economic policies. The authorities also saw *kye* as diverting funds that would otherwise finance the industrial sector away from state-controlled banks, which served as the official conduit of government funding.

To reduce *kye* fever and underscore the regime's desire to control the unofficial economy, the National Tax Service leaked to the media a tentative plan to tax *kye*.[20] This occurred just three months before Park Chung Hee's Emergency Decree on Economic Stability and Growth of August 3, 1972.[21] The main purpose of this decree was to relieve ailing corporations of the debilitating high interest rates they had incurred from unregulated private curb market loans and to extend the repayment period for those loans. But the decree also pushed citizens to dramatically increase the amount of money they put aside in their savings accounts in banks. In other words, this decree sought to concentrate individual resources in savings accounts held at public-sector banks so that the significant influx of money that would result could then be funneled as loans to large companies in crisis or used to finance the national shift to heavy industrialization. Through this strict financial policy, the state wanted to reduce the influence of *kye* on individuals and their household finances, and to shift *kye* members to banks and other official financial institutions. Contrary to the Park regime's anticipation, however, people resisted following the decree and savings rates rose only briefly. Public-sector banks failed to make as many loans as expected both because the huge surge in revenue anticipated from increases in savings never materialized and because banks saw a golden opportunity to dramatically increase their interest rates on loans at this time, which scared off many potential business clients. Consequently, bank profits increased very little and contributed only marginally to the nation's overall economic development (Kim 2013, 102–5).

In fact, favoritism shown to select corporations, coupled with state intrusion into people's financial affairs, fostered considerable public resentment toward this decree. Given the difficulty in getting bank loans as individuals, people continued to rely on private moneylenders or grassroots groups such as *kye*. In addition, many small- and medium-sized business enterprises (SMEs) turned to *kye* as well because the August 3 Decree, which gave preferential treatment to big business to help ailing corporations restore solvency and allow them to expand their operations (Park 2013, 138), was noticeably slower to come to their rescue. These SMEs then turned to *kye* managers for the crucial financing that banks had refused them.[22] As the provider of capital to SMEs, some *kye* far exceeded the scale of small, informal credit associations composed of friends and neighbors. In fact, an article that appeared in the January 1980 issue of *Yŏsŏng Tonga*, a prominent women's magazine, attests to the role of *kye* in providing considerable support for many financially strapped SMEs. According to this article, numerous female *kye* managers were known for their ability to move and manage extremely large sums of money. Located in downtown Chongno, Kugilgwan was the first Western-style club in South Korea, and it became the favorite place for *kye* managers to conduct their business. As highly successful women in a predominantly male world, these *kyeju* may have favored meeting their clients at Kugilgwan because it was a swanky bar that catered to high-ranking politicians and wealthy businessman.

Opportunities to rub elbows with such powerful men may have lent this bar a certain cachet that appealed to upstart women who held similar power in their own economic spheres. Approximately a hundred *kye* managers gathered there every morning to meet their SME clients, lend them money, and buy and sell corporate bonds. Their daily exchange volume was so large—it exceeded the equivalent of two million US dollars—that these women were nicknamed the "invisible vault." Some *kye* managers also issued corporate bonds at discounted prices, which were circulated in nearby markets and commercial districts.[23]

The state's effort to squelch *kye* was itself a backhanded compliment and grudging acknowledgment of the broad influence of *kye* on the financial well-being of individuals, modest-sized businesses, and the economy as a whole.[24] But when neither the August 3 decree nor any other state economic policy managed to cool down *kye* fever the authorities unveiled proposals intended to strengthen the secondary banking system to compete against *kye*. Just four months after issuing the August 3 decree, the government announced a plan to establish mutual trust banks (*sangho sinyong kŭmgo*) under the auspices of the Department of the Treasury.[25] On December 20, 1972, 299 mutual trust banks were set up for the purpose of "establishing financial order, facilitating access to financing for low-income families, and stimulating household savings."[26] The savings plans of these banks imitated the ground rules of *kye* and even incorporated the term *kye* into the names they gave their services, for example, *sangho sinyong kye* (mutual credit *kye*), choosing not to use the conventional term for "loan," *taech'ul*, presumably because of public antipathy toward bank loans. In fact, mutual trust banks were advertised as a kind of *kye*, only better, since they would be under the protection and patronage of the state. Prominent articles in women's magazines presented comparisons between mutual trust banks' interest rates and those of *kye*. It goes without saying that these comparisons favored the banks.

The mutual trust banks were not an instant success, despite their ambitious beginning, ample state support, and favorable reviews in magazines. The key factor was their lack of flexibility relative to *kye*. *Kye* allowed members to freely determine the size of their loans and payment schedules, the number of members, the tenure of membership, and so on. In contrast, the "mutual credit *kye*" structured by these banks preset the number of members to thirteen, the repayment period to six, ten, thirteen, or twenty-six months, and the amount of money for each loan from two hundred to a thousand dollars. The rotation order was determined roughly every month.[27] Since they lacked the autonomy and flexibility of genuine *kye*, they had little success in convincing *kye* members to open accounts with them.

The tepid response of the public to mutual trust banks may have caused the Park regime some concern.[28] Other state-led economic campaigns implemented throughout the 1970s also strove to eclipse public interest in *kye*. These measures pushed people to practice austerity so that they could save as much as possible and put what they saved into bank accounts. Through these campaigns, the Park government sought to link ordinary people's desire for a more affluent life and a better tomorrow to the national discourse of becoming an "advanced nation." Redefining individual action in national terms provided the basis for the economic mobilization of South Korean society. The most comprehensive of these campaigns was the New Village movement (Saemaŭl Undong), initiated in 1970. The campaign employed many financial strategies, including Saemaŭl kŭmgo (New Village credit unions) and cooperatives. "Let us be better off" became a mantra; every morning a song containing these words was played on the public address system in every corner of the country. Everyone was exhorted to save. Even children were instructed to deposit money in their savings accounts at the New Village credit union set up in the school's administration office. According to one interviewee, she was awarded the honor of being *chŏch'uk wang* (queen of savings) at her elementary school, not because of the actual amount she saved but because she deposited something into her savings account every day.[29] Those children who could not afford to save money were humiliated in front of their classmates. Homeroom teachers continually exhorted their students to save because the class that saved the most was awarded the much-coveted title of *mobŏm hakkŭp* (exemplary class).

Naturally, students wanted their own classes to shine, so everyone tried to save as much as they could each day. From an early age, students became accustomed to having an economic routine as part of their daily lives, which fostered an interest in capitalism. Every morning, a female official of a New Village credit union stopped by each classroom to return students' bankbooks. The front cover was illustrated with an image of a neat pile of green bricks with a few loose bricks beside it. The green color matched the green used for the logo of the New Village movement, and the bricks symbolized the nation's economic development. These pocket-sized bankbooks had narrow-lined tables drawn on long, narrow folding sheets. Each deposit was marked with a red stamp, which consciously imitated the practice of most moneylenders, who also marked their borrowers' deposits with a red stamp in a small book. Schoolchildren's bankbooks simply copied the style used for adults. Teenage students were especially pleased if they collected a lot of stamps because they could boast about the number of stamps to their classmates. Although the deposited amount was documented on each line, the exact amount did not matter to them, since the important thing was getting the stamp. This daily savings routine instilled in these young impressionable students a strong desire to "have more than others," preparing them for a life of competition. These were the qualities deemed advantageous for South Korea's drive to become a modern capitalist nation and what the state sought to foster in young people.

The authorities adopted a reward system for both young people and adults. Each village and district searched for the family that had saved the most and crowned the parents "king and queen of saving" (*chŏch'ugwang*). The last Friday in February was Family Day, and the chief of police would give the exemplary family an award.[30] *Chŏch'ugwang* families were common topics in news reports. With the help of the Ministry of Finance and Economy, associations of homemakers led *kagyebu ssŭgi undong* (nationwide campaigns that encouraged the keeping of household account books). All this emphasis on savings showed immediate economic benefits as savings capital flowed into banks and credit unions and then out to businesses and industries, but those benefits did not last long (Kim 2013, 103–4). The fact that the state coerced people into saving large amounts of money had adverse effects on most South Koreans because this overemphasis on savings put even more pressure on already strained family budgets.

The strong national emphasis on the virtue of saving and the implementation of a daily savings routine had the effect of heightening the general public's appreciation of the importance of money. While the Park regime's goal was to shift people's allegiance away from private *kye* toward state-sanctioned financial institutions, the general awareness thus raised found an outlet in alternative methods of moneymaking. Many joined *kye* or sought financial help from friends and family. The pressing need to borrow a lump sum stemmed from the crisis in housing; the harsh experience of *setpang sari* (living in a rented room) fueled people's desire for homeownership. One interviewee, who was in her sixties and currently living in Panp'o (an affluent middle-class neighborhood in Seoul), recalled the difficult times she had as a renter. "The time of *setpang sari* early in my marriage was terrible," she said. "My family had to share the lavatory with the landlord's family. I really hated that arrangement, so every night I put a 'piss pot' in the room. Hardship and a strong desire to end *setpang sari* may have driven me to buy my home more quickly."[31] In order to purchase an apartment at an affordable price, this interviewee had to visit one real estate agency after another, which made realizing the dream of homeownership almost a full-time job in and of itself. She had no other choice but to ask her mother to live with her and take care of her three children. Because the state did not enact economic policies that helped ordinary citizens, urban working- and middle-class families had to rely on their own resources and those of their relatives, and they had to develop their own financial safety net, such as participation in *kye*, rather than depending on a state welfare system.[32]

The Culture of Capitalist Investment: *Are You Satisfied with What You Have?*

As state propaganda emphasized savings, thrift, and other "rational" economic behaviors in citizens' individual lives, as well as the nation as a whole, it became commonplace to openly discuss ways to make money and where to invest it. Securities, the real estate market, lucrative investments, and general knowledge about the economy were popular topics for discussion. Feature articles in newspapers cited experts and interviews with both men and women who had succeeded in accumulating wealth. Between 1974 and 1975, for example, *sallim sari* became a media item, and news reports about it greatly increased. A term implying overall housekeeping, *sallim sari* increasingly took on an economic valence of meaning such as managing a household budget. Reports on *sallim sari* tended to emphasize austere methods of managing household finances as a way to combat inflation during this time. News reports also highlighted the lucrative investment strategies of salaried men who had limited resources. Tapping into this interest, real estate agencies took groups of interested clients on weekend expeditions to rural areas likely to have state-subsidized development in the near future. Salaried men in particular used these weekend tours to look for investment opportunities.[33] Another common economic practice was exercising collective buying power. Housewives teamed up with close neighbors to make a group purchase of various household goods at discounted prices or to arrange installment payment plans. *Kye* members did the same. These pragmatic approaches to capitalism contributed much to creating a general culture of money and investment. Keeping updated on contemporary trends in investments and other economic issues was recognized as a necessary step in becoming a rational and modern citizen.

In most families, women tended to manage the household budget. Men generally agreed that their spouses were far more adept at that task than they were. One male interviewee, who identified himself as a retiree in his early sixties and a resident in the Panp'o section of Seoul, recalled that he gave full control over the management of his family's finances to his spouse from the beginning of their married life because he grew up seeing his mother successfully running his boyhood home and overseeing the family budget. Passing the financial torch from one generation to the next gave housewives more opportunities to hone their financial skills.[34]

Experience with *kye* provided crucial financial grounding and knowledge that enabled housewives to venture into other financial activities. This was especially true in regard to consumer culture. The Keynesian idea that "consumption is a virtue" was featured in many TV commercials throughout the 1960s. People brought modern technology into their homes by buying televisions, radios, and telephones. The exorbitant prices of these products—a television set cost the equivalent of a month's wages for an urban working-class salaried worker (Son 2008, 319)—did not stem the growing demand, especially as these electronic goods came to be seen as signifying a rational modern home at a time when modernization was understood as a synonym for progress. When the South Korean government, worried that overconsumption could adversely affect the national economy, instituted assertive measures to control consumption, including a new luxury tax on televisions and telephones, a prominent newspaper editorial criticized the government's move. These goods, argued the editorial, had become necessary for members of the middle class seeking to live a modern "civilized life." Working-class families also aspired to such a lifestyle. A high price was no longer prohibitive since families could now pay for them in installments.[35]

It was familiarity with the use of credit in the *kye* system that made married women and much of the South Korean public more willing to purchase items via installment plans. Their receptivity to consumer credit, in turn, spurred the consumer goods industry to adopt installment plans aggressively as the best way to sell its products. Advertisements for everything from pianos to chinaware described the payment system as *kyesik chŏkkŭm* (*kye*-style installment savings).[36] *Halbup'anmae*, as the installment purchase was called in Korean, became quite fashionable by the late 1960s and was applied to consumer goods ranging from small appliances like irons and radios to big-ticket items like stereos, televisions, and refrigerators. Even sets of books for children—an entire library of world literature classics, for example—could be bought on an installment plan.[37] Middle-class urban housewives were keen to fill their homes with modern goods and installment plans proliferated even more in the 1970s.

Installment plans were popular because consumers, manufacturers, and banks alike found them beneficial (Editorial Bureau 1975, 104–7). For consumers, whose real income declined in the 1970s due to inflation, installment plans served as credit cards in effect, allowing them to own goods that they would not have been able to afford up front. Manufacturers preferred to sell their products on credit because it speeded up the turnover of their stock and increased sales of diverse consumer goods. Banks also profited handsomely. Through contracts with manufacturing companies, they could secure a steady stream of clients. For instance, if consumers wanted to buy a Samick piano on an installment plan, they would have to open an account at the Chohŭng Bank through which to make their payments, guaranteeing the bank a secure source of interest income.[38] Installment purchases were a convenient way to buy necessary or desirable goods on credit, but companies charged interest, so the amount paid in installments always exceeded the asking price. Since *kye* provided members with lump-sum loans, people could purchase goods at the asking price and avoid the additional fees. Many preferred to buy consumer goods with the aid of *kye* for that reason. Stereos were one of the most popular dowry items in the 1970s, and women organized *kye* solely for the purpose of buying one (Son 2008, 254). Such examples reveal the reciprocal relationship that existed between *kye* and the consumer goods industry. In sum, *kye* familiarized people with the concept of credit and made them more receptive to purchasing goods via installment plans. Installment plans were also incorporated into select *kye*, and the economic pragmatism shown by members of these *kye* paved the way for other novel financial strategies in their everyday lives as well.

Popular media frequently depicted the deleterious consequences of overconsumption caused by installment purchases and blamed any excessive consumption on housewives' negligent and unwise management of their family budgets.[39] However, the receptivity of many South Koreans to engaging in various financial activities could also dovetail with government initiatives as financial institutions began to receive vigorous state support in the 1970s in an effort to mobilize domestic capital more effectively. The Park regime needed to increase national savings and raise the country's credit rating, so it aggressively tried to grow the financial sector. In 1972 a law was enacted to foster short-term money market. In 1973–74, six such companies were founded.[40] Except for insurance and general savings, they were qualified to deal with most financial transactions, including securities, bonds, commercial paper, and overseas investments. Various investment products offered by these companies had a term limit of six months, and the amount of investment per unit was much larger than that of typical savings accounts. Aware of the important role women played as financial managers, these companies advertised heavily in women's magazines to target those willing and able to invest. An advertisement for Daehan Investment Finances that appeared in the April 1978 issue of the women's magazine *Yŏsŏng Tong'a*, for example, contained a long list of portfolios and products, including issued notes, corporate paper, treasury bills, and securities. Another company featured the catchy phrase *kajŏng ŭi kyŏngyŏngja* (CEO of the family) in its ad, clearly aiming to flatter housewives and thereby encourage them to use its products. As a further enticement, the company claimed that the amount of interest income generated by its products could go as high as a thousand dollars.[41] The market share of these investment and financial companies grew quickly, jumping from 1.3 percent in 1972 to 30 percent in 1980, the biggest increase seen among nonbanking financial institutions (Yi 2004, 457).

In addition to these ads for products offered by financial companies, women's magazines of the 1970s prominently featured stories about women's lucrative management strategies. Success stories about housewives ran alongside stories about *kye*, installment "savings," and insurance. These stories celebrated *kye* as a flexible tool with swift results because *kye* members could take out loans on short notice to get urgently needed funds and then adjust their repayment schedules depending on their financial situation. For enterprising women, *kye* also offered a rare opportunity to generate extra income. *Kye* were not tainted by the negative images associated with loan-sharking, which made it easier for housewives to choose to become *kye* managers (*kyeju*). Recognized by their fellow *kye* members for their diligence and credibility, competent *kye* managers oversaw the smooth running of rotating credit. Success with one *kye* enabled *kyeju* to increase the number of *kye* they oversaw as well as the size of the membership within each *kye*. My research uncovered many stories about successful female *kyeju* told to me by relatives or acquaintances. One *kyeju*, for example, started with a small *kye* that had only a few housewives as members; then she gradually expanded until she oversaw several large-scale *kye* with hundreds of small shopkeepers as members. She later became rich enough to purchase several buildings in downtown Seoul.[42]

Investment companies noted the success of these women and saw them as potential clients. In the early 1980s, these investment firms greatly increased the number of ads they placed in women's magazines. Such ads tapped into the financial competitiveness that had been instilled in these women since their school days with the slogan "Are you satisfied with what you have now?" In order to attract customers, these investment companies provided very detailed descriptions of their products and emphasized their high rates of return compared with the savings rates of banks. Ads for finance classes appeared alongside those for investments. Newspaper companies that owned affiliated women's magazines hosted *yŏsŏng kyŏngje taehak* (women's economy colleges) and offered short intensive courses on different aspects of managing household finances such as paying for children's education, taxes, insurance policies, and insurers' protection along with informative classes on the global economy.[43] The large number of ads for investments and finance classes that appeared in women's magazines in the 1980s suggests a continuing enthusiasm for accruing wealth that had already permeated South Korean society by the 1970s. Women's participation in *kye* had paved the way.

Conclusion

With rapid industrialization and urbanization as the backdrop, a new culture of money and investment emerged and took hold of South Korean society in the 1960s and 1970s. Feverish construction of massive apartment blocks and the widespread desire to own a home drove real estate speculation to unprecedented levels in Seoul. Words like *pokpuin* (female real estate speculator) and *cholbu* (the nouveaux riche) entered everyday parlance, and many families purchased consumer goods such as televisions and telephones on installment plans. In traditional Korea, the notion of profit had been disparaged in gentle society and the pursuit of money regarded as the unseemly preoccupation of the vulgar. "Interest income" had long been considered an unjust and exploitative way to acquire money; negative images of usurious men and greedy landlords were deeply engrained in the public psyche. In the 1970s, however, advertisements for diverse financial products promising more and more attractive interest rates routinely appeared on the pages of newspapers and women's magazines alongside ads for goods that such interest income would enable consumers to purchase. Modern capitalism had arrived in South Korea with a vengeance.

Though largely overlooked by scholars, *kye* played a tremendously important role in establishing this moneyed culture. A means of encouraging cohesion within a traditional community, *kye* were transformed into associations with a primarily economic function in modern times. With more than 70 percent of working- and middle-class families participating in them as one of the best ways to solve their financial problems, *the* impact of *kye* exceeded that of public-sector banks during the Park Chung Hee era. Despite some prominent cases of swindling and fraud reported about *kye*, their popularity among ordinary Koreans remained unchallenged and became a veritable social phenomenon, as encapsulated in the expression *kyebaram*. The enormous and enduring popularity of *kye* was due to three major factors: *kye* were autonomous, remaining outside governmental control; they were flexible, allowing members to set the agenda and rules of operation; and they made much-needed capital accessible because they provided members with credit without requiring collateral. All these desirable qualities drew people to *kye* and away from banks. Until banks could win back customers by adopting reasonable interest rates and loan services in the 1980s, *kye* would remain a popular means of garnering more income.

Kye provided the avenue for women's participation in the economy beyond management of their household finances. *Kye* was, by and large, the domain of women's activities. The prominent role played by housewives in *kye* activities came about because of the financial acumen they showed while managing their own household finances. As regular members and as *kyeju*, women gained confidence in financial matters, which inspired them to pursue other lucrative financial activities such as investments, sideline businesses, and real estate. *Kye* empowered women and made them a force to be reckoned in the South Korean economy. Even though patriarchal biases against successful women persisted and sometimes tarnished *kye*'s image—*ch'inmok kye* (social *kye*) were especially belittled as frivolous social gatherings of housewives—*kye* played a vital role as an institutional safety net and a practical tool with which women contributed to the economic growth and modernization of South Korea. The widespread success of *kye* demonstrated that women could work together to achieve crucial financial gains for themselves, their families, and the nation as a whole.

Kye also emboldened people to engage successfully in various other financial activities, exerting a favorable and reciprocal impact on the consumer goods industry. Greater economic awareness taught people that consumption and investment are inseparable, and consumption is neither immoral nor naive. *Kye* helped tutor members of the the public on using credit so that they would be more willing to engage in related activities such as installment purchases. Thus, the popularity of *kye* fostered interest in other economic practices and supported the drive toward capitalistic modernization in South Korea.

The Park regime's attitude toward *kye* remained alarmed and disapproving throughout. For the most part, *kye* were seen as an obstacle to the government's desire to mobilize all private resources toward forming a nationalized economy either directly or indirectly. And yet, ordinary people stayed with *kye*, and when, in the 1970s, the Park regime's effort to legalize the private bond market, strengthen secondary financial institutions, and raise the national savings rate resulted in stringent economic policies for individual citizens, it was *kye* that helped many individuals protect their property and reap the benefits of that grassroots lending system. Likewise, the disparity between the government's objections to *kye* and the public fervor for them illustrates that the national pursuit of prosperity motivated the public to seek self-help schemes, rather than depending solely on government aid, and to secure monetary stability through diverse financial strategies. To the extent that the expressed goal of the Park Chung Hee regime was modernization and capitalization of the South Korean economy, it was actually the grassroots organizations so despised by the Park regime, like *kye*, that ironically helped instruct the Korean people in the ways of modern capitalism. The overall contribution of *kye* to the economy and social fabric of South Korea during the decades of rapid modernization and economic development was both significant and positive; it taught everyday citizens how to thrive, not just survive, in the brave new world of modern capitalism that had engulfed them.

NOTES

1. RCAs are known as *kye* in South Korea, *tandas* in Latin America, *cundinas* in Mexico, *susu* in West Africa and the Caribbean, *panderiros* in Brazil, *chit* funds in India, *bisi* committees in Pakistan, *partnerhand* in the United States, and by many other names across the globe. Classic comparative studies on RCAs include Geertz (1962) and Ardener (1964).

2. *Kyŏnghyang sinmun*, August 27, 1970.

3. Most scholarly works about *kye* have focused on case studies of local communities during the Chosŏn period. Modern era *kye* are still relatively unexplored. A few papers examine the role played by *kye* in household economies, but due to limited resources and figures the range of studies is limited. To offset these shortcomings, I used the contents of interviews of middle-class subjects that I conducted in South Korea from August 2013 to April 2014. About *kye* in the modern period, see Campbell and Chang 1962; Kennedy 1977; Janelli and Yim 1988; and Light and Bonacich 1988.

4. At the end of Taehan Cheguk (the Great Han Empire), *puin kye* (housewives-only *kye*) and *singni kye* (financial-purposes-only *kye*) were widely used. Some types of *kye* operated like lotteries, but they continued to be considered *kye*. Because the colonial era made it difficult for the Korean public to borrow money and make their money grow, *kye* became widespread as a popular financial method. I was able to obtain invaluable knowledge and the latest scholarly works about *kye* in the colonial period thanks to a Humanities Korea workshop, Kye rŭl t'onghan kongdongch'e kusŏng ŭi yŏksa wa nolli t'amgu (History and Dialectics of Community Formation through Kye), held at the Kyujanggak Institute for Korean Studies, Seoul National University, on May 20, 2014.

5. *Mujin*, also known as *Tanomashi*, was a form of rotating savings and credit practice that originated in Japan. In the 1950s, *mujin* remained widespread and functioned similarly to *kye*, but *mujin* gradually disappeared because many *mujin* companies were financially unstable and their high interest rates damaged their businesses (Yi 2004, 384).

6. *Kyŏnghyang sinmun*, May 21, 1970.

7. The average monthly income of urban households was 211,640 Korean won (439 dollars) as of fall 1979 (*Tong'a ilbo*, October 1, 1979). The range of apartment prices varied, but apartments in the Kangnam area cost around 7.4 million won (15,352 dollars) (*Tong'a ilbo*, October 18, 1975). This average price for apartments was calculated based on a range of prices and the exchange rate of Korean won and US dollars. The won-to-dollar exchange rate was fixed at 482 won from 1972 to 1979 (Lee 2006, 70).

8. *Kyŏnghyang sinmun*, March 23, 1973.

9. *Tong'a ilbo*, June 11, 1973; *Kyŏnghyang sinmun*, June 11, 1973.

10. This adverse situation lasted throughout the 1970s, and citizens criticized state policies primarily because they did not properly reflect the actual housing shortage (*Tong'a ilbo*, January 8, 1976; *Maeil kyŏngje*, March 15, 1977; *Tong'a ilbo*, February 10, 1978; *Tonga ilbo*, December 16, 1978).

11. *Maeil kyŏngje*, January 16, 1971.

12. *Sin Tong'a*, May 1973, 60. This article also estimated that the total amount of private loans was equivalent to twenty billion dollars, which equaled the amount of all public-sector bank loans.

13. Among a total of thirty-nine subjects, I conducted thirteen in-person interviews and twenty-six anonymous questionnaire surveys (one in-person interview was conducted in August 2011 when I conducted preliminary research in South Korea). Because

my interview topic touched on the sensitive subject of personal finances, I carefully crafted my questions to avoid invading the subject's privacy, so I only identified interview subjects with their approximate age and location. Some subjects voluntarily provided the names of their towns, but others avoided identifying the precise location where they lived by naming a nearby large city such as Seoul.

14. *Yŏsŏng Tong'a*, January 1969; *Yŏsŏng Chungang*, October 1970.

15. Retired female schoolteacher, interview with the author, Seoul, South Korea, April 15, 2014.

16. Middle-class housewife, interview with author, Seoul, South Korea, 23 January 2014.

17. Female bookstore owner, interview with the author, Seoul, South Korea, January 23, 2014.

18. Numbers of fraudulent *kye* increased noticeably during the colonial period and the 1980s. My interviews indicated that *kye* with high interest rates were often engaged in dubious schemes. Those interviewees who participated a lot in *kye* tended to continue to do so even after being swindled. They said that the *kye* and its rules were not the source of the problem but that certain *kye* managers or members broke the rules in order to scam others.

19. The Yusin Constitution gave Park Chung Hee dictatorial powers and lent its name to this time period. The Yusin period saw the emergence of voices critical of the authoritarian rule, especially among urban residents (Diamond and Kim 2000, 74–75).

20. *Kyŏnghyang sinmun*, April 21, 1972. However, the plan could not be put into action because many pragmatic concerns existed regarding how to measure the actual amount of profit each *kye* earned and how to survey the membership. The report pointed out three major obstacles to taxation of *kye*. First, the authorities planned to tax the margin on the lump sum received by each *kye* member at his or her the last turn. That member was supposed to receive the largest amount, including the highest interest. However, that profit should not be regarded as interest only, for it includes payment for any risks incurred. There is always the possibility that a *kye* could be dissolved prematurely. Second, to properly tax *kye*, current income tax laws needed to be revised, which would be difficult to do in a timely fashion. Third, this method of assessing taxes could violate individual privacy. Also the small loans (less than one hundred dollars) issued by some *kye*, such as friendship *kye*, made taxing them not worthwhile.

21. Banks suffered losses because they were ordered to drastically reduce the interest rates they charged for all short-term business loans and to accept longer repayment periods. Other financial institutions were ordered to issue special financial bonds, which helped compensate banks for their interest rate losses. Although studies on the decree are numerous, most concentrate on its political and economic effects and agree that the impact of individual moneylenders on the private bond market was considerable. Due to the lack of precise official figures and limited surveys, few studies clearly illustrate the relationship among the decree, the bond market, and *kye*.

22. It is widely considered that *kye* money constituted a significant proportion of the

private bond market, but regarding the actual influence of *kye* money on SMEs, the scarcity of sources also demonstrated the disparity between the reality of the considerable influence of *kye* on the Korean economy and the amount of coverage about it. Many SMEs were excluded from the state-led corporate loan program. Frozen out of the state-sponsored programs, SMEs turned to *kye* for financial help. By issuing corporate bonds for these small companies and giving them loans at reasonable interest rates, the *kye* exerted considerable influence on SMEs throughout the 1970s.

23. *Yŏsŏng Tonga*, January 1980, 270–73.

24. Interviewees agreed that *kye* played a crucial role in allowing them to wisely deal with crucial financial moments such as purchasing homes and swiftly reacting to urgent financial needs. From the late 1960s onward, the authorities had invented ways to encourage more national savings and attempted to legalize nonbanking financial institutions. It may not have been the original intention of the authorities, but as a result they attempted to eliminate *kye* or at least reduce their influence on the household economy. Those who participated in *kye* did less business with banks. I believe that *kye* should be reassessed as important grassroots financial institutions, much like cooperatives or mutual trust banks.

25. *Sangho sinyong kŭmgo* (mutual trust banks) consisted of numerous small-scale people's banks or so-called *sŏmin kŭmgo*. *Sŏmin kŭmgo* had a long history of individual businessmen and noncommercial customers loaning others small amounts of money. Even though their interest rates were a little higher than those of most banks, many customers who needed money urgently or could not put up the necessary collateral got loans from them.

26. *Sin yŏwŏn*, March 1973, 269–72.

27. Ibid.

28. Due to the state's support, nonbanking institutions grew more than banks during the 1970s. Park's regime during the Yusin era tended to encourage the growth of the whole financial sector, but it maintained restrictive policies toward banks as they provided the capital for state economic development plans (Yi 2004, 463–64).

29. She deposited five cents every day from the third to the sixth grades. The amounts deposited by other students varied. She recalled that some rich students deposited as much as a dollar a day. Middle-class housewife, interview with the author, Seoul, South Korea, January 30, 2014.

30. *Yŏsŏng Tonga*, May 1970, 202–5.

31. This interview was conducted in Seoul on April 15, 2014. When she recalled her *setpang sari* experiences she said, "Don't say a word about it. Fine thing! You know." She did not want to explain in detail what those hardships were. Even though she did not elaborate, she presumed that fellow Koreans would recognize the difficulties of *setpang sari*.

32. Some scholars believe that family ties in Korea were strengthened to ensure the survival of each family and to achieve minimum living conditions (S. Cho 2003, 114).

33. *Yŏsŏng Tonga*, December 1967, 424. In the 1970s, there occurred more newspaper advertisements about investing in property, including *chumal nongjang* (vacation homes). These real estate investment companies offered "regular" tours that departed from offices located in downtown Seoul. They seemed to actively engage in these types of marketing activities on both weekdays and weekends.

34. The interview was conducted at the Panp'o Community Center on April 15, 2014. The interviewee repeatedly emphasized that his wife took a full responsibility for financial management and that her real estate investments made a great contribution to the family's accumulation of wealth. He also stressed the importance of homeownership as a middle-class standard and took pride in the possession of his own apartment in Panp'o, a representative upper-middle- and middle-class apartment town.

35. *Kyŏnghyang sinmun*, September 6, 1966. Many urban families considered it essential to have at least one of these items—a radio, a refrigerator, or a television (*Yŏsŏng Tonga*, August 1968, 229).

36. The term *kyesik chŏkkŭm* (*kye*-style installment savings) might seem confusing, but it refers to installment payments not savings. This confusion in terminology was widespread in installment sales during the 1960s and 1970s. The advertisements only stated the amount of the monthly payment, not the interest rate. After the final payment was made, the product belonged to the buyer. In other words, here *savings* is the same as *payment*.

37. Installment purchases became popular at somewhat different times for different products. For example, installment sales of publications had already peaked by the mid-1960s. Home appliance and piano companies advertised their installment plans prominently in newspapers in 1968 and 1969.

38. Women's magazines, especially from the late 1960s through the 1970s, contained advertisements for many brands that utilized the marketing ploy of installment purchase. Most piano makers competed with one another for potential customers through magazine ads, including Samick Piano, Handok Piano, and Schimmel Piano.

39. The frequency of installment purchases varied depending on the kinds of products. For example, because installment sales of publications peaked in the 1960s, publishing companies began to adopt new marketing strategies in 1969 (*Kyŏnghyang sinmun*, May 7, 1969).

40. These six companies were Han'guk, Hyŏndae, Saehan, Hanbul, Asea, and Hanoe. Other big companies, such as Dongyang (Tongyang) and Daehan (Taehan), were founded at roughly the same time. See Naver Encyclopedia: http://terms.naver.com/entry.nhn?docId=9478&cid=43659&categoryId=43659

41. *Yŏsŏng Tonga*, December 1974 (page number unidentified).

42. Middle-class housewife, interview with the author, Seoul, South Korea, April 16, 2014.

43. *Yŏsŏng Tonga*, October 1984, 452.

REFERENCES

Primary Sources

Chosŏn ilbo
Kyŏnghyang sinmun
Maeil kyŏngje
Sin Tongʾa
Sin yŏwŏn
Tongʾa ilbo
Yŏsŏng Chungʾang
Yŏsŏng Tongʾa

Secondary Sources

Ardener, Shirley G. 1964. "The Comparative Study of Rotating Credit Associations." *Journal of the Anthropological Institute* 94, no. 2: 201–29.

Campbell, Colin D., and Chang Shick Ahn. 1962. "Kyes and Mujins. Financial Intermediaries in South Korea." *Economic Development and Cultural Change* 11: 55–68.

Cho Hŭi-yŏn. 2003. *Hanʾguk ŭi chŏngchʾi sahoejŏk chibae tamnon kwa minjujuŭi tonghak: Hanʾguk minjujuŭi wa sahoe undong ŭi tonghak, 3* [Dominant political and social discourses and dynamics in relation to democracy in Korea, 3]. Seoul: Hamkke Ingnŭn Chʾaek.

Cho Sun-gyŏng. 2003. *Hanʾguk ŭi kŭndaesŏng kwa kabujangje ŭi pyŏnhyŏng* [Korean modernity and the transformation of patriarchy]. Seoul: Ihwa Yŏja Taehakkyo Chʾulpʾanbu.

Diamond, Larry Jay, and Byung-kook Kim. 2000. *Consolidating Democracy in South Korea*. Boulder, CO: Rienner.

Editorial Bureau. 1975. "Wŏlbu pʾanmae ŭi silmu" [Issues in installment sales]. *Wŏlgan kyŏngyŏng kwa makʾetʾing* 9, no. 10: 104–7.

Geertz, Clifford. 1962. "The Rotating Credit Association: A 'Middle Rung' in Development." *Economic Development and Cultural Change* 10, no. 3: 241–63.

Janelli, Roger L., and Dawnhee Yim. 1988. "Interest Rates and Rationality: Rotating Credit Associations among Seoul Women." *Journal of Korean Studies* 6: 165–91. https://doi.org/10.1353/jks.1988.0001

Kennedy, Gerard F. 1977. "The Korean Kye: Maintaining Human Scale in a Modernizing Society." *Korean Studies* 1: 197–222.

Kim, Eun Mee, and Pil Ho Kim. 2014. *The South Korean Development Experience: Beyond Aid*. Hampshire: Palgrave Macmillan.

Kim Ki-tʾae. 1993. *Hanʾguk kyŏngje ŭi kujo* [The structure of the South Korean economy]. Seoul: Hanul Academy.

Kim To-gyun. 2013. "Hankuk ŭi chaepunpae chŏngchʾi ŭi yŏksachŏk kiwŏn" [The historical origin of re-distributional politics in Korea: Tax policy and savings encouragement in the Park Chung Hee era]. *Sahoe wa yŏksa* 98: 85–119.

Kim Yun-hwan. 1981. *Han'guk kyŏngche ŭi chŏn'gae kwajŏng: Haebang ihu esŏ 70 nyŏndae kkaii* [The procedure of South Korean economic development: From postliberation to the 1970s]. Seoul: Tolbegae.

Lee, Byeong-cheon (Yi Pyŏng-ch'ŏn). 2006. *Developmental Dictatorship and the Park Chung-hee Era: The Shaping of Modernity in the Republic of Korea.* Paramus, NJ: Homa and Sekey.

Lee, Chung H. 1992. "The Government, Financial System, and Large Private Enterprises in the Economic Development of South Korea." *World Development* 20, no. 2: 187–97.

Light, Ivan Hubert, and Edna Bonacich. 1988. *Immigrant Entrepreneurs: Koreans in Los Angeles, 1965–1982.* Berkeley: University of California Press.

No Sang-hŏn. 2013. "Pin'gon kwa kungmin yŏngŭmpŏp" [Poverty and the National Pension Act]. *Sahoe pochang pŏphak* 2, no. 1: 5–42.

Pak Tae–gyun (Park Tae Gyun). 2013. "8.3 choch'i wa sanŏp hamnihwa chŏngch'aek— Yusin ch'eje ŭi kyŏngjejŏk t'odae kuch'uk kwajŏng" [The 8.3 measure and industrial rationalization policy, the economic foundation of the Yusin system]. *Yŏksa wa hyŏnsil* 88: 101–44.

Son Sŏng-jin. 2008. *Lŏkk'i Sŏul bŭrabo Taehan Min'guk: 20-segi Han'guk ŭl ingnŭn 25-kaji p'ungsok k'iwŏdŭ* [Lucky Seoul bravo South Korea: Twenty-five keywords of Korean customs through which to read twentieth-century South Korea]. Sŏul-si: Ch'usubat.

Wang Hye-suk. 2013. "Kajok injŏng t'ujaeng kwa pokchi chŏngch'i—Han'guk ŭi ŭiryo pohŏm p'ibuyangja chedo ŭi pyŏnhwa kwajŏng ŭl chungsim ŭro" [Recognition struggles in welfare politics focused on the dependent system of the National Health Index in South Korea]. *Han'guk sahoehak* 47, no. 4: 67–106.

Yi Tŏk–chae. 2009. "Pak Chŏng-hŭi chŏngbu ŭi kyŏngje chŏngch'aek: yangnal ŭi k'al ŭi chŏngch'i kyŏngjehak" [The economic policies in the era of the Park Chung Hee government: Political economy of a double-edged sword]. *Yŏksa wa hyŏnsil* 74: 79–112.

Yi Yŏng-hun. 2004. *Han'guk ŭi ŭnhaeng 100 nyŏnsa* [Hundred-year history of Korean banks]. Seoul: Sanha.

"My" Sweet Home in the Next Decade

The Popular Imagination of Private Homeownership during the Yusin Period

Han Sang Kim

Toward the end of the 1960s, a new word appeared in South Korean mass media as a designation for privately owned houses. First seen in 1967, *maihom*, a Korean transliteration of "my home," quickly became the centerpiece of an entire host of trendy neologisms referring to different aspects of the domestic space. The coinage had come from Japan where, already in the mid-1960s, *maihōmu* was in wide use in the media.[1] But while *maihōmu* coincided with the beginning of the phenomenon among members of postwar Japan's emerging middle class of moving to the suburbs and into residences tailored for nuclear rather than extended families, the Korean *maihom* was an aspirational term rather than a descriptive one. In 1970 the housing-shortage ratio in Korea's urban areas hit 46.3 percent; 51.6 percent of urban households lived in rented rooms.[2] The government policy of encouraging the construction of multifamily housing did not solve the problem fundamentally.[3] Nor was the apartment construction boom in the 1970s without its own problems, as we will see later in this chapter. In short, for most Koreans throughout the Yusin period, "my sweet home" indicated a luxury that might be enjoyed sometime in the future only with considerable luck rather than a bountiful reality that already existed in the present.

The persistent gap between the dream of private homeownership—articulated in English and imported from Japan—and the reality of the housing shortage in Korea at the time demonstrates that the term *maihom* was less indexical than symbolic. One possible reason for its importation may have been to create positive media around the government's blueprint for the future, thereby encouraging the people to embrace state-led modernization and its promise of future—and thus deferred—affluence. But what *maihom* also stood for was individual freedom, the kind that had not yet arrived in authoritarian South Korea. Within those private spaces delineated with English words, individuals might be able to own objects they desired, decorate rooms to their taste, and build worlds of their own impervious to outside influences. Utterly incongruous with the Yusin Constitution, under which individual lives were left impervious to no demand that the state saw fit to make, such a desire was, of course, a practical impossibility for large swaths of the population. But far from being dismissed altogether, the impracticability of the desire only fueled the dream, as the association of "my home" with values of liberalism and individuality strengthened the symbolic power of the coinage and militated against the collectivist exhortations of the Yusin state.

This essay explores how the popular imagination of private utopias, precisely in their state of perpetual deferment, became the locus of a compromise between a number of mutually conflicting paradigms in Yusin Korea. Reading the *maihom* discourse from the second half of the Park Chung Hee (Pak Chŏng-hŭi) era as it appears in the period's fiction and film against the backdrop of the Park regime's housing policy and media coverage, I analyze the precise ways in which representations in these texts both encode a constellation of personal desires around the trope of home-ownership and record the frustrations of these desires. The negotiated compromises that result help us to see how South Korea's modernization during the Park Chung Hee era fostered contradictory attitudes toward the idea of individual freedom and generated a twisted vernacular ideal of private ownership.

"My Home": Private but Elusive Spaces

> Home, my home. Every day, babies are born. More houses ought to be built as the population grows, but since they are not, we are short of houses. So let's build more houses. A cottage would be fine. One-bedroom bungalow with a small kitchen wouldn't be so bad. As long as it's my home, built on my land . . . my home, my happy home.

So opines the protagonist of *The Woman Who Wanted an Apartment* (*Ap'at'ŭ rŭl katko sip'ŭn yŏja*), a 1970 comedy film directed by Chŏng In-yŏp. In this story of misadventures in homesteading, conventional expectations about modern lifestyles are turned on their heads in a number of telling ways. The backdrop for these misadventures is a company-owned apartment building in which a young couple is given a much coveted opportunity to live when the husband (played by Sin Sŏng-il) is employed by the company. The condition of occupancy, however, is eligible bachelorhood. The company president (Hŏ Chang-gang) gives the new male employees a chance to live in the apartment building in the hopes of monitoring them intimately to see whether any would be suitable for marriage with his daughter (Yun So-ra). The daughter participates in the observation of residents–turned–inmates. This means, of course, that the protagonists of the film have to conceal their marital status, with the wife (Yun Chŏng-hŭi) hiding herself in the apartment. The elaborate hide-and-seek that ensues creates moments of tense comedy, though the film ends somewhat predictably with the couple's secret divulged. The husband's continued devotion to his wife moves the boss to offer the apartment to them anyway, but the couple politely refuses the offer and sets forth to find a house of their own good enough to call *maihom* in the closing sequence of the film.

In this rather madcap story, we witness both the desire for homeownership—especially when the home in question is a modern apartment depicted as a prize worth seizing even at the price of having to disguise one's identity—and the practical impossibility of realizing this desire for the working class. For the young couple, the apartment is a modern space liberated from the obligations associated with the traditional organization of the extended family, a space where they can achieve the true romance of *maihom* as a signifier for individual freedom. The film brilliantly situates this space, however, in a plot setting that robs it of all privacy for the couple, as evidenced by the fact that the boss's daughter can walk through the door at will with the master key. "My home" does not bring the sought-after individual freedom for the young couple, whose modest means makes it easier for the audience to empathize with them. After treating the viewers to *fantastic* images of a high-rise apartment building for much of the story, the film returns the protagonists to the ground where *real* life will unfold. *The Woman Who Wanted an Apartment* ends as the young couple pledge that they will be homeowners yet, though not immediately, this time with their own money.

Despite the levity of its comic narrative, *The Woman Who Wanted an Apartment* well reflects the bitter despondency that nonhomeowners experienced during the 1970s. With the declaration in 1967 of "il kagu il chut'aek" (a house for every household) as a policy goal by the Park Chung Hee government, accompanied by the launch of a home-loan financing program through the Housing Financing Agency, "A House for Every Family" became a widespread slogan throughout Korean society (Kim 2013). The aggressive expansion of the housing supply, however, proved to be premature and ill-advised.[4] The project met with financial difficulties, which led in the end to the government's overreliance on private capital to increase the housing stock (Government Information Agency 2007). Speculation followed, squeezing out the lower class as the housing economy began to revolve around the pursuit of high profit margins rather than the professed goal of making it possible for every family to own a home. The "lifelong dream" of "my home" became literally that, a dream that would remain just beyond reach for many (Kim 2013).

Notwithstanding the difficulty of actually owning a home, the discourse of *maihom* thrived, attached initially to stand-alone houses. Articles and columns in newspapers and magazines of the late 1960s and early 1970s routinely dispensed advice on how to design, construct, and inhabit these single-family houses, under the assumption that readers would come to see the wisdom of such a living arrangement if only they could familiarize themselves with it. A weekly column in *Maeil kyŏngje sinmun* entitled "Maihom ŭi ch'odae" (Invitation to My Home), which ran from April 5 to July 19, 1971, introduced good examples of space organization and architectural design. Financial advisers counseled readers about how to secure loans for purchasing land and building a house (Yu 1970; Pak et al. 1971; Sŏng 1974, 6).

In the mid-1970s, however, the *maihom* discourse started to change as apartments emerged as the new focal point. The shift coincided with the development of massive apartment complexes in the Kangnam area south of the Han River, the cornerstone of the decades-long process that transformed the Republic of Korea into what Valérie Gelézeau has aptly termed the "Republic of Apartments" (Gelézeau 2007). The result of a symbiotic relationship among the Park regime, budding conglomerates like the Hyundai (Hyŏndae) Engineering and Construction Company, and real estate speculators, the development of Kangnam in the 1970s turned farm fields and reclaimed marshlands of Panp'o, Apkujŏng, Chamsil, and Togok into a forest of concrete that could accommodate nearly 125,000 households (Chŏn 2012). While the apartment construction projects that took place in the 1960s north of the Han River tended to target specific populations such as civil servants (*kongmuwŏn ap'at'ŭ*) or evictees from slum areas of Seoul zoned for redevelopment (*simin ap'at'ŭ*)—the most notorious example of *simin ap'at'ŭ* was the Wau Apartments, which collapsed within a few months of being completed, killing thirty-four in the process—Kangnam developments were aimed at the middle class for the most part, with the largest number of units falling in the "middle" range of 915 to 1,600 square feet. The government incentivized the middle class to move to the new developments by relocating to Kangnam many of the city's top high schools, including the most prestigious, Kyŏnggi, and key transportation depots such as the long-distance express bus terminal. As recounted by the famed urban geographer Son Chŏng-mok, who worked in the Bureau of City Planning from 1970 and 1977, Ku Cha-ch'un, the mayor of Seoul, took less than twenty minutes to unilaterally transform Metropolitan Subway Line 2, which had initially been set to run in a straight line from Wangsimni to Yŏngdŭngp'o, into a circular line running through Kangnam (Son 2003).

The periodicals of the day allow us to chart the process by which the apartment boom became wedded to the *maihom* discourse. In a 1975 news article, for example, five office workers, all white-collar employees of large companies, contributed their personal stories after the successful conclusion of what the paper called "Maihom chakchŏn," or Operation My Home (*Maeil kyŏngje* February 19, 1975, 7). With the exception of one female accountant who did not mention the type of real estate she ended up owning, all the workers had managed to buy an apartment. Such success stories of "salarymen" who became apartment owners made the news frequently, strengthening the association between white-collar jobs and apartment ownership (*Kyŏnghyang sinmun*, December 13, 1974, 5; *Maeil kyŏngje*, April 10, 1974, 6; *Maeil kyŏngje*, February 18, 1976, 6). While not all of these entries were glowing celebrations of apartment living, they had the effect of reinforcing the view that apartments represented the normative form of middle-class homeownership (*Kyŏnghyang sinmun*, July 13, 1978, 3; *Tong'a ilbo*, November 29, 1975, 5; *Tong'a ilbo*, February 16, 1977, 4; *Maeil kyŏngje*, September 20, 1974, 6; *Maeil kyŏngje*, February 19, 1975, 6).

Indeed, the *maihom* discourse was specifically middle-class, with housewives frequently serving as the target readership.[5] Selling the "middle-class fantasy," periodicals primed housewives to desire "sweet home" and thus seek to familiarize themselves with the purported lifestyle and etiquette appropriate for such a space in the hopes of one day becoming its actual inhabitants (Kim 2007). Women's magazines carried manuals for leading a "well-organized and rational lifestyle" and provided guidelines for home economics such as "saving," "living frugally," and "keeping a home budget book" (Kim and Kim 2008). In addition, between 1972 and 1977, *Kajŏng paekkwa* (Encyclopedia of Housekeeping) became a popular title in the publishing marketplace.[6] As vehicles for spreading normative ideas about the nuclear family, these publications urged housewives to internalize specific attitudes about finance and hygiene as the basic qualification for someone who would deserve "my home." In this regard, the *maihom* discourse drew on the dual meaning of the word *house* that Bourdieu (2005) has noted: a house is a "dwelling" but also "the totality of its inhabitants," such that its purchase is not only an economic action but also "a biological and social reproduction project" (20–24). To the extent that the discourse led housewives to uphold and reproduce a gendered division of labor within the domestic space, the desire to enjoy individual freedom in "my home" paradoxically led its would-be female residents to submit themselves to rigorous self-discipline as a means of obtaining a promising future.

In Japan, where newspapers and magazines devoted pages to detailed reports on *maihōmu*, the expression *maihōmu shugi* (maihōmuism) emerged as a term to describe "the widespread commitment to family life" (Vogel 1971, 279–81). While some criticized the "selfish indifference" and "family-centered hedonism" that the term came to imply, the critique did not diminish the craze over domesticity (Emmerson 1969, 3). The "three sacred treasures" (*sanshu no jingi*) that constituted the landscape of "my home"—namely, television, washing machine, and refrigerator—exemplified the consumer culture and affluence of everyday life in postwar Japan (Hotta 2014).

Japan was a frequently invoked point of reference in Korean newspapers and magazines, with the housing culture in Japan as it actually existed in the 1970s providing the future image of "my home" in South Korea. A 1977 newspaper article, for example, reported on the results of an attitude survey conducted in Japan that found that Japanese people in their twenties and thirties preferred to start out in an apartment but hoped to move to a single-family house later in life, suggesting that such a pattern might be replicated in Korea (*Maeil kyŏngje*, December 6, 1977, 3). Several headlines drew attention to the difficulty of achieving private homeownership in Japan, thereby relating the degree to which homes were desired, for example, "Japan May Be Rich, but the Housing Situation Is Still [Poor] . . . [and People's] Lifelong Dream Is to Own a Home" (*Kyŏnghyang sinmun*,

September 16, 1978, 4), and "Homeownership Is Like Asking for the Moon" (*Kyŏnghyang sinmun*, May 6, 1978, 4). These negative pronouncements on the housing situation in Japan should thus be seen as resulting from admiration rather than a critique of the overall trend toward homeownership. *Maihōmu* was the future that *maihom* hoped to achieve.

A Normal Woman: Apartment Living as the Middle-Class Norm

> It was never his money that I was after. What I wanted was to be loved by someone, to find a place to rest. And yes, I wanted a room decorated to my own taste.
> —*O Yang ŭi apʹatʹŭ* (Miss O's Apartment, 1978)

The 1970s raised the curtain on the era of television in South Korea. No longer a commodity whose rarity made it "the most treasured possession of any family," which it had been in the 1960s, television had become "a necessity of life, no different from a piece of furniture" by 1972 (*Chosŏn ilbo*, November 22, 1972, 2). As the number of households owning a television grew sharply, the annual box office numbers in the nation decreased precipitously from 193,628 in 1969 to 122,748 in 1972, a decrease of 36.6 percent in just three years (*Maeil kyŏngje*, March 8, 1973, 7). The blow to the movie industry caused by this transformation in the media environment had an unexpected impact on the content of 1970s films as well. With its growing popularity and ability to penetrate into the very living rooms of viewers' homes, television quickly absorbed the lion's share of Yusin censors' attention. The government argued that in order to cultivate a "wholesome" family culture, television needed to be "cleansed of decadent trends" (Kim 2009). Tight government control over the content of what could be aired on the Braun screen (as the cathode-ray-tube screen was called in Korea) had the effect of relaxing censorship of the silver screen somewhat so that cinema could secure some room for erotic and sexually provocative expression. It was precisely in this context that the so-called hostess genre in South Korean cinema—romance films that featured heroines with a background in the sex industry—gained popularity in the mid-1970s as it became the destination for the kinds of desires exiled from the domestic media (Byun 2007, 7). Such desires would be given a brief moment on the silver screen before being flushed down the drain.

For this reason, Yusin era cinema has been widely referred to as the "plughole of desire" (*yongmang ŭi paesugu*).

The apartment served as a frequent setting in these hostess films, including *Pyŏldŭl ŭi kohyang* (Hometown of the Stars, 1974) and *O Yang ŭi ap'at'ŭ* (Miss O's Apartment, 1978), and similar melodramas such as *Pot'ong yŏja* (The Kept Woman, 1976) and *Kyŏul yŏja* (Winter Woman, 1977). The last two films shared the typical plot of an ill-fated love affair between a lower-class woman and a middle-class man, although the heroines were not "hostesses" per se.[7] All four films feature the apartment as the space where the paramours meet for their secret trysts. The space serves a dual signifying function. For the man at least, the apartment promises powerful, albeit temporary, relief from the pressures of maintaining social respectability and family obligations, and provides him a space where he can assert his individual freedom and romantic choice. At the same time, the apartment spatializes the man's superior economic background, transforming a social difference between the lovers into a physical one and thus presenting the gap between the middle and lower classes as ultimately unbridgeable.

In such representations, the middle-class lifestyle associated with the apartment space is signified as "normal" but seldom permitted for long to the female protagonists from the lower class. In *The Kept Woman*, Pyŏn Chang-ho's 1976 film based on the renowned screenwriter Kim Su-hyŏn's original script, Ŭn-hŭi (Kim Cha-ok) is the mistress of a successful entrepreneur (Ch'oe Mu-ryong) and lives in an apartment he has provided for her. Even though he is gentle and considerate enough to guarantee her a peaceful life, her simple dream of starting a family ignites a chain of arguments with him (Kim 2009). Her neighbors in the apartment building provide her with a model of such normalcy and fill her with a deep sense of shame at not being able to meet that standard. The Korean title of the film, *Pot'ong yŏja*, which literally means "a normal woman," is an ironic play on the dream of the middle-class nuclear family denied to the kept woman.

The powerful association between apartment living and "normal life" for women was established in these films not only in terms of the nuclear family but also in terms of taste. In *Miss O's Apartment* (1978), Miss O, a prostitute, speaks in envy of middle-class women and their refined listening habits while denouncing as vulgar the musical genres with which she is familiar: "I didn't buy this apartment to listen to such cheap music as jitterbug, go-go, tango, or trot. I wanted to rest quietly as a good woman, at least while living in this apartment." Elegant music, a quiet and peaceful apartment, and sophisticated neighbors serve as "indices of upward mobility" for Miss O (Bourdieu 2010, 262). While she desires "a room decorated to [her] own taste," a comment that suggests the association between the apartment space and individual freedom, taste becomes for Miss O the very medium for producing conformity in relation to her middle-class neighbors. Taking on the tastes shared broadly by the residents of the apartment building, Miss O hopes to "rest quietly as a good woman," but the use of the subordinating conjunction *as* already reveals that she can never be a good woman truly since it requires that she become a genuine "Mrs." rather than a "Miss" parading about as one. Taste in this regard becomes a matter of social mimicry rather than an expression of individual authenticity.

The fact that these films rarely deliver a happy ending to the heroines suggests the difficulty of charting an upward path for lower-class women, even on the silver screen. The primary affect that the audience was supposed to feel toward the women's frustrated aspirations for social acceptance and material comfort was empathy. Following the pattern established by the so-called *sinp'a* films that gained popularity in the late 1960s, hostess films featured "poor and deprived" heroines as objects of audience identification and voyeurism at the same time (Lee 2007; Kim 2009). Their despair is made all the more intensely tangible at the end of the film when they are ejected from the space of the apartment and lose the brief access they had been given to the middle-class stability and modern elegance associated with apartment living during the middle space of the film. The immense popularity of this plot convention in Korean cinema of the 1970s suggests by its mechanism of audience identification the elusiveness of the dream of apartment ownership for many Seoul residents at the time.

When Normative Turns Oppressive: From Conformity to Standardization

If an apartment is the elusive space of middle-class dreaming for the "hostess" who finds herself a brief sojourner in that space, what does it become for the middle-class housewife who finally achieves the dream of "sweet home"? Several fictional works of the mid-1970s that explore this question offer an answer that is far from reassuring: when the dream becomes a reality, a nightmare sets in. Narrated from the viewpoint of a middle-class resident of a new urban apartment complex, Pak Wan-sŏ's short story,

"*Talmŭn pangdŭl*" (Identical Apartments, 1974), describes the monotony and insipidness of everyday life in an apartment despite the material comfort and convenience the space offers. Uniformity characterizes the apartments above all—wallpapers, home appliances, and furniture of similar design and function turn a dream played out on the pages of the *Encyclopedia of Housekeeping* into a ready-made good.

It is this uniformity that turns life oppressive for the first-person narrator of "Identical Apartments" who suffers from the "vain, tiresome competition" of everyone within the society to resemble one another. She "shudder[s] in disgust at this behavior," but soon finds herself copying others to "live exactly like them, only better." She sees from the woman next door "how bored, empty, and dispirited" she herself is since they "lead mirror-like existences." Seeking to escape their weary, monotonous, and repetitive daily life in the apartments, the two women become addicted to the lottery and dream of building a house of their own out in the country. But the narrator soon recoils from the dream, realizing that even their dreams resemble each other.

This feeling of deep repulsion toward the architectural uniformity of the apartment units, which also produces uniformity in habits and tastes of the residents, is shared by the male narrator of Yi Tong-ha's short story "*Hongso*" (A Roar of Laughter, 1977). As the narrator steps out of a taxi into the huge apartment complex of identical buildings in which he lives with his family, he feels both envy and contempt toward the residents of the complex. In a flashback, he remembers the day he first moved into the complex, his entire family and their life possessions in tow. For the right to purchase the apartment, he had paid a premium to members of a poor family whose home had been zoned for demolition in the process of the city's redevelopment but who could not afford to buy a unit in the newly built apartment complex that they had been granted priority status to buy as compensation for being evicted from their home. Looking out at the maze of strikingly identical buildings, coldhearted and impersonal in their impeccable order, into which a ragtag parade of people was moving, the narrator has a sinking feeling that "something awful" will happen to him here.

His disturbing premonition does indeed come true, and it takes the form of neighbor envy. Among the housewives in the apartment complex, any new trend spreads with the speed of lightning. When someone buys a new set of furniture, all the other housewives on the floor become anxious that they are not furnishing their homes with furniture of equal quality.

From tea service to refrigerator, washing machine, cosmetics and beauty treatments, and even dancing skills, a trend sweeps over the residents of the apartment in a dynamic of competitive consumption and mutual surveillance. The narrator's wife becomes so obsessed with following the latest trends that she ultimately leaves home altogether.

What both "Identical Apartments" and "A Roar of Laughter" share is recognition of the central contradiction that marks the living space of these new apartments. Despite its initial association with independence and individualism, an apartment complex turns out to be a place of deindividualization and ready-made consumption. In that regard, representations of apartments that had appeared to differ so markedly across the genres of film and literature—apartments as the aspirational space of domestic fantasy and social acceptance for the "hostesses" of hostess films and as the oppressive nightmare of surveillance and conformity for middle-class housewives in fiction—turn out to be not so different after all in their understanding of the contemporary reality of rapid urban development.

To the extent that the attempt to own one's unique space may be seen as a form of self-expression or a drive toward self-realization, the repulsion resulting from the uniformity of apartment living that the fictional texts record can be understood as arising from the frustration of not being able to achieve "my home" in the true sense of the word. Here we might also come to understand the standardization of apartment complexes, which established middle-class nuclear families as the basic normative unit of society, in relation to the Park-era ideology of economic development. As a replaceable unit for the reproduction of the labor force, the middle-class nuclear family became the backbone of the image of the industrialized modern society propagated by the Park regime. According to Gelézeau, "this type of dense and standardized collective housing is very well adapted to the Fordist production system on which a growing economy, such as the Korean economy from the 1960s to the late 1980s, is usually based" (2008, 299). What such an idealized social imaginary hid from view was the reality of labor performed by women, whose bodies were harnessed directly, rather than indirectly through reproduction, to the industrial machine. *Yŏgong* (female factory workers) were precisely the suppressed figures in popular cultural texts of the 1970s, the unavowed other of "hostesses" who offer their bodies for sexual rather than factory work or of housewives oppressed by the drive to consume the very goods that have commoditized women's physical labor. These works of fiction and film thus reveal the actual absence of "my home" in the craze over apartment ownership that became a noticeable social phenomenon in 1970s Korea.

Housing Lottery and Suburban Villas:
The Twisted Vernacular

> What I find, though, is not an adulterer but a lottery ticket. / Lips parched, one hand clutching the ticket, the other beckoning who knows what, she sits on the floor watching a number wheel on the television, and every time the arrow settles on a number she leans forward as if she'll jump right into the television and become the arrow herself, and then her fleshy bottom pounds back onto the floor. All the while she groans in a strange, breathy way. / I realize immediately the reason for this woman's striking transformation, for her glow of fullness. It's the possibility of release from these endless identical apartments. . . . With the eight million won riding on that ticket, she can go out and buy herself a hillside plot in a beautiful city out in the country where the air is clean, I tell myself. And she can design her own house.
> —Pak Wan-sŏ, "Identical Apartments"

Suffocated by the "normal life" that has turned oppressive in its very uniformity, the occupants of the "identical apartments" in Pak Wan-sŏ's story dream of escape. What enables this dream is the housing lottery system, with the lottery ticket functioning as an emblem of the desire to achieve self-realization otherwise than through a life of standardized consumption. The apartment dwellers of Pak's story are clearly in possession of "my home"; like the white-collar contributors to the magazine described earlier, they have succeeded in "Operation My Home." They find, however, that the coveted prize of "my home" still eludes them in the self-alienating space of the apartment. The real "my home," therefore, must now be imagined as a detached, single-family house in the country, but this dream can only be financed by lottery, that is to say, an act of speculation.

The coupling of the lottery with the dream of "my home" reveals the important semantic change that *house* underwent in the mid-1970s. The first "Chut'aek Pokkwŏn" (Housing Lottery) was conducted by the Korea Housing Bank in September of 1969 as an extension of veterans' welfare. Nearly 40 percent of the funds accumulated through the Housing Lottery were to be used to finance home mortgages for war veterans and families of the war dead (*Kyŏnghyang sinmun,* August 26, 1969, 3). The explosive popularity of the Housing Lottery among members of the general public, however, helped to recode homeownership, linking it to fortune and fortuitousness. A "house" had always been a place to live and build a family within, but now it acquired another meaning: the means of accumulating wealth and, as such, the privileged object of speculation (Kim 2013).

Apartments were at the center of such speculation in real estate, as reflected in the period's films. An early example is *Chett'ŭ puin* (Madame Jet, 1967), set in the Map'o Apartments, one of the earliest apartment complexes to be constructed in South Korea. Madame Jet is a moneylender whose usurious practices drive a couple living in one of these apartments to commit suicide out of despair. Madame Jet's reaction on hearing of the couple's death is neither sorrow nor remorse but glee; with one of her henchmen, she celebrates the fact that the couple's death will allow her to purchase the couple's apartment for only six hundred thousand won when its fair market price would be over a million. In the 1960s, apartments had not yet attained the kind of popularity that would make them the prime object of speculation in the later decades, but this scene may be seen as a harbinger of the Republic of Apartments that South Korea would become, where each apartment unit's price is marked as a manufactured good, and its owner might have to mortgage his or her life in a cycle of speculation and private loans to obtain a piece of the action (Gelézeau 2007, 29–42).

The Park Chung Hee government's housing policy, which relied heavily on private enterprise, had the effect of fanning real estate speculation and its attendant corruption (Kim 2013). Instead of seeking to meet its proclaimed goal of "a house for every household" by increasing public sector housing or affordable rental housing stock, the Park regime emphasized homeownership and built apartment complexes as "an urban middle-class production factory" (Gelézeau 2008, 305). A couple of unique features of South Korean housing policy further drove apartment speculation after the mid-1970s. The first was the price ceiling instituted by the Park regime for units in new apartment complexes, which fixed their price below their market value in order to further incentivize homeownership. After the mid-1970s when the association of apartments with modern living became firmly entrenched in public opinion, this economic incentive drove Seoul's aspiring middle class to flock to the first public offering of new apartments, such that a lottery system had to be instituted starting in 1977. The second feature had to do with the way the construction of apartments was capitalized. Prior to construction, companies raised capital by selling allotment subscriptions (*punyang*). Prospective owners, selected by lottery, paid into the construction project with their deposits at the first public offering, then made an intermediate payment at the midpoint of the project, and finally paid the balance in full on taking possession of the apartment unit. From the initial lottery that decided who the prospective owners of apartments to be constructed would be to the final taking of possession, there were multiple opportunities for the purchasing rights to be sold and resold, each time at an additional premium. Every sale increased the value of the apartment unit, such that the actual final price far exceeded the official price ceiling set by the government. The entire process was rife with opportunities for exploitation by speculators, making the dream of homeownership that much more elusive for the underclass (Kim and Kim 2008). Such speculation over apartments, which reached a frenzied level in the subsequent decade, became the subject of several films of the 1980s, including Im Kwŏn-t'aek's *Pokpuin* (Mrs. Speculator, 1980) and Kim Ki-yŏng's *Yuksik tongmul* (Carnivorous Animal, 1984).

As the title *Mrs. Speculator* suggests, real estate speculation became increasingly gender specific. The representations of female speculators in these cultural texts did not merely reflect an existing phenomenon in a neutral way but implied a sharp critique of the crisis of family being fostered by the state of the housing market in Korea. As we have seen, the narrator of "Identical Apartments" ends up committing adultery, unable to bear the tedium of apartment living. The wife of the narrator in "A Roar of Laughter" leaves home after becoming a slave to the latest consumer trends observed religiously by her neighbors. Even though the compartmentalized living space of apartments was supposed to support the reorganization of the household around the nuclear family, the housewives at the heart of the changed domestic space find themselves hystericized by that very space. The hysteria is based on the suppressed recognition that standardization of living spaces is an aspect of the Fordization of the society at large and that their private dreams of domestic bliss are participating in the "production of urban middle-class factory." "My home," a private utopia within whose walls one would be free and unique, thus turns dystopic for middle-class female subjects; for these women dystopia culminates in a sense of alienation from the very reproductive labor that is supposed to define their role as housewives. It is in this sense that the narrator of "Identical Apartments" finds that she can no longer tell her identical twins apart. The discovery simultaneously signals a crisis in mothering and reveals an unavowable desire to reject her position as a reproducer of interchangeable labor in a capitalist industrial economy. In the same vein, the cruel female speculators in *Madame Jet, Mrs. Speculator,* and *Carnivorous Animal* are housewives whose attempts to escape the opprobrium of their lives within the domestic sphere and vitalize the household economy by participating directly in the world of real estate speculation outside end up turning them into monsters responsible for the ultimate breakdown of their own families.

When a dream becomes a nightmare, the escape from the nightmare takes the form of another act of dreaming. We can read the narrator's dream of owning a house outside the city in "Identical Apartments," quoted at length at the beginning of this section, precisely in this context as encoding a desire to build an ideal family beyond the capture of the Yusin state and modern industrial economy. What would such a home look like? It would most likely be a single-family suburban house with "a large backyard, a gas-fired barbecue, swings and slides, shiny bicycles, a big family room, and spacious individual bedrooms," in short, the dream house promoted in postwar America as summarized by Dolores Hayden. The "utopian ideal" in postwar America, she argues, was "based on the house rather than the city or the nation" (2002, 33–34). That architectural embodiment of postwar American utopia as centered on the ideal nuclear family became part of the popular imagination in Korea by being constantly featured in American films and television serials, such as *The Lucy Show* (CBS, 1962 / MBC, 1974) and *Little House on the Prairie* (NBC, 1974 / MBC, 1976). While neither show replicated Hayden's suburban house exactly—*The Lucy Show* featured a pseudonuclear family with two women, a widow and a divorcée, living together with their children rather than a married couple, and *Little House on the Prairie* retrojected the postwar utopian ideal a century back to Minnesota of the 1870s and 1880s—they nevertheless contributed to consolidating the prototype of "my home" outside the city as the American dream house (Hayden 2002, 33–55). It goes without saying that such a house was far from an existing reality even for the middle class in 1970s Korea.

In fact it was only the upper class that had the economic resources to even approximate this American dream; the suburban house obtained its vernacular meaning in South Korea in the 1970s as upper-class Seoulites started to build nature-friendly "villas" in the suburbs of Seoul as second homes in a move that paralleled the construction boom in massive apartment complexes. As the use of the term *villa* suggests, however, the house was associated with luxury rather than middle-class life. A survey conducted by the provincial government of Kyŏnggi-do in May of 1979 found that the majority of the owners of luxury villas within the province were in high-income groups residing in Seoul (*Chosŏn ilbo*, June 29, 1979, 7). By the early 1980s, the association between the suburban villa and the culture of the upper class had become strong; a 1983 article criticized promotional schemes designed to lure rich people into purchasing suburban villas (*Chosŏn ilbo*, August 18, 1983, 6).

Interestingly, it was the genre of the horror film that made the suburban villa its favored setting. A 1975 film, *Nŏ ttohan pyŏl i toeŏ* (You've Become a Star Too), is an especially fascinating text to examine in this regard. In the film, an economically struggling couple wins the housing lottery and decides to buy a house in the suburbs rather than an apartment in Seoul. But what appears at a first glance to be a fantasy come true of sudden wealth and home acquisition for a poor family turns into a confession about the impossibility of realizing such a utopian ideal. The house has a tragic history of betrayed love—a young woman once committed suicide there after being betrayed by her social-climbing lover. The young woman's spirit haunts the house and then possesses the couple's little daughter. The wife becomes increasingly isolated after the move to the suburbs, left alone in the house after her husband leaves for the city for work, and the husband begins a love affair with a mysterious woman who turns out to be a reincarnation of the dead young woman.

By staging the anxiety of homeownership through the generic conventions of the horror film, *You've Become a Star Too* reveals the gap between the Americanized ideal of the suburban dream house and the reality of the housing situation in South Korea. The country house was already a space of fantasy for most Koreans, its spaciousness and modern amenities representing a level of luxury that even those who aspired to become apartment owners could not dream of. The various levels of estrangement from one another and ultimately from reality that the residents experience in the space bespeak just how fantastic a thing the postwar American dream became when transplanted in Yusin Korea. Several other horror films made in the early 1980s, after the formal end of the Yusin regime, expanded on this theme, including *Kwihwa sanjang* (The Haunted Villa, 1980), *Mangnyŏng ŭi weding tŭresŭ* (The Haunted Wedding Dress, 1981), and *Kip'ŭn pam kapchagi* (Suddenly in Dark Night, 1981). All three films feature a young lower-class woman violated by an older, wealthier man (in actuality or imagination). The luxurious suburban villa becomes the scene of both the young woman's violation and her subsequent revenge, and as such the space dramatizes the gap between social classes.

It was Richard Nixon who famously identified the "availability" of the "model home" to "Americans of all classes" as the most important feature of what made American capitalism superior to communism in the so-called "Kitchen Debate" with Soviet Premier Nikita Khrushchev in 1959 (May 1988, 162). A "model home" in suburbia, as an ideal for "consumer-oriented family life" in postwar America (166), was frequently publicized in the South Korean media. The prototype of the ideal home taken from the American idiom was resignified, however, into its very opposite in the process of vernacularization. In the context of South Korean economic development and urbanization, "my home" became a true fetish object—forever desired because forever beyond reach.

Conclusion

> The past year has been the toughest of our nine years of marriage. In the aftermath of the IMF [International Monetary Fund] crisis, my husband's salary was frozen and the small clothing shop I ran on the side was hit by the recession too. We are now in danger of losing our longtime dream of "owning a home of our own (nae chip maryŏn)." . . . Our only thought nowadays is how to tighten our belt more. It is the only way to ride out the IMF crisis.
> —*Kyŏnghyang sinmun*, November 16, 1998

This letter to the editor submitted by a female reader of a daily newspaper following the Asian Financial Crisis of 1997–98 reveals the persistence of the discourse of "my home" in South Korea, albeit in its vernacular version of "nae chip maryŏn," almost two decades after the end of the Yusin era. Entwined with various collateral discourses, such as "new town in town" (*sinsigaji*), "new city" (*sindosi*), and "school district" (*hakkun*), the discourse continues to fuel the desire for homeownership and to shape the real estate market in the 2010s (Pak 2013, 15–65). The Park regime's provocative declaration of "a house for every household" as a policy goal, reborn in different guises many times over since the regime's end, has not brought about the desired result in the housing market; one lasting legacy of the Yusin era housing policy, in fact, is the deep entrenchment of structures of inequality. In the absence of meaningful government policies intended to curb speculation and ensure the inclusion of low-income groups in the housing market, the construction industry's pursuit of excessive profitability, combined with the popular desire for "my home" aggressively fanned by the government, the real estate industry, and the media, has made homeownership the locus of class polarization. A series of temporary expedients implemented by every regime since Park Chung Hee's has not significantly altered the fundamental pattern. A 2014 nationwide survey by Statistics Korea and the Statistical Research Institute showed that only 48.3 percent of couples in their tenth year of marriage owned a home (KOSTAT 2014, 11). Fifty years after the slogan "a house for every household" first went viral in South Korea, the long-deferred utopia of "my home" shows no signs of arrival.

During those five decades, apartment living became the norm and profoundly transformed everyday lives and *mentalité* of the Korean public. Through their strong association with the middle class, apartments have bred normative habits of consumption not only for those who seek to confirm their identity as middle class but also those who aspire to attain that status. Writing about the "bureaucratic society of controlled consumption" that France became after World War II, whose characteristics are most clearly seen in the so-called new towns, Henri Lefebvre has argued, "Whatever the size of his income or the class to which he belonged, the inhabitant of the new town acquired the generalized status of proletarian" (1971, 59). In the case of South Korea, we might say that apartment complexes became these "new towns," allocating the residents' everyday lives to the conveyor belt of the consumption-labor system. Largely as a consequence of the urban development programs of the Park Chung Hee regime, private homeownership became widely perceived as a form of self-realization and thus a goal to be achieved even at the risk of alienation, speculation, and even bankruptcy. The supreme irony is that one achieved this self-realization by subjecting oneself to a life spent before identical assembly lines.

NOTES

1. Hotta 2014.

2. The shortage became more pronounced during the Yusin period. According to a news article published just before Park Chung Hee's death, the housing shortage ratio hit 56 percent in urban areas and 35.5 percent total (*Tong'a ilbo*, October 23, 1979, 5). This means over 2,427,000 households did not have their own homes. *Setpang sari* (living in

a rented room) was a common solution to this problem, and a single house accommodating multiple families became a popular type of residence (AKS 2014).

3. AKS 2014.

4. The Park government's impractical plan for addressing the housing crisis brought about the forced migration of residents to and from areas zoned for urban renewal. Yun Hŭnggil's short story "Ahop k'yŏlle ŭi kudu ro namŭn sanae" (The Man Who Was Left as Nine Pairs of Shoes, 1977) alludes to a three-day civil uprising that took place in Kwangju, Kyŏnggi-do, in August 1971. The residents of the new housing complex in Kwangju, numbering nearly one hundred thousand, consisted of both the urban poor relocated from various slum areas of Seoul slated for development and those who had bought land from real estate speculators in the hopes of finally owning their own home. The new complex, however, had neither infrastructure to accommodate the population influx nor sufficient public transportation to allow the residents to get to work. Thus isolated in the middle of nowhere and living mostly in makeshift tents, the residents became further incensed when the provincial government sought to collect land payments at a rate multiple times over the initial agreed-upon price, and as a one-time payment rather than in installments. The residents' grievances exploded into violent action.

5. According to sociologist Hagen Koo (2012), the Korean concept of the middle class, "chungsanch'ŭng," cannot be defined by means of precise Marxist class analysis, but rather should be considered a discursive product: "The advent of the concept of chungsanch'ŭng in South Korea was related to the Park Chung Hee government's economism and deeply connected with the strategy of the military regime to secure legitimacy by achieving the so-called society of chungsanch'ŭng. . . . Chungsanch'ŭng was a concept that represented such experiences and desires of individual upward mobility" (405).

6. The National Library of Korea and the National Assembly Library hold seventeen books that include "Encyclopedia of Housekeeping" in the title, all of which were published between 1972 and 1977 (three in 1972, four in 1973, one in 1974, four in 1975, three in 1976, and two in 1977). There are no such holdings in either library published in 1970, 1971, 1978, or 1979. Before and after the 1970s, there seem to have been only occasional publications bearing the title.

7. I use the term *hostess films* to refer not only to those films whose heroines actually engage in sex work but more broadly to a group of melodramas of the 1970s that feature a female protagonist who has fallen on hard times and enters into a sexual relationship with multiple men across the class divide.

REFERENCES

Primary Sources

Literary Writings

Pak Wan-sŏ (Park Wan-suh). 1997. "Identical Apartments." In *Wayfarer: New Fiction by Korean Women*, edited and translated by Bruce Fulton and Ju-Chan Fulton, 139–60. Seattle: Women in Translation. Originally published in 1974.

Yi Tong-ha (Lee Dong-ha). 1977. "Hongso" (A Roar of Laughter). *Hyŏndae Munhak* 267. November, 1977.

Yun Hŭng-gil (Yun Heung-gil). 2007. "*The Man Who Was Left as Nine Pairs of Shoes.*" In *Land of Exile*, edited and translated by Marshall R. Pihl, Bruce Fulton, and Ju-Chan Fulton, 145–75. Armonk, NY: M. E. Sharpe. Originally published in 1977.

Films

American Working Women (USIS, n.d.)
Carnivorous Animal (Kim Ki-yŏng, 1984)
The Haunted Villa (Yi Tu-yong, 1980)
The Haunted Wedding Dress (Pak Yun-gyo, 1981)
Hometown of the Stars (Yi Chang-ho, 1974)
The Kept Woman (Pyŏn Chang-ho, 1976)
Madame Jet (Yi Kyu-ung, 1967)
Miss O's Apartment (Pyŏn Chang-ho, 1978)
Mrs. Speculator (Im Kwŏn-t'aek, 1980)
Suddenly in Dark Night (Ko Yŏng-nam, 1981)
Winter Woman (Kim Ho-sŏn, 1977)
The Woman Who Wanted an Apartment (Chŏng In-yŏp, 1970)
You've Become a Star Too (Yi Chang-ho, 1975)

Television Shows

Little House on the Prairie [*Ch'owŏnŭi chip*]. NBC, 1974 / MBC, 1976.
The Lucy Show [*Lusi syo*]. CBS 1962 / MBC 1974.

Newspapers

Chosŏn ilbo
Han'guk ilbo
Kyŏnghyang sinmun
Maeil kyŏngje
Tong'a ilbo

Articles in Newspapers and Magazines

Emmerson, John K. 1969. "70 nyŏnda ŭi chŏnch'ojŏn (1) 70 nyŏn ŭl hyangan Ilbon" [A prelude to the 1970s (1): Japan toward 1970]. *Kyŏnghyang sinmun*, January 6.

Pak Chŏngja, et al. 1971. "Sae haeenŭn kiŏhi tangsinege chip ŭl maryŏnhage hanŭn chut'aek chŏngbo! Mai houm chakchŏn" [Housing information that will lead you finally to buy a house! Operation My Home]. *Chubu saenghwal* [Housewife's life] 7, no. 1: 429–51.

Sŏng Yŏngso. 1974. "Pomch'ŏl saenghwal paekkwa (1): Maihom chakchŏn" [Spring encyclopedia of living (1): Operation My Home]. *Tong'a ilbo*, March 11.

Secondary Sources

AKS [Academy of Korean Studies]. 2014. "Seppang." In *Encyclopedia of Korean Culture,* edited by the Academy of Korean Studies, October 13. Accessed October 20, 2014. http://encykorea.aks.ac.kr/Contents/Item/E0029900

Bourdieu, Pierre. 2005. *The Social Structures of the Economy.* Translated by Chris Turner. Cambridge, UK: Polity.

Bourdieu, Pierre. 2010. *Distinction: A Social Critique of the Judgement of Taste.* Translated by Richard Nice. New York: Routledge.

Byun In-shik. 2007. "The Authoritarian Period and a Depression in the Film Industry, 1972–1979." In *Korean Cinema: From Origins to Renaissance,* edited by M. Kim, 221–29. Seoul: Communication Books.

Chŏn Kang-su. 2012. "1970-yŏndae Pak Chŏnghŭi chŏnggwŏn ŭi Kangnam kaebal" [The Development of Kangnam by the Park Chung Hee Regime in the 1970s]. *Yŏksa munje yŏngu* [Critical studies in modern korean history] 28: 9–38.

Gelézeau, Valérie. 2007. *Apat'ŭ konghwaguk: P'ŭrangsŭ chirihakcha ga pon Han'guk ŭi apat'ŭ* [Seoul: Giant city, radiant cities]. Trans. Kil Hye-yŏn. Seoul: Humanit'asŭ.

Gelézeau, Valérie. 2008. "Changing Socio-Economic Environments, Housing Culture and New Urban Segregation in Seoul." *European Journal of East Asian Studies* 7, no. 2, 295–321.

Government Information Agency (GIA). 2007. "Sillok pudongsan chŏngch'aek 40 nyŏn (9): Anjŏngjchŏk chut'aek konggŭp" [Chronicle of the forty years of the real estate policy (9): The stable supply of housing]. *Chŏngch'aek pŭrip'ing* [Policy briefings], March 2. Accessed October 20, 2014. http://www.korea.kr/special/policyFocusView.do?newsId=148620166&pkgId=49500196&pkgSubId=&pageIndex=2

Hayden, Dolores. 2002. *Redesigning the American Dream: Gender, Housing, and Family Life.* New York: Norton.

Hotta Yoshihiro. 2014. "'Maikā' to 'maihōmu' o meguru jūtaku chi dezain nitsuite: Sengo jūtaku chi no keishachi kaihatsu nikansuru shiteki kōsatsu" [On designing residential sections regarding "my car" and "my home": A historical investigation of the postwar development of slope lands]. *Tochi sōgō kenkyū* [Journal of the Land Institute] 22, no. 1: 59–67.

Kim A-ram. 2013. "1970-yŏndae chut'aek chŏngch'aek ŭi sŏnggyŏk kwa kaebal ŭi yusan [A Study on Characteristics of Housing Policy and Legacy of Development in the 1970s]." *Yŏksa munje yŏngu* [Critical studies in modern korean history] 29: 47–84.

Kim Han Sang. 2009. "Pak Chŏng-hŭi chŏnggwŏn'gi kajok sŏsa ŭi kyunyŏl kwa chŏhang - Kim Su-hyŏn ŭi mello yŏnghwa rŭl chungsim ŭro [Cracks and Resistance in the Family Narrative of the Park Chung-Hee Regime: On Kim Su-Hyun's Melodrama Films]." *Taejung sŏsa yŏn'gu* [Journal of popular narrative] 22: 283–313.

Kim Han Sang. 2016. "*My Car* Modernity: What the U.S. Army Brought to South Korean Cinematic Imagination about Modernization." *Journal of Asian Studies* 75, no. 1: 63–85.

Kim Chŏng-hŭi, and Kim Yŏng-ch'an. 2008. "1960–70-yŏndae yŏsŏngji e nat'anan kŭndaejŏk chugŏ konggan mit chugŏ munhwa tamnon e kwanhan yŏngu" [Formation of the cultural discourses of "modern home" in women's magazines of the 1960s through the 1970s]. *Midiŏ, chendŏ & munhwa* [Media, gender and culture] 10: 109–60.

Kim Ye-rim. 2007. "1960-yŏndae chunghuban kaebal naesyŏnŏllijŭm kwa chungsanch'ŭng kajŏng p'ant'aji ŭi munhwa chŏngch'ihak [The Cultural Politics of Developmental Nationalism and Middle-Class Home Fantasy in the Late 1960s]." *Hyŏndae munhak yŏngu* [Journal of Korean modern literature] 32: 339–75.

KOSTAT. 2014. "Saeng'ae chugibyŏl chuyo t'ŭksŏng punsŏk" [An analysis of the characteristics at different stages of the life cycle]. Press release, November 18. Accessed January 11, 2015. Statistics Korea, http://kostat.go.kr/edu/sri_kor_new/5/6/index.bo ard%3Fbmode%3Ddownload%26bSeq%3D%26aSeq%3D334840%26ord%3D2+& cd=1&hl=ko&ct=clnk&gl=us

Ku Hae-gŭn (Koo Hagen). 2012. "Han'guk ŭi chungsanch'ŭng ŭl tasi saenggak handa" [Rethinking the middle class in South Korea]. *Ch'angjak kwa pip'yŏng* [Creation and criticism], Spring, 403–21.

Lee, Soon-jin. 2007. "The Genealogy of Shinpa Melodramas in Korean Cinema." In *Korean Cinema: From Origins to Renaissance*, edited by M. Kim, 37–44. Seoul: Communication Books.

Lefebvre, Henri. 1971. *Everyday Life in the Modern World*. Translated by Sacha Rabinovitch. London: Allen Lane.

May, Elaine Tyler. 1988. *Homeward Bound: American Families in the Cold War Era*. New York: Basic Books.

Pak Hae-chŏn. 2013. *Ap'at'ŭ keim* [The apartment game]. Seoul: Humanist Books.

Son Chŏng-mok. 2003. *Sŏul tosi kyehoek iyagi* [Tales of Seoul's Urban Planning]. Seoul: Hanul.

Vogel, Ezra F. 1971. *Japan's New Middle Class: The Salary Man and His Family in a Tokyo Suburb*. Berkeley: University of California Press.

Yu Pyŏng-sŏk. 1970. "Saenghwal kwalli: Maihom eŭi chirŭm kil" [Life management: A shortcut to my home]. *Chibang haengjŏng* [Local administration] 19, no. 204: 190–94.

Peripheral Visions of Yusin

Techniscope Action Cinema and the Anxiety of the State

Irhe Sohn

> In darkness, then, it is looking askance that is needed.
> —Yi Yŏng-hŭi, "Movies I Want to Watch."

Action Cinema and Peripheral Vision

Contrary to what viewers might expect from the title, there is no one-legged man in *Toraon oedari* (The One-Legged Man Returns), one of six action movies directed by Lee Doo-yong (Yi Tu-yong) in 1974. Typical of the "Manchurian western" of the 1960s and 1970s in South Korea, the film features bandits, Japanese villains, and incognito Korean freedom fighters but no one-legged man.[1] The hero of Lee Doo-yong's film fights for love and revenge against the backdrop of Manchuria, the proverbial "Wild West" of the Japanese empire in the 1920s and 1930s. Played by Han Yong-chŏl, a Korean American actor also known as Charlie Shell, the hero stands securely on his own two feet throughout the entire film when not flying through the air with his leg outstretched to deliver a deadly kick to his enemies.

So strong is the title's suggestiveness, however, that even Soyoung Kim, the preeminent South Korean film scholar, assumes the presence of a crippled male protagonist in the film. The assumption in turn allows Kim to see the possibility of "decolonizing choreography" in such "blatantly handicapped action cinema" set in Manchuria under Japan's control (Kim 2005, 101).[2] This common error is perhaps understandable when we consider that *The One-Legged Man Returns* was not available for screening until the recent restoration of the film's original reels by the Korean Film Archive. Before then discussion about the film depended largely on a short synopsis of it on the Korean Movie Database: "As Yong-chŏl in despair breaks his leg, he leaves Hyang-suk and drowns his sorrow in wine." The absence of the one-legged man in *The One-Legged Man Returns* is a telling sign. Far from being an inconsequential fact to be corrected in an errata that no one will read, the oxymoronic absence is emblematic of the critical misrepresentation of lives that remained at the margins of society during the decade of 1970s in South Korea, a misrepresentation that has persisted in subsequent decades. Delving into this misrepresentation, this chapter begins at the point of intersection where film genre, cinematic technology, and spectatorship come together.

The genre in question is the action film produced in the brief period between 1971 and 1979, of which the above-mentioned Manchurian western is perhaps the most prominent subgenre. Used to film these works was an affordable variant of widescreen technology called Techniscope. Even though the state decried them loudly as *p'ongnyŏk yŏnghwa* (violent movies)—the films featured extended sequences of martial arts combat choreography—the genre gained tremendous popularity among urban working-class males. All of Lee Doo-yong's six films produced in 1974 fall into the category of the Techniscope action film.

As suggested by the decades-long persistence of the erroneous interpretation of the title *The One-Legged Man Returns*, the Techniscope action film was a genre relegated to obscurity in South Korean cultural history for years. Indeed, compared to the 1960s, the 1970s has long been considered a dark period by film critics in a number of respects. First, there was the reality of censorship. As Kim Won's chapter has shown, film was an integral part of the Park Chung Hee (Pak Chŏng-hŭi) regime's cultural policy of hypernationalization, which began in earnest in the late 1960s. The industry became subject to infelicitous attempts by the authoritarian state to yoke cinema's mass appeal to the regime's propaganda needs, even as the state exercised strict censorship over all cinematic content. Second, the rapid cycle of production and consumption that characterized the 1970s film industry became a damning mark of compromise where aesthetic value was concerned. For film critics, the 1960s was the "golden age of South Korean cinema," characterized by the sophisticated brilliance of such films as *Aimless Bullet* (dir. Yu Hyun-mok (Yu Hyŏn-mok), 1961),

Housemaid (dir. Kim Ki-young (Kim Ki-yŏng), 1961), and *Late Autumn* (dir. Lee Man-hee (Yi Man-hŭi), 1966), while the 1970s fare of "cheaply produced" action movies and "hostess melodramas" featuring prostitutes with hearts of gold provided vulgar and inferior entertainment that pandered to the uneducated tastes of the urban underclass.[3] Third, due to the advent of television, the 1970s saw a significant drop in the number of moviegoers.

Thus besieged by the authoritarian government, leeched of its creative energy by the relentless race to the very bottom of popular taste, and unable to cope with the rise of a formidable rival in the media market, 1970s South Korean cinema is seen as saturated with darkness. Accordingly, the decade's contribution to the development of South Korean cinema is frequently dismissed as negligible. While such a representation delivers a sharp critique of the negative impact that the Yusin state had on the film industry, it shares with the Yusin state a fundamental orientation toward the main consumers of 1970s action cinema. For both the state and the film scholars critical of the state alike, the urban underclass was a population whose base propensities needed to be criticized or reformed.

Over the last decade, such negative characterizations of 1970s action cinema have undergone an important revision, if not in critical circles then at least among filmmakers themselves. Most notably, the genre has been brought back to life as a cheerful, self-parodying supplement to the directors' more "serious" works in the filmographies of Kim Jee-woon (Kim Chi-un) and Ryoo Seung-wan (Ryu Sŭng-wan), two members of the internationally acclaimed cohort of filmmakers who came of age within the emerging cinephile culture of the 1990s in South Korea. Kim's *The Good, the Bad, the Weird* (2010), for example, makes an explicit reference to Lee Man-hee's 1971 Techniscope continental action movie *Soesasŭl ŭl kkŭnŏra* (Break the Chain). In two films with the same title *Dachimawa Lee* (2001, 2008), Ryoo's cinematic revaluation revitalizes the Techniscope action genre's playfulness and popular appeal, exploiting its kitsch quality at full capacity.

The merry revival in the twenty-first century of the 1970s Techniscope action film is based on a self-conscious and stylized celebration of the genre's lowbrow pop quality. Kim Jee-Woon's sophisticated recreation of the "continental action movie" in *The Good, the Bad, the Weird* refurbishes the genre's hybridity under the rubric of the global western; the pleasure it affords the audience is deeply intertextual and contingent on the audience's recognition of the film's multiple reference points to westerns ranging from the spaghetti to the Manchurian. Ryoo's extreme citation of the techniques of 1970s action movies creates a wild adventure that is part exercise in nostalgia and part cinematic experimentation with the limits of kitsch. But in the end what the studied lightheartedness of both films achieves, despite their intense intertextuality, is radical decontextualization. As self-parodies, the films can neither acknowledge nor transmit the profound resonance that 1970s action films achieved with their audiences, which were overwhelmingly male, lower class, and urban.

Whether denied agency by the characterization of the Techniscope action cinema of the 1970s as vulgar and violent or rendered invisible amid the decontextualized celebrations of the bygone genre, the viewers who so avidly flocked to the second- or third-run theaters on the city's peripheries to watch projections of films made ragged by overuse are profoundly marginal to the existing narratives of South Korean cinema's heyday, decline, and rebirth. Nevertheless, our understanding of this "dark period" of South Korean cinema, and of cultures of Yusin more broadly, would remain incomplete or distorted without an attempt to examine the political and aesthetic import of this particular spectatorship.

In an essay called "Movies I Want to Watch," published at the height of the Yusin regime in 1976, Yi Yŏng-hŭi, then the culture section editor at *Han'guk ilbo*, related the science of optics to the experience of moviegoing, focusing on what happens to the faculty of vision in a dark auditorium: "[To] see clearly in the dark, one has to avert one's eyes and glance sideways" (1976, 78). The human eye, wrote Yi, has two different types of photoreceptors. While cones are sensitive to color, rods are sensitive to motion; in order to perceive objects in dim light, one has to rely on the rods rather than cones. And since rod cells are distributed around the periphery of the retina, one has to glance sideways to make the most effective use of them. Using optics as a metaphor and harnessing it to social critique, Yi argued that in order to properly perceive the grim reality of the times, one needs to develop the facility to look askance. In other words, in order to grasp the shape of reality in darkness, one should activate one's peripheral vision.

Following Yi Yŏng-hŭi's suggestion to look askance, I take South Korean action cinema of the 1970s as an opportunity to activate a peripheral vision of the Yusin era. What would it mean to utilize the rods distributed at the margins of our retinas, rather than focalizing on the central elements dominating the field of vision, when viewing South Korean film history? What would such an exercise with reference to film history enable us to understand about the Yusin era in turn? This essay seeks to provide answers to such questions by examining a sociocultural field of vision created by the convergence of three different "rod cells" of South Korean film history: (1) action movies produced during the Yusin era, particularly between 1973 and 1976 when the Presidential Emergency Decrees that made Yusin synonymous with oppression went into full effect; (2) an affordable widescreen technology called Techniscope on which action movie production was highly dependent; and (3) the lower-class male audience that patronized action cinema. In other words, by "Techniscope action cinema," I refer not simply to a group of action movies produced in the 1970s in South Korea but to an entire field of vision that was contingent on a specific technology, genre, and audience. This chapter thus weaves together textual analysis, the political economy of cinematic production, and questions of audience reception.

For the Yusin regime, which labeled Techniscope action cinema *p'ongnyŏk yŏnghwa*, there was little doubt that these films would be detrimental to society at large. No wonder, then, that the state regulated the genre heavily, using such derogatory branding to produce a social discourse on the correlation between the act of viewing action cinema and committing acts of juvenile delinquency. A central argument of this chapter is that the Yusin state's attempt to expel Techniscope action cinema from what it considered the realm of desirable and respectable films attests to its anxiety over its inability to control the kinds of aberrancy hinted at in these movies. As we shall see, the aberrancy was articulated in gender and class terms as it concerned the movement and governability of male bodies that were coded as specifically working class, even within the fantastical setting of Manchuria in the 1930s. The popularity of these films among urban working-class males during the Yusin period must therefore be understood in relation to the "ideal" male bodies that the Yusin state aspired to create and discipline.

Techniscope Action Cinema: Technology and Genre

Techniscope action cinema emerged in the early 1970s in South Korea in a media climate undergoing a profound transformation. The rise of television, in particular its growing appeal to middle-aged women who had been the film industry's major target audience in the 1960s, meant that filmmakers needed to find ways to offer a differentiated viewing experience while looking for new audiences. A widescreen system that made the cinematic experience more spectacular was a natural answer—indeed, widescreen spectacles had become the global industrial standard since its introduction in the 1950s—but the cost of producing such widescreen films was prohibitively high for most Korean filmmakers. Two factors contributed to these high production costs. First, most widescreen technology required a whole new set of equipment, including an anamorphic lens and sophisticated lighting apparatus. Second, many widescreen systems, such as Cinemascope, were monopolized by giant Hollywood film companies like Fox and necessitated the payment of high royalties. It was under these constraints that the Techniscope system was invented by producers who wanted to provide a widescreen cinematic experience for their audiences without having to pay royalties. Originally introduced by Technicolor Italy in 1960, Techniscope was a unique widescreen technology in that it did not require an anamorphic lens to materialize a screen of a 1:2.35 or 1:2.40 ratio. In widescreen systems like Cinemascope, a camera typically made use of an anamorphic lens, which squeezes widely distributed objects into the full frame of 1:1.33-ratio film. In contrast, Techniscope created a widescreen image by using only half a frame for a single shot. This way, it reduced the required amount of negative film stock and allowed the filmmaker to reduce the total budget. Not unsurprisingly, Techniscope became the go-to technology for low-budget movies. Revisionist westerns made in Italy, the so-called spaghetti westerns, for example, were filmed using Techniscope and went on to gain great popularity throughout the world.

South Korea's domestic Techniscope technology was developed around the late 1960s by cinematographers who remodeled a regular camera to adopt half of a frame, or two perforations, for each shot. For this reason, the technology was alternately referred to in the film industry as "half size" (*hap'ŭ saijŭ*), or "two perf" (*t'u p'ŏp'oreisyŏn*). It came into popular use after 1971 when the Korea Color Film Laboratory (Han'guk Chŏn'yŏn P'illŭm Hyŏnsangso) developed its own printing and developing equipment for Techniscope. According to Kim Mi-hyŏn (2004), the Korean Film Archive now houses 139 films made in the 1970s with Techniscope.

Figure 1. A comparison between Cinemascope and Techniscope. (*Kyŏnghyang sinmun*, December 28, 1964.)

At 14 percent of the total of 992 films produced in the 1970s that are now preserved at the archive, this number may not seem terribly significant at first. However, when we consider that Techniscope movies were mostly considered vulgar entertainment not worthy of preserving, the actual number of Techniscope movies produced was likely much higher. According to some estimates given by filmmakers of the time, more than 300 films produced between 1974 and 1976 could have been shot using Techniscope, which translates to almost 80 percent of the total number of films produced during the period.

According to Kim Mi-hyŏn, however, the cost effectiveness of Techniscope was not its primary attraction. In her dissertation (2004), the only technological history of South Korean cinema to date that traces the transformation and historical significance of the widescreen system, Kim suggests that the common argument that the domestic Techniscope system helped reduce production costs should not be taken at face value.[4] Techniscope helped save 565,000 won at best, which was not a significant reduction since the total production budget hovered usually around 10 million. Kim emphasizes instead Techniscope's sociopolitical connotations within the discourse of export-led economic growth. The technology was exported to overseas markets in Hong Kong, Indonesia, and Venezuela, and it was the impression of their competitiveness in outside markets that fueled the domestic demand in turn. In other words, "[T]he value system around Techniscope was shaped by the interaction between a form of technology and the social discourse directed outward . . . a result of the dominant discourse that disguised itself as an economic effect" (104). Techniscope's *true* value, according to Kim, did not rest with its ability to reduce production costs but rather with its projected global marketability, which would in turn prove the South Korean film industry's contribution to the project of national prosperity.

While it is important to underscore Kim's argument about the ideological dimension of what might appear to be a purely economic calculation—especially given the ubiquity of the Yusin ideology of developmentalism at the time—I want to refrain from dismissing the economic question altogether. Kim's calculation gives an overly simplistic picture when it equates the price of negative film stock and developing fees to the entirety of financial motivations that might have led movie producers to adopt Techniscope. Because the supply of negative film stock was controlled by the government through a single agency, the Korean Motion Picture Promotion Corporation (Yŏnghwa Chinhŭng Kongsa, or KMPPC), securing a steady supply was a real and serious problem for every South Korean filmmaker at the time. The supply problem became even more critical in 1973 when KMPPC stopped importing Kodak film and the price of negative film stock rose as a result. In addition, it is noteworthy that the Techniscope system affected not only the amount of negative film stock that had to be used to make a movie but also the entire production system. For anamorphic widescreen systems like Cinemascope, lighting was of the greatest importance because an anamorphic lens, compared to standard lenses, not only distorts an image by squeezing it but also loses the depth of field to a substantial degree. Because Techniscope did not require an anamorphic lens, filmmakers could also achieve significant cost savings in lighting equipment. For this reason, Techniscope was especially attractive to small film studios that wanted to trim the budget while still producing movies in a widescreen format.

While Techniscope made movies cheaper to produce, the reduced price tag came at a cost in terms of the quality of the images generated. Anamorphic systems produced the higher-quality images much preferred by South Korean cinematographers in general. In addition, the use of half a frame was not appropriate for creating grand spectacles onscreen, the kind that might entice audiences back into the theaters and away from their living rooms, because such scenes required larger frame fields. Nevertheless, Techniscope was found to be very effective for the action genre because the camera became so much lighter with half the weight of a magazine, such that its mobility could be enhanced. Combined with a zoom lens, the lighter camera was perfectly suited for capturing rapid movements. These factors made Techniscope ideally suited for lowbrow genre films such as the action movies produced in small film studios with limited budgets. Among the 139 Techniscope titles housed at the Korean Film Archive, 54 are classified as action-related, compared to 59 melodrama, 11 "enlightenment" (*kyemong*), 5 horror, 3 comedy, and 6 literary/artistic (*munye*).[5] The actual number of action movies produced must have been even higher considering that lowbrow action movies were less likely to be preserved, as previously noted.[6]

The film director Lee Doo-yong's six action movies made in 1974 can probably be considered the most representative of Techniscope action movies: *Yongho taeryŏn* (Manchurian Tiger, released on March 15), *Chugŏm ŭi tari* (The Leg of Death, April 21), *The One-Legged Man Returns* (July 20), *Punno ŭi oenbal* (Left Foot of Wrath, September 7), *Sok toraon oedari* (The One-Legged Man Returns 2, October 16), and *Paesinja* (The Turncoat, October 26). These movies bear a strong resemblance to one another in several respects due to their shared mode of production. The plot is formulaic, as noted earlier, and all six films are set in the colonial period somewhere in China, where a Korean action hero takes his revenge against a Japanese villain. All the titles except for *The Turncoat* were filmed using the domestic Techniscope system and bear its technical imprint: the use of a zoom lens and swifter camera movement. Han Yong-chŏl appeared in all six movies as a Taekwondo hero. Film producers and marketers may have found his Korean American identity attractive; most advertisements refer to him by his English name, Charlie Shell. After Han Yong-chŏl left the industry in the late 1970s, the same strategy of hiring a Korean American Taekwondo star continued with Bobby Kim. And last, as seen from their release dates, these movies were made very quickly. The fast cycle of production and consumption attests to the existence of a high demand for this genre of films. It also suggests a kind of preformatted taste that knit the audience together.

Hidden in Plain Sight: Lower-Class Men Go to the Movies

In his account of fantasies of labor power inscribed in American action cinema, Paul Willemen (2005) boldly argues that until the 1980s in the United States, *action cinema* did not exist as a film genre in the way film studies would now understand the term, that is to say, as a production category. In *Variety*, a US trade journal, for example, the term *action* was used to denote ingredients that could appear in any type of film rather than as the designation of a content genre. *Action* functioned instead as a marketing category that "*preformatted* audience expectations in terms of ingredients specific audience segments are supposed to be willing to pay for" (227). Audiences, in turn, were defined in terms of "identity categories" such as young urban working class, middle-class urban youths, black urban working class, and so on. Willemen concludes that there is a strong connection between action movies and audiences with lower levels of education.

Willemen's insight about the action genre as a marketing category helps us to better understand the relationship between a film genre and its audience, as well as the political representation of an identity group that the genre can manifest. Although Willemen's analysis is too contingent on the specific context of American action cinema to apply immediately to the South Korean action cinema of the 1970s, it is suggestive of the way a genre can be constituted by the identity categories of its audience rather than conceptualized exclusively in terms of elements internal to the produced content. To understand the relationship between genre and audiences in 1970s South Korea, we can turn to an important public opinion survey conducted in 1973 by *Yŏnghwa* (Cinema), a monthly periodical issued by KMPPC. The magazine hired five polltakers to interview one thousand people at six locations in Seoul, including three first-run movie houses at the city's center, two second-run theaters near train stations, and even one third-run theater on the outskirts of the city. The survey results were published in its November issue. Different film genres were grouped in two large categories, melodrama and action, and then further divided into subgenres. Under the heading action genre, for example, there were five subgenres: *ch'uri* (detective), *chŏnjaeng* (war), *hwalgŭk* (action), *muhyŏp* (martial arts), and western. For melodrama the three subgenres were *romangsŭ* (romance), *pigŭk* (tragedy), and *sagŭk* (costume drama).[7] The taxonomy of genres used in the survey reveals that the notion of the film genre itself was conceived as a marketing category for each target group in South Korea in the 1970s rather than as an aesthetic system. The two large category headings bore strong correlations to male and female audiences. Melodrama, especially in the 1960s, was overwhelmingly patronized by middle-aged women who were called the "rubber-slippered audience" (*komusin kwan'gaek*), a derogatory term that implied judgment against the moral values and cultural tastes of women who sought entertainment outside the home. Action movies, on the other hand, was the genre for young men.

Of the five subgenres identified as belonging to the larger "action" umbrella by the magazine, my own definition of "Techniscope action cinema" encompasses only the three subgenres of hwalgŭk, muhyŏp, and the western. Hwalgŭk, the Korean-style action genre, offered a historically specific narrative for action movies in the 1970s; muhyŏp (Chinese wuxia) introduced a cinematic mode of representing martial arts with the Korean Taekwondo variation emphasizing the leg kick; and western, particularly its Italian variation, paved the way for imagining the colonial landscape of northern China as the Wild West. Grouping these three subgenres together foregrounds the question of class by making visible the nature of the audiences that favored these movies (see table 1). Unlike the detective subgenre, for example, which was preferred by those with larger incomes and higher levels of education, as seen in the table, the three subgenres of Techniscope action films were preferred by 34.6 percent of those whose highest level of education was middle school, 26.6 percent of high school graduates, and 25.3 percent of college graduates. Living standards appear as an even more decisive factor. Among those with lower living standards, 31.7 percent affirmed their preference for Techniscope action cinema, while the percentage dropped

Table 1. Percentages of the analysis of the 1973 survey on spectatorship

	Living Standards			Academic Backgrounds		
	High	Medium	Low	College graduate	High-school graduate	Middle-school graduate
Mystery	16.3	13.2	7.9	15.7	14.6	3.8
Hwalgŭk	8.2	10.5	13.9	11.5	8.7	15.1
War	10.2	10.2	11.9	13.1	9.8	7.5
Wuxia	2.0	8.7	11.9	4.3	10.2	12.6
Westerns	6.1	8.5	5.9	9.5	7.7	6.9
Sum	42.8	51.1	51.5	54.1	51.0	45.9
Techniscope action cinema (Hwalgŭk, wuxia, and westerns only)	16.4	27.7	31.7	25.3	26.6	34.6

Source: "P'aendŭl i paranŭn Han'guk yŏnghwa." Yŏnghwa, November 1973.

to 16.3 percent among respondents in a higher income bracket. My readjustment of the data more clearly brings to the fore the class issue involved. The lower a respondent's living standard and level of education were, the more likely he was to find *hwalgŭk*, *muhyŏp*, and westerns appealing. In sum, urban lower-class males made up the lion's share of the audience for lowbrow action movies.

Despite the large percentage urban working-class men that made up of the audience at the movies throughout the 1970s, it is extremely difficult to find any contemporary written accounts of their presence. They are either lumped together as the new younger generation, which elides class distinctions among them, or represented simply as ignorant viewers who blindly follow film studios' commercialism. We see this dismissal at work in the writing of Ho Hyŏn-ch'an, a film critic. In his essay "What Do Audiences Want from Movies?" Ho argues for the urgent need to entice middle-aged women away from television and bring them back to the movies.

> Recent movies ignore romance, warm affection, and sentimentalism; instead, what prevails is brutal action drama of no known national origin and commercialism that stimulates a peripheral nerve. This is how I would like to explain the drop in the number of female moviegoers. (1975, 32)

Ho's call to female moviegoers previously belittled as "rubber-slippered" is especially noteworthy here, given the patronizing tone that cultural critics often adopt toward the so-called masses writ large. The appeal comes in the context of the film critic's attempt to revive the golden age of melodrama, which, according to Ho, represents "the dreams and romantic aspirations of the moviegoing public at all times." This elevation of the genre of melodrama and its predominantly female audience rests, however, on the dismissal of Techniscope action cinema as "brutal," "commercial," and "peripheral." The very patrons who in all probability saved South Korean film studios from financial ruin in the 1970s are thus overlooked in the critic's search for a more "ideal" spectatorship.

The erasure of Techniscope action cinema's audience occurs in yet another way in Ho's essay. "The population of the postwar generation has increased exponentially," Ho notes. "The age factor seems to have a profound correlation with the recent popularity of Korean movies" (1975, 32). In linking the baby boomer generation to film spectatorship, however, Ho makes no mention of the class distinctions within this generation. When taken as a single group, the generation tends to be represented disproportionately by college students, with an emphasis placed on the novel, western, and consumerist "youth culture" (chŏngnyŏn munhwa) of their so-called jeans-beer-guitar (t'ong-p'ŭl-saeng) lifestyle. College students, many of whom hailed from privileged economic backgrounds, belonged to the elite in South Korean society at a time when only a quarter of the eligible population advanced to college. Even if they did not come from well-off families, their future as the socioeconomic elite was often a foregone conclusion by virtue of their scarcity. Where movies were concerned, college students favored more "sophisticated" titles shown at the first-run movie theaters downtown. Needless to say, however, the baby boomer generation consisted also of the growing population of lower-class males living in the city's underbelly and outer limits. Coming to Seoul to take low-paying jobs, these men typically settled into cheap housing around the industrial areas or in shantytowns. Unlike college students, their avenues of temporary escape from work were limited to second- or third-run theaters located in an underdeveloped residential area or an industrial complex, which also featured a variety of live shows such as dance performances, concerts, and comedy acts.

In his reminiscences, Pae Pyŏng-jo, who worked in the 1970s in the sales division of the Kyŏngwŏn Theater located near Yŏngdŭngpo Station, drew an explicit connection between action movies and working-class viewers: "This area [Yŏngdŭngpo] was an industrial zone, so a bit lagging [in terms of cultural taste]. Probably for that reason, the action genre did well" (Yi et al. 2004, 133). The action movies that did well in his theater were not Star Wars or Rocky, the foreign titles that "enjoyed a great run at the first-run theaters" in the more fashionable urban areas, but what Ho Hyŏn-chan had denounced as "brutal action drama of no known national origin." These mongrel works of hwalgŭk, wuxia, and the western were produced rapidly and cheaply for an audience that cared more for the pleasure to be found in the beauty of the precisely delivered spin kick than aesthetic purity or purposiveness.

Precisely because the question of class is so commonly elided in discussions of spectatorship in 1970s film culture, it is important to take the cheapness of the technology as a productive point of departure for adopting a peripheral vision of Yusin. As we have seen, Techniscope action cinema emerged at the intersection of a cheap technology, a vulgar entertainment genre that presumed little about its aesthetic merit as an end product, and male audiences with lower-class backgrounds. However, notwithstanding the fact that the action movie genre was clearly a marketing category in the sense that Willemen has discussed it, its lower-class male audiences were given little representation in the 1970s. Statistical data concealed them by lumping their preferences under the umbrella category of "action." Elitist discussions of spectatorship also subsumed class differences between those who favored Western "youth" culture and those with motley "vulgar" tastes under the generation marker "baby boomers," making youth culture stand for the entire generation. Thus, the presence of lower-class male audiences at the movies in the 1970s can only be confirmed by looking askance at these "objective" data. What sustained such invisibility of a key demographic? If cultural critics saw no contribution worth highlighting in the constellation of genre, technology, and audience that sustained Technoscope action cinema, the Yusin state saw in its "vulgar" energy a potential threat that it sought to contain. It is to legal and institutional aspects of the Yusin film culture that we now turn in order to explore the measures the state took to expel Techniscope action cinema from the domain of desirable *and* controllable film culture.

Regulating "Violent Movies"

Regulations regarding film during the Yusin period were extensive to say the least. From production to distribution to exhibition, these regulations covered every detail of every aspect of the film industry. Concerning the movie theaters, for example, there were detailed provisions about architecture, management, programming, and even hygiene. The basis for these regulations was the expansive Film Law (Yŏnghwabŏp), first enacted the year after Park Chung Hee came to power and amended several times during the eighteen years of his reign. The degree to which the Park regime concerned itself with cinema can be appreciated from the fact that the government announced a new film policy (yŏnghwa sich'aek) every year to supplement the existing law. In addition, on August 31, 1975, the Ministry of Culture and Information announced a policy that targeted action cinema specifically. Seeking to control modes of film production with the professed aim of enlightening moviegoers as a public good, the new set of regulations singled out action cinema as detrimental to society. Its designation as p'ongnyŏk yŏnghwa by the state had the effect of institutionalizing film critics' general contempt for action cinema, creating a feedback loop that further justified state regulation as part of a united front against Techniscope action cinema.

The policy declared its purpose to be the prevention of the production and importation of "extremely violent movies that only had entertainment value and which were produced with the exclusive goal of generating profit." According to the state, these films were harmful to society because they resulted in the "introduction [to the innocent audience] of methods of outrageous crimes, the diffusion of disrespectful ideas about human life, and the spread of juvenile delinquency." The law mandated four steps for *p'ongnyŏk yŏnghwa*: submitting the screenplay for government approval before shooting begins, detailed reporting of the production schedule, review of the finished film by censors in a screening room, and rating of the properly censored content by the Commission on Performance Ethics (Kong'yŏn Yulli Wiwŏnhoe) before its release to the public. The policy defined a violent movie as follows.

1. For-entertainment-only movies with obscure themes and no discernible aims.
2. Action movies that feature evil-on-evil violence and the revenge theme.
3. Movies in which violent content overpowers elements of "promoting virtue and reproving vice" (*kwŏnsŏn ching'ak*).
4. Content that is repellent to audiences because of the extreme brutality and cruelty of scenes or content that urges [audiences] to lean toward disrespectful ideas about human life by highlighting illegal and murderous actions.
5. Content that may destroy social discipline, harm law and order, or nurture the spread of criminal methods by depicting an illegal activity in excessive detail.
6. Movies that contain sheer nonsense and utter fantasy.
7. Vulgar action movies that make a pretense of promoting anti-communist or anti-Japanese sentiments.
8. Content that could invite trouble internationally with descriptions of criminal acts and investigations of international scope.

("Mun'gongbu p'ongnyŏk yŏnghwa e taehan kyuje naeyong" 1975)

Notable is the fact that the policy must *define* what is to be regulated in the very process of seeking to regulate it. The various definitions of violent cinema that these articles offer weave together elements belonging to two different levels of film culture: the production of cinematic content *before* the movie's release (articles 1, 2, 3, 6, and 7) and the movie's possible influence on the public *after* its release (articles 4, 5, and 8).

How would the five categories pertaining to prerelease regulation apply to Techniscope action cinema? We can examine the plot of *The One-Legged Man Returns* as an example. The movie begins with three men looking to kill a man known as Shanghai Tiger. Yong-chŏl, once famed for his prowess, is now wasting away and wallowing in alcohol, a toothless tiger at best. A mystery man named Kim Sŭng comes to Yong-chŏl's rescue and informs him that the assassins were sent by a Japanese man named Yamamoto, to whom Hyang-suk, Yong-chŏl's former fiancée, is now married. The film then flashes back to Harbin in the 1930s where Yong-chŏl had grown up as an adopted son of Master Wang. When Yong-chŏl decides to leave his master's fold and marry Hyang-suk, Master Wang gives Yong-chŏl one last mission to carry out in collaboration with the Yamamoto gang—a stagecoach heist. During the mission, the Yamamoto gang kills the coach owner. When Yong-chŏl discovers that the dead man is actually Hyang-suk's brother, he is overcome with guilt and leaves Hyang-suk to become a drifter. As the action returns to the present, Yong-chŏl realizes that it was Yamamoto who had schemed everything from the start. Seeking revenge, Yong-chŏl penetrates the enemy's camp with Kim Sŭng, who turns out to be a Korean Independence Army soldier. Together the men defeat Yamamoto's thugs, only to discover that Hyang-suk has already committed suicide.

The One-Legged Man Returns is clearly a "violent film" according to the definitions set out in the 1975 regulations. Most of the characters are gangsters who perpetrate aimless violence (article 1). Their fights have nothing to do with a greater cause like the anticolonial struggle but are motivated instead by personal grievances. Even though Kim Sŭng, the Independence Army soldier, tries to enlighten Yong-chŏl about his duty as a patriotic Korean, such moments are immediately overwhelmed by the story of Yong-chŏl's revenge against Yamamoto for ruining his love and life (article 2). While justice appears to prevail at the end of the movie when Yamamoto is defeated, it is not a full-fledged victory over Yamamoto's vice; the suicide of Hyang-suk for reasons unknown leaves Yong-chŏl deeply scarred (article 3). Moreover, the film is filled with moments of nonsense, and notable gaps appear in the plot. In fact the absence of a one-legged man in the movie makes the title of the film itself nonsensical (article 6). The plot caters to popular anti-Japanese sentiment by making the villain a

Japanese, which only works as a specious pretense for exhibiting Yong-ch'ŏl's martial arts skills (article 7). Indeed, the appropriation of anti-Japanese sentiment was one of the most frequently employed narrative strategies for Techniscope action movies, but this very strategy also became a favorite target of attack by critics who bemoaned the low quality of action movies. For example, Im Yŏng wrote in 1976 that "action movies under the mask of anti-Japanism are simply imitations of Hong Kong kung fu movies and offer nothing but a cheap thrill.... Like all Taekwondo movies, they are vapid and meaningless" (Im 1976).

Reinforcing the state policy on p'ongnyŏk yŏnghwa, the contemporary discourse on the harmful social effects of violent movies focused on adolescents especially as the group most susceptible to the potential harmful influence of the genre. In the same issue of Yŏnghwa in which the new government policy on violent movies was announced, Pak Hyŏn-sŏ (1975), a member of the review committee of the state-owned television station KBS, argued that there was a clear connection between movie watching and juvenile delinquency. According to Pak, whereas "normal" middle school and high school students typically went to see a movie once every couple of months, juvenile delinquents went to the movies much more frequently, averaging more than four times a month. For Pak it was even more problematic that theater managers did not abide by the rating system and allowed young students into the theaters to watch violent movies.

A report in the daily Kyŏnghyang sinmun also suggested a causal relationship between violent movies and juvenile delinquency. It reported that imitating Bruce Lee and Bobby Kim—Han Yong-ch'ŏl's successor—was so popular among middle school boys that students were buying nunchucks instead of school supplies. What's more, these "playthings" could become weapons used to commit actual crimes: "*Fists of Wind, Duel of Life and Death, The Last Five Fingers, The Leg of Death*—just a glance at such titles is enough to strike me with horror.... This is a trend that 'does nothing but trifle with audiences,' according to Cho Sŏk-ho, the chief of the Film Department at the Ministry of Culture. Cho Yŏn-hyŏn, the chair of the Committee for the Ethics of Arts, insists on promoting healthy movies by radically revising the Film Law" (Kyŏnghyang sinmun, November 27, 1975).

Although such concern over the relationship between representations of violence in popular media and the susceptibility of teenagers to such representations is not uncommon even today, it is important to note that the hyperawareness of the adolescent spectatorship in the

Yusin era discourse had the concomitant effect of rendering lower-class males invisible. While some adolescents could indeed be found at the movies, the actual audience for Techniscope action movies consisted by and large of adult working-class males. The discourse on juvenile delinquency revealed the authorities' preoccupation with the future; their concerns over the present were actually oriented toward the time when their dire forecasts would materialize if the movies were allowed to have their full run without state intervention. Prerelease definitions of the violent movie were drawn largely from concrete and specific features of Techniscope action movies as they were screened in the present. However, what made the violent movie violent was not only what it contained in the here and now but its potential role in the imagined troubles that would afflict the nation in the *future*. This anxiety found expression in those articles of the policy that addressed the postrelease management of action movies.

Here, then, we can see how the two levels of definition engaged different temporalities. At the first level of prerelease definition, a violent movie was established as such in its distinction not only from other genres, such as the melodrama, but also ideological constructions such as "films of excellence" (*usu yŏnghwa*) recognized by the government. This definition was most concerned with what the film looked like as a finished product in the present. The second level, which concerned the postrelease definition of violent cinema, brought the question of cinema's educational efficacy to the fore while making a connection *in potentia* between action movies and juvenile delinquency. The process transformed a class problem into a generational one and justified the state's heavy-handed regulation of the film industry as a means of protecting the future of the nation from vulgar entertainment. The process resulted in the marginalization of lower-class audiences.

Thus, Techniscope action cinema did not simply refer to a group of action movies with a distinct style but was instead defined in relation to what the government and cultural critics identified as its essential vulgarity. As we saw, vulgarity was not simply a matter of the genre's content but was made applicable to the technology itself, as well as the audience for the films. The attempt to single out action movies like *The One-Legged Man Returns* as a prime example of violent movies eventually led to the exclusion of lower-class male audiences from the discourse about contemporary film culture in the 1970s. Such future-oriented discussions about action films, in turn, reinforced the state policy by providing an additional rationale for the government to impose prescriptive measures on Techni-scope action cinema.

The Laboring Male Body and the Anxieties of the Yusin State

What I have called "Techniscope action cinema" in this chapter refers to a cinematic triptych in the 1970s that emerged out of contingent encounters among action movies, widescreen technology, and lower-class male audi-ences. The domestic Techniscope system satisfied the increasing demand for widescreen cinema, which had already become the standard of the film industry, at a lower cost. Most action movies of the time, such as *The One-Legged Man Returns*, took advantage of the technology and its affordabil-ity. It was precisely the cheapness of this technology that broadened access to the movies and allowed action movies to accommodate the tastes of lower-class male audiences, which had little significance in the dominant discourse on cinema in the 1960s.

With the onset of the Yusin era, Techniscope action cinema quickly became one of the state's concerns. As the regime sought total control over the film industry, it labeled those visions that unfolded at the margins of society as violent cinema, thereby seeking to expunge them altogether. The state's concern over Techniscope action cinema was immediately echoed by contemporary critics who articulated the genre's harmful im-pact on teenagers, creating a negative discursive climate for action movies. To a large extent, they succeeded. After 1979 filmmakers stopped using the Techniscope system, and the aggregate number of action movies pro-duced began to drop. Even Lee Doo-yong, who made six such action mov-ies in 1974, stopped making action films altogether. He would not make another until *Torai* (Crazy Boy) in 1985. On the surface, therefore, the ef-ficacy of the Yusin state in containing social elements that it deemed un-desirable appears to have been proven again in regard to Techniscope ac-tion cinema.

Why was Techniscope action cinema identified as a potential social ill by the Yusin state? What were the peripheral visions that the state sought to drive out even from the fringes of society? In other words, what did Techniscope action cinema speak of and against in the era of Yusin? These questions take us to the heart of the Yusin state's anxiety, which we can unpack by focusing on the physical body of the action hero in Techniscope action cinema. As Willemen (2005) has noted, bodies of heroes in action cinema manifest socioeconomic fantasies about labor as value and thus the modalities in which labor power is inscribed in the films. However, my concern with the male body in Techniscope action cinema is with its nonrepresentation rather than representation of labor power, those critical points in the film when a representation no longer represents what it purports to. In Techniscope action movies, the male body remains in perpetual excess of the regulatory imagination concerning labor power; I argue that this excess destabilizes the yoking of the laboring male body to the authoritarian state's narrative of nation building and industrialization.

In this regard, Yong-chŏl's body in *The One-Legged Man Returns* is profoundly ambivalent. His toned and muscular body manifests power but remains a diamond in the rough; in order to serve the nation's great cause, such a body must be trained and disciplined. This narrative arc references the familiar plot line of Hong Kong action cinema in which the film's hero is transformed from a talented hoodlum into a righteous martial arts master through a rigorous course of training. As Ng Ho has put it, "[T]his emphasis on individual achievement and on outdoing one's own master undoubtedly parallels the ethos of capitalism" (quoted in Willemen 2005, 245). Indeed, it is well known that Hong Kong action cinema served as one of the major points of reference for South Korean action movies throughout the 1970s. In light of such intertextuality, we should note the curious difference that emerged in South Korean cinema. As Soyoung Kim has observed with acuity, action movies of the 1970s depict their heroes as "natural born street fighters without professional training" (2005, 108). From the movie's beginning to the end, Yong-chŏl never relies on any kind of training to hone his deadly kick as a weapon. While the presence of Master Wang, his adoptive father, gives a nod to the established convention of the *wuxia* genre, which emphasizes the process of training, Yong-chŏl remains in the rough to the end, refusing to be carved.

The need to discipline Yong-chŏl's body for nationalist ends is expressed in the voice of Kim Sŭng, the Independent Army soldier. Kim accuses Yong-chŏl of not committing himself to Korea's independence, and when Yong-chŏl apologizes for his errant ways, the ensuing cooperation between the two men appears to hint at Yong-chŏl's repentance. However, the movie does not allow Yong-chŏl to proceed to the great national cause and forecloses the possibility that he will elevate personal grievance into a political act. Hyang-suk's death at the end of the movie strands Yong-chŏl in a perpetual state of personal grief and private revenge.

Women, either as the violated love object or the maternal bosom forever lost, have often stood allegorically for the fragile nation. *The One-Legged Man Returns* deploys this familiar leitmotif by featuring a villain who dons the Japanese kimono. The film's reference to nationalism, however, remains curiously hollow. The colonial past that the movie depicts has nothing to do with any vision of the future Korean nation nor with the desire to break free of a wretched past. By means of flashbacks, the movie repeatedly takes the audience back to the tragic past; the return establishes the past as the origin of both the present and another present of sorts, indeed the past that persists as the present. What further complicates the nationalist resignification of Yong-ch'ŏl's action is that he never learns who is to blame for Hyang-suk's death. He successfully defeats Yamamoto, but Hyang-suk still commits suicide. The possibility thus lingers that without his belated quest for revenge Hyang-suk might still be alive, albeit married to his enemy. In this regard, it is not the parameters of nationalism that circumscribe the pathos of the characters in *The One-Legged Man Returns*; such an imagination of the colonial past exceeds the imperative of the postcolonial nation-state and its industrialization movement. Yong-ch'ŏl's body is thus detained in the repetitive cycle of the past and the present, which does not point to a future. It remains unusable for achieving the nation's independence and irreducible to anything that might have been conceived as desirable, and thus ungovernable. And this ungovernability emanating from a useless body that refuses to be domesticated is an anxiety-ridden prospect for the authoritarian regime.

To appreciate the ambivalence of such a body fully, we need only contrast it to the way a working-class male body was represented in *kukch'aek yŏnghwa*, the so-called national policy films that the Yusin state sought to disseminate as promoting the ideal subject. These films invariably told the story of an enlightened hero driven by a great cause whose sacrifice results in the triumph of the nation. The government flooded the movie theaters with national policy films; however, the audiences remained less than enthused about such anticommunist, developmentalist narratives onscreen. While this "wholesome" fare provided by the government languished in the theaters, "vulgar" movies like *The One-Legged Man Returns*, expunged from the discourse of mainstream film culture and denounced as mere *p'ongnyŏk yŏnghwa*, continued their shadowy existence in second- and third-run theaters. Today only the frayed edges of their prints remain as a sign of their journey, which became so extended that the films became ragged from being played over and over again. In this sense, the ungovernable bodies in the action movies of the 1970s parallel other ungovernable elements that persisted even at the height of Yusin state control. Perhaps it was this very anxiety over the ungovernable movements that Techniscope action cinema might engender that spawned the derogatory discourse about it in the first place.

Cultures of Yusin, looked at directly and narrated straight, reveal the ubiquity of state power in South Korea of the 1970s. And although this mode of narration frequently denounces the illegitimacy of state power that seeks to subsume all resistance into itself, the effect of such analyses often end up highlighting the efficacy of the very state that it seeks to critique. This is precisely one of the unintended effects of the recent reassessment of 1970s action cinema. The playful stylization of these movies in twenty-first-century revivals domesticates in retrospect the ungovernable vitality that animated Yusin's peripheries, a vitality that also lay at the heart of Techniscope action cinema. Ironically, perhaps it was the authoritarian Yusin state that best appreciated the presence and potential power of what lay at the margins of the society over which it sought such complete control. In its attempts to render these "aberrant" margins invisible, we find paradoxical acknowledgment of the state's own limits of power over those margins. Almost four decades after the end of the Yusin era, it is by looking awry that we might redeem such a peripheral vision from what might appear to be pitch darkness.

NOTES

1. Hye Seung Chung (2011) defines Manchurian westerns as "a cycle of 1960s and 1970s South Korean action films set in Manchuria during the 1920s and 193s, a space populated by members of the Korean colonial diaspora (consisting of disparate groups, such as peasants, bandits, freedom fighters, and hired guns)." 288–89. Jinsoo An (2010) sees Manchuria as a deterritorialized space on which the ambivalence of South Korean nationalism in the 1960s is mapped in the Manchurian westerns of the 1960s.

2. Kim writes, "It is, however, the infested and fantastic space of *Hwalkuk* that provides an arguably decolonizing choreography and landscape through the figure of the one-legged fighter acting against the Japanese authorities in 1930s Harbin" (2005, 101).

3. Yi Yŏng-il (1969) identifies the early 1960s as one of the few glorious moments in Korean film history in his 1969 historiography entitled *Han'guk yŏnghwa chŏnsa*. Taking a feminist spin, Kathlyn McHugh and Nancy Abelmann (2005) have also called the 1960s the South Korean golden age for melodrama.

4. Namhee Han (2014) has examined widescreen cinema in both Japan and South Korea. If Kim is more concerned with a technological development and its sociocultural engagement, Han's study of widescreen cinema gravitates toward films' aesthetic effects

on what she calls "postcolonial modernity." Han's discussion on Techniscope is limited since her interest lies more in the anamorphic widescreen cinema.

5. It seems natural that melodrama should account for the highest number since it has been the dominant mode throughout Korean film history.

6. Two factors in particular that compromised the preservation and archiving of Techniscope action cinema should be noted here. First, film producers did not have to submit copies of the movies to the government agency for preservation purposes until the establishment of Korean Film Archive in January 1974. Second, some technical issues in screening Techniscope films due to the peculiarities of the format made it difficult to actually determine how many Techniscope movies should be classified as action. Thanks to recent digital restorations of Techniscope films, we will soon have a better picture of the diversity of the works that the format encompassed.

7. *Hwalgŭk*, which literally means "action drama," is a term that has been in use since the early days of cinema in Korea. But the term's usage here as a subgenre of action cinema references a specific set of generic coventions. Interesting to note here is that three subcategories of action cinema, *hwalgŭk* (South Korea), *muhyŏp* (Hong Kong), and western (Italy/United States), are based on the countries of origin. This is another reason why I have grouped the three subgenres together in my analysis in this chapter. Although their aesthetic and stylistic systems vary according to their geographic distributions, all three genres were in fact highly influenced by one another. For *hwalgŭk*'s significance as a concept for modes of production during the colonial period, see Yi Sun-jin 2009.

REFERENCES

An, Jinsoo. "The Ambivalence of the Nationalist Struggle in Deterritorialized Space: The case of South Korea's Manchurian action film." *China Review* 10: 2 (2010): 37–61.

Chung, Hye Seung. "The Man With No Home/Musukja: *Shane* Comes Back in a Korean 'Manchurian Western.'" In *Westerns: The Essential 'Journal of Popular Film&Television' Collection*, edited by Gary R. Edgerton and Michael T. Marsden. 288–309. New York: Routledge.

Han, Namhee. 2014. "Technologies of Anamorphic Vision." PhD diss., University of Chicago.

Ho Hyŏn-ch'an. 1975. "Kwan'gaek ŭn yŏnghwa esŏ muŏt ŭl wŏnhanŭn'ga." *Yŏnghwa*, September.

Im Yŏng. 1976. "Han'guk yŏnghwa ŭi hwallo ch'akki wihae pusim." *Yŏnghwa*, December.

Kim Mi-hyŏn. 2004. "Han'guk sinemasŭkopŭ e taehan yŏksajŏk yŏn'gu." PhD diss., Chung-Ang University.

Kim, Soyoung. 2005. "Genre as Contact Zone: Hong Kong Action and Korean *Hwalkuk*." In *Hong Kong Connections: Transnational Imagination in Action Cinema*, edited by Meaghan Morris, Siu Leung Li, and Stepehn Ching-kiu Chan. 97–110. Durham, NC: Duke University Press.

McHugh, Kathlyn, and Nancy Abelmann, eds. 2005. *South Korean Golden Age Melodrama: Gender, Genre, and National Cinema.* Detroit: Wayne State University Press.

"Mun'gongbu p'ongnyŏk yŏnghwa e taehan kyuje naeyong." 1975. *Yŏnghwa*, October.

O Sŭng-uk. 2003. *Han'guk aeksyŏn yŏnghwa.* Seoul: Sallim.

"P'aendŭl i paranŭn Han'guk yŏnghwa." 1973. *Yŏnghwa*, November.

Pak Hyŏn-sŏ. 1975. "P'ongnyŏk yŏnghwa (TV p'oham) ka chŏngsonyŏn ege mich'inŭn yŏnghyang." *Yŏnghwa*, October.

Willemen, Paul. 2005. "Action Cinema, Labour Power, and the Video Market." In *Hong Kong Connections: Transnational Imagination in Action Cinema*, edited by Meaghan Morris, Siu Leung Li, and Stepehn Ching-kiu Chan, 223–47. Durham, NC: Duke University Press.

Yi Sun-jin. 2009. "Chosŏn musŏng yŏnghwa ŭi hwalgŭksŏng kwa kongyŏnsŏng e taehan yŏn'gu." PhD diss., Chung-Ang University.

Yi Yŏng-hŭi. 1976. "Pogo sipŭn yŏnghwa." *Yŏnghwa*, October.

Yi Yŏng-il. 1969. *Han'guk yŏnghwa chŏnsa.* Seoul: Sam'aesa.

Yi Kil-Sŏng, Yi Ho-gŏl, and Yi U-sŏk. 2004. "Pae Pyŏng-jo kusul charyo." In *1970-yŏndae Sŏul ŭi kŭkchang sanŏp mit kŭkchang munhwa yŏn'gu*, 126–39. Seoul: Korean Film Council.

Dissident Dreams

Science Fictional Imaginations in 1970s South Korean Literature and Film

Sunyoung Park

In the historical study of science fiction in South Korea, the decade of the 1970s is often regarded as a sort of black hole in the local evolution of the genre. In a recent account of the state of the genre, for example, the literary critic Kim Chae-guk recognizes Mun Yun-sŏng's novel *Perfect Society* (*Wanjŏn sahoe*, 1965) as the first mature science fiction to appear in postwar South Korea, only to then skip ahead to Bok Geo-il's *In Search an Epitaph* (*Pimyŏng ŭl ch'ajasŏ*, 1987) to account for the genre's development. Similar views have been proposed by critics such as Ko Chang-wŏn and Cho Sung-myeon (Cho Sŏng-myŏn), who also regard the 1970s as a period of quantitative, rather than qualitative, development of science fiction.[1] In this wide-ranging historical narrative, the 1970s is written off as a rather unexciting period that saw the continued publication of science fiction stories, mostly for children and teenagers, but without notable developments in adult science fiction.

The popularization of science fiction often follows the industrial and technological transformation of a society. This was true in Britain at the time of H. G. Wells's *The Time Machine* (1895) and also in the United States with Hugo Gernsback's *Amazing Stories* (1926). It may thus seem strange that the 1970s should have been such an unremarkable period in the history of Korean science fiction. The decade was after all an era of development for Korea's heavy industry. It began with the establishment in 1971 of the Korea Advanced Institute of Science and Technology (KAIST), the nation's first research-oriented university for science and engineering majors. Having inaugurated a new heavy-industry-oriented economic policy for national development, President Park Chung Hee (Pak Chŏng-hŭi) in 1973 launched a nationwide campaign for the promotion of general scientific knowledge among Koreans (chŏn'gungmin kwahakhwa). The subsequent government sponsorship reinforced science education for youths, established a science film library, and significantly boosted the publication of science-related books, more than doubling their number from that of the previous decade.[2]

The flourishing of science and scientific culture in 1970s Korea, however, was apparently not accompanied by remarkable developments within local science fiction. In the period's publication boom in youth science fiction, translated works accounted for the majority of new titles.[3] At theaters and on television, Japanese superrobot animations—in particular Nagai Go's Mazinger Z (1972)—and Hollywood sci-fi films and television series—for example, The Six Million Dollar Man (1974–78), Wonder Woman (1975–79), and Star Wars (1977)—enjoyed immense popularity among Koreans across all age groups. These imported science fiction products had the effect of stimulating the domestic production of sci-fi animation and comics, especially those for children, such as Yi Chŏng-mun's Iron Man Kangtau (Chŏrin K'angt'au, 1976) and Kim Chŏng-gi's blockbuster animation Robot Taekwŏn V (Robot'ŭ T'aekwŏn V, 1976).[4] With regard to more critically relevant, adult-oriented science fiction, however, the 1970s did not see the appearance of the kind of future-bound works that have come to define the genre. The apparent discrepancy between general advancement in scientific knowledge and the lack of its fictional representation raises questions for our understanding of 1970s cultural dynamics. Why did science fiction fail to attract serious interest from the period's cultural intellectuals? What social or psychological barriers account for writers' and directors' lack of interest in science fiction? And what forms of alternative science fictional imaginations, if any, were cultivated in the shadow of the decade's regime-led industrialization?

Answering these questions, I believe, requires first of all some rethinking of the notion of "science fiction" and what is generally accepted as such. It is true that contemporary Korean intellectuals did not produce any readily recognizable works of "hard SF," whose narratives are typically founded on futuristic scientific knowledge and its explorations. Still, some of them did rely on popular tropes of science fiction—such as the mad scientist, aliens, parallel universes, time travel, and utopia/dystopia—to create texts in which the science fictional element played a definite critical and countercultural function. The three examples that I discuss in this essay are Choi In-hun's (Ch'oe In-hun's) alternate history *Typhoon* (*T'aep'ung*, 1972), Cho Se-hŭi's dystopian proletarian novel *A Little Ball Launched by the Dwarf* (*Nanjangi ka ssoaolin chagŭn kong*, 1975–78), and Kim Ki-young's (Kim Ki-yŏng's) sci-fi horror film *Killer Butterfly* (*Sarin nabi rŭl tchonnŭn yŏja*, 1978). These works may not be considered science fiction in the conventional sense, yet they are all shaped at their core by science fictional inspirations, or "science fictionality" in Istvan Csicsery-Ronay Jr.'s words.[5] As I shall argue, all three works are representative of the application of science fictional themes and tropes to the political and cultural challenges of their era. Each is uniquely expressive of the culture of the 1970s, a product of the convergence between the cultural cosmopolitanism of contemporary young intellectuals and the rising tides of dissident social activism that began with the April 19 Student Uprising of 1960. Far from being an unexciting period devoid of qualitative innovation, I submit, the decade of the 1970s gave rise to the first wave of critical science fiction in Korea. In the formation of Korean counterculture, science fiction played an important role, and this renewed knowledge casts a new light on a decade whose cultural history has hitherto been represented almost exclusively by the realist and nationalist mainstream.

A Postnational Anti-imperialist Fantasy: Choi In-hun's Alternate History *Typhoon*

With his abstract, experimental, and socially conscious narratives, Choi In-hun epitomizes the innovative cultural sensibility of the decade that began in Korea with the April 19 Student Uprising and remained relatively liberal throughout even after Park Chung Hee's 1961 coup d'état. Having made his literary debut in 1959, Choi established his fame with *The Square* (*Kwangjang*, 1960), a novel featuring a young prisoner of war during the Korean War who can feel at home in neither the corrupt South nor the totalitarian North and instead chooses to emigrate to India, a neutral country.[6] Written amid the Manichean social atmosphere of postwar Korea, such a narrative could be taken to be radically provocative for its protagonist's rejection of both Koreas. In his subsequent works, such as *The Dream of Nine Clouds* (*Kuunmong*, 1962), *A Grey Man* (*Hoesaegin*, 1964), *The Journey to the West* (*Sŏyugi*, 1966), and *A Day in the Life of Kubo the Novelist* (*Sosŏlga Kubo Ssi ŭi iril*, 1970–72),

Choi continued to evoke his memories of the North during its social revolution while also maintaining his critical distance from South Korean society, where he lived as a refugee.[7]

If Choi's literary subject matter centered on collective national experiences such as the division, the war, and student uprisings, then his writing style, distinctive in its dreamy fantastic quality, was shaped by international inspirations. In many of Choi's novels, basic elements of realist fiction, such as characters, plot, time, and setting, are all dissolved into a nebulous and fluid psychological reality. This writing style partly harks back to 1930s modernists such as Yi Sang and Pak T'ae-wŏn, but antirealism in postwar Korea was a distinctive inflection of the French *nouveau roman*. The *nouveau roman*, also called *antiroman*, had its most articulate advocate in Alain Robbe-Grillet, then an internationally renowned intellectual who was well known in Japan and Korea. Robbe-Grillet called for a new literature that would defy the "ready-made," supposedly "objective" signification of classic fiction, focusing instead on reporting reality through a character's thoughts, observations, and sensations—that is, a reality as "a total subjectivity."[8] Such a call for antirealism found its resonance in Choi's own motto, "The real is the fantastic, and the fantastic is the real."[9] While Choi's works shared some formal similarities with those of Robbe-Grillet—such as the blurring of reality and fantasy, a labyrinthine narrative structure, and the use of mise-en-abyme, their stylistic resemblance was limited because of the considerable disparity between their respective social and cultural contexts.[10] It seems that Robbe-Grillet's proposition of antirealism, rather than his individual aesthetic style, appealed to Korean literary intellectuals.[11]

After a series of antirealist literary experiments, Choi turned to writing alternate history novels in the late 1960s. Alternate history (also known as alternative history, parahistory, and uchronia) can be defined as a nonrealistic historical fiction that speculates on how our present—and future—might have turned out as a result of some hypothetical changes in the past.[12] Choi wrote two novels in this genre. The first work, *The Governor-General's Voice* (*Ch'ongdok ŭi sori*, 1967–68), consists of four episodes, each of which is the record of a day's radio broadcast by the ex-governor of Japan's former colonial administration in Korea. The faceless leader is now the head of an underground network of Japanese who chose to remain in liberated Korea with the aim of reclaiming the lost colony. The novel is illustrative of Choi's antirealist writing style, as the narrative almost entirely consists of the disembodied voice. In comparison, *Typhoon*, the second alternate history, was written in plain prose, possibly because it was a newspaper-serialized novel targeted at a general readership. Set in a fictional location in South Asia in the last months of the Pacific War, the novel also shares the theme of Japanese imperialism.[13]

Choi wrote his two alternate history novels ten years after the publication of Philip K. Dick's *The Man in the High Castle* (1962), whose commercial and critical success made alternate history an internationally popular genre in the post–World War II period. The two writers' common preoccupation with Japanese imperialism, however, appears to have been more the result of historical contingencies than international cultural exchange. Dick's classic science fiction was not translated into Korean until 2001. Although its Japanese translation existed from 1965 on and many Korean intellectuals could read Japanese the work's generic nature precluded its becoming the object of critical attention among Korean literati.[14] Indeed, the author is to be believed when he affirms that he had not yet read P. K. Dick when he wrote his novels.[15]

Typhoon tells the story of Otomenak (Ot'omenak'ŭ), who finds himself caught in the Pacific War as a twenty-six-year-old lieutenant in an imperial army.[16] The prologue of the novel introduces its fictional chronological and geographic setting. The time is "early 1941," and the location is "the islands in the South Pacific," which "looked to Europeans as wondrous objects of conquest but were just ancestral hometowns for native inhabitants." "Which of them is barbaric is determined," adds the third-person narrator, "by who wins the battle at their first encounter" (7). The narrative then moves on to "the region called East Asia" and names three countries, "Anich, Aerok, and Napaj," inversions of the words *China, Korea,* and *Japan*. Otomenak is from a pro-Napaj Aerok family, his grandfather having been a famous collaborator in Napaj's successful annexation of Aerok and his father the chief executive officer of a state corporation. A follower of Ikitada Kitanat, the author of *Ideology of the Divine Country*, Otomenak passionately believes in Napaj's destiny to save the Asian people from the evils of Western empires such as Nibrita (Britain) and Acirema (America). Amid the thickening clouds of war, Otomenak is assigned to guard enemy hostages—Aisenodin independence fighters and forty Nibrita women—in Ropagnis (Singapore), one of Aisenodin's islands and a former colony of Nibrita. The young lieutenant moves into a mansion where Karnosu, the charismatic leader of the Aisenodin independence movement, has been under house arrest along with his female companion, Amanda, also a native of Aisenodin.

During Otomenak's stay in Ropagnis, however, a series of events causes him to become disillusioned and to undergo a transformation into a contrite, self-critical colonial subject. First, Mayaka, a renowned pro-Napaj journalist from an Aerok newspaper and a family friend, visits him to leak the news of Napaj's impending defeat. More important, Otomenak discovers in a hidden chamber next to his bedroom, a trove of Nibrita's colonial government's documents on Aisenodin's independence fighters as well as its looted treasures. From the documents, which include police reports on suspected nationalists, prisoners' pledges of "an ideological conversion" (chŏnhyang), compensation records for converts, and follow-up instructions for the arrest of newly identified nationalists, Otomenak learns "the real history of Aisenodin for the past hundred years" (121). He discovers that the friendly, innocent, and seemingly helpless faces of the natives tell but half of the story of Aisenodin, the other half being the indignant, blood-stained faces that loom from the police documents. Otomenak soon feels the intensity of their fury himself, and he barely survives the bombing of his military vehicle by a rebel force. He also witnesses vengeful Napaj soldiers' mass execution of five hundred Aisenodins of the Anich minority, including women and children. In his shocked mind, the tormented faces of Aisenodin rebels and victims overlap with those of Aerok independence fighters, whom he has thus far dismissed as misguided souls. Now that he realizes that Nibrita and Napaj are the same kind of exploitative empire, he feels that the side of independence fighters is where he belongs.

Otomenak does not return to Aerok after the end of the war, rather settling in Aisenodin under the pseudonym of Banya Kim. (Otomenak, or Kanemoto, is a Japanized version of the Korean surname Kim.) He is then charged with the mission of overseeing the exchange of forty Nibrita women in a location across the sea, but his voyage is first interrupted by the prisoners' riot and then by a typhoon that wrecks the ship and sweeps survivors onto an uninhabited island.

The epilogue skips thirty years ahead. A diplomat from the Aerok embassy in Ropagnis is now visiting a certain Kim, a mysterious local man of influence, who is rumored to be of Aerok origin. The narrative follows the diplomat through his walk past a leafy square named after Karnosu, now known as a legendary leader of Aisenodin as well as Asia. Under his charismatic leadership and egalitarian vision, several former colonies routed out imperial powers such as Nibrita and gained their independence (479). Aerok, which had been divided after the war, was unified twenty years later "thanks to the united power of these minor countries, which successfully struggled against the tyranny of superpowers to set a new paradigm for the international order" (475). The diplomat is visiting Kim to thank him for his own contribution to Aerok's unification and also to solicit his continued support. He is warmly welcomed by Kim's family: his wife Mary, a Nibrita woman, and Amanda, the daughter of Karnosu, whom Kim adopted after her father's death. Kim, however, politely declines the award of a consul general's title. Seeing off Aerok's messenger, Kim reminisces over Karnosu having arrived at the island just in time to persuade him out of a suicide attempt and Kim's subsequent assistance to Karnosu's anti-imperialist campaign: he had shared his own intimate knowledge of Napaj's military secrets and the treasures of Nibrita. He also reflects on how he came to marry his current wife, one of the women prisoners who were protected from lustful soldiers by his own command (498).

A thinly disguised alternate history, *Typhoon* projects an idealized version of postwar Asia onto our own world. The figure of Karnosu is unmistakably modeled after that of Sukarno, the founder and president of Indonesia as well as the leader of the Bandung Conference of decolonized Asian and African states. The character of Ikitada Kitanat refers instead to Kita Ikki, the author of *An Outline Plan for the Reorganization of Japan* (*Nihon kaizō hōan taikō*, 1919), who urged Japan to wage war against western imperial powers for a free and united Asia. These hidden references would have been familiar to informed readers in 1970s Korea. Choi's alternate history, however, substantively reconfigures the postwar history of Asia, presenting a heroic tale of successful revolutions and political triumphs in place of the region's bloody saga under successive military dictatorships sponsored by western powers within the global order of the Cold War. Notably, in this alternate world, the two Koreas have managed to unify into a single country.

Just as important as its envisioning of a new world order, Choi's alternate history also highlights the possibility of bringing about historical change through an individual's agency. What enabled the happy ending of postliberation Asian history was none other than Otomenak's decision to accept Karnosu's advice to transcend his native ethnic affiliation and join the Aisenodin's anti-imperialist struggle. This breakthrough is narrated through a dialogue recorded in indirect speech.

> I have sinned against my compatriots. How can I go back to my
> home country? Karnosu answered his seemingly unresolvable
> question. Why don't you become an Aisenodin? But I'm an Aerok
> man. Until recently, you thought yourself to be a Napaj, but you are
> now saying that you're an Aerok. You can also become an Aiseno-
> din or even a man of Nibrita. You just need to discard a name that
> has become no longer relevant. A man is born only once, but as a
> social subject, he can be born many times over. (492)

Persuaded by the Karnosu, Otomenak allows himself to survive and assist
Aisenodin in its war for independence. When the Aerok diplomat first
meets Banya Kim, the young man finds the dignitary physically indistinct
from the locals: "Even Aisenodin natives would have taken him as one of
them" (481). In fact, the former Japanese soldier has morphed into Karnosu's successor and double, with his identical laughter and his custody of
the late president's daughter. The possibility of individual rebirth, according to Karen Hellekson, is a generic premise of alternate history, which
tends to foreground "the individual's role in making history" along with
"the constructedness and narrativity of history."[17]

The utopian vision of *Typhoon* is not, however, without its own complicity in the hegemonic discourse of orientalism. For all its critique of imperialism and its advocacy of a Third World alliance, the novel ultimately represents the South Asian country Aisenodin through an orientalist lens. Choi's
narrative does counter Otomenak's initial impression of "bright and child-
like" natives with his later awakening to the complex social reality of the
colony. Yet the narrative betrays its own prejudice in depicting the protagonist's love affair with Amanda. This heroine of the romantic subplot is described as a tropical goddess who personifies the natural beauty of her land:
her body, which smelled fresh, like "a young, brown palm tree" with "two
round, heavy fruits," is said to be "as big and joyous as the land of Aisenodin"
(209). During their intercourse, the narrative compares Amanda to a tropical sea and Otomenak to a canoe passing through its islands (178–80). That
their relationship is also sublimated into comradeship between two colonial
subjects—Amanda turns out to be the daughter of a martyred nationalist—
does not offset the subimperial conquest of the future first lady of the South
Asian country by an Aerok agent of imperial Napaj. In a more sinister interpretation, this subplot sharply undercuts the narrative's elevation of Karnosu above Otomenak, who assumes an uncanny resemblance to the late
leader and indeed takes his place.

Anchoring Choi's anti-imperialist novel is the colonial fantasy of the South Sea (*nanyang*), which predated Japanese imperialism but became most prominent in Korea only after Japan's invasion of western colonies in South Asia in the early 1940s.[18] In the popular culture of the Japanese empire, the South Sea was represented as a fantasy landscape: a cluster of islands replete with the sensual pleasure of its natural—also translated as "uncivilized"—riches and its sexually promiscuous brown-skinned beauties.[19] In this cultural imagination of the South Sea as a primitive utopia, South Asian countries were rendered as, we might say, East Asia's own Orient. For its territorial composition of islands and its association with Karnosu, Choi's fictional utopia of Aisenodin is strongly reminiscent of Indonesia, but this supposed prototype of a South Asian colony was actually created based on the author's weeklong travel experience in Vietnam, where he visited Korean soldiers.[20] It is only within the framework of the imperial fantasy of the South Sea that Choi could fuse Vietnam, Indonesia, and Singapore into an imaginary amalgam while keeping his fantastic clones of western and East Asian nations distinct from each other.

If *Typhoon* offered an ambiguous literary critique of global imperialism, it still had a clearer counterhegemonic discursive function in its transcendence of 1970s nationalist politics. Its newspaper serialization began within a year of Park Chung Hee's 1972 proclamation of the so-called Yusin Constitution. The amendment extended Park's presidential tenure to his lifetime and sanctioned severe repression of any criticism of the government or its policies. In one of its totalitarian measures, the regime also introduced the National Charter of Education (Kungmin kyoyuk hŏnjang, 1968), which emphasized the obligation of all Koreans to dedicate themselves to "the historical mission of nation building." This document was distributed to all elementary and junior high schools throughout the 1970s for students to memorize and recite.[21] Read against this political and social context, Choi's protagonist, an Aerok who chooses to become an Aisenodin, and his postnational dialogue with Karnosu assume a refreshingly liberating significance for their flouting of official ethnonationalism. We can also appreciate anew the critical import of Choi's alternative international vision of the world and its emphasis on the anti-imperialist egalitarian alliance among Third World countries. Such a vision was antithetical to both a developmentalist nationalist worldview, in which nations were seen as competitors in the rat race for the survival of the fittest, and a Cold War binary division of the world into the US-led capitalist sphere and the Soviet-led communist bloc.[22]

Choi's radical political imagination in *Typhoon* could be represented—and in fact conceived—only through the mediation of such a fantastic narrative mode as alternate history. After all, in a society where intellectuals were routinely harassed, arrested, and tortured, any expression of dissent needed to be carefully camouflaged. Beyond this logistical necessity, however, Choi's science-fictional, narrative strategy also seems to have allowed the writer to set his imagination free to an extent from the constraints of hegemonic ideologies inculcated within himself. A comparison of *Typhoon*'s epilogue with the ending of 1960's *The Square* makes a telling point supportive of such a hypothesis. The latter complies with the usual demands of nationalist discourse by having the protagonist, who betrays the nation, commit suicide in the end. Whereas the former defies such a discursive constraint by letting Otomenak not only survive his disloyalty to the nation but also thrive far more than he would have had he returned to his home country, which was soon to be riven by civil war. In the novelist's own words, the writing of this fantasy novel inspired in him a sense of optimism, a hope for "resurrection," amid the frozen atmosphere of 1970s South Korea.[23]

Typhoon was one of the first instances in which a science fictional mode of imagination was critically appropriated in postwar South Korea. In retrospect, its fantastic literary imagination derived from 1960s cultural idealism hitting the hard wall of 1970s politics. Throughout the postwar decades, cultured Koreans had to cope with the stark disparity between their ideals—which were nourished by international popular and intellectual culture—and their life experiences. Schizophrenic as they felt, they also maintained the hope for a better future during the 1960s, when Korea enjoyed relative political stability, economic expansion, and cultural growth. But with the inauguration of the Yusin regime in 1972, history seemed to derail from its promised path: reality became too repressive and even absurd. It seems no coincidence that the alternate history of *Typhoon*, at once a fantastic flight from and a critical rewriting of reality, should have been written at such a moment. After *Typhoon*, Choi In-hun stopped publishing prose fiction for nearly two decades until his memoir-novel *Speech* (*Hwadu*, 1994).[24] In the period between, however, more fantastic writings with science fictional elements were published by others, and we shall now turn to examining one of its most famous examples.

Alienated Labor in the City of Machines: Cho Se-hŭi's Proletarian Dystopian Novel *The Dwarf*

Cho Se-hŭi's *A Little Ball Launched by the Dwarf* (1975–78, hereafter *The Dwarf*), arguably the best-known Korean novel of the 1970s, epitomizes the decade through its combination of formal experimentalism and proletarian cultural sensibility. The early 1970s saw the revival of proletarian literature in South Korea, where the literary tradition had gone dormant since the division of the two Koreas. *The Dwarf* was part of a new wave of socially engaged texts, which included workers' own testimonial writings, as well as stories about urban laborers and slum residents by authors such as Hwang Sok-yong (Hwang Sŏk-yŏng) and Pak T'ae-sun.[25] Cho's novel, however, differed from both contemporary works and the later literature of *minjung* realism—which aimed at a faithful, reportagelike depiction of life experiences and struggles—in its experimental and fantastic writing style. Alternating between multiple perspectives and temporalities, *The Dwarf*'s narrative presents various characters' intertwined life stories. Together they form a mosaic of different walks of life, with settings ranging from luxurious mansions of the cream of society to middle-class households and the unauthorized housing in urban hills that is lyrically known as a "moon village" (*taltongne*). Through its dreamy tones, Cho's narrative questions and deliberately blurs the boundary between the real and the fantastic. At the heart of this literary fantasy stands the evocative, fablelike, and quasi-sci-fi image of a dwarf leaving the earth, a hostile planet of giant aliens, for a lunar utopia.[26]

The Dwarf has a circular narrative structure. The prologue, titled "The Möbius Strip," begins with a scene in a classroom where a mathematics teacher is lecturing high school seniors; the epilogue returns to the same scene. These bookends divide into the frame story and the embedded story of an urban crime, the narrative shifting between the two story lines with few transitional markers. The story follows Hunchback and Squatlegs, two slum residents with congenital physical disabilities, on their nightly adventures. In the prologue, they attack a real-estate speculator who has previously embezzled money from them. Largely consisting of dialogue between the two unlikely robbers, the narrative obliquely suggests that the two take from the man only the exact amount owed to them and afterward set his car on fire with him inside. In the epilogue, we find the pair again on the road, this time trying to hitchhike in order to chase after another swindler, a drug peddler who had previously exploited them.

The reader is not given any explanation about the mutual relevance of these two stories, which draw a stark contrast: one is educational, civilized, and orderly, the other brutal, criminal, and chaotic. Hinting at the possible interconnections between the two separate worlds are the two scientific tropes centrally placed in the teacher's lectures: the Möbius strip and a space voyage. After observing that the curved surface of the Möbius strip "conceals many truths," the teacher declares that "human knowledge is often put to extraordinarily evil use" (12). His remark, and the juxtaposition of the two contrasting story lines, foreshadows the remainder of the novel: a tale about industrializing Korea's tyrannical use of scientific reason and its human costs. In the epilogue, the teacher refuses the school's request that he teach ethics in place of mathematics. Instead of instilling in his students the hegemonic doctrines that would "smother [their] creativity," he bids them farewell and announces his plan to "leave on a space voyage" for another planet (218).

The metaphorical assimilation between the disabled, the proletarian, and the alien—all figures of physical, economic, and biological alienation—resonates throughout the main part of the novel. In its originary narrative event, a dwarf's family receives an order to evacuate from their house, which had been built illegally on one of the many hills in Seoul that had turned into urban slums. The family is given occupancy rights for a new apartment, yet it cannot afford the required down payment. With the dwarf father working as a day laborer and his two sons just laid off from a printing factory for their participation in a labor strike, the evacuation is bound to leave them homeless. On their final day in the "Paradise" district (Haengboktong), the family invites Chi-sŏp, a college dropout who has befriended the dwarf, to their last supper. When the demolition squad arrives, Chi-sŏp fights with them and is dragged away. That night, weary of his lifetime of hardship, the dwarf "leave[s] this dead land" for the moon, and his pretty teenage daughter, Yŏng-hŭi, also disappears, presumed by her neighbors to have been taken by "a flying saucer" (63, 67). In an alternative account, the dwarf throws himself into a factory smokestack, and Yŏng-hŭi follows a real-estate speculator to become his secretary-cum-mistress with the goal of recovering her family's occupancy rights. After their fall from "Paradise," the rest of the family members are banished to nearby Ŭngang, where the two brothers find jobs as mechanics at a new automobile factory in a gigantic industrial complex.

Unfolding in the latter half of the novel is a proletarian bildungsroman of the dwarf's three children—or their own process of "extraterrestrial" transformation—in Ŭngang, the "City of Machines." The city is described as a frontier of Korean industrialization and an epitome of all its vices. As an international trade port, the city is reminiscent of Inch'ŏn, but it is also an imagined place filled with all kinds of factories, producing everything from clothes, paper, and ceramics to chemicals, electronic goods, cars, and ships. The industrial complex in the north of the city is wrapped in thick layers of smog that wall it off from the outside world. Within the complex, a different set of ethical standards applies, and in this sense, Ŭngang is "an abandoned city" and its residents "extraterrestrial" (159). At their workplaces, the dwarf's children are exposed to the rampant violation of labor laws and the routine practice of labor and sexual exploitation: "The machines that operated in the factories were things of precision, but society was full of peculiar habits, surveillance, inefficiencies, and dangers." To Yŏng-ho, the dwarf's eldest son, "everything looked black, like the steam engines you see in photographs" (164). Eventually, the siblings become involved in a labor movement. During their struggle, they meet activists such as a Christian minister at Workers' Church, and also reunite with Chi-sŏp, who has since become a veteran union organizer. Their union movement is, however, soon crushed by the police force. Out of indignation, the now blacklisted Yŏng-ho attempts to assassinate the powerful corporate head of Ŭngang's factories, but he misidentifies the man and kills his brother instead. In the epilogue, we learn of Yŏng-ho's execution.

Emerging from Cho's mosaic omnibus novel is a dystopian, apocalyptic vision of South Korean society at the height of its industrialization. The country appears to be increasingly polarized into haves and have-nots, who regard each other as "otherworldly" beings. Members of the proletariat—not just industrial workers but also the weak and marginalized in general—are abused, neglected, and discarded like disposable mechanical parts. After a supervisor pricks her arm with a clothespin during her night shift, for instance, Yŏng-hŭi comments that 1970s Korea seems similar to nineteenth-century Britain, when Marx was documenting the plight of urban laborers during the Industrial Revolution (143). Yet, although Yŏng-hŭi imagines that the poor like herself are born with "screams" whereas rich children draw their first breaths "sweet and snug" (113), the world of the bourgeoisie is no utopia either. Accumulating their wealth through corruption and exploitation, upper-echelon ctitzens educate their heirs in the principle of the survival of the fittest. Learning "useful" subjects such as economics and "human engineering," the young bourgeois live in constant anxiety about falling behind and losing the trust of their elders, since they know all too well that "love alone cannot earn [you] anything" (263). In this divided and iniquitous society, those who protest—"those who tell the truth"—are simply "buried alive" (98). It is a "monstrous" world (125) where "everyone was making a mistake. There could be no exception. In Ŭngang, not even god was faultless" (203). This godforsaken world seems bound for an apocalypse.

The Dwarf, however, suggests no blueprint for a structural, let alone scientific, reform of this dystopia; in its stead, the novel offers only fragmentary poetic fantasies. Yŏng-hŭi tells Yŏng-ho, for instance, about the fabled town of "Lilliput" in Germany near Lake Hasbro, where no oppression, inequality, or violence threaten the multinational dwarf inhabitants. Dwarves live happily ever after in this autonomously ruled place, which has "no dictator" and is also free of "big corporates," "factories," and "their managers" (169). Also the dwarf father dreams of a lunar utopia whose residents "work with love, raise their children with love, [and even] make the rain fall with love" (185). To love would be the only duty of the citizens of this utopia, and the greedy would be judged as having lost their love and would be deprived of the necessities of life—"the sunshine, wind, electricity, and water." Such abstract, romantic utopian dreams require no technological innovations and even seem nostalgic for a preindustrial past.[27] Along with the novel's seemingly superficial, diluted appropriation of the generic conventions of science fiction, this lack of a scientific vision in its utopian dreams—or "a novum" that can be validated by "scientifically methodical cognition" in Darko Suvin's words—may seem to disqualify *The Dwarf* as a science fictional work.[28]

Yet, despite its apparent divergence from more conventional forms of science fiction, the novel is profoundly shaped by a science fictional mode of imagination. For one thing, regardless of what specific contents its utopian dreams may have, the novel's utopianism is itself inspired by science fiction. Although utopian literature has ancient antecedents, its practice in modern times has been closely associated with science fiction—so much so that utopian literature can be conceived, as Suvin himself notes, as "the sociopolitical subgenre of science fiction."[29] A good textual illustration of this generic affinity is the repeated reference to the dwarf and Chi-sŏp, two utopian dreamers, obsessively reading a science fictional work titled *The World after Ten Thousand Years* (102). In this and other parts of the novel, *The Dwarf*'s narrative is punctuated and infused with science fictional leitmotifs, including chapter titles such as "The City of Machines," "Space Travel," and "Orbital Rotation." By relying on tropes such as the planet, space travel, and alien beings, the novel effectively communicates to readers its proletarian characters' acute sense of social alienation and their desperate hopes for the amelioration of the status quo. *The Dwarf* thus achieves an eloquent critique of Korean society under Park's developmental dictatorship—depicted here as "a dystopian planet"—that would have been impossible without its science fictionality.

Cho's proletarian dystopian novel showcases both the potential and the limitations of science fiction in 1970s Korean literature. The genre could not quite thrive, because its perceived commercial and conformist character failed to attract many serious writers, who harbored countercultural sentiments. At the same time, the genre did inspire a distinctive critical literary work like *The Dwarf*, thus proving its potential as a camouflaged, metaphorical vehicle for poignant social commentaries. As was the case with *Typhoon*, the science fictional aspect was crucial in enabling the critical discursive function of Cho's novel, especially under the constraints of the period's intense censorship. Admittedly, such crossbreeding between mainstream fiction and science fiction was more the exception than the norm in 1970s Korea, yet as the other examples in this chapter attest, *The Dwarf* was not an entirely isolated instance either.

Subversive Spectacles: Kim Ki-young's Sci-Fi Horror Film
Killer Butterfly

Kim Ki-young's *Killer Butterfly* is arguably one of the weirdest films ever made. At first viewing, the film confounds the audience with a fragmented, incoherent narrative, grotesque visual excess, and a generic hybridity that eludes easy categorization. Its unconventional, experimental quality is striking, especially because the film was made in the so-called dark age of Korean cinema, during which period the government's newly reinforced censorship suppressed cinematic creativity. In some aspects, the film bears the unmistakable trademarks of its auteur director: a surrealist blurring between material and psychological reality; an expressionist mise-en-scène with artificial use of settings, color, and lighting; and a thematic preoccupation with the degeneration of a model bourgeois family. Yet an auteurist approach would be insufficient to interpret the film, whose lack of a coherent narrative and abundance in sci-fi fantasy tropes are uncharacteristic of Kim's filmography. Perhaps for this reason, the director himself once took a dismissive attitude toward the work: "[T]he film has neither a logic nor any definite meaning. In fact, I don't even want to remember it."[30] When pressed to rationalize his work, he characterized it as "a deformed (*kihyŏng*) product of the mass hysteria" of 1970s Korean society, "a nightmare of a vegetative people who had their limbs severed and their brains lobotomized by the military dictatorship."[31]

In placing this cult film in the 1970s cultural scene, it is best to approach it as a collaborative product of two cosmopolitan cinephiles, director Kim and scenarist Yi Mun-ung. As is well known, Kim Ki-young drew seminal inspiration for his filmmaking from Japanese films (Mikio Naruse's and Kurosawa Akira's in particular) and European avant-garde cinema (especially Robert Wiene and Luis Buñuel), as well as theatrical arts, during his college days in Tokyo in the colonial era.[32] After the 1945 liberation, the majority of foreign films screened in Korea were from Hollywood, but Kim kept up with international cinemas, including those of the Eastern European Communist bloc, by reading smuggled Japanese film magazines and books.[33] Best known today for his masterpiece *Housemaid* (*Hanyŏ*, 1960), a domestic horror film that has been celebrated in Korea as a critical realist film, Kim has also been recently reevaluated by critics such as Soyoung Kim and Chris Berry as an early master of Korean fantasy cinema for works such as *Iŏdo* (Iŏ Island, 1977) and *Killer Butterfly*.[34]

If the film owes its visual aesthetic to the director, its narrative is a brainchild of Yi Mun-ung, who was twenty years Kim's junior and belonged to the "April 19 generation" that led the 1960 student uprisings. Yi is perhaps better known for his screenplay for the 1980s erotic film *Madame Aema*, but during the 1970s he was a versatile and prolific screenwriter of a variety of genre films. Having majored in French literature—an appealing subject due to the popularity of existentialism in postwar Korea, he worked as a journalist at the established film magazine *Kukche yŏnghwa* (International Cinema) before turning to screenwriting. His filmography includes a number of B-movies, including the martial arts *Yusŏnggŏm* (The Yusŏng Sword, 1977), the SF animation *Koesu taeraesŭp* (A Monster's All-Out Attack, 1977), the historical horror *Hŭphyŏlgwi yanyŏ* (A Female Vampire of the Night, 1981), and the ghost horror *Sahu segye* (The Netherworld, 1981), which variously reflect the influence of American, Japanese, and Hong Kong cinemas.[35] While Kim was notorious for radically altering original texts in adapting them to his films, he made an exception for Yi's screenplay in making *Killer Butterfly* because he found it "unusually imaginative," though incomprehensible at first.[36] The film's affinity with existentialist philosophy and sci-fi horror cinema, as well as its appropriation of the youth codes of *chŏngch'un yŏnghwa* (youth cinema), was thus more Yi's contribution.[37]

What kind of nightmare, then, did this cosmopolitan duo create in *Killer Butterfly*? The first of the film's three fragments shows the protagonist, Yŏng-gŏl, an impoverished college student, wavering between life and death after having been unwittingly embroiled in a love-suicide pact. The opening of the film offers a panoramic view of a college campus shot from various angles before the camera tracks Yŏng-gŏl, his friend Mun-ho, and their classmates on an out-of-town picnic trip. During the trip, Yŏng-gŏl chases after a butterfly, only to run into a mysterious woman wearing a golden butterfly pendant who tricks him into drinking a cup of poisoned soda with her. The woman dies, but Yŏng-gŏl survives. After returning to his lodging in a mountain village, however, Yŏng-gŏl begins to suffer from unrelenting suicidal impulses. His multiple suicide attempts are all blocked by an old bookseller, who preaches "a will to live," urging Yŏng-gŏl to read a (fictional) book titled *The Triumph of the Will* (*Ŭiji ŭi sŭngni*). The man recites ideas drawn from, among others, Arthur Shopenhauer's *The World as Will and Idea* and Elvin Toffler's *Future Shock,* and he counters the latter's concern about rapid social change with the former's emphasis on the importance of individual desire.[38] Yŏng-gŏl soon grows tired of these harangues and he ends up stabbing the chattering bookseller. The man's corpse, however, is soon revived, forcing Yŏng-gŏl to try to kill it again and again. He buries the still talking corpse and then burns the maggot-infested yet still moving carcass. In the end, Yŏng-gŏl surrenders to the immortal man of will, whose living skeleton then finally crumbles into dust. The film cuts from its close-up on Yŏng-gŏl's pale, dust-covered face to a scene at a police station, where the chief detective discharges Yŏng-gŏl and tells him that all was but his delusion.

The second episode features Yŏng-gŏl in a necrophilic love affair with a revived corpse. Yŏng-gŏl follows Mun-ho into a cave and collects an ancient skeleton, which he assembles in the hopes of securing a job as an assistant to Professor Lee, a renowned paleontological archaeologist. Once put together, the skeleton turns into a beautiful woman who claims to have died while hiding from her parents to avoid an arranged marriage in the kingdom of Silla two thousand years prior. Reminiscent of the traditional folk monster of a fox lady, the woman professes her love for Yŏng-gŏl but demands that he procure for her a fresh raw human liver or be killed himself. In order to support his new lover, Yŏng-gŏl purchases a puffed rice cake maker, and in the following sequence, the two have sex amid flying rice cakes. In their moment of lethargy, the starved vampiric woman considers killing him but decides to sacrifice herself instead. After she turns back into bones, Yŏng-gŏl takes her skeleton to Lee and is employed as his assistant.

In the final and longest episode of *Killer Butterfly*, we find Yŏng-gŏl himself transformed into the living dead. The setting has now shifted from Yŏng-gŏl's shack to the scientist's Western-style mansion, its gothic interior complete with a basement lab for the chemical processing of specimens. Lee regularly receives new specimens from an unidentified benefactor who supports Lee's nationalist ambition of proving that Koreans are direct descendants of Genghis Khan. Soon Yŏng-gŏl begins to suspect the scientist of using his connections to murder rivals. He reports his suspicion to the police and also confronts Lee. Meanwhile, Yŏng-gŏl also dallies with Kyŏng-mi, the scientist's only daughter, who turns out to be a close friend of the mysterious woman in the first episode and wears an identical butterfly pendant. When Kyŏng-mi falls terminally ill with cancer, her father asks Yŏng-gŏl to take her to "a young couple's love camp." The couple go but return without having consummated their relationship, and Kyŏng-mi soon develops an obsessive desire for the young assistant. To fulfill her dying wish, Lee has Yŏng-gŏl killed and has his severed head delivered to his home. The now satisfied Kyŏng-mi strangles herself in front of her lover's head, but Yŏng-gŏl suddenly revives and yells with shrill laughter, "I am not dead. My will to live will never succumb to death!" In furor, Lee plunges a knife into the undead only to stab himself to death during the ensuing struggle. The camera then closes up on Yŏng-gŏl's triumphant face in a wide-angle shot. His blood-streaked head rocks with increasingly louder peals of laughter, while his cheeks comically puff up to blow out the numerous candles on the table. The film then cuts to the evil doctor, now turned into a gigantic black butterfly, flying away with Kyŏng-mi hanging onto his legs. Following this sequence is a brief epilogue in which both Yŏng-gŏl and Mun-ho wake up from their nightmare and cheerfully stride down the streets of Seoul in broad daylight.

Killer Butterfly can be read as the protracted nightmare of a young man of humble social origin. Yŏng-gŏl's sexual fantasies and frustrated desire for social advancement find their expression in his hallucinatory encounters with three femme fatales, the embodiments of "the monstrous-feminine," whose life-threatening power derives from their sexual attraction.[39] Despite their differences, the women characters can be seen as mirror images of one another: Kyŏng-mi and her nameless friend are bound by a sisterly, if not lesbian, bond hinted at by their common butterfly pendants, and the Silla lady and Kyŏng-mi share a identity as unruly daughters who rebel against their fathers' authority. Although Lee poses as a caring father who indulges his temperamental daughter's whims, he actually reigns over his family as a domineering patriarch, as is exemplified by his arrangement of his daughter's deflowering without her consent. In fact, Kyŏng-mi accuses her father of "suffocating" her mother to death by turning her gradually into "a mummy" in her domestic cage. Accordingly, these monstrous women are themselves unhappy victims of the domestic—and social—patriarchy. In this sense, at the darkest heart of Yŏng-gŏl's nightmare stands Lee, the antagonistic mad scientist who epitomizes the tyranny and corruption of authoritarian patriarchy in an allegorical reference to Park Chung Hee's regime.

Given the centrality of the scientist character as the prime antagonist, *Killer Butterfly* can also be read as a late variation of what Song Hyo-Joung calls "Gothic SF," a group of 1960s horror films that featured a mad scientist as a villain.[40] As Song explains, this genre thrived from the 1960s to the mid-1970s, from Yi Ch'anggŭn's *The Death of an Invisible Man* (*T'umyŏng in'gan ŭi ch'oehu*, 1960) to Kim Ki's *Half Human and Half Beast* (*Pansu panin*, 1975). Having initially expressed the popular fear and suspicion of scientific modernity through the Frankensteinian trope of a failed experiment and its horrifying consequences, the genre was gradually tamed to include a happy ending in which the villain is overpowered by another benign scientist, typically a paternal or patronizing figure to the persecuted heroine. Produced after the passing of the genre's popularity, *Killer Butterfly*, which is notably left out of Song's account, deviates from this domesticated type, as it leaves the evil scientist without a matching rival.

Without denying its complicity in the male intellectual anxieties about the feminine, we can see in the nightmarish fantasy of *Killer Butterfly* a critique of the militarized modernity of contemporary South Korea—or, more specifically, of Park Chung Hee's dictatorial regime.

Here I am in general agreement with Chris Berry's analysis of the film as "an apt characterization of South Korean modernity as an experience more delirious than rational."[41] As Berry suggests, the fantastic aspects of the film may be seen as representing the irrational, discontinuous, and self-contradictory character of South Korea's modernity, which was violently imposed on the masses by foreign imperial powers and dictatorial governments to provoke the ambivalent popular response to it as the object of both allure and repulsion. More specifically, the evil scientist and his degenerate westernized household suggest an allegorical critique of Park Chung Hee's regime—which led the campaign for national modernization and scientification under militarist social control—and the Korean society shaped by it. The film thus highlights the effects of uneven development in 1970s Korean society not only by focusing its narrative on an impoverished youth living in a slum house but also by undermining the linear, progressive temporality of developmentalism through the disruption of the present with the ghostly figures of the living dead. As Bliss Cua Lim notes, the fantastic or supernatural reveals that "homogenous [national] time is not a 'reality' but rather a translation" that may or may not reflect the life experience of everyone in the national community.[42]

This subversive imagination of Killer Butterfly finds its visualization chiefly in the aesthetic of the grotesque, whose liminality between reality and fantasy challenges normative thinking. The grotesque as an aesthetic mode can be characterized by "distortion or unnatural combinations," especially of human and animal or nonhuman, which creates the effect of the fantastically bizarre, at once terrifying and ludicrous.[43] Such an aesthetic prevails throughout the film as a creative principle found in its most memorable fantastic spectacles, from the ranting skeleton of the bookseller and the puffing and laughing of Yŏng-gŏl's severed head to Lee's metamorphosis into a giant black butterfly. The grotesque aesthetic was popular during the 1970s not only in horror-fantasy films, including science fiction, but also European avant-garde films such as Yugoslavian director Dušan Makavejev's W.R.: Mysteries of the Organism (1971), which also featured a talking severed head. Observing the popularity of the grotesque in 1970s international cinema, Ruth Perlmutter has interestingly characterized its dark allure: "In its representation of the unthinkable and the suppressed, [the modern grotesque film] violates all our taboos, disorients our unexamined views, and unbalances the stability of our structured lives.... Like comedy, the grotesque demands reassessment of what we accept as normal."[44] The grotesque spectacles of the undead in *Killer Butterfly*, we may say, had the critical discursive function of questioning the period's social and cultural norms and belying the falsity of conventional thinking, similar to that of the Möbius strip in *The Dwarf*, whose twisted shape defies the distinction between the interior and the exterior, connoting moral ambiguity.

Not less, importantly, the grotesque aesthetic of *Killer Butterfly* had a subversive significance for its playfulness amidst the rigidly disciplinarian society of 1970s Korea. Its ludic quality assumes a polemical edge, especially considering the government's heavy-handed regulatory control over the period's film industry. Not only did the Yusin regime subject all film studios to its licensing system, but it also induced them to promote the twin official ideologies of nationalism and anticommunism by awarding those that were compliant with a greater opportunity to import foreign movies, which were generally more profitable than domestic films. Moreover, the so-called Ethics Committee of Arts and Culture (Yesul Munhwa Yulli Wiwŏnhoe), which was established in 1966, installed in 1970 a separate bureau for censoring screenplays, and by 1975 the proportion of censored or banned scripts reached as high as 80 percent.[45] In a "Winter Republic" where all cultural media were mobilized to promote the state agenda and dissenting intellectual could be tortured to death, the grotesque fantasy of *Killer Butterfly* was a positive expression of cultural resistance to the militarist regime. Its playful air was its director and screenwriter's daring exercise of individual creative freedom, which could turn into a collective enactment of a momentary release from the hegemonic order in its mass consumption. It is for this dissident esprit that the carnivalesque laughter of skeletons and corpses in *Killer Butterfly* still appeals to many fans and viewers, who see a most radical rejection of the established authoritarian social order, then and now, in the clownlike bluish rolling head—at once ghastly and funny.

Rethinking the Cultural History of 1970s Korea: The Critical Turn of Korean Science Fiction

Rather than a time of regress, the 1970s was the decade when science fiction took a critical turn in South Korea. Among the most daring writers and filmmakers were Choi In-hun, Cho Se-hui, Kim Ki-young, and Yi Mun-ung, who drew from mainstream science fiction culture some of its generic tropes and conventions to create their own experimental narratives with critical sensibilities. By reimagining the present through an alternate history, projecting a utopian desire through the dystopian depiction of "the city of machines" or visualizing a grotesque nightmare with an evil scientist at its dark center, their works challenged the social status quo of 1970s Korea and the myth of its historical inevitability. It is notable that all these texts engaged in temporal play, disrupting the linear progressive time of the official ideology of developmentalism with the representation of fractured, heterogeneous, or multiple temporalities. Shaped by science fictional imaginations, these works defied the regime's disciplinarian control over national culture not only with their nonconformist themes, such as antiauthoritarian existentialism, postnational anti-imperialism, and proletarian utopianism, but also with their playful, unruly forms.

Rediscovering the history of 1970s science fiction also compels us to reconsider the nature of the decade's dissident culture, which in the past has sometimes been regarded as a mere precursor of 1980s *minjung* cultural activism. Here we may appeal to Fredric Jameson's distinction between utopian fancy and utopian imagination in order to develop a more nuanced understanding of how the two decades' countercultures relate to each other. Jameson distinguishes utopian imaginations, as grand visions of social redesign, from utopian fancies, which are instead fragmented, anarchic everyday fantasies of a better life. In his theorization, utopian fancies are "placeholders and symptoms of a more fundamental repression," but they do not achieve the systematic character of utopian imaginations.[46]

The intense political repression of 1970s Korea, I submit, led to the projection of utopian fancies via experimental literary and visual forms, including science fiction. These fancies were reflective at once of the growing aspirations for a more democratic society and of the difficulty of imagining an alternative political vision. With the fall of Park's regime and another military coup in 1979, however, Koreans gained more confidence and conviction in the possibility of changing their society. Through conflict and debate among growing forces, the utopian fancies of the 1970s congealed into a more concrete and structured utopian imagination to be projected in the language of social science and literary criticism rather than creative fiction. The 1980s utopian imagination was not necessarily singular, but its general aspirations were broadly shared by the majority of participants in the democratization movement. This indisputable achievement had its own cost in the rigidifying of political and aesthetic doctrines as oppositional activist camps began to require cultural intellectuals' explicit political commitment. Once a consensus developed about an immediate direction for social change, however, rigidification was but a necessary part of a cultural movement aimed at social change.

Seventies culture, then, was not just an anterior and minor part of the *minjung* cultural activist era. Rather, the decade was distinctive in South Korean cultural history for its stirring artistic experimentation with mass cultural genres, albeit on a repressed scale, when the combination of economic prosperity and the growth of a new generation of educated youths created an atmosphere of cultural innovation that was at the same time fanned and hampered by the period's political repression. It is telling of the decade's originality that Choi In-hun's alternate history did not find its successor until the 1987 publication of Bok Geo-il's *In Search of an Epitaph*. Cho Se-hŭi's hybrid narrative of science fiction and proletarian realism did not see another of its kind until the appearance of Jang Joon-hwan's (Chang Chun-hwan's) film *Save the Green Planet* (*Chigu rŭl chik'yŏra*, 2003). And the fact that Kim Ki-young's nightmarish vision, a delusion of "a lobotomized people" is yet to be matched in postdemocratization Korea only testifies to the idiosyncrasy of the time's science fiction and confirms 1970s cultural distinctiveness.

NOTES

Unless noted otherwise, all Korean-language titles were published in Seoul, South Korea. The writing of this essay was supported by a gratefully acknowledged research grant of the Daesan Foundation. I would also like to thank Kyung Moon Hwang, Woosung Kang, Yumi Moon, Youngju Ryu, and Dafna Zur for their feedback on its early drafts.

1. Kim Chae-guk, "Han'guk kwahak sosŏl ŭi hyŏnhwang" [The current state of Korean science ciction] in *Kwahak sosŏl iran muŏssin'ga*, ed. Taejung Munhak Yŏn'guhoe (Kukhak Charyowŏn, 2000), 1013. Kim cites as his main reference the Korean SF Archive website run by Park Sang Joon (Pak Sang-jun), a science fiction (SF) fan and independent researcher. See also Cho Sung-myeon (Cho Sŏng-myŏn), "A Chronicle of Korean Science Fiction," *LIST* 20 (Summer 2013): 1012, and Ko Chang-wŏn, "Han'guk SF

rŭl chʼajasŏ" [In search of Korean science fiction], *The Science Times*, 2011, http://www. sciencetimes.co.kr/article.do?todo=series&pageno=1&searchatclass2=111&seriesidx= 1754&atidx=&backList=sList In the latter serial column, see in particular Koʼs "Namjadŭl i hwasŏng ŭro tchokkyŏnan yutʼopʼia?" [A utopia without men?], May 18; and "Munʼgopʼan kwahak sosŏl pŏnyŏngmul ŭi pit kwa ŏdum" [The light and darkness of the publication boom in translated science fiction series], May 23.

2. See "73 kyŏlsan: Ponʼgwedo e orŭn pŏmgungmin kwahakhwa undong" [Report on 1973: The national science campaign is well on track], *Kwahak kwa kisul* 6, no. 12 (1973): 5–7. A search of the catalog of the Korean Library of the National Congress for books with "science" in their titles yields 849 from the period of 1971 through 1980 versus 325 from 1961 through 1970.

3. For the publication boom in youth science fiction, see Ko, "Munʼgopʼan kwahak sosŏl." As Ko notes, while the 1960s saw the domestic growth of the genre by writers such as Han Nak-wŏn, translated SF works dominated in the 1970s publication boom. Also Cho Kye-suk observes that, although the magazine *Student Science* (*Haksaeng kwahak*) continued to serialize science fictional novels for its teenage readership in the 1970s, translations increasingly outnumbered original literary works. See Cho Kye-suk, "Kukka ideollogi wa SF, Hanʼguk chŏngsonyŏn kwahak sosŏl: *Haksaeng kwahak* chi surokchak ŭl chungsim ŭro" [National ideology and SF: Korean youth science fictional works in the magazine *Student Science*], *Taejung sŏsa yŏnʼgu* 20, no. 3 (2014): 415–42.

4. A comprehensive history of Koreaʼs imports of foreign films has yet to be written. I grew up in the 1970s and remember how popular these sci-fi series were. The given years refer to their American and Japanese release dates. For the history of 1970s Korean sci-fi animation, see Hŏ In-uk, *Hanʼguk aenimeisyŏn yŏnghwasa* [A history of Korean animation] (Sinhan Midiŏ, 2002), 61–70. According to Hŏ, the first work of the genre was Pak Yŏng-ilʼs *The Golden Iron Man* (*Hwanggŭm chŏrin*, 1968). The genre had a burst of growth after *Taekwŏn V*ʼs success, which produced its sequels as well as classic works such as Im Chŏng-gyuʼs *Maruchʼi Arachʼi* (*Maruchʼi Arachʼi*, 1977).

5. Istvan Csicsery-Ronay Jr., *The Seven Beauties of Science Fiction* (Middleton, CT: Wesleyan University Press, 2008), ix.

6. Chʼoe In-hun, *Kwangjang/Kuunmong* [The square/the dream of nine clouds], vol. 1, in *Chʼoe In-hun chŏnjip* [Collected works of Choi In-hun] (Munhak kwa Chisŏngsa, 1976). In my study of the authorʼs works, I have generally referenced this twelve-volume collection.

7. For a recent comprehensive study of the writer, see Kim In-ho, *Hechʼe wa chŏhang ŭi sŏsa: Choi In-hun kwa kŭ ŭi munhak* [Narratives of deconstruction and resistance: Choi In-hun and his literature] (Munhak kwa Chisŏngsa, 2004).

8. Alain Robbe-Grillet, "New Novel, New Man" (1961), in *For a New Novel: Essays on Fiction*, trans. Richard Howard (1965; Freeport, NY: Books for Libraries Press, 1970), 139–40. According to Robbe-Grillet, the term *nouveau roman* is "not to designate a school, nor even a specific and constituted group of writers working in the same

direction; the expression is merely a convenient label applicable to all those seeking new forms of the novel, forms capable of expressing (or of creating) new relations between man and the world, to all those who have determined to invent the novel, in other words, to invent man." Alain Robbe-Grillet, "The Use of Theory" (1955, 1963), in *For a New Novel*, 9.

9. Ch'oe In-hun, "Kamjŏng i hŭrŭnŭn hasang" [A river of flowing emotions], in *Yut'op'ia ŭi kkum* [Utopian dreams], *Ch'oe In-hun chŏnjip* 11 (1976): 191.

10. For a comparative study of the two writers, see Sŏ Ŭn-sŏn, "Ch'oe In-hun sosŏl kwa Robbe-Grillet sosŏl ŭi pigyo yŏn'gu" [A comparative study of the novels of Choi In-hun and Robbe-Grillet], *Han'guk munhak nonch'ong* 32 (December 2002): 395–431.

11. Robbe-Grillet's ideas about the *nouveau roman* were introduced to Korea by Kim Pung-gu (1922–91), a founding figure in local French literary studies. A graduate of Waseda University and a professor of French literature at Seoul National University (1953–87), Kim significantly contributed to popularizing French literature among Korean intellectuals. In 1961 he edited the papers from a symposium on the *nouveau roman* for *Sasanggye*, then the most influential journal, which carried, among other essays and translated short stories, his own "Angtti romang ŭi pip'an" [A critique of the anti-roman], *Sasanggye*, March 1961, 329–40. See also his other writings on the subject: "Munmyŏng ŭi wigi wa sosŏl ŭi wigi: Nubo romang ŭi munhwasajŏk ŭiŭi" [The crisis of civilization and the crisis of the novel: The cultural historical significance of the *nouveau roman*], *Sasanggye*, February 1962, 328–34; and "Nubo romang pi'pan" [A critique of the *nouveau roman*], in *Sae pulmunhak san'go* [Reflections on French literature], rev. ed. (Minjosa, 1964 [1962]), 117–34.

12. See Karen Hellekson, "Alternate History," in *The Routledge Companion to Science Fiction*, ed. Mark Bould et al. (New York: Routledge, 2009), 453–57.

13. See Ch'oe In-hun, "Ch'ongdok ŭi sori" [The governor-general's voice], in *Ch'ongdok ŭi sori*, vol. 9, *Ch'oe In-hun chŏnjip*; and *T'aep'ung* [Typhoon], vol. 5. Page numbers in in-text citations refer to the latter's reprint, *T'aep'ung*, vol. 5, *Ch'oe In-hun chŏnjip* (Munhak kwa Chisŏngsa, 2009).

14. Philip K. Dick, *The Man in the High Castle* (New York: Putnam, 1962). For its Japanese and Korean translations, see *Takai shiro no otoko* (Tokyo: Hayakawa Shobo, 1965); and O Kŭn-yŏng, trans., *Nop'ŭn song ŭi sanai* (Sigongsa, 2001).

15. I interviewed Choi in his house on July 4, 2016. The writer readily acknowledged the *nouveau roman*'s influence on his works, but he showed no sign of recognition at my mention of Dick's work. I have also found no reference to Dick or his works in periodical publications.

16. In romanizing the names of fictional countries and characters in *Typhoon*, I chose to diverge from the McCune-Reischauer system at times in order to convey Choi's wordplay.

17. Hellekson, "Alternate History," 453.

18. For the Chinese colonial fantasy of the South Sea, See Brian Bernards, *Writing the*

South Seas: Imagining the Nanyang in Chinese and Southeast Asian Postcolonial Literature (Seattle: University of Washington Press, 2016).

19. See Jennifer Robertson, *Takarazuka: Sexual Politics and Popular Culture in Modern Japan* (Berkeley: University of California Press, 1998), 89–138 in particular.

20. Choi In-hun mentions writing the novel based on his experience in Vietnam in *Hwadu* [Speech] (Minŭmsa, 1994), 2:29. For his remembrance of his trip to Vietnam, see "Pet'ŭnam ilchi" [Vietnam diary], in *Yut'op'ia ŭi kkum*, 115–30.

21. For the introduction of the charter and its impact on school education, see Sin Chu-baek, "Kungmin kyoyuk hŏnjang ŭi yŏksa, 1968–1994" [A history of the national education charter, 1968–1994], *Han'guk minjok undongsa yŏn'gu* 45 (2005): 295–328.

22. See also Kwŏn Podŭrae's reading of the novel within the context of Cold War Korea in Kwŏn Podŭrae, "Chungnip ŭi kkum, 1945–1968: Ch'oe In-hun sosŏl ŭi chŏngch'ijŏk sangsangnyŏk kwa 'che 3 ŭi kil' mosaek" [A dream of neutrality, 1945–1968: The political imagination of Choi In-hun's novel and his search for 'a third way'], in *1960-yŏn ŭl mutta: Pak Chŏng-hŭi sidae ŭi munhwa chŏngch'i wa chisŏng* [Questioning the year 1960: Cultural politics and intellect in Park Chung Hee's era], ed. Kwŏn Podŭrae and Cheon Jung-hwan (Chŏn Chŏng-hwan) (Chŏnnyŏn ŭi Sangsang, 2012), 221–74.

23. Ch'oe, *Hwadu*, 2: 29.

24. The writer left Korea and stayed in the United States for three years before returning as a playwright in 1976.

25. For a study of the period's testimonial labor literature, see Ruth Barraclough, *The Factory Girl Literature: Sexuality, Violence, and Representation in Industrializing Korea* (Berkeley: University of California Press, 2012). See also Pak T'ae-sun, *Chŏng tŭn ttang ŏndŏk wi* [On the hill where my hometown is] (Minŭmsa, 1973); and Hwang Sŏk-yŏng, *Kaekchi* [Strange land] (Ch'angjak kwa Pip'yŏngsa, 1974).

26. Cho Se-hŭi, *Nanjangi ka ssoaollin chagŭn kong* [A little ball launched by the dwarf] (1978; Munhak kwa Chisŏngsa, 1996). Part of the novel was serialized in *Munhak kwa Chisŏng*, a quarterly publication by the same publisher that sponsored Choi In-hun. Page numbers in in-text citations refer to its English translation, *The Dwarf*, trans. Bruce Fulton and Ju-Chan Fulton (Honolulu: University of Hawai'i Press, 2006).

27. According to Choi's own account, he wrote his first alternative history in response to the 1964 normalization of Korea's diplomatic relations with Japan, which set off intense popular protests in Korea due to the perceived inadequacy of Japan's atonement of its imperial past. See Choi, *Hwadu*, 2:26.

28. Darko Suvin, *Metamorphoses of Science Fiction: On the Poetics and History of a Literary Genre* (New Haven, CT: Yale University Press, 1979), 65–66.

29. Ibid., 61.

30. See Yu Chi-hyŏng, *24-yŏn-kan ŭi taehwa: Kim Ki-yŏng kamdok int'ŏbyujip* [24 years of conversation: Interviews with director Kim Ki-young] (Sŏn, 2006), 65, 231.

31. Ibid., 231–32.

32. Ibid., 50, 227–28.

33. Ibid., 49. Kim also recalled having studied Alfred Hitchcock's films through Japanese books (94).

34. See Kim So-yŏng (Soyoung Kim), *Kŭndaesŏng ŭi yuryŏngdŭl* [Ghosts of modernity] (Ssiat ŭl Ppurinŭn Saramdŭl, 1999); and Chris Berry, "Salinnabileul Ggotseun Yeoja/Killer Butterfly," in *The Cinema of Japan and Korea*, ed. Justin Bowyer, 111–18 (New York: Wall Flower, 2004).

35. For Yi Mun-ung's filmography, see his entry in the Korean Movie Data Base (KMDB), http://www.kmdb.or.kr/vod/mm_basic. asp?pgGubun=02&tabmov=T&person_id=00006411

36. Yu Chi-hyŏng, *24-yŏn kan ŭi taehwa*, 223.

37. *Chŏngch'un yŏnghwa* refers to the 1970s and 1980s youth cinema, which is represented by Lee Chang-ho's *Heavenly Homecoming Stars* (*Pyŏldŭl ŭi kohyang*, 1974) and Ha Kiljong's *March of Fools* (*Pabodŭl ŭi haengjin*, 1975). *Killer Butterfly* recalls the latter in particular for its buddy movie theme of two friends about town.

38. Toffler's *Future Shock* (New York: Random House, 1970) was translated and propagated by the Korean Productivity Center, a public organization for business education and consulting sponsored by the Ministry of Commerce and Industry. Its Korean translation, the three volumes of *Mirae ŭi ch'unggyŏk* (Han'guk Saengsansŏng Ponbu, 1970–71), was reprinted once in 1973 before commercial publishers introduced new translations of the popular title in the early 1980s. Kim Ki-young mentions the book as a reference in Yu Chi-hyŏng, *24-yŏn kan ŭi taehwa*, 225. Schopenhauer's *The World as Will and Idea* was translated into Korean no less than three times throughout the 1970s: *Ŭiji wa p'yosang ŭrosŏ ŭi segye* [The world as will and idea], trans. Kim Chung-gi (1972; Chimmundang, 1979); *Susangnok: Ŭiji wa p'yosang ŭrosŏ ŭi segye* [The world as will and idea], trans. Kim Yun-sŏp (Chŏngsan Munhwasa, 1974); and Arthur Schopenhauer and Edmund Husserl, *Ŭiji wa p'yosang ŭrosŏ ŭi segye, hyŏnsanghak sŏsŏl* [The world as will and idea and an introduction to phenomenology], trans. Kim Pyŏng-ok and Pak Sang-gyu (Taeyang Sŏjŏk, 1978). In his aforementioned essay, Berry misidentifies the source of the bookseller's inspiration as Hitler's *Mein Kampf*.

39. Barbara Creed, *The Monstrous-Feminine: Film, Feminism, and Psychoanalysis* (New York: Routledge, 1993).

40. Song Hyo-Jŏng (Song Hyo-Joung), "Sirhŏmsil ŭi mich'in kwahakcha wa cheguk chuŭijŏk hyangsu: 1960-yŏndae Han'guk kodik SF yŏnghwa yŏn'gu" [Mad scientists' laboratories and imperialist nostalgia: The study of Gothic SF films of the 1960s], *Taejung sŏsa yŏn'gu* 20, no. 3 (2014): 271–378.

41. Berry, "Salinnabileul Ggotseun Yeoja/Killer Butterfly," 112.

42. Bliss Cua Lim, *Translating Time: Cinema, the Fantastic, and Temporal Critique* (Durham, NC: Duke University Press, 2009), 26.

43. The quote is from the *Oxford English Dictionary*, s.v. "grotesque," http://www.oed.

com/view/Entry/81794?rskey=3pS6Hv&result=1&isAdvanced=false#eid. See also Justin D. Edwards and Rune Graulund, *Grotesque* (New York: Routledge, 2013), 2–5.

44. Ruth Perlmutter, "The Cinema of the Grotesque," in *Focus on the Imagination*, special issue, *Georgia Review* 33, no. 1 (Spring 1979): 193.

45. Pae Su-gyŏng, "Han'guk yŏnghwa kŏmyŏl chedo ŭi pyŏnhwa" [The evolution of Korean film censorship], chapter 7 of Kim Tong-ho, ed., *Han'guk yŏnghwa chŏngch'aeksa* [A history of Korean film policies] (Nanam Ch'ulp'an, 2005), 489.n

46. See Fredric Jameson, *Archaeologies of the Future: The Desire Called Utopia and Other Science Fictions* (New York: Verso, 2005), 53.

Alluvium of Dreams

The 1969 Master Plan and the Development of Yŏŭido

Se-Mi Oh

A three-channel projection artwork entitled "An|other River,"[1] by Sim Cheol-Woong (Sim Chŏl-ung), depicts a view of the Han River from a peculiar perspective. He coined the term *Landseasky* to describe the ways in which he grafted two videos of the river together. The bottom of the screen shows a still-shot video of water lapping onto the riverbank covered with dirt and pebbles. On the top of the screen, a panoramic view of the riverbank, crowded with high-rise apartment buildings, is placed upside down. These contrasting images show two different sides of the river: nature and artifice. The precarious placement of apartment buildings hung upside down collapses the boundary between land, water, and sky and reminds us that the sky has been replaced with skyscrapers that dominate the skyline. In this juxtaposition, it is the buildings that pan and move while the image of water in the bottom half remains static. Nature is depicted as time stopped, and artifice represents time on the move, which is the time of modernity.

Through this projection art, Sim Cheol-Woong alerts viewers about a landscape that is so unnatural that it can only be called a "derivative spectacle of a new civilization."[2] What Sim refers to is a drastic change that the Han River underwent in a matter of decades in the latter half of the twentieth century, which caused the natural landscape of sand dunes and swamps to disappear beneath concrete riverbanks, highways, and apartments. The work is a potent reminder of the mad dash to modernization that South Korea pursued. However, the new landscape of the river is synonymous with development today, as it erases any traces of destruction and multiplies itself all around the country. Therefore, Sim urges viewers to feel estranged by the two-panel view of the river. It is our perception, he says, that recognizes space as place for all the history and personal stories attached to it, but the colossal spectacle has colonized our vision so that we no longer perceive the different interests and powers that have shaped the place. Rather, Sim suggests, the spectacle of modernity blinds our vision and capacity for introspection so that we idolize the power that produced the spectacle. For Sim, the power of the urban spectacle lies in its control not only of the identity of a given place but also of our critical engagement with it.[3]

Yŏŭido, an island located in the western part of Han River, is an urban spectacle of Korea's insatiable appetite for development and perhaps best illustrates how the artificial landscape of the river has been naturalized. Today it is the main financial hub of Seoul with skyscrapers hovering over the river. Yŏŭido boasts many of the largest buildings in the city. In the center, new skyscrapers, including the International Financial Center, the Korean Exchange Center, and LG's corporate headquarters define what Yŏŭido is today. To the west, older but equally monumental structures such as the National Assembly, Korean Broadcasting Company, and the Yŏŭido Full Gospel Church showcase earlier megascale development, and the 63 Building, a landmark of the Seoul Olympic Games of 1988, stands on the eastern side of the island.

Such ostentatiousness makes it easy to forget that Yŏŭido was once an alluvial island, a large sand deposit originally made up of two islands, Yŏŭido and Pamsŏm, which would connect to and separate from each other depending on the water level. In times of flood, most of the island was submerged, leaving only the peak of the Yangmal Mountain in Yŏŭido visible, and in other seasons a large sandy beach would spread in the middle of the river, stretching from Yongsan to Map'o to Tang'illi in the north and to Noryangjin and Yanghwari in the south. Literally meaning "your island," Yŏŭido is said to have gained its name due to its arid and infertile sand deposits. "You can have it" sums up the long-standing neglectful attitude toward the island and its inconspicuous place throughout history.[4]

Few people today seem to remember that Yŏŭido had such humble origins. The urban spectacle of Yŏŭido, both monstrous and quotidian, conceals the processes of how this landscape became naturalized. What is lost is the *longue durée* of nature that created the layers of sandy sediment. The idea of "over time" has been blotted out of memory so that we do not even recall that this urban complex was once an alluvium. In that forgetting of the accumulative space and time of Yŏŭido, we have also disallowed the amorphous nature of the island to take its course and only come to remember it in its fixed and controlled form—an ode to the power that created it.

This chapter, therefore, looks into the forgotten stories of Yŏŭido in the late 1960s and early 1970s, shortly before Yusin rule began. The stories are a testament to a particular moment in South Korea's history, an era known for rapid modernization aptly termed the "Miracle on the Han River." They tell of a city, as well as a nation, that struggled to reinvent itself in the face of exploding urban growth, state-directed industrialization, and strengthening grip of the authoritarian regime. Of particular interest is the plan called the Development of Yŏŭido and the Shores of the Han River of 1969, an urban-planning proposal that never went into effect. Through a closer look at the visions, debates, and executions of this plan, this chapter hopes to illuminate a moment of history when different dreams collided on urban and national levels and how this collision presages the ways in which Yusin came to work later. The chapter pays particular attention to competing interests of the state, the city, and the architects by examining three major participants: Park Chung Hee (Pak Chŏng-hŭi), Kim Hyun-ok (Kim Hyŏn-ok), and Kim Swoo-geun (Kim Su-gŭn). The first section discusses the events leading up to the 1969 proposal drafted by Kim Swoo-geun and the collaborating and conflicting relationship of Kim Hyun-ok and Park Chung Hee that shaped the urban planning of Seoul. The second section looks at the 1969 master plan more closely and discusses in detail Kim Swoo-geun's modernist vision and its failure to materialize in the face of Park Chung Hee's increasing grip on power.

Yŏŭido Triumvirate

On a cold winter day in 1967, a groundbreaking ceremony was held on the shore of Yŏŭido to implement the Three-Year Plan for the Development of the Han River, which had been drafted a few months earlier. This was a momentous event in the history of urban planning in Seoul because of the inconspicuous status that Yŏŭido had held in the past. In attendance were President Park Chung Hee, accompanied by his wife Yuk Young-soo (Yuk Yŏng-su), Secretary of Defense Kim Sŏng-ŭn, and the mayor of

Seoul, Kim Hyun-ok.[5] This ensemble cast underscores the importance of this occasion as the Han River and Yŏŭido took their place at the forefront of national development. However, beneath the facade of this collaborative venture lies a more complicated story. The unity displayed among these characters in terms of their personal ties and the shared goal of national development and defense was marred by different interests and visions.

Kim Hyun-ok was a graduate of the Korean Military Academy (Yuksa) and a close confidant of Park Chung Hee. After his retirement from the military, Kim served as the mayor of Pusan from 1962 to 1966, in which capacity he enjoyed enormous success, especially in regard to redistricting the port areas. Thanks to his success in Pusan, he was appointed as the mayor of Seoul in 1966. Before Kim, urban development projects in Seoul had mainly focused on rebuilding the city after the Korean War (1950–53), but Kim proceeded to redefine the nature of urban planning. The common problem that the urban projects under Kim Hyun-ok addressed was population growth. The congestion that Seoul experienced during this time is well conveyed by the phrase "Seoul has reached its quota" (Sŏul ŭn manwŏn ida), popularized by the eponymous novel by Yi Ho-ch'ŏl. Despite the increase in the national population, the rural population actually decreased during this time as urban centers absorbed much of the population growth. Seoul, for example, more than doubled its population, from 2,240,000 in 1961 to 5,530,000 in 1970. An immediate solution was called for to address many problems that arose as a result of such rapid growth.

The list of the projects that Kim oversaw demonstrates some major changes that took place in the way the flow of the city was managed. In order to address heavy congestion in the downtown area, two tunnels were blasted through Namsan to ease the flow of traffic into downtown. Underpasses in Myŏngdong and Sejongno were created in order to offer multilevel traffic access. On a much bigger scale, the first elevated motorway, Ahyŏn, and the controversial Chŏnggyech'ŏn Motorway were built for the same purpose and came to define what modern megaconstruction would look like in Seoul. He also oversaw major housing and subdivision projects to replace some of the shantytowns springing up all around the city. Sewoon Mall (Seun Sangga) in particular, designed by Kim Swoogeun, was a project that transformed the area in front of Chongmyo. Designated for fire evacuation during the Pacific War (1941–45), the area had been occupied by refugees' makeshift housing since the Korean War. Similar efforts to maximize the use of space with multilevel structures drove Kim Hyun-ok's predilection for apartments as a solution to the housing problem. He introduced an affordable housing option called the "citizen apartment" (*simin ap'at'ŭ*) and planned to build more than 90,000 apartment complexes in Seoul and its vicinity. In the year 1969 alone, he commissioned the construction of 406 apartment complexes containing 15,000 units. Throughout his career, Kim Hyun-ok came to be known as much for his forceful management style as for the projects that he oversaw, the style that earned him the nickname "The Bulldozer."

Initially, for Kim, Yŏŭido was not a pressing priority as he concentrated on the problems in the city center. At an exhibition of urban planning held shortly after his inauguration as the mayor of Seoul in 1966, for example, most of the projects presented focused on the city center north of Han River. The keystone projects proposed for the Great City Planning of Seoul and New City Planning of Seoul in this exhibition included the construction of underpasses in Sejongno and an underground plaza in front of the City Hall. Yŏŭido was only the twenty-first exhibit out of twenty-three, and it was introduced as simply 2.7 million *p'yŏng* of low-lying land prone to flooding.[6] The metropolitan government's modest goal for Yŏŭido, a land of no utility as far as the exhibition was concerned, was to improve its usability for the area's residents. The proposed embankment was 3.7 kilometers long and the new shoreline highway 4.3 kilometers, a much smaller project than the actual construction that would later take place. The total planned area was 1.2 million p'yŏng to be divided into 780,000 p'yŏng of residential area and 420,000 set aside for public use, with key facilities such as parking areas and public parks.[7]

As mentioned, part of the reason why Yŏŭido existed outside the purview of urban planning for so long had to do with its unstable condition due to frequent flooding. Most of the island was deemed unusable because it would disappear with the rising water level of the river. Urban planning in Yŏŭido, if we can even use the word *planning*, had existed only for the purpose of flood control. The Japanese colonial government, for example, took up many survey projects on the rivers in Korea, including the Han River. The meticulous measuring and recording of water levels culminated in the first recorded construction of an embankment, completed in 1923. In the area just north of Yŏŭido, today's Ich'on-dong area in Yongsan district, the construction of an embankment began in 1920 and was completed in 1925. However, the embankment was destroyed during the great flood of 1925, a historic natural disaster that debilitated urban infrastructure and displaced more than ninety thousand residents, in addition to the hundreds of casualties it caused. The second phase of construction took place during 1927 and 1928, resulting in a thirty-two-kilometer-long embankment in the same area.[8]

The unruly nature of the Han River evident in these earlier measures continued to haunt and shape subsequent urban-planning efforts in postliberation Korea. In that regard, Kim Hyun-ok's 1967 proposal was a major departure from the previous measures. A pamphlet distributed to newspaper reporters by the city states the purpose of the development of Yŏŭido and the Han River as follows: "According to the plan laid out for the total use of the Han River, the project aims to control floods and solve traffic congestion in the city. It seeks to serve as an innovative foundation for urban development by the shoreline through the construction of embankments, expressways, and a modern, multilevel city in Yŏŭido."[9] Like those of his predecessors, flood control continued to be an important aspect of Kim's plan, so the first project that he implemented was the construction of ring bunds around the island. He also continued to address the congestion in the city and sought to ease traffic problems by building multilane expressways along the shoreline of the Han River. However, his plan was more ambitious because it factored in land development on the embankment. Inspired by the Law on Public Land Reclamation (Kongyu sumyŏn maerippŏp) of 1962, the development plan sought to erect residential buildings on the land secured by the embankment in order to attract private investment. For a city—and a country for that matter—that had little capital with which to fund such a large-scale project, attracting private investment through land sales helped alleviate the financial burden. These new functions of the embankment—not simply to provide walls higher than rising water levels but to secure land and build roads—heavily guided the Three-Year Plan for the Development of the Han River of 1967.

The construction of ring bunds on Yŏŭido was carried out in a manner that befit Kim Hyun-ok's nickname "The Bulldozer." As mentioned, Yŏŭido was originally an island that did not have a stable boundary and fluctuated in size and shape depending on the variable water levels. Other than 650,000 p'yŏng of land designated for an airport and 300,000 of farmland, 1 million p'yŏng of sand beaches made up the island, which increased by another 20 million p'yŏng during its seasonal emergence. After the construction that began in December 1967, embankments came to clearly demarcate the island's boundary, which decreased in size because it was now limited to 870,000 p'yŏng (2.9 square kilometers). Building the ring bunds was no easy undertaking, however. They were 20 meters wide, 16 meters high, and 7.6 kilometers long and required 520,000 workers and 584,000 pieces of heavy equipment from major construction companies such as Hyundai, Daelim, Donga, Daehan, and Kyunghyang. The 400,000 cement blocks used for the construction would have paved 300 kilometers of highway, the distance between Seoul and Taegu.[10] And the most drastic change took place when Pamsŏm was blown up to supply soil for the construction. At three o'clock in the afternoon on February 10, 1968, Kim Hyun-ok pressed the button to commence the explosion of Pamsŏm, and a mere one hundred days later the construction of the ring bunds saw its completion.

For Kim, the purpose of the new Yŏŭido was to take on some of the functions of the city center. In fact he envisioned the division of Yŏŭido into four sections, with the National Assembly Hall placed in the west and City Hall in the east. Kim also saw Yŏŭido and the Han River as a model for future urban development, and he used some grand rhetoric to characterize his plan. Evidently, in an interview with newspaper reporters just a few days before the groundbreaking ceremony on Yŏŭido in 1967, Kim talked about the development of the Han River as "the art of the nation" (*minjok ŭi yesul*).[11] This is the phrase that he continued to use, which suggests that Kim saw the urbanization of Seoul as a national project—a project that would showcase the strength of the Korean nation. In a pamphlet entitled *Construction on the Han River*, published in May 1968, he reiterated this point: "The endeavors of the four million people will create a miracle. First, we build on the river. Second, we reap material and immaterial benefits from the construction. The material benefits gained from the construction are the land, and the immaterial benefits are a sense of pride and ownership. And, third, we turn these great resources for reinvestment, which will be directly linked to social welfare and the establishment of a new social order."[12] Interestingly, however, while attesting to the shared rhetoric of national development, this statement by Kim hints at an even greater ambition for the city. It places Yŏŭido beyond the purview of urban planning and presents it as a model for society. In other words, Kim Hyun-ok thought that the change for the nation must begin with Seoul. In his inauguration address, he famously said, "[T]he modernization of the nation must be achieved through the modernization of Seoul."[13] He argued that, as Seoul was the capital city, its administration represented the potential of the nation as a whole and would serve as the motor for national development. *Total administration* was the term he used to describe how Seoul would decide the overall governance of the country—politics, economy, society, culture, and military.[14] For this reason, throughout his tenure, Kim remained unapologetically pro-Seoul in the policies he pursued, and he focused on practical solutions to the problems that Seoul faced even when such solutions would prove deleterious for other areas of the country.

Park Chung Hee did not always see eye to eye with Kim Hyun-ok. The divergence between the two men became especially pronounced after a momentous event in 1968 when a group of armed agents from North Korea infiltrated Seoul with an order to assassinate Park Chung Hee. The plan was foiled in a violent confrontation with police that occurred on January 21, and resulted in twenty-nine of the thirty-one North Korean men being killed. Of the two survivors, one was captured and the other made it back to North Korea. The event is referred to as the 1.21 Incident or the Kim Sin-jo Incident, following the name of the captured agent. In the aftermath of the attempted raid on the Blue House, national security came to take priority in the island's development as demonstrated by the presence of the secretary of defense at the earlier described groundbreaking ceremony on Yŏŭido. Architectural historian Ahn Changmo (An Ch'ang-mo) argues that this was the point of anticommunist turn in how Park Chung Hee viewed urban planning. Anticommunism was not a new ideology suddenly introduced to urban development by this incident. However, before the incident, anticommunism was limited to architecture and had mostly to do with monuments, such as the Freedom Center, which served as a convention center for the Asian People's Anti-communist League (APAC); statues of historical figures erected in accordance with the state's understanding of anticommunist genealogy; and the traditional architectural style adopted in the design of the National Performing Arts Center in a conscious attempt to counter the way North Korean architecture incorporated traditions. In contrast to the symbolic, representational, or ornamental function that anticommunism performed in these monuments, the anticommunist element of urban planning added by this incident had, according to Ahn, everything to do with military defense. The fortification of the city in preparation for war now became more pressing and personal for Park. Unveiled shortly after the incident was a plan to build the Pugak Skyway along the ridge of Pugak Mountain, north of Kyŏngbok Palace and the Blue House, which would entail paving the road for military access and increasing the visibility of activities that would otherwise be hidden in the mountains. In March of the same year, a plan to build eight underground bunkers was announced, and in the following year, Namsan was selected as a strategic location for urban development in order to fortify the city and facilitate the evacuation of nearly four million residents of Seoul in the event of war.[15] "Construction is defense" was the motto that guided Park's strategic rethinking of the city in terms of its survivability in wartime. "This will be the year of fighting and building for Korea," Park announced in the presidential New Year's address of 1969.[16]

According to Ahn Changmo, another aspect of anticommunist urban planning urgently fueled by the 1.21 Incident was the need to develop the area south of the Han River.[17] How to disperse the population and relieve congested activities in the city center in order to reduce the scale of damages and casualties in case of war became an important factor in urban planning. Similar ideas had been introduced earlier when a development plan of Seoul was drawn up in 1961, but the plan had gained little traction up to this point. The 1.21 Incident highlighted the strategic importance of defense-oriented thinking and changed the trajectory of the development of the Han River. A plan that Kim Hyun-ok had laid out on April 4, 1968 called for "a second Seoul" to be built between Yŏŭido and Suwŏn by 1972, which would serve largely as a new administrative complex of one million residents. Later the focus of the development shifted to the Kangnam area. As Kangnam rose in prominence as an alternative to the proposed second Seoul, a new plan was developed based on a three-core model. The old city center within the city walls north of the Han River and two urban areas south of the river—the Yŏngdŭngp'o core in the west, which would include Yŏŭido and the eastern core of Yŏngdong in what is today the Kangnam area connecting to Chamsil—comprised the three cores. The plan called for massive relocation of the executive, legislative, and judicial branches of the government, along with major financial institutions. It is in this context that Yŏŭido was mentioned as a candidate site for the relocation of City Hall and the National Assembly Hall.[18]

A plan introduced in this context was the Development of Yŏŭido and the Shores of the Han River in 1969.[19] It was a proposal put forward by the Korean Engineering Consultants Corporation (KECC), which Kim Swoo-geun led as vice-president from 1966 to 1968 and as president from 1968 to 1969, as well as the chief engineer throughout. Though it was not a state-run organization, KECC was the primary engineering consulting firm working with Park's regime. Therefore, it was in charge of large-scale national development plans (kukt'o kaebal), which included some of the most enduring architectural constructions commissioned by the South Korean government, as well as massive projects for the heavy and chemical industries. KECC provided, for instance, blueprints for Seoul-Pusan Highway and the Soyang Dam, and was responsible for selecting the main plant site for Pohang Steel Company. Kim's partnership with the state was also reinforced by personal relationships. Especially well known was Kim's close friendship with the then prime minister Kim Jong-pil (Kim Chong-p'il), who reportedly helped him win major contracts for KECC.

Kim Swoo-geun is arguably South Korea's most important modern architect. He entered Seoul National University in 1950, but due to the Korean War he finished his education in architecture at Tokyo University of the Arts. There he was heavily influenced by the traditionalism and modernism of Tange Kenzo and Yoshimura Junzo, and immersed himself in studying the modernism of Le Corbusier.[20] The competition for the design of the National Assembly Hall in 1959 was what brought Kim back to Korea. His winning proposal was highly praised for combining a concrete structure with traditional lines of Korean architecture, though it was never built because of the coup d'état in 1961. Kim would go on, however, to become the main architect for some of South Korea's most recognizable architecture of the modern era: Hill Top Bar of the Walker Hill Hotel (1961), a commission that he landed with the help of Kim Jong-pil; as well as the aforementioned anticommunist icon, the Freedom Center (1963), composed of a seventeen-story tower and convention hall that show a great deal of resemblance to Le Corbusier's Palace of Justice in Chandigarh. Kim then caused some controversy with Puyŏ National Museum (1967). In this building, he continued to experiment with traditionalism, but his interpretation of Korean traditional architecture raised eyebrows for being heavily influenced by the Japanese architecture of his training. Nevertheless, Kim was called to duty again with the Sewoon Mall project (1967) and Chŏnggyechŏn Elevated Motorway (1967–76). These projects showcased how Kim Swoo-geun came to fully embrace modernism. The Sewoon Mall project in particular proposed restructuring the urban axis in the downtown area through the construction of a single structure that not only combined commercial and residential quarters but distributed pedestrian and motor traffic onto different levels.[21] This megastructure did not realize its full potential of creating a new urban space but nonetheless became a signature of Kim's style and laid an important foundation for his Yŏŭido master plan.[22]

Projects like the Sewoon Mall and Chŏnggyechŏn Elevated Motorway brought together Kim Hyun-ok and Kim Swoo-geun, who were no strangers to each other to begin with. Kim Hyun-ok, a fan of Kim Swoo-geun's modernist approach, applied the latter's concept of the multilevel city to the construction of roads in Seoul and built elevated motorways, overpasses, and underground walkways for multitier traffic access. In early 1968, Kim Hyun-ok approached Kim Swoo-geun about Yŏŭido.[23] What Kim Hyun-ok asked for—"an ideal, artistic, and ultramodern urban planning that will be commemorated for the generations to come"[24]—became the mandate for a group of young architects working under Kim Swoo-geun at KECC. The plan, completed on March 19, 1968, was published in *Chosŏn ilbo* on March 21 in an article entitled "The Seoul of Our Dreams Brought to Life In a Blueprint: Yŏŭido of the 1980s." This article featured a photo of a scale model that showcased many key features of Kim Swoo-geun's modernism—multilevel streets and vertical space planning—and incorporated Kim Hyun-ok's earlier vision for Yŏŭido, which had the National Assembly building and the City Hall on opposite ends of the island. Reportedly, Kim Hyun-ok did not take it very well that the plan was published in the newspaper before it was sent to him, so the second version was submitted to the city in the Development of Yŏŭido and the Shores of the Han River plan of 1969.[25] Interestingly, this revision came to sport more modernist, and some would say idealistic, features than the original plan published in *Chosŏn ilbo*. A closer look at this plan will allow us to gain some insights into how the architect's vision of Yŏŭido differed from those of the city and the state and how that dream was altered in the process of its implementation.

The Master Plan, 1969

The 1969 Master Plan for Yŏŭido, as its formal name suggests, was part of a larger plan for developing the Han River. Similar to the ways in which both Kim Hyun-ok and Park Chung Hee located Seoul in the larger context of national development, this plan stated that the goal of the development of Yŏŭido was to "reestablish the central place that Seoul occupied in the capital region and the nation."[26] Such a move was warranted, in turn, because "the nation as a whole was experiencing heightened urbanization."[27] This master plan, therefore, aimed to create a symbiotic relationship among Yŏŭido, the Han River, and Seoul. The Master Plan of Yŏŭido was part and parcel of the Seoul Master Plan, as Yŏŭido would serve as a stimulus for new urban development in Seoul and beyond.[28]

Kim Swoo-geun used the term *total urbanization* to talk about this overarching idea, which placed Yŏŭido in the context of the Han River, the Han River in the context of Seoul, and Seoul in the context of the nation. As he put it, total urbanization was an effort to overcome "the conventional fundamentals of the city" and seek new possibilities for urban planning beyond reactive approaches to urban problems.[29] Therefore, Kim Swoo-geun found fault with the ways in which the saturation of the city center had been handled. The saturated center could:

> be likened to the ways in which the trunk of an aged tree collectivizes in its center. No longer able to carry out its normal functions, the city core loses its meaning as the center, and urban life becomes stagnant. This results in the development of slums within the bloc, and the only solution is found in blocking the influx of traffic to the city center. This is a drastic condition, the opposite of the mechanism of a modern city. It is time to rethink and overturn this irrational theory, which has grown rampant.[30]

Kim Swoo-geun's master plan was thus a study of the contemporary problem of urban expansion in Seoul and its negative impact on the surrounding area. As such it offered proposals to turn existing problems into solutions, which would then contribute to the creation of a new urbanity. As it existed, Seoul was organized in concentric circles radiating outward from a single nucleus. The nucleus was the area within the old city walls, and every plan of urban development ever proposed had simply expanded the city's outer limits, first by destroying the city walls and then by expanding outward to accommodate the growing population and activities. Such development models were based on the idea of dispersing urban functions from the city core, and the development of Yŏŭido here would merely serve as land development.[31]

The alternative laid out in the Master Plan of 1969 proposed a linear axis for the city in place of expanding concentric circles as the new spatio-temporal structure of Seoul.[32] The theory of the linear city, it argued, was derived from working out the contradictions between the theories of modern urbanization and the actualities of urbanization in Seoul. The new master plan differed from the existing plan in that it relied on "the logics with future perspectives."[33] The irrationality of the existing plan was noted in its inability to accommodate the long-term development of Seoul, whose population would reach ten million by the year 2000. Thus, rather than reactively accommodating the overgrowth of the city, the master plan aimed to guide the city's course of development along the linear axis and eventually induce organic growth of the city. This plan was based on the assumption that reorganization of the spatiotemporal structure of the city would cause changes in its socioeconomic growth. For its attempt to produce a new model of urbanity rather than merely addressing existing problems, we can easily consider the 1969 master plan as the first urban planning project in Korea. Or, as articulated by Kim Seok Chul (Kim Sŏk-chŏl), an architect colleague of Kim Swoo-geun's, the plan was not supposed to be urban engineering but urban management, driven as it was by the desire to provide guiding principles rather than solutions to specific problems. Therefore, for Kim Seok Chul, the 1969 master plan was a case of comprehensive and total urban planning, which would result in the complete restructuring of the urban space.[34]

The proposed linear model connected the city center to the Kyŏng'in Industrial Belt in Inch'ŏn by establishing the main axis of the city along the six-lane expressway between Map'o and Yŏngdŭngp'o via Seoul Bridge (present-day Map'o Bridge). It was an ambitious, perhaps even unrealistic, proposal because the linear model connecting Seoul to Inch'ŏn would not have been possible without addressing the serious problem that the Han River came to pose in the postwar division of Korea. The Han River, in the newly drawn division between North and South Korea after the war, came to have a limited function as its downstream entry into the Western Sea was blocked by the Demilitarized Zone (DMZ). Therefore, the master plan proposed the revitalization and restoration of the Han River through the construction of an alternate route to the sea. In this model, the dams constructed on the upper stream would control the water supply, effectively turning the river into a lake, and a canal would be constructed connecting the Han River to the Western Sea via Inch'ŏn.[35] Seoul, a city of four million residents, would then grow and expand along this linear axis, stimulating further development along the Western Sea around Inch'ŏn. This is quite a different picture from the three-core model mentioned above. Instead of having Kangnam function as a new home to share the burden of a growing population, the plan pointed westward for the future growth of Seoul. This was an unusual move, considering that almost all discussions during this time about moving the administrative function of the city center pointed to the area south of the river, or south of Seoul. Kim's linear model brought the future orientation of Seoul perhaps a little too close to the DMZ, suggesting that the Cold War mentality and anticommunism so prevalent in Park Chung Hee's vision might not have weighed as heavily for Kim Swoo-geun.

The linear model of the 1969 master plan echoed the language of the Tokyo Plan of 1960, which also sought to address problems associated with rapid urban growth in the postwar era. The Tokyo Plan revised a previous proposal of 1958, which modeled itself after London in envisioning a city with the three concentric elements of core city, greenbelt, and satellite city. Whereas the previous plan concerned itself with how to prevent a high concentration of population in Tokyo and uncontrolled expansion of the city, the 1960 plan actively accommodated the growth of the city and presented a model for urban growth. It proposed three principles (the linear city, urban communication, and a structural urban system) and turned the urban space into a communication system among clusters of loops that carried out specific urban functions. In anticipating the increase in human activities and the circulation of goods, this plan hierarchized different levels of movement: high speed, low speed, walking, and stationary. Therefore, relationship was the key concept in facilitating movement and growth. In essence, what this plan proposed was a modernist city that bridged the historical and the modern, on the one hand, and the natural and the artificial on the other.[36]

Kim Swoo-geun was most impressed by the idea of the linear city and communicative spatial planning in the Tokyo plan, so in his master plan, he made a proposal for multiple "center cities," with each of these located in the larger collectives called "function cities." In this model, the hierarchical organization of units, or "density fields," was formed surrounding the center city and connected to the core of the center city according to the functions they performed. Then the center cities were connected to one another in linear linkages of equal distance and influence rather than having one core in the city center. The basic principle of the linear city, in sum, consisted of distributing functions across the base urban core and "the functional urban collective" of center cities within function cities.[37] Yŏŭido in this model was to serve as a center city, and the Han River was to be the network connecting the areas north of the river (Kangbuk) and south of the river (Kangnam). So Kim Swoo-geun designed an intercity highway that passed through the center of the island. According to Kim Seok Chul, Yŏŭido was not supposed to be a terminal city like Manhattan (although it is often dubbed the "Manhattan of Seoul") but rather a station city that connected and choreographed the relationships of the surrounding areas with one another.

The inner-city highway created another north-south axis connecting

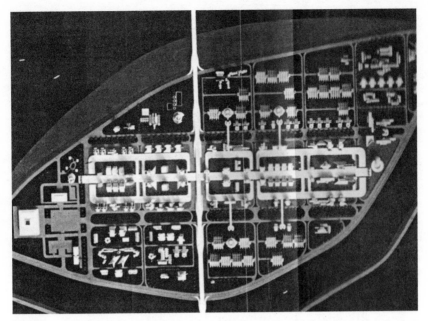

Figure 2. The Master Plan of Yŏŭido, *Yŏŭido mit Han'gang yŏn'an kaebal kyehoek*, p. 397.

Yongsan and Suwŏn in addition to the main linear axis between Yŏngdŭngp'o and Inch'ŏn. As mobility was an important component in integrating the blocs that separated commercial, administrative, and residential zones, and in creating a linkage between the opposite ends of the island, each zone was carefully placed in balance with the others. The inner-city highway was to function as the main axis of the island by dividing the city into two parts. And the National Assembly Hall was to be built in the west and City Hall in the east, giving each side equal weight in importance. These two sections were then to be connected through three public spaces: the city plaza in the east, the plaza of the citizens in the middle, and the national plaza in the west. Each of these public plazas was to have a representative structure—City Hall, the Supreme Court, and the National Assembly Hall, respectively—all connected to the core blocs in the center. Overall, symmetry and balance were what this design sought to achieve (fig. 2)[38]

Another important aspect of this plan was the construction of multidimensional space, consisting of artificial lands called "urban fronts" that would make it possible to vertically separate vehicular and foot traffic into

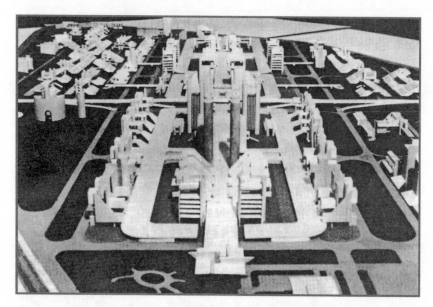

Figure 3. A plan for the center city, *Yŏŭido mit Han'gang yŏn'an kaebal kyehoek*, p. 24.

different tiers. It was a plan premised on the advent of new technology and the predominance of automobiles in the urban space. The speed and mobility that this multilevel planning set out to achieve would eventually help integrate the four blocs that separated different zones.[39] Architecture played an important role in harmonizing the two levels, so the core blocs in the center of the island were placed next to each other on a horizontal line and connected through five loops. These five loops were also linked by the core spine running through the island vertically on multiple levels (fig. 3). This was a notable addition to the first plan published in *Chosŏn ilbo*, as it envisioned that only a megastructure like this could allow a careful choreography of movement and synchronize that movement at different speeds. Kim Seok Chul called this "the architecturization of the city, the urbanization of architecture."[40]

The scale of this plan was grand, so Kim Swoo-geun and his team expected that it would take twenty years to complete. Construction would be spread out into four periods of five years from 1967 to 1986, estimated to cost over one billion dollars.[41] In fact, the report noted that even twenty years might not be enough for a city to grow into an advanced urban form, but intensive investment of modern capital could hurry things along.[42]

For the critics of this plan, such long-term investment was simply impossible. Sohn Jung-mok (Son Chŏng-mok), who served as the chief of urban planning in the municipal government of Seoul in the 1970s, was one such vocal critic. In his memoir of 2003, he expressed dismay at the unfeasibility of this plan given the economic conditions in Korea during the 1960s and 1970s and argued that the plan would be difficult to realize even in the 2000s. He also noted that the original plan published in *Chosŏn ilbo* was more "realistic and dynamic" than the revised version of 1969. His harshest criticism was reserved for the five loops placed in the center of the island and their multilevel design. This feature was "too idealistic" and "dreamy" for Sohn, a virtual creation, like a storybook, fashioned out of theory rather than reality.[43]

Sohn Jong-mok's criticism of Kim Swoo-geun's Master Plan of 1969 comes in part from his personal reservations about the idealistic zeal of Kim's cohorts as well as his skepticism of their elite backgrounds. Kim Swoo-geun surrounded himself with a close group of young architects, including Yu Sŭng-jung, Park Sŭng-gyu, Kim Kyu-o, Kim Wŏn, Kim Mun-gyu, and Kim Seok Chul. These were men in their early thirties by and large. Kim Seok Chul, in particular, who had to take up the bulk of the work for the master plan when Yu Sŭng-jung and Kim Wŏn were called away to oversee the design and construction of the Korean pavilion at the Osaka International Expo, was only twenty nine years old. Sohn branded these architects the "KS," invoking the "Korea Standard mark" given to products that met the industrial standard set by the government. Sohn used the KS brand, however, as an acronym for Kyŏnggi High School and Seoul National University and thus took a swipe at the elite educational background of Kim Swoo-geun's group. Sohn commented that these architects had a strong elite mentality as the select few, and Kim Swoo-geun in particular exhibited a star syndrome and "was self-indulgent to the extent that he had to act differently from ordinary people."[44]

Sohn Jung-mok further raised an interesting question as to why there was no debate about the Master Plan for Yŏŭido among his contemporaries. And he noted that, despite many newspaper articles publicizing the development of Yŏŭido, the earliest assessment of the plan appeared in an article in *Sin tong'a* only in October 1984.[45] Sohn attributed this glaring absence of discussion or critique to the elitism of the architects and the exclusivity of their profession, as betrayed by the fact that the only architectural magazine in Korea until the 1970s was *Space* (*Konggan*), published by Kim Swoo-geun's own architectural group. Sohn also cited what he called "the Confucian comradeship" among the participants as a factor that discouraged critical feedback.[46] In his study of *Konggan*, Alain Delissen also characterizes Kim Swoo-geun as a "modernizing cultural elite" and argues that *Konggan* "had a realm of its own, neither mainstream nor marginal, neither official culture nor counter-culture."[47] These comments refer to a culture in which the architectural profession operated on the basis of its exclusive ownership of specialized knowledge in a country where such knowledge was hard to come by. Bound by their educational and personal ties, which also translated into shared ideas and ideals, Kim Swoo-geun and his peers acted as agents that presented the future of the Korean nation without civic engagement or feedback from the citizens.

Kim Swoo-geun always maintained an idealistic vision of the role of an architect representing the citizenry, however. In an article about the master plan, he said that the responsibility of the urban planner was to serve society, that is to say the citizenry, with creativity: "An urban planner should always be able to get back to the position of an ordinary citizen and breathe and empathize with them. All of his thoughts and knowledge should start with the citizens."[48] "Human-oriented urban planning" was what he advocated here, which he emphasized by saying that urbanization without citizens would be the greatest error: "The subject of urban planning is human, not simply the convenience of everyday life. The numbers of the urban engineers and the regulations of the urban administrators will not matter even if they all indicate the immediate outcome of convenience. If urban planning cannot be ascertained in terms of a human scale fit for the time, it becomes meaningless."[49] However, the humans referred to here were not supposed to be participants or partners in the architectural venture. Rather, for Kim, the architect occupied a position of privilege as the one who should consider the needs of ordinary people. Kim Swoo-geun's human-oriented urban planning thus had a rather abstract and theoretical outlook, as opposed to reflecting the practical concerns about convenience in the everyday life. The proposal of artificial land, megastructure, and multidimensional city in the 1969 master plan supports this point. It was the architect who defined the needs of the time and the direction for the future and took up the responsibility to lead the citizenry.

Therefore, many people attributed the failure of the 1969 Yŏŭido master plan to its adoption of a modernist vision not rooted in political, social, and economic conditions specific to Korea. Some people even accused Kim of merely transplanting the Tokyo Plan of 1960.[50] For the critics, it was overall a blueprint for the future that privileged theoretical implications without considering the particular needs of the city. Hyungmin Pai (Pae Hyŏng-min), an architectural historian, offers similar criticism: "The KECC, with all its modernist language, was unable to link its plans to a specific ideological and cultural formation. Lacking was a concept of a modernist urban culture. i.e. an internalized, quasi-autonomous notion of what a modern city can be: aware of its specific economic and political conditions yet not totally subsumed within them. . . . In the rapidly changing relation between concentration and centrality, the original project by Kim Swoo Geun was ultimately unable to deal with the new economic realties of urban land. The Sae'oon Sang'ga [Sewoon Mall] complex stands alone in the dense urban fabric of the city center, neither part of the surrounding area nor able to affect it. It is a fragment of a utopia that was re-iterated in its full scale in the original plans for Yŏŭido."[51] The problem for Kim Swoo-geun was that he could not realize his goal of creating a new urbanity through his plans for a specific site. Rather, the existing urban frame persistently exerted its power, so much so that Kim's creations disconnected from their surroundings. It is interesting to see Pai introducing a new term, *modernist urban culture*, to discuss Kim Swoo-geun's modernism because this term underscores the importance of the local context absent in Kim's work. Perhaps all these critiques attest to the fact that nationalism was the driving force behind modernization in South Korea, not the other way around. Kim Hyun-ok and Kim Swoo-geun shared a vision of Yŏŭido that was a potent symbol of modernity. Park Chung Hee pursued modernization and industrialization in the city and the countryside. The critiques of the 1969 master plan, however, show that modernism only in theory, that is to say, modernization that did not conform to nationalist goals was a mere utopian vision.

In the end, however, the difficulties that the 1969 master plan ran into had more to do with issues on the ground than its theoretical soundness and local interpretation—or lack thereof. Throughout the process, the development of Yŏŭido suffered from financial trouble despite Kim Hyun-ok's effort to attract private investment. The situation only worsened in 1970 when the Wa'u apartment complex in Map'o, one of the citizen apartment projects constructed under Kim, collapsed only four months after it was completed, killing thirty-four and injuring forty. When it was revealed that hurried construction, as well as the use of poor and insufficient building materials, was the cause of the collapse, Kim Hyun-ok had to resign from the mayorship and take responsibility. After Kim's departure, the new mayor of Seoul, Yang Yŏn-t'aek, changed the course of development in Yŏŭido, increasing the area dedicated to apartment construction and allotting the land reserved for the Supreme Court and City Hall to address the financial difficulties that the project had encountered. In order to broaden the appeal of the apartments, which were still a rather unfamiliar form of housing for the majority of Koreans at that time, Yang changed their name from "mansion apartments" to "demonstration apartments (sibŏm ap'at'ŭ)."[52] This is when Sohn Jung-mok was brought in to rectify the city's finances and oversee urban development projects. Sohn was quick to find fault with the aggressive urban planning proposed by Kim Swoo-geun due to the slow sale of land. From the perspective of the city, the development of Yŏŭido needed to supply funds for the continuous development of Seoul. Developed land needed to be parceled out and sold to fund other development projects in the city. Urban space was to be treated like a commodity for sale, and economic efficiency was regarded as the most important criterion.[53]

Eventually, the most drastic alteration to Kim Swoo-geun's plan happened in a way that no one in the urban planning community or the city had anticipated. It was neither opposition from Sohn nor the persistence of financial troubles that forever changed the trajectory of the 1969 master plan. In a meeting with Yang Yŏn-t'aek in October 1970, Park Chung Hee handed out a plan with a large square he had drawn himself with a red pen. The square, to be erected in the center of the island, would be 1,350 meters long and 350 meters wide. Ideologically inflected and motivated by personal ambition, Park's stipulation of a largely monumental public space paid no heed to the city's financial troubles, requiring as it did that the amount of land available for sale be dramatically reduced. In order to draw up a new plan in accordance with the president's wishes, Yang consulted Park Byung-ju (Pak Pyŏng-ju), a professor at Hongik University. Park Byung-ju toyed with the idea of modeling the square after Red Square in the Kremlin or Tiananmen Square in Beijing; in the end, relying on his travel experience, he drew up a plan for the square based on the National Mall in Washington, DC. Park Chung Hee rejected this plan, which called for a plaza with greenery and a connecting park area, and ordered a large, open area paved in asphalt. Park also rejected the names proposed by Yang, the "national square" (minjok ŭi kwangjang) or "unification square" (t'ongil ŭi kwangjang), and named it the 5.16 Square to celebrate the military coup that he himself had led.[54] On its completion, 5.16 Square became the main stage for the regime's subsequent displays of power and propaganda such as military parades. The first Military Day parade took place a mere two days after the completion of the square in 1972 and continued until 1990.

The revised plan drafted by Park Byung-ju in 1971 to accommodate Park Chung Hee's demands made Kim Swoo-geun's 1969 master plan basically ineffectual. It disconnected the flow of the city between the two axes of the National Assembly Hall and City Hall, and disrupted the multilevel construction in the core loops. In addition, the interdependent relationship among the three local plazas had to give way to one massive space that dominated the center space of the island. In the 1971 plan, Yŏŭido came to retain only the contours of the blocs and zoning ideas from the 1969 plan. Gone were its core principles of a linear, multidimensional, and modernist city. However idealized it might have looked, the 1969 master plan was based on the recognition of fundamental problems of conventional urban development in Seoul. It took issue with the ways in which previous urban planning had simply accommodated outward expansion of the city to diffuse and disperse the concentration of human activity in the city center. Its goal was thus corrective, not reactive. The linear model was designed to stimulate, guide, and frame the development of Seoul as a whole, and to decisively elevate the city's role in nation building. The failure of this master plan resulted in the demotion of Yŏŭido's status from a center city with a vital role in shaping the growth of the city along the linear axis of the river to a mere regional support center that supplemented the local functions of Yŏngdŭngp'o. With the completion of the Seoul-Pusan Highway and the development of Kangnam, Yŏngdŭngp'o simply became one of the multiple cores of the city.[55] The development of Kangnam trumping the Seoul-Inch'ŏn linear development is a testament to the anticommunist policies of the Park Chung Hee regime overwriting the urban design and visions proposed by the architects. Years later, ruminating on what might have been, Kim Seok Chul could not hold back his disappointment: "The failure of the master plan was a painful reminder that urban planning and design will remain a dream if they are not supported by the highest power and the system of the government.... Urban planning is not what one can do as an individual. It has to accommodate the limitations of the nation."[56]

Given the monstrous monumentality of Yŏŭido today, it might be easy to dismiss it as a creation of nationalist fervor at a specific time in Korean history. The rash pursuit of modernization, grand rhetoric about *minjok*, and the hyperbolic performance of military propaganda for which Yŏŭido became the main stage all seem to validate this point. However, the blanket term *nationalist* fails to adequately describe all the entangled visions and interests—developmentalist, anticommunist, personal, and otherwise—that competed, lost, and ultimately won in the creation of the Yŏŭido we know today. On a closer look, Yŏŭido's nationalist mythology seems to unravel into a story of different visions colliding against and collaborating with one another. At the heart of this story, as seen in its final stages of planning and construction, an invisible enemy in the north forced the reevaluation of the health of the city in a divided Korea and the rise of a dictatorship. If, however, we remain attuned to the uncomfortable coexistence of 5.16 Square—a product of the anticommunist agenda of Park Chung Hee—and high-rise buildings—fragments of the 1968 and 1969 plans pursued by Kim Hyun-ok and Kim Swoo-geun respectively, we can still glimpse the traces of a different city that was once dreamed of and almost realized. We can learn how architects forged a complicated relationship with the city and the state, ranging from cooperation to accommodation to active disagreement. Indeed, Kim Swoo-geun's close relationship with government officials ensured commissions for public structures and sustained his architectural reputation. However, the competing visions of urbanity seen in the 1969 master plan shows fissures beyond personal partnership. Architects also occupied a precarious position between state and citizenry. While Kim Swoo-geun's philosophy put him on the side of the citizens, endowing the architects with the responsibility and authority to define the needs of the time, Kim inevitably made himself a stranger to the citizenry, though not completely complicit in the national agenda of the state.

The foreshadowing of what was to come in the Yusin era, then, might be found in the ways in which this story of multiple casts connected by personal ties but divided by different ideas became forgotten, completely overshadowed by the dictatorial rule of Park Chung Hee. Yusin implemented a narrow and singular channel of decision making, that would unify, often brutally, any differences in vision and method. Whether reactive (for the city) or corrective (for the architects), all visions of urban planning had to be mandated and then sanctioned by the state. Nevertheless, the story of multiple casts also teaches us that we should not posit an absolute rupture between the Yŏŭido of the 1969 master plan and the Yŏŭido that came to be under Yusin rule. The 1969 master plan was harshly criticized as utopian and unnationalistic for disregarding Korea's cultural foundation and privileging theory over local interpretations and needs. But to my mind it is in this utopianism that we can locate some of the same energy that drove Park Chung Hee's nationalist developmentalism, his utopian gospel of making the impossible possible.[57] In a similar fashion, Kim Hyun-ok's pursuit of a seamlessly functioning city can be seen as just as utopian as the modernist city of Kim Swoo-geun.

But the greatest parallel can be found in the ways in which utopia had the same kind of totalizing effect on the respective visions of development that the three men harbored. Reckless and even violent, utopia's homogenizing tendency has little patience for local dissent—the rickshaw driver whose movements can be classified as neither vehicular nor pedestrian, the squatter who cannot afford the middle-class dream of apartment ownership, the political dissident who insists 5.16 was a military coup and not a national revolution. On that level, Kim Swoo-geun's urban dreams are not so distinct from Park Chung Hee's dictatorship or Kim Hyun-ok's aggressive management style. All these ideas referred to something as all encompassing as "total administration" and "total urbanization" and envisioned a top-down transformation of space and society. Park Chung-Hee, Kim Hyun-ok, and Kim Swoo-geun may not have agreed on their approaches as to how to create a new urban form in Yŏŭido, but they were indeed collaborators in sharing a dream that would create a homogenizing urban landscape. The city's growing pains, the architect's modernist dream, and the state's dread of the enemy all collided on an alluvial island that disappeared under the totalizing dream of development.

From these stories, it is possible to see how the island of sand deposits called Yŏŭido changed its form into a glorious manifestation of violence staged for utopian dreams. The mad dash to the future showed little regard for the island and its memory and created a strange amalgam of power that combined developmentalist and militarized modernity. Therefore, Yŏŭido exemplifies an urban structure that dominates rather than assimilates and stands today disconnected not only from history in its forgetting of the past but also from the present in its fixation on the future. Its touting presence, existing without a sense of belonging on the part of the people, estranges onlookers. Doing so, it may have just validated its name, "your island."

NOTES

1. Sim Cheol-woong (Sim Chŏl-ung), An|other River: Dream, Blood, History, 2011. 3 Channel HD video projection, National Museum of Modern and Cotemporary Art, South Korea.

2. Sim Chŏl-ung, Changso wa munhwa ŭisik kwa chŏngch'esŏng: Sim Chŏl-ung

chakp'umjip 1996-2013 [*Place and Culture, Consciousness and Identity: The Works of Sim Cheol-Woong, 1996–2013*] (Pep'ungch'e, 2013).

3. Ibid.

4. One of the first historical records mentioning Yŏŭido appeared in the sixteenth century. It called the island Inghwado and described it as a pasture that the government used for sheep and goats, thereby giving the name Yangmalsan (or Yangmasan) to the small hill in the middle of the island. Over the course of the Chosŏn dynasty, due to its proximity to nearby ferry ports, it developed some auxiliary industries such as ship-building, fishing, and agriculture. Pamsŏm, which had been a place of exile initially, in particular became a vibrant center for these industries. At the onset of the modern era, however, Yŏŭido was left out of the initial modernization projects because the main transportation routes came to be defined by the Seoul-Inch'ŏn railway, which passed through Yongsan. In 1916, under Japanese colonial rule, an airport was built on Yŏŭido, and the first Korean pilot, Ahn Ch'ang-nam, tested aircraft from there in 1922. However, Yŏŭido remained largely excluded from major urban development during the colonial period, even after it was included in the jurisdiction of Seoul (Keijo) along with Yŏngdŭngp'o by Great Keijo Urban Planning in 1936. Yŏŭido also maintained its peripheral status after the liberation in 1945 despite government projects that attempted to relocate tens of households to Pamsŏm. In 1956 it seemed like a new era was beginning for Yŏŭido when an international airport was completed and national airline's first flight took off. But it was also short-lived because a new airport was built in Kimp'o in 1958. Only after 1963 did Yŏŭido come to occupy a central place geographically as the city limits expanded south of the Han River, and only in 1968 did the urbanization of Yŏŭido become a realistic project. See An Ch'ang-mo, "Sŏul tosihwa kwajŏng esŏ Yŏŭido ŭi sooe wa kaebal," *Han'guk tosi sŏlgye hakhoeji* 11, no. 5 (December 2010): 53–68.

5. Ibid., 124.

6. One p'yŏng is 3.3058 square meters.

7. Son Chŏng-mok (Sohn Jung-mok), "Manwŏn Sŏul ŭl haegyŏl hanŭn ch'ŏttangye, Han'gang kyebal (chung)," *Kukt'o* 190 (August 1997): 132–41.

8. Sŏul sisa p'yŏnch'an wiwŏnhoe, *Han'gang ŭi ŏje wa onŭl* (Seoul: Sŏul sisa p'yŏnch'an wiwŏnhoe, 2001.

9. Quoted in Son, "Manwŏn Sŏul ŭl. haegyŏl hanŭn ch'ŏttangye, Han'gang kyebal (chung)," 136–37.

10. Son Chŏng-mok, "Yŏŭido kŏnsŏl kwa sigaji ka hyŏngsŏng toenŭn kwajŏng (sang)," *Kukt'o* 192 (October 1997): 131.

11. Ibid.

12. Ibid.

13. Kim's speech, delivered on April 1, 1966, is reproduced in Sŏul Yŏksa Pangmulgwan, *Tolgyŏk kŏnsŏl: Kim Hyŏn-ok sijang ŭi Sŏul* (Sŏul Yŏksa Pangmulgwan, 2013), 7.

14. Son Chŏng-mok, "Yŏŭido kŏnsŏl kwa sigaji ka hyŏngsŏng toenŭn kwajŏng (sang)," 131.

15. Ahn Ch'ang-mo, "Pundan ch'eje wa Sŏul tosi kujo," *Hyangt'o Sŏul* 81 (2012).

16. The full text of this address is available on the website of the Blue House, http://15cwd.pa.go.kr/korean/data/expresident/pjh/speech12.html

17. Ibid.

18. Ibid.

19. Sŏul T'ŭkpyŏlsi, *Yŏŭido mit Han'gang yŏn'an kaebal kyehoek* (Sŏul T'ŭkpyŏlsi, 1969).

20. Chŏng In-ha, *Kim Su-gŭn kŏnch'ungnon: Han'guk kŏnch'uk ŭi saeroun inyŏmhyŏng* (Migŏnsa, 1996), 39.

21. The core concept of the Sewoon Mall project can be traced to the paradigm continuum from Le Corbusier's contemporary city of three million inhabitants to the 1960 Tokyo Plan and Japanese metabolism architecture. See Yi Tu-ho and An Ch'ang-mo, "Seun Sangga e taehan tosi kŏnch'ukchŏk chaehaesŏk," *Han'guk kŏnch'uk yŏksa hakhoe ch'ugye haksul palp'yo taehoe nonmunjip* (November 2011), 355–67.

22. For more discussion of Kim Swoo-geun's career, see Kang Nan-hyŏng, "Sŏul mega sŭtŭrŏkchŏ Seun Sangga ŭi tosi tanmyŏn yŏn'gu, *Han'guk kŏnch'uk yŏksa hakhoe ch'ungye haksul palp'yo taehoe nonmunjip* (May 2011), 63-75; Kim Chŏng-dong, "Kim Su-gŭn kŏnch'uk 25-yŏn chaego," *Han'guk kŏnch'uk yŏksa hakhoe ch'ugye haksul palp'yo taehoe nonmunjip* (November 2012), 173-185; and Kim Kyŏng-t'ae and An Kyŏng-hwan, "Kim Su-gŭn ŭi kŏnch'ukchŏk p'aerŏdaim pyŏnhwa wa kŭ paegyŏng yŏn'gu," *Taehan kŏnch'uk hakhoe nonmunjip* 13, no. 1 (January 1997): 69-77.

23. Sohn Jung-mok notes a discrepancy between KECC Yearbook and an article published in the magazine *Space (Konggan)* regarding when KECC signed the contract with the city. KECC Yearbook gives the date of September 25, 1968, while the article in *Space* states that the signing took place in early 1968. See Son Chŏng-mok, "Yŏŭido kŏnsŏl kwa sigaji ka hyŏngsŏng toenŭn kwajŏng (chung)," *Kukt'o* 192 (December 1997): 122–34.

24. Son, "Yŏŭido kŏnsŏl kwa sigaji ka hyŏngsŏng toenŭn kwajŏng (chung)," 124.

25. Ibid., 126.

26. Sŏul t'ŭkpyŏl-si, *Yŏŭido mit Han'gang yŏn'an kaebal kyehoek*, 9.

27. Ibid.

28. Kim Su-gŭn, "Yŏŭido kyehoek," *Kŏnch'uksa* 5, no. 1 (1970): 35-37.

29. Ibid.

30. Kim Sŏk-ch'ŏl, *Kim Sŏk-ch'ŏl ŭi 40-yŏn tosi kyehoek/tosi sŏlgye: Yŏŭido esŏ 4 taegang ŭro*, reprint (Seoul: Saenggak ŭi namu, 2010), 381.

31. Kim Seok Chul, in his criticism of the way the 1969 master plan was later altered, maintained that it was urban planning, unlike the real-estate development plan proposed by Kim Hyun-ok. See Kim Sŏk-ch'ŏl and O Hyo-rim, *Tosi rŭl kŭrinŭn kŏnch'ukka* (Ch'angbi, 2014).

32. Kim Sŏk-ch'ŏl, *Kim Sŏk-ch'ŏl ŭi 40-yŏn tosi kyehoek/tosi sŏlgye*, 379.

33. Kim Sŏk-ch'ŏl, "Yŏŭido kyehoek."

34. Kim Sŏk-ch'ŏl and O Hyo-rim, *Tosi rŭl kŭrinŭn kŏnch'ukka*, 98.

35. Kim Sŏk-ch'ŏl, *Kim Sŏk-ch'ŏl ŭi 40-yŏn tosi kyehoek/tosi sŏlgye*, 391–93.

36. Chŏng In-ha, "Yŏŭido tosi kyehoek e kwanhan yŏn'gu: Kim Su-gŭn ŭi 1969-yŏn kyehoeg'an ŭl chungsim ŭro," *Taehan kŏnch'uk hakhoe nonmunjip* 12, no. 2 (1996): 125.

37. Kim Su-gŭn, "Yŏŭido kyehoek."

38. Sŏul t'ŭkpyŏlsi, *Yŏŭido mit Han'gang yŏn'an kaebal kyehoek*, 9–20.

39. Ibid., 38–39.

40. Kim Su-gŭn, "Yŏŭido kyehoek," 396.

41. The exact figure given was over a hundred billion won. It called for the use of private funds as much as possible but also pressed the city to invest 10.8 billion won up front. See Sŏul t'ŭkpyŏlsi, *Yŏŭido mit Han'gang yŏn'an kaebal kyehoek*, 70–79.

42. Ibid., 72.

43. Son Chŏng-mok, "Yŏŭido kŏnsŏl kwa sigaji ka hyŏngsŏng toenŭn kwajŏng (chung)," 126.

44. Ibid., 124.

45. It included only a brief comment suggesting that Kim Swoo-geun's plan pushed the boundaries too far with its ideas and scale and mainly discussed the revised plan of 1971 because the 1969 plan was considered have been erased from history. See Son Jung-mok, "Yŏŭido kŏnsŏl kwa sigaji ka hyŏngsŏng toenŭn kwajŏng (ha)," *Kukt'o* 194 (December 1997).

46. Ibid.

47. Alain Delissen, "Aesthetic Past of *Space* (1960–1990)," *Korean Studies* 25, no. 2 (2002): 258.

48. Kim Su-gŭn, "Yŏŭido kyehoek."

49. Ibid.

50. Son Chŏng-mok, "Yŏŭido kŏnsŏl kwa sigaji ka hyŏngsŏng doenŭn kwajŏng (chung)," 132.

51. Hyungmin Pai, "Modernism, Development, and the Transformation of Seoul," in *Culture and the City in East Asia*, ed. Won Bae Kim et al. (Oxford University Press, 1997), 122.

52. Ibid., 110.

53. Chŏng In-ha, "Yŏŭido tosi kyehoek e kwanhan yŏn'gu," 133.

54. See Son Chŏng-mok, *Sŏul tosi kyehoek iyagi* (Han'ul, 2003), 2:67–72. Son carefully recollects the events and suspects that Park secretly planned to use this square as a military runway. Such a defense-minded decision is well supported in the recent discovery that Park built an underground bunker below the square. See "Pak Chŏng-hŭi chŏnggwŏn ttae mandŭn chiha pŏngkŏ," *Chosŏn ilbo*, July 26, 2015.

55. An Ch'ang-mo, "Sŏul tosihwa kwajŏng esŏ Yŏŭido ŭi sooe wa kaebal," 53–68.

56. Kim Sŏk-chŏl, *Tosi rŭl kŭrinŭn kŏnch'ukka*, 396.

57. The report, Sŏul t'ŭkpyŏl-si, *Yŏido mit Han'gang yŏn'an kaebal kyehoek*, has a preface listing Park Chung Hee's presidential instructions. It reads, "1. The one who quits cannot succeed, and the one who succeeds does not quit. 2. There is future where belief is. There is a way where the will is. 3. A new era of governance has come that values effort over status and creativity and execution over experience." All these items, and the second one in particular, show the utopian zeal that drove South Korea's development.

BIBLIOGRAPHY

An Ch'ang-mo. "Sǒul tosihwa kwajǒng esǒ Yǒŭido ŭi sooe wa kaebal." *Hanguk tosi sǒlgye hakhoeji* 11, no. 5 (December 2010). 53–68.

An Ch'ang-mo. "Pundan ch'eje wa Sǒul tosi kujo." *Sǒul kwa Yǒksa* 81 (June 2012): 161–208.

Chǒng In-ha (Jung In-ha). *Kim Su-gǔn kǒnch'uk ron: Han'guk kǒnch'uk ǔi saeroun inyǒmhyǒng*. Migǒnsa, 1996.

Chǒng In-ha. "Yǒŭido tosi kyehoek e kwanhan yǒn'gu: Kim Su-gǔn ǔi 1969-yǒn kyehoeg'an ŭl chungsim ŭro." *Taehan kǒnch'uk hakhoe nonmunjip* 12, no. 2 (1996): 123–35.

Delissen, Alain. "Aesthetic Past of *Space* (1960–1990)." *Korean Studies* 25, no. 2 (2002): 243–60.

Kang Nan-hyǒng. "Sǒul mega sŭtŭrǒkch'ǒ Seun Sangga ǔi tosi tanmyǒn yǒn'gu. *Han'guk kǒnch'uk yǒksa hakhoe ch'ugye haksul palp'yo taehoe nonmunjip* (May 2011), 63–75.

Kim Chǒng-dong. "Kim Su-gǔn kǒnch'uk 25-yǒn chaego." *Han'guk kǒnch'uk yǒksa hakhoe ch'ugye haksul palp'yo taehoe nonmunjip* (November 2012), 173–85.

Kim Kyǒng-t'ae and An Kyǒng-hwan. "Kim Su-gǔn ǔi kǒnch'ukchǒk p'aerǒdaim pyǒnhwa wa kŭ paegyǒng yǒn'gu." *Taehan kǒnch'uk hakhoe nonmunjip* 13, no. 1 (January 1997): 69–77.

Kim Sǒk-ch'ǒl (Kim Seok Chul). *Kim Sǒk-ch'ǒl ǔi 40-yǒn tosi kyehoek/tosi sǒlgye: Yǒŭido esǒ 4 taegang ŭro*. Seoul: Saenggak ǔi namu, 2010.

Kim Sǒk-ch'ǒl, and O Hyo-rim. *Tosi rŭl kŭrinǔn kǒnch'ukka*. Ch'angbi, 2014.

Kim Su-gǔn (Kim Swoo-geun). "Yǒŭido kyehoek." *Kǒnch'uksa* 5, no. 1 (1970): 35–37.

Pai, Hyungmin. "Modernism, Development, and the Transformation of Seoul." In *Culture and the City in East Asia*, edited by Won Bae Kim, Mike Douglass, Sang-Chuel Choe, and Kong Chong Ho. Oxford University Press, 1997.

Sim Cheol-woong (Sim Ch'ǒl-ung). *An|other River: Dream, Blood, History*. 2011.3 Channel HD video projection. National Museum of Modern and Cotemporary Art, South Korea.

Sim Ch'ǒl-ung (Sim Cheol-woong). *Changso wa munhwa ǔisik kwa chǒngch'esǒng: Sim Ch'ǒl-ung chakp'umjip, 1996–2013*. Pep'ungch'e, 2013.

Son Chǒng-mok. "Manwǒn Sǒul ŭl haegyǒl hanŭn ch'ǒttangye, Hangang kaebal (chung)," *Kukt'o* 190 (August 1997): 132–41.

Son Chǒng-mok. "Yǒŭido kǒnsǒl kwa sigaji ka hyǒngsǒng toenŭn kwajǒng (sang)." *Kukt'o* 192 (October 1997): 117–31.

Son Chǒng-mok. "Yǒŭido kǒnsǒl kwa sigaji ka hyǒngsǒng toenŭn kwajǒng (chung)." *Kukt'o* 193 (November 1997): 122–34.

Son Chǒng-mok. "Yǒŭido kǒnsǒl kwa sigaji ka hyǒngsǒng toenŭn kwajǒng (ha)." *Kukt'o* 194 (December 1997): 108–25.

Son Chǒng-mok. *Sǒul tosi kyehoek iyagi; Sǒul kyǒktong ǔi 50-yǒn kwa na ǔi chŭngǒn*. Vol. 2. Seoul: Hanul, 2003.

Sǒul Sisa P'yǒnch'an Wiwǒnhoe. *Han'gang ǔi ǒje wa onŭl*. Seoul. 2001.

Sŏul T'ŭkpyŏlsi. *Yŏido mit Han'gang yŏn'an kaebal kyehoek*. Seoul. 1969.

Sŏul Yŏksa Pangmulgwan. *Tolgyŏk kŏnsŏl: Kim Hyŏn-ok sijang ŭi Soul*. Sŏul Yŏksa Pangmulgwan, 2013.

Yi Tu-ho, and An Ch'ang-mo. "Seun Sangga e taehan tosi kŏnch'ukchŏk chaehaesŏk." *Han'guk kŏnch'uk yŏksa hakhoe ch'ugye haksul palp'yo taehoe nonmunjip* (November 2011): 355–66.

"Oh Jesus, Now Here with Us"

Literary Christology in 1970s and 1980s South Korea

Serk-Bae Suh

The literary critic Kim U-ch'ang's (Kim Uchang's) 1977 essay entitled "Han Yong-un: The Poet in Time of Need" begins with a brief discussion about Lucien Goldmann's study of Blaise Pascal and Jean Racine.[1] In his book *The Hidden God*, Goldmann examines a tragic worldview manifested in the work of Pascal and Racine, who lived in seventeenth-century France, a time of turbulent transition.[2] During this period, the modern state emerged in France as the Bourbon kings consolidated power against the aristocracy and clergy. The centralization of state power coupled with the advance of natural science and the rise of individualistic rationalism created a tragic worldview among members of the status group called the nobles of the robe. Unlike the old nobility, with possession of traditional prestige and land as its political and economic power base, the nobles of the robe were ennobled for their services as administrators for the king. Being economically and politically at the mercy of the kings, they were caught in a more precarious position due to the changes accompanied by centralization, which would push the nobility, whether it was old or new, away from the center of power. The hidden God, as famously presented by Pascal in his *Pensées*, is the God of the tragic sentiments emanating from this sociopolitical situation.

Goldmann finds the best expression of this Pascalian God in Jansenism, a religious movement within the Catholic Church, of which many nobles of the robe and those affiliated with them, including Pascal and Racine, were followers. God is hidden because he is supposed to be omnipresent but absent in this untruthful world. God never answers the supplications of man in desperation, and God never intervenes in man's worldly affairs, although he will judge man in the last days.

In his essay, Kim highlights Goldmann's idea of the tragic vision as a worldview that emerges when an individual's conviction conflicts with the demands of the world. In such a time, a man of conscience is forced to choose between the truth of his own conscience and the untruth of the world. The tragic vision is one of the three attitudes one can take without permitting oneself to surrender to the demands of the world. One may fatalistically withdraw from the immanent world to seek consolation in transcendence or actively resist the world by attempting to change it. The person of the tragic vision takes neither stance. He absolutely refuses the world and yet remains in it because he knows there is no place outside this world where he exists. Pascal's hidden God represents a tragic worldview of those who are caught between two contradictory demands on them, the truth of their consciences and the untruth of the world. On that point, Kim finds it relevant to understanding how Han Yongun and his work were situated in colonial Korea. Kim's essay is a eulogy for the poet who refused to compromise his ethical and artistic integrity in the untruthful world of colonial rule. Given that the essay was written at the peak of the Yusin regime, it is hard not to consider Kim's essay to be a commentary as much on what was expected of writers and poets under the oppressive rule of Park Chung Hee (Pak Chŏng-hŭi) as it was on Han Yong-un's poetry during the colonial period.

I began this chapter by calling attention to Kim's essay and its highlighting of Pascal's tragic vision because what I attempt to do in this chapter is respond to a series of questions to which the Pascalian hidden God leads. What if God comes down from the realm of transcendence once again as a helpless and even abject being in flesh? What if God frankly admits, then, that he cannot save the oppressed from their suffering? In other words, what if Jesus comes again not in glory but in misery and reveals his total lack of divine power? Put differently, what if, even in the second coming, God still remains humanly weak or even weaker than man?[3] Thus, what if he is miserably defeated by evil in the world, which proves to be stronger than his kingdom? In a word, what if God comes again not as the Messiah who will bring everlasting justice, freedom, peace, and reconciliation to the world but as someone who is as helpless and impotent as men in their unjust and violent world? The grim view expressed by these questions, much grimmer than Pascal's in some sense, is conjured up by the literary texts I examine in this chapter. As further discussed however, the grim view of God helps us envisage a more affirmative view of man's capacity to bring his own liberation.

This chapter examines a conjuncture in which literature, politics, and religion intersected under the oppressive regime of Yusin and in its immediate aftermath. More specifically, it deals with literary texts by Kim Chi Ha (Kim Chi-ha), Yi Mun-yol (Yi Mun-yŏl), and Kim Chŏng-hwan. In a sense, the provenances of these texts mark the beginning, end, and aftermath of the Yusin regime. Kim's play *The Gold-Crowned Jesus* was staged for the first time in 1972, the same year in which Park Chung Hee declared a state of emergency and revised the constitution to stay in power indefinitely.[4] Yi's novella *The Son of Man* came out in 1979, the same year in which the dictator perished at the hands of his own right-hand man, the head of Korean Central Intelligence Agency, which was the most feared weapon of repression wielded by Park's regime.[5] On the other hand, Kim Chŏng-hwan's series of poems collectively entitled "The Story of Yellow Jesus" (1981) were published in the aftermath of the Yusin regime, culminating in Kwangju, May 1980.[6]

Despite the differences between the texts in genre, style, and theme, they share in common the portrayal of a Jesus who is weak and impotent. He, with all human fragility, could not be further from the divine power of the Christian God, who is the Supreme Being, omnipotent and infinitely perfect. Neither is he presented as the mediator who reconciles God and humanity for a new covenant. Despite his compassion for humanity, he is too weak to intervene in human history as the God of the Old Testament did. He does not free humanity from its suffering. He does not lift up humanity from its sins, nor does he promise eternal life. Instead he weeps over the suffering of men. To be more precise, he suffers with men, but his suffering does not bring about their salvation.

In Kim Chi Ha's play, Jesus desperately begs a leper to liberate him. Without the help of the wretched of the earth, he cries, he cannot return to save humanity. Being helpless but compassionate, however, he inspires the oppressed to realize that only they can liberate themselves. In a sense, Yi's novella and Kim Chŏng-hwan's poems can be read as responses to Kim Chi Ha's Jesus, who is weak but compassionate and inspirational.

In an attempt to explore the meaning of religion for society, Yi's novella *The Son of Man* implicitly criticizes the view of Jesus as an emancipatory inspiration.[7] Yi calls into question the idea that God that will help humanity liberate itself from such worldly predicaments as political repression and economic inequality. In that sense, the novella can be read as an implicit criticism of Kim Chi Ha's play.

In contrast, "The Story of Yellow Jesus" further highlights the emancipatory aspect of the figure of Jesus by depicting him as the universal spirit of love incarnated in individuals of the oppressed in the course of modern Korean history. Jesus does not come again as the Messiah who will liberate humanity from suffering. Rather, he suffers with men and dies. And he is born again, incarnated in flesh among the oppressed. In the repeated and overlapped cycles of rebirth, suffering, and death, he turns into the universal spirit of love residing in the oppressed. In the end, anyone who suffers for others in the painful history of modern Korea is identified with Jesus in the poetry.

The Gold-Crowned Jesus

The play opens with a song, which would hold iconic status in South Korean underground music scenes well into the 1980s. Composed by the legendary folksinger Kim Mingi, it expresses the unbearable suffering and feeling of abandonment beleaguering the people of a repressive society. A part of the lyrics toward the end sums up the overall sentiment of the play.

Where can he be?
Where can he be?
Where is Jesus?
. . .
He who could save us
Where can he be?[8]

The song ends with a repeated supplication.

Oh, Jesus
Now here with us
Oh, Jesus, with us[9]

As the story goes on, it is revealed that Jesus cannot be "here with us" because those in power prevent him from coming again and bringing justice and peace to the world. Thus, the play is a damning indictment of a society in which justice and peace are trammeled in the interest of those in power.

Set in a ghetto in a provincial city in 1970s South Korea, the play features a leper, a beggar, and a prostitute who represent the oppressed and a Catholic priest and a nun who stand for two sides of the Church, one hypocritically concerned only about the spiritual salvation of the oppressed, and consequently collusive with the status quo, and the other concerned about their suffering in this world as well. The ghetto is about to be redeveloped, and its residents will be driven away. The nun implores the priest to join a demonstration protesting the redevelopment, but he refuses to get involved, saying that the Church's mission is to help people spiritually not politically. As their argument proceeds, it turns out that the priest is a narrow-minded bigot who despises the unprivileged of society whom he calls "lepers, beggars, thieves, and other undesirables."[10]

The beggar not only hates religious hypocrites like the priest and mistrusts the Church, but he also denies Jesus because the latter does not offer him any practical help. In contrast, the leper holds onto his faith in Jesus. Interestingly, Jesus appears to him when he is losing his belief and starting to doubt. When he comes across a gold-crowned Jesus pietà, the leper bursts out, somewhat intoxicated from drinking, "I cannot bear it any longer." Reminiscent of Job's complaint to God in the Old Testament, the leper complains about the unbearable hardships inflicted on the poor and powerless. He asks why Jesus keeps silent when the powerful and the Church are selling him out by telling the poor and powerless in his name that they should be obedient to authority and endure earthly hardship for heavenly rewards. He cries out, asking why Jesus has abandoned him and why he does not answer. When he plops down before the statue of Jesus, he feels a drop of water falling on him. He finds the cement statue of Jesus weeping. Befuddled, he notices for the first time that the crown on Jesus's head is made of gold. As he is imagining all the things he could do and buy with the gold, the Jesus statue suddenly breaks its silence and tells him he should take it.

Jesus explains to the leper that he is responding to him because he is an honest and poor man. Far from saving the leper from his hardship and suffering, however, Jesus asks the leper to free him from his suffocating prison, the stone in which he is kept. Jesus further explains that "they" want to keep him imprisoned by ossifying him as a god for the rich and powerful, and only the oppressed like the leper can liberate him and make him live. The gold crown on his head, Jesus continues, is a ploy of the rich and powerful to prevent him from coming down to the oppressed. Jesus begs the leper to remove the gold crown from his head and thus liberate him. In other words, Jesus needs the oppressed to save him first. Only after that will he be able to save them. Jesus frankly admits that he is weak and impotent without the help of the oppressed. He says he cannot come again because "My power alone is not enough."[11] In other words, God depends on men to be complete. Without men's participation in his completion, he is as weak as or even weaker than men.

Jesus tells the leper to take the gold crown and share it with others. The leper is soon joined by the nun and his friend the prostitute in the presence of Jesus. As the leper removes the gold crown from Jesus's head, Jesus declares that his kingdom will come down to earth and he will bring peace to the world, rescuing his true disciples and repelling the evils of the world. At the moment of Jesus's declaration however, those in power, represented by the priest, a policeman, and a rich businessman, show up and take the gold crown from the leper's hands. The policeman arrests the leper for theft, and the priest and the businessman put the gold crown back on Jesus's head. As soon as the crown is returned to his head, Jesus grows stiff.

As seen in this synopsis, the play portrays Jesus as a weak and impotent being that cannot free himself from his prison, the ossification imposed on him by the rich and powerful, let alone liberate the oppressed from their suffering. On his own he even cannot lift a finger. He needs the oppressed to liberate him from his prison first. The oppressor does not allow the oppressed to do so however. Accusing the rich and powerful of making Jesus's second coming impossible, the play takes a pessimistic view of 1970s Korea, where state violence, injustice, and inequality prevailed; the status quo fed off people's apathy; and no prospect of change came into view.

Probably to ameliorate the original version's pessimism, O Chong-u, a dramatist, added one more act in his more popular version. Kim's original version ends with the scene in which Jesus returns to immobility and silence. In the added act, on the other hand, the businessman, the policeman, and the priest tell their sides of the story and justify themselves in turn. In the end, a new character, a college student, appears and comments on the situation. He says it shows what South Korean society is like. The poor become poorer, and the rich become richer; the powerful stay in power, and the powerless are abandoned to despair. He fatalistically sighs that it cannot be changed and there is nothing he can do about it, although he is well aware of what is expected of him. He goes on to say that only those who are not afraid of killing themselves can be heroes in a society like this. As soon as he ends his commentary, curiously saying that all the material components of a human body are worth a dollar in terms of their monetary value and it takes just one match to set fire to a one-dollar bill, the leper returns to give him a match. He tries to run away from the leper, who chases him around. The spotlight follows them. The college student finally cries out, "Don't put that spotlight on me. Please, I beg you not to do that."[12]

The scene must have reminded audiences of the death of Chŏn T'ae-il, which had shocked South Korean society a couple of years before the staging of the play. A sweatshop worker and workers' rights activist, Chŏn immolated himself in protest over the poor working conditions in South Korean factories and the prevalent violation of workers' rights by both the government and business. His death ultimately galvanized dissident intellectuals and student activists to reach out to workers. They felt that they had failed exploited workers especially because Chŏn allegedly wanted to make friends with student activists who could help him better understand labor law and teach him how to organize public demonstrations.[13]

Given that the memory of Chŏn T'ae-il's death was still vivid among many audiences, the leper's act of forcing the college student to take a match must have been intended to encourage Korean intellectuals to awake from defeatism and political dormancy and take the lead in protesting oppression, injustice, and inequality. In that sense, the added act can be seen as an attempt to suggest what should be done to change the status quo. The scene is deeply problematic for the following reason however.

The last scene of the added act suggests that the liberation of the oppressed requires a heroic figure whose sacrifice will eventually open the path to liberation. This insistence on sacrifice ultimately suggests that Jesus, a failing god, should be replaced with a human messiah who will lead the oppressed out of their suffering through his sacrifice. Longing for heroes who take action and can bravely embrace even death in the course of their struggles, the last scene signals the yearning for the messianic figure, the role Jesus fails to take in the play. In that sense, the emphasis on the heroic leader rejects the weakness and impotence of Jesus, who cannot do anything for the oppressed, and reverts to the conventional image of the Messiah to which Jesus fails to live up in the play. As long as emphasis is placed on a messiah, whether he is divine or human, the conclusion is identical; the oppressed need to be guided to their liberation by a heroic leader who is spiritually, morally, and politically more advanced than them in their struggles against oppression.

The scene thus distracts audiences from a more radical possibility implied by the original version, which ends on a more poignant note with Jesus's return to silence. Although the play features a weak and impotent

Jesus who cannot do anything without the help of the oppressed, it does not necessarily lead us to conclude that Jesus is meaningless to the oppressed. Out of the play's portrayal of Jesus as a weak and impotent being, we can envision another meaning, one that is possibly powerful and subversive. Surely his power is not that of a divinity associated with the traditional view of the Christian God. His power rather lies in the people. It comes alive only when the people realize that no one but themselves can liberate them from the shackles in which they are chained . In other words, God's power is palpable only when his absence is exposed. God's self-emptying, the notion that canonically explains God's incarnation, as well as his death on the cross, awakens the people to the fact that it is they who must lead the struggle against oppression.[14] By emptying himself out, God reveals his powerlessness and impotence; thus his own absence as an almighty god leads men to a true freedom that lets them decide their fate rather than waiting for intervention on their behalf by a higher authority.[15] Jesus, though weak and impotent, inspires men to realize that only they can save themselves from their suffering. As will be discussed later, by identifying Jesus with those who suffer for others in the course of the traumatic history of modern Korea, Kim Chŏng-hwan's poems further this emancipatory possibility of Jesus glimpsed in the exposure of his impotence in Kim Chi Ha's play. Before moving onto Kim Chŏng-hwan's poems, however, we will examine Yi Mun-yol's novella *The Son of Man*, which offers an implicit criticism of the liberationist aspect of Jesus implied in *The Gold-Crowned Jesus*.

The Son of Man

Part murder mystery, part commentary on Christianity set in 1970s South Korea, *The Son of Man* revolves around the homicide victim Min Yo-sŏp, a seminary dropout, adulterer, migrant day laborer, labor organizer, and preacher of a religious cult. While tracing his past whereabouts to find clues, Sergeant Nam, the police detective in charge of the case, comes across a manuscript Min wrote about the life of Ahasuerus, a fictional composite based on such characters from the New Testament as the devil who tested Jesus in the wilderness and the possessed man who confronted Jesus, as well as the legend of the wandering Jew, who was condemned to eternal wandering for taunting Jesus on the way to the Crucifixion.

A precocious child, Ahasuerus was groomed to become a rabbi by his family. Fate, however, leads him to a different path. At the age of twelve, he encounters Thedos, one of many self-proclaimed messiahs of the time. Ridiculed by others as a false messiah, Thedos earns young Ahasuerus's sympathy however. After showing the boy around a workplace staffed by slaves, a dungeon, and the valley of lepers, Thedos tells him that the word of God preached by rabbis and priests cannot save the people from hardship, poverty, violence, and disease, the very real suffering of humanity. The real messiah to come, Thedos goes on, should be one who can solve the real problems of humanity in this material world. Later it turns out that the encounter foreshadows the rest of Ahasuerus's life in which he wanders around the known world from India to Rome in pursuit of truth. Disappointed by all the religious teachings and philosophical wisdom he has encountered during his journey, he eventually founds a new religion premised on the idea of a God who will help men save themselves from their suffering.

As Sergeant Nam continues to read the manuscript, he finds that many episodes of Ahasuerus's story mirror the murder victim Min's real life events, including an affair with the wife of Elder Mun, a fellow churchgoer. With the help of the story, Sergeant Nam, as well as the readers, comes to understand why Min was disillusioned with Christianity and its God and why he was possessed with the idea of a God who ministers to the earthly needs of humanity and does not demand anything in return. Much like Ahasuerus, Min came to be skeptical about the Christian God once he was exposed to all the absurdity of the human world, which God supposedly created but has been distant from ever since. Along with his first disciple, Cho Tong-p'al, Min came up with his own religious teachings and preached them to a small number of followers. His teachings, glimpsed in the sketchy information that Sergeant Nam obtains, suggest that Min wanted to replace the Christian God with a new god, one that frankly admits his impotence and modestly lets men help themselves. They include "Do not worship me," "Do not squander your wealth and effort on building an altar, performing rituals, and making sacred garments for me," "Save yourself first," and "Love your neighbor and he will return your love. Do not do it for me. Do not impoverish your neighbor by having too much."[16] In other words, instead of despairing at the silence of God or arguing for atheism, Min attempted to found a religion that would enable men to help themselves. In that sense, Min's view of God is not far from the emancipatory potential of Kim's Jesus.

The points of contention Min and Cho have with the Christian understanding of God are further gleaned from Ahasuerus's confrontations with Jesus. They cross paths several times throughout the story, and their first confrontation shows most explicitly their differences in understanding God. Ahasuerus encounters Jesus for the first time when the latter is fasting and meditating for forty days in the wilderness, a rendered account of the Bible episode in which the devil tempts Jesus to perform three miracles.[17] Ahasuerus, standing in for the devil, challenges Jesus to show his divine power.[18] Reminiscent of the famous grand inquisitor in *The Brothers Karamazov*, Ahasuerus blames Jesus for giving humanity freedom to choose.[19] For the majority of men, it is not easy to hold onto their faith in God, who is distant and silent about their suffering. What Ahasuerus highlights in challenging Jesus is the impotence of God about the earthly suffering of humanity. Ahasuerus proposes to Jesus that the latter become a strong military and political leader who will, together with Ahasuerus himself, lead the Jewish nation out of Roman rule and revive the glory of David. Ahasuerus reasons that if Jesus succeeds in building an earthly kingdom, he will spread his religious teachings among his people more effectively.[20] To Ahasuerus, religion should provide people with practical solutions to their problems. Spirituality is only a secondary priority for him.

In response to Ahasuerus's question What is God's redemption for if it cannot save men from suffering in this world?, Jesus repeats the divine mystery theory that it is futile for man to attempt to understand the unfathomable depth of God and insists that man should not judge God's will with his limited knowledge. He goes on to claim that material life in this world is temporal, nothing when compared to the eternal life of one's soul after death. In the face of Ahasuerus's persistent demand for a more convincing answer, Jesus finally asserts that true faith or submission cannot come with material blessings and miracles.[21]

For Ahasuerus, miracles would be indications of the power with which God could save humanity from its misery. Without proof of God's divine power, God is not meaningful to the people. In response to Ahasuerus's denouncement, Jesus insists that God has to be silent. If he shows his presence to man through material blessings and miracles, it will deprive him of freedom to choose between belief and disbelief because he would know for certain that God exists. Positive knowledge about truth obviates faith in it. Those who know God exists do not need to believe in his existence. Without the freedom to believe, there is no true faith. Put differently, Jesus suggests that true faith emerges only when one overcomes one's despair over the silence of God. This despair exceeds the angst of an affluent existentialist, who lives in a materially comfortable environment but cannot find any meaning in the absurdity of the world from which God is inevitably banished. The despair comes only after one realizes that there is no immediate coming of a Messiah who will rescue one from the bottomless abyss of material as well as spiritual misery, which one cannot escape on one's own. To remain a true believer, one must first fall into deep despair over the silence of God, who never answers a cry for help, and then one must rise triumphantly from the abyss of despair by embracing God's silence and believing in his ultimate saving grace. In other words, true faith not only presupposes but requires God's failure to answer one's supplications. For the true believer who keeps his faith in God and endures earthly sufferings, heavenly rewards are waiting.

To Ahasuerus's ears, Jesus's answer sounds like either a cruel demand from a cold, remote god on those in misery or a cunning excuse that God makes for justifying his impotence in this world. In either case, God leaves them suffering and offers only an uncertain promise of otherworldly rewards.

The impotence of God is pronounced once again in a scene in which Ahasuerus is witnessing Jesus dying on the cross. Noticing Ahasuerus among the spectators, Jesus, in unbearable agony, pleads to the Father Almighty for mercy, wishing to live on. Dejected by the silence of God, he cries out "eli eli lema sabachthani." His cry of despair "My God, my God, why have you forsaken me?" speaks volumes about God's impotence. God fails to answer his beloved son's heartbroken plea.[22] By resorting to Sabellianism, a heretical belief that there are no real differences between the Father, the Son, and the Holy Spirit, the three persons of the Godhead, one may further argue that this cry of despair proves the impotence of God even more clearly because God fails himself.[23]

Given that Ahasuerus's criticism of Jesus's teachings and Min's disillusionment with Christianity pivots on the impotence of God, one might conclude that the novella echoes the image of a weak and impotent Jesus as manifested in *The Gold-Crowned Jesus*. However, the unfolding of the novella turns back on its affinity with the play. As the story proceeds toward its end, it turns out that Min and Cho took matters into their own hands to help the unfortunate and poor around them. They finally resorted to burglary and robbery to put their teachings of neighborly love into practice. Despite their lofty vision of a religion that will help humanity save itself, they turned into petty criminals, and they could hardly help others with their meager booty. Their religious experimentation has proved to be a complete failure. In the end, it is revealed that it is Cho that murdered Min because he felt betrayed by the latter, who recanted his new religion and decided to return to Christian beliefs. The fall of Min and Cho parallels that of Ahasuerus. Instead of giving in to the exacting demands of true faith, Ahasuerus plotted against Jesus with other like-minded Jews who were disappointed in him and got involved in Jesus's arrest and crucifixion.[24] With the rise of Christianity, Ahasuerus was doomed to the damnation of eternal life in the legend of the wandering Jew, and his religious vision was reviled.

By alluding to the futility of an attempt to create a new religion in opposition to Christianity, whose God is aloof when men need his help but stringent when it comes to his demands on their flesh, the novella actually suggests under the surface of its criticism of Christianity that no religion will flourish if its priority is to free humanity from its material misery. In that sense, *The Son of Man* can be read as an implicit criticism of the emancipatory possibility of Jesus's impotence put forward in *The Gold-Crowned Jesus*.

"The Story of Yellow Jesus"

In the 1980s, a significant number of poets invoked religious images associated with Christianity in their poetry.[25] One of the reasons for the surge of poetic interest in Christianity can be attributed to the Kwangju massacre of May 1980 and the government's suppression of the democratization movement. As "Oh, Kwangju, the Cross of Our Nation," the title of a poem written immediately after the massacre, exemplarily shows,[26] the poets must have felt that the sacrifice of Jesus and the message of redemption underlined in the Bible resonated with the political situation of 1980s South Korea.

Among the 1980s poems that drew on Christian images, Kim Chŏng-hwan's series of poems collectively entitled "The Story of Yellow Jesus" stands out as the most sustained attempt to reflect on the emancipatory possibility that the figure of Jesus and his message of redemption open up. In that sense, it can be said that the series of poems carries on Kim Chi Ha's Jesus as an emancipatory inspiration.[27] The third poem of the series, entitled "Book of Birth," reveals its unifying theme.

Book of Birth

I was born in Bethlehem and
laid in a filthy manger two thousand years ago,
but for your unbearable sorrow,
I am also born now in a poor family in the countryside.
I entered into your life for love,
but for bigger love,
I am born, suffer, and resurrect
in moments of your life.
I chose history for love,
but I choose your life
for love again.
It means the moment of despair lasts unbearably long,
but it also means you need innumerable instances of resurrection
    in your life
to complete love in its true sense.
Before my eyes,
your history has turned not even halfway yet,
but I am not eternal.
The only eternal truth is nothing is eternal.
Even if I am eternal, you are temporal
so you need to prove my eternity
in your temporality.
At this moment, I am born fatherless in some shabby inn
and dying with you
in your sin of pride.
My birth, death, and resurrection is not history,
but it is the moments of horrors
to be perpetrated and redeemed endlessly
for the history of you whom I love.
It is for your revolution,
for your humanness,
for betrayal and resurrection,
and finally
for the completion of love both you and I need.
However, you are the power of love
in itself

that is too deep to be torn apart
like some rapturous contact of fingertips and the tips of toes,
kisses, and whispers in one's ear.[28]

The first-person narrator of the poem, Jesus, is the personification of love for those who suffer. He is misunderstood, persecuted, and finally abandoned by the world. Unlike the orthodox understanding of Jesus, he is trapped in the incessant cycle of birth, suffering, and death because he sympathizes with the nameless who suffer because of their love for others amid the violence of history. He is not outside human history. Neither does he intervene in human history with supreme divine power. Rather, he is born as a man among those who suffer over and over again.

Jesus appears in flesh, suffers, and dies simultaneously and indefinitely as long as there are those who suffer. In a dialectical fashion, Jesus is both a singular individual incarnated and the universal spirit of love living among those in despair. To be more exact, Jesus must be plural. He is all of those who live, suffer, and die for others. Incessantly resurrected in the lives of those who suffer for others in a series of traumatic events in modern Korean history, such as the Korean War, Jesus transcends his particularity as a Jewish man who was born in the land of Palestine more than two thousand years ago and was condemned to death on a cross. In other words, through the repeated and overlapped cycles of birth, suffering, death, and resurrection, Jesus turns into the universal spirit that resides with those who suffer in this world.

What is the love that makes the repeated and overlapped cycles possible? It is not a cosmic mystery beyond human understanding. Rather it is the unstoppable care for those who suffer. Love enables Jesus to enter into the life of a singular individual who is also suffering. Love overcomes the essential difference between man and God: man's temporality and God's eternity. Jesus incarnated in flesh is temporal like any other man. God's eternal, universal truth of love can be proved only by a temporal, singular man. Jesus's universality as the spirit of love for those who suffer comes to stand out in relief through the identification of him with a multitude of singular individuals among the oppressed of history. This is a different mode of universalization than Saint Paul's, which turned the religion of a nation into that of humanity by placing the death of Jesus on the cross at the center as the ultimate sacrifice for the sins of humanity. People can be identified with Jesus not because they religiously follow his teachings and worship him as their lord but because they suffer for the sake of others. In other words, they can be identified with Jesus as long as they live in his spirit even if they have never heard who he is.

Thus, what unites Jesus and men is suffering. Jesus does not come in glory but in suffering. He is born among those who suffer and lives and suffers with them.[29] This highlighting of suffering should not be mistaken for the glorification of Jesus's suffering however. As the following poem from "The Story of Yellow Jesus" warns, we should not commit the idolatry of suffering.

About the Idolatry of Suffering

Blessed are you when people revile you and persecute you and ut-
    ter all kinds of evil against you falsely on my account. Rejoice
    and be glad. (Matt. 5:11–12)

If you fix your eyes on my suffering every day,
only on me,
my suffering already becomes your idol.
Being with you from the beginning,
I am always willing to be your pain
through suffering the pain of very familiar times.
But you end up being engulfed by the idolatry of my suffering,
I am where you used to be,
and you are where I used to be.
Thus, we are far from each other.
Because you reflect only on me,
you idolize my love,
my flesh, and tears.
Thus, I am driven far from where you are.
Suffering is not a microuniverse.
Suffering is scattered everywhere.
Although, in the microuniverse of my suffering,
you tear your clothes
and weep bitterly over my death every day,
I walk away from your idolatry
and groan and wander from one place to another.
If you want to find me,
do not let my suffering lead you

to see the world as that of suffering.
Instead, find my corpse
scattered in the suffering of the world,
in the cry of the weak near you.
And then,
I will be wailing
in tune with the sound of your cry in everyday life.[30]

As the poem suggests, we should not be fixated on the suffering of Jesus. The point is how to liberate the oppressed from their suffering. The first step toward the liberation of the oppressed is to find Jesus, the universal spirit of love, in the suffering of the world. On that point, Kim Chŏng-hwan's Jesus is comparable to Kim Chi Ha's. Both are the inspiration for human liberation from the social, political, and economic misery of men in history. Kim Chi Ha's Jesus is external to humanity and its history is unlike Kim Chŏng-hwan's however. Though weak and impotent, he is more a God who grieves over the suffering of his creations than a man incarnated in flesh. His inspiration for human liberation ironically goes along with his appearance as a weak and impotent being. As discussed above, his presence as a weak and impotent being proves the absence of God as the omnipotent and supreme being. No longer able to expect intervention from a higher authority on their behalf, those who suffer cannot help but realize that they are on their own and should help themselves solve the problems they face. In contrast, Kim Chŏng-hwan's Jesus is singular individuals who suffer and live in the universal sprit of love. In other words, Jesus is not external to but immanent in this material world. He is those who suffer for others in history. That means he has already been and will continue to be engaged in the struggle for human liberation. In that sense, Kim Chŏng-hwan's poetic imagination makes more tangible the radical possibility of Jesus that is only latent in Kim Chi Ha's play.

In Lieu of a Conclusion

At the end of our discussion on the figure of Jesus appearing in the literary texts of 1970s and 1980s South Korea, one might raise the following question. Even though writers and poets in 1970s and 1980s South Korea found parallels between the biblical stories about Jesus and the situation in their society under dictatorship and drew on his image to comment on the social, political, and economic issues of the time, what is still relevant about it to contemporary South Korean society where electoral democracy has been in place since the 1990s? In other words, is Jesus as an emancipatory inspiration still relevant in South Korean society today?

In lieu of a conclusion, I would like to respond to the question by returning to Kim Chi Ha's play *The Gold-Crowned Jesus* and discussing it in relation to one of his best-known poems, "In Burning Thirst." As mentioned earlier, Jesus in the play cannot come here to bring peace, freedom, and justice to the world and save those who suffer because those in power do not allow him to do so. Karl Marx's critique of religion can help us articulate the political and social meaning of Jesus in the play. Often quoted in an unjustifiably truncated form as a crude criticism of religion, Marx's famous dictum actually exhibits his nuanced thought on the subject. It reads as follows. "Religious suffering is at the same time the expression of real suffering and a protest against real suffering. Religion is the sigh of the oppressed creature, the sentiment of a heartless world, and the soul of soulless conditions. It is the opium of the people."[31] Rather than simplistically reducing religion to a product of human consciousness in which man projects the best of himself onto the image of God or an ideology through which the ruling class justifies the status quo and keeps the ruled docile, Marx points out that people turn to religion because they cannot spell out real solutions to the problems of their world. Furthermore, he implies that religion expresses humanity's hope of liberating itself from its current suffering and its yearning for a better world. Thus, what is at issue for Marx is not harking back to the invalidity of religion but endeavoring to realize the emancipatory vision latent in religion and changing a world where humanity cannot but resort to religion. Kim Chi Ha's Jesus in this context can be said to express a yearning for what will enable peace, freedom, and justice to prevail in society against the political system that currently prevents the vision of a better society from coming true. The leper's call for Jesus's help is thus the yearning for the realization of that vision. If so, can we not call the leper's plea to Jesus the cry of the oppressed for democracy, a democracy that will ensure a more peaceful, free, and fair society? The poem "In Burning Thirst," which Kim published in 1975, helps us establish the connection between Jesus and democracy further. The first stanza reads as follows.

Before dawn in a back alley
I write your name, Democracy.

My thoughts long ago turned from you,
and long, long ago my steps turned away.
The single fragment remaining, memory
of my burning heart-thirst.
Where no one knows, Democracy,
I write your name.[32]

Reminiscent of the leper's frustration with Jesus's silence in the play, the narrator of the poem laments that he is losing the memory of democracy due to its long absence. Nevertheless, he longs for it and cannot give up on it, much like the leper whose protest to Jesus is a desperate gesture of holding on to his faith in the latter.

The connection between Jesus and democracy is crucial in thinking about the relevance of our discussion to South Korean society today. *Democracy* is a fuzzy term, the meaning of which cannot be confined to etymological or legalistic interpretations. What is for certain in the context of our discussion is that its meaning goes beyond the political system based on such principles as free elections, freedom of speech, the separation of powers, and so on. They are necessary but not sufficient conditions for democracy as longed for in Kim Chi Ha's poem, in which it refers to the spirit that leads society to peace, freedom, and justice.

What deserves our special attention in discussing the connection between Jesus and democracy in 1970s and 1980s literary texts is the weakness and impotence of democracy. Democracy is as fragile as Jesus in Kim Chi Ha's play. As Chong Sun Kim and Shelly Killen point out in their preface to the English translation of Kim's play, Kim Chi Ha shares the vision of God with Nikos Kazantzakis, who wrote, "It is not God who will save us—it is we who will save God, by battling, by creating, and by transmuting matter into spirit."[33] The same can be said of democracy.

Democracy as a political institution cannot save us from violence, oppression, or injustice. As is well known, democracy did not prevent the Nazi party from rising to power in interwar Germany. On the contrary, under the democratic constitution of the Weimar Republic, the Nazi party won the federal elections of 1932, and it paved the way for the total destruction of the country in the end. Has the United States, supposedly one of the most democratic nations in the world, not been also the most aggressive one, having been at constant war, if not the most belligerent one in recent history? Instead of passively believing that democracy will solve all the problems we face, we should save democracy so it can help us make our society more peaceful, free, and fair. Potentially powerful, democracy can do nothing without the help of the people. It is as weak and impotent as Jesus as portrayed in Kim's play.

Democracy is also tantalizingly incomplete.[34] There is always the unbridgeable gap between present democracy, which is never present in complete form, and complete democracy, which is always in the future tense, much like the Kingdom of God, which is to come but nobody knows when. Democracy is dependent on the people's engagement with constant and consistent efforts to keep it moving toward its future completion, much like the weak and impotent Jesus in the play who cannot do anything without the help of men who suffer. What if the play does not end depressingly pessimistic as Kim's original version or troublingly problematic as O's expanded version does, but closes with a blissfully utopian ending in which Jesus comes back in response to the leper's supplications to bring peace, freedom, and justice to the oppressed? The revision would not only ruin the poignancy of the play. Its implication is also antidemocratic. If we want God to solve our problems on behalf of us, which is unrealistic, why should we not go for the second-best thing, the authoritarian rule of a wise despot who astutely decides what is good for the nation's safety and welfare and can execute his decisions much more efficiently without being constrained by the people's involvement in governance?

Again, democracy will not save us. It is we who can save democracy by taking it closer and closer to perfection, although its completion can never be achieved. The only possible democracy lies in the constant efforts of the people. On that point, Kim Chŏng-hwan's Jesus as the universal spirit of love among those who suffer is especially suggestive. Although one may not entirely agree with his politics and his view of history manifested in the poems "The Story of Yellow Jesus," we still can see the relevance of his Jesus as the universal spirit to the survival of democracy. In the same manner as the Jesus who lives as spirit immanently in the lives of the oppressed, democracy should be constant movement that permeates the lives of the people. To keep democracy alive, that is, to keep it moving toward perfection, we should live in its spirit. Otherwise, it will be ossified like the gold-crowned Jesus, who is abused to legitimize those in power. It will be reduced to an empty and even pernicious ritual through which whoever gets the most votes in an election is legitimized to rule no matter how many shameless and treacherous tricks she or he has pulled to win.

NOTES

1. Kim U-ch'ang, *Kungp'iphan sidae ŭi siin* (Seoul: Minŭmsa, 1977), 126–47. An English translation of the essay was published in 1979, Uchang Kim, "Han Yong-un: The Poet in Time of Need," *Korea Journal* 12 (1979): 4–12.

2. Lucien Goldmann, *The Hidden God: A Study of Tragic Vision in the Pensées of Pascal and the Tragedies of Racine* (London: Routledge and Kegan Paul, 1964).

3. Needless to say, this goes against the grain of the well-known verse from the bible, "For the foolishness of God is wiser than human wisdom, and the weakness of God is stronger than human strength" (1 Cor. 1:25).

4. *The Gold-Crowned Jesus* has a complicated production history. Yi Tong-jin, a dramatist who was also a professional diplomat, wrote a first draft of the play on the basis of Kim Chi Ha's previous work *The Copper Yi Sun-sin* (1971) when his troupe decided to go on performance tours for the Korean Catholic Church. Ch'oe Chong-nyul, the stage director, revised Yi's draft during preproduction. Kim Chi Ha himself rendered the revised version and came up with the final version, which consists of three acts. The most popular version, however, has four acts, the last of which was added by O Chong-u when the play was staged at the Seoul Drama Center following the performance tours. Kim Sŏng-man, "Saeroun ch'ŏnji rŭl kidarimyŏ" [Waiting for a new world], annotation of *Ttongttakki Ttongttak*, by Kim Chi Ha (Seoul: Tonggwang Ch'ulp'ansa, 1991), 248–49.

5. Yi Mun-yŏl (Yi Mun-yol), *Saram ŭi adŭl* [The son of man] (Seoul: Minŭmsa, 1979). Yi expanded the novella into a full-length novel and published it in 1987. The expanded version was translated into English by Brother Anthony of Taizé. *Son of Man*, accessed December 24, 2014, http://hompi.sogang.ac.kr/anthony/SonofMan.htm. In this chapter, I use the 1979 edition.

6. The series of poems were originally published in the literary journal *Silch'ŏn Munhak* [Literature of praxis] in 1981. The previously published poems and one new poem entitled "Ipsŏng" [Entering the city] came out in book form under the tile of *Hwangsaek Yesujŏn* [The story of yellow Jesus] two years later. Kim Chŏng-hwan, *Hwangsaek Yesujŏn* (Seoul: Silch'ŏn Munhaksa, 1983). Kim went on to publish three more volumes of poetry under the same title as sequels, one in 1984 and two in 1986. According to the literary critic Ch'ae Kwangsŏk, who was in the same prison as the poet for political activism in 1975, Kim came up with an idea about the series of poems during his incarceration. Ch'ae Kwang-sŏk, "Kim Chŏng-hwan's Jesus," annotation of *Hwangsaek Yesujŏn*, by Kim Chŏng-hwan (Seoul: Silch'ŏn munhaksa, 1983), 1, 105–6.

7. Yi Nam-ho argues that *The Son of Man* concerns more the meaning of religion for society than theological issues of Christianity. I agree in principle with Yi's assessment. As discussed later in the chapter however, the story looks into the social and political meaning of religion by way of tackling the problem of God's absence in the immanent world of humanity. In that sense, Song Sang-il correctly frames the story as a literary endeavor to explore the issue of the absence of God. Yi Nam-ho, "Sin ŭi ŭnch'ong kwa in'gan ŭi chŏng'ŭi: Yi Mun-yŏl ŭi "Saram ŭi adŭl" [God's grace and man's justice: Yi Mun-yŏl's Son of Man], annotation of Yi Mun-yŏl, *Saram ŭi adŭl* (Seoul: Minŭmsa,

1979), 299–322; Song Sang-il, "Pujaehanŭn sin kwa sosŏl" [Absent god and literature], in Hanguk kidokkyo munhak yŏngu chŏngsŏ 2 [Collected papers on Christian literature in Korea 2], ed. Han Sŭng-ok and Cha Pong-jun (Seoul: Pangmunsa, 2010), 331–53.

8. Chi Ha Kim, The Gold-Crowned Jesus and Other Writings, ed. Chong Sun Kim and Shelly Killen (Maryknoll, NY: Orbis, 1978), 87.

9. Ibid.

10. Ibid., 91.

11. Ibid., 123.

12. Ibid., 131.

13. Cho Yŏng-nae, Chŏn T'ae-il p'yŏngjŏn [Biography of Chŏn T'ae-il] (Seoul: Tolbegae, 1991), 167–68, 220.

14. "Let the same mind be in you that was in Christ Jesus, who, though he was in the form of God, did not regard quality with God as something to be exploited, but emptied himself, taking the form of a slave, being born in human likeness, and being found in human form, he humbled himself and became obedient to the point of death—even death on a cross" (Phil. 2:5–8).

15. Probably to many of us living in this secular era, the hint of the death of God is nothing new or inspiring. Didn't Friedrich Nietzsche famously declare that God is dead in Gay Science (1882) and Thus Spoke Zarathustra (1883)? A much more detrimental blow to the conventional understanding of God as a transcendent being came from Georg Wilhelm Friedrich Hegel, however. Not only did Hegel write about the death of God before Nietzsche, but he also offered a much more radical view of Christianity, which hollows it out by detaching it from its conventional theism. For him Christianity is the true religion because its doctrine of the Incarnation and its understanding of God as the Holy Spirit implicitly hold the truth that absolute reason, which is metaphorized as God in Christian thought, is immanent as spirit in the world. G. W. F Hegel, Phenomenology of Spirit (Oxford: Oxford University Press, 1976), 454–55, 462, 475–76. Hegel's influence has been crucial in the development of a radical strain of modern political theology. Ernst Bloch, the German Hegelian Marxist thinker, went beyond Hegel's point of God's immanence in the world and read the narrative of liberation into the Bible. Ernst Bloch, Atheism in Christianity (London: Verso, 2009). Bloch's thought influenced Jürgen Moltmann, a major figure in modern theology, who emphasizes the importance of God's suffering with humanity. Moltmann's theology in turn has influenced liberation theology in Latin America. Hegel's influence is strongly felt also in the theological movement sensationally called the death of God theology. Thomas J. J. Altizer and William Hamilton, Radical Theology and the Death of God (Indianapolis: Bobbs-Merrill, 1966).

16. Yi Mun-yŏl, Saram ŭi adŭl, 97–98.

17. Matt. 4:1–11; Luke 4:1–13.

18. Yi Mun-yŏl, Saram ŭi adŭl, 107–14.

19. The influence on the novella of the grand inquisitor scene in The Brothers Karamazov has been noted by Yi Po-yŏng. Yi Po-yŏng, Hanguk sosŏl ŭi kanŭngsŏng [The possibility of Korean fiction] (Seoul: Chŏngyewŏn, 1998), 39.

20. Yi Mun-yŏl, Saram ŭi adŭl, 111.

242 | Cultures of Yusin

21. Ibid., 110.

22. Matt. 27:46; Mark 15:34.

23. In the dominant theological tradition, Jesus's cry of despair, as well as his suffering and death on the cross, does not disprove the omnipotence of God. Jesus, God incarnated in flesh for his love of humanity, suffers as man and embraces death to overcome it and resurrect. Through his sacrifice, men can be saved from their sins, and the reconciliation between God and man becomes possible. In that sense, Jesus is God's grace to transcend his aloofness from human suffering.

24. Yi Mun-yŏl, *Saram ŭi adŭl*, 146.

25. Kim Su-i, "1980-yŏndae si e nat'anan kidokkyo ŭi ŭimi wa t'eksŭt'ŭhwa yangsang" [The meaning of Christianity and its textualization in 1980s poetry], *Han'guk hyŏndae munhak yŏngu* [Studies in contemporary Korean literature] 24 (2008): 445–68.

26. Kim Chun-t'ae, "Ah, Kwangju yŏ urinara ŭi sipchaga yŏ" [Oh, Kwangju, the cross of our nation], *Chŏnnam maeil sinmun* [Chŏnnam daily], June 2, 1980, 1.

27. It should also be noted that Kim Chi Ha's writing, including *The Golden-Crowned Jesus*, had a significant impact on the development of *minjung* theology, the Korean political theology that emerged in the 1970s and 1980s in protest against growing political repression and economic inequality in South Korea. It is well known that Sŏ Nam-dong, one of the pioneering *minjung* theologians, developed his theology by reflecting on the ideas of *minjung* (multitude) and *han* (ressentiment) first articulated by Kim. The other crucial influence over the development of Sŏ's theology is the death of Chŏn T'ae-il. Sŏ Nam-dong, *Minjung sinhak ŭi t'amgu* [Investigation into *minjung* theology] (Seoul: Han'gilsa, 1983), 78–82. Chŏn's death also had a decisive impact on the thought of An Pyŏngmu, another pioneer of *minjung* theology. Kim Nam-il, *An Pyŏng-mu p'yŏngjŏn* [Biography of An Pyŏng-mu] (Seoul: Sagyejŏl, 2007), 30–31, 229.

28. Kim Chŏng-hwan, "T'ansaeng ŭi sŏ," *Silch'ŏn munhak* 2 (1981): 127–28.

29. The focus on suffering as the inseparable link between Jesus and men resonates with the increasing emphasis on a suffering God in modern theology. For a brief introduction to the idea of a suffering God in modern theology, see Richard Bauckham, ""Only the Suffering God Can Help": Divine Passibilityin Modern Theology," *Themelios* 9, no. 3 (1984): 6–12. One of the most prominent contemporary theologians who have worked on the theme of God's suffering" is Jürgen Moltmann, whose work was introduced to Korea in the 1970s. The Korean translation of his essay "The Crucified God," based on one of the chapters of his influential book with the same title, was published in a Korean theology journal in 1973. Jürgen Moltmann, "Sipchaga e chŏhyŏngdoen hanŭnim" [The crucified God], *Sinhak chŏnmang* [Theological View] 22 (1973): 141–54. The book was also translated and published in 1979. Jürgen Moltmann, *Sipchaga e chŏhyŏngdoen hanŭnim [The crucified God]* (Seoul: Han'guk Sinhak Yŏnguso, 1979). God's suffering was an important theme of *minjung* theology as well. For example, Sŏ Namdong highlights "Jesus's identification with the poor, the oppressed, the despised, and the sick" in his seminal essay "Yesu, kyohoesa, Han'guk kyohoe" [Jesus, church his-

tory, and the Korean church], *Kidokkyo sasang* [Christian thought] 201 (1975): 53–67. Slavoj Žižek, who has developed an atheistic understanding of Christianity, also has worked on the idea of a suffering God. In recent years, critical theory has shown increasing interest in religion. Special attention has been paid to Christianity as a source of inspiration that may lead us to envision a radical alternative both to the tyrannical circuit of commodity exchange increasingly intensified by the dominance of global capitalism and to the pernicious trap of political nihilism fanned by the obstinately unchanging status quo in society. Žižek is one of the leading figures in critical theory today who draw on Christianity to put forth their criticism of the entrenched system of global capitalism. For him Christianity is important because it helps explicate his materialist criticism of liberal democracy, global capitalism, and postmodern thought. He sees that liberal democracy is not only unable to prevent the detrimental effects of capitalism, which are even more strongly felt on a global scale than ever, but also constitutive of capitalism's mechanism of domination. For him postmodern thought also should be denounced for its denial of universal truths and its fetishization of alterity, which results in its failure as critical theory and its collusion with the status quo. Žižek is clear about his lack of interest in affirming Christianity as a religion and its transcendent divinity. For him Christianity is a discursive frame in which he can explicate his advocacy for radical changes in this immanent, material world. He finds Christ himself manifesting the atheistic aspect of Christianity. God became man and died. Christ's suffering and death on the cross bore witness to God's forsakenness. There is no transcendent God beyond this world. Following in Hegel's footsteps, he insists that the death of Christ shifted the focus of Christianity to the Holy Spirit, which resides in the community of believers bound by love. For him the death of Christ indisputably signals the absence of God or the big Other whom one should obey. Slavoj Žižek, "The Fear of Four Words: A Modest Plea for the Hegelian Reading of Christianity," in *The Monstrosity of Christ*, by Slavoj Žižek and John Milbank (Cambridge, MA: MIT Press, 2009), 24–109; Slavoj Žižek, "Dialectical Clarity versus the Misty Conceit of Paradox," in ibid., 234–306; Slavoj Žižek, "Christianity against the Sacred," in *God in Pain*, by Slavoj Žižek and Boris Gunjevic (New York: Seven Stories Press, 2012), 43–72; Slavoj Žižek, "Only a Suffering God Can Save Us," in ibid., 155–92.

30. Kim Chŏng-hwan, "Kot'ong ŭi usanghwa e taehayŏ," *Silch'ŏn munhak* 2 (April 1981): 138–39.

31. Karl Marx, "Contribution to the Critique of Hegel's Philosophy of Right: Introduction," in *The Marx-Engels Reader*, ed. Robert C. Tucker (New York: Norton, 1978), 54.

32. Kim Chi Ha, "In Burning Thirst," in *The Columbia Anthology of Modern Korean Poetry*, ed. David R. McCann (New York: Columbia University Press, 2004), 223–24.

33. Chong Sun Kim and Shelly Killen, "Preface," in *"The Gold-Crowned Jesus" and Other Writings*, by Kim Chi Ha (Maryknoll, NY: Orbis, 1978), xxii.

34. According to Jacques Derrida, democracy is self-destructive because of its opposite directions. For example, democracy depends on sovereignty to protect itself from

outside threats, but sovereignty sustains itself only by closing off the community of its base and thus tends to suffocate the openness of democracy. The same tension exists between equality and freedom, both of which democracy needs for its survival. Democracy cannot help but be incomplete, incapable of resolving the tensions and antimonies inherent in it. Thus, democracy is never fully present but is always to come. Jacques Derrida, *Rogues: Two Essays on Reason* (Stanford, CA: Stanford University Press, 2005).

Why Performance in Authoritarian Korea?

Joan Kee

Consider the black-and-white photographs taken of *Body Drawing 76–01.* It was a performance conceived and executed by Lee Kun-yong (Yi Kŏn-yong), one of the foremost early champions of performance art in Korea. (fig. 5) The work took place on the rooftop of the Seoul studio belonging to his friend Sung Neung-kyung (Sŏng Nŭng-gyŏng). Taken by Sung at Lee's specific direction, they show the order in which the performance took place. Against a nondescript background, a panel of plywood stands upright, steadied by two hands reaching over its top edge. The hand on the far left goes over the edge, apparently in the midst of repeatedly marking the panel with a permanent black marker. Diagonally oriented, the lines vary in length, the result of the maker not being able to see his handiwork from the front. Another photograph reveals the body to which the mysterious hands belong, the hands now attached to arms that wield a long saw. Standing next to a piece of thin plywood roughly the same height as himself, a bespectacled Asian man in his thirties saws the marked portion, calling attention not only to the material nature of the plywood but also to the manual labor involved in creating the work. The marked portions he saws are placed on the ground and then progressively stacked until the original plywood board is reconstructed as an accumulation of marked bands with what was once the uppermost band at the bottom.

The year is 1976, a profoundly difficult time for artists and audiences in Korea. It is almost four years since South Korean president Park Chung Hee declared martial law in the name of protecting the South Korean citizenry from the communist threat embodied by North Korea's very existence. Euphemistically framed as a "restoration," or in Korean "Yusin," this period of martial law lasted almost seven years, from October 1972 to Oc-

Figure 4. Lee Kun-yong, *Body Drawing 76–01*, 1976. (Courtesy of the artist. Photo by Sung Neung-kyung.)

tober 26, 1979, when Park was assassinated. In many respects, it was but a symbolic benchmark, the culmination of what since the 1960s had been the steady expansion of government power and the commensurate diminution of alternate forms of authority. Life in Yusin Korea was irrevocably marked by the radical suppression of civil rights, including the right of public assembly, by a tightly controlled state elite. At the same time, the South Korean economy—helped in large part by the United States and its need for material support during the Vietnam War—increasingly affected the general direction of national policy. The state was run by a technocracy whose "paramount concerns were effectiveness and performance" and whose policies were intended to mold individual behavior to better achieve the economic goals it set.[1]

Visual art was by no means exempt from this pursuit of efficacy and achievement. From approximately 1973, the national documentary paintings project, the Korean state's largest continuous visual arts project, which resulted in the production of hundreds of figurative oil paintings commemorating various scenes of military and historical glory, was expanded to include scenes of economic achievement.[2] The Kukjŏn, the juried National Art Salon annually held in Seoul since 1948, tended to include artworks that featured images of a rapidly industrializing Korea; this was particularly well demonstrated in the many photographs of factories, pipelines, and ships selected to represent Korean art. In January 1972 the government enacted the Cultural and Arts Promotion Law, yet another state directive aimed at helping "national culture flourish."[3] The law supported cultural preservation in the name of upholding Korean traditional culture but also established a central funding body, the Korean Culture and Arts Foundation.[4] However, artists working outside the recognized categories of western-style oil painting, ink painting, and sculpture received little government support. Many instead pooled their resources and formed unofficial support networks of their own. Largely self-funded, groups like the A.G. (Avant-Garde Group) and S.T. (Space and Time) held public exhibitions, which, like any form of public display or opportunity for public assembly in Yusin Korea, was subject to police surveillance.

These groups also attracted the notice of foreign audiences, a point not lost on a state eager to improve its perceived standing in a shifting world order. Certainly, one of the goals of the Cultural and Arts Promotion Law was to improve the quality of contemporary Korean art so that it could "hold" its "own in international cultural circles."[5] Thus it was not surprising that the state might look askance at artists like Lee Kun-yong yet still allow him to participate as a national delegate in what during the 1960s and 1970s was an extensive international network of biennials and triennials.

But these were confusing, and often dangerous, times for it was not always clear to artists what in fact was acceptable. Making work outside a recognized exhibition space could result in continued surveillance or even imprisonment, though not always. Park's instigation of new emergency decrees in the spring of 1975 so expanded the latitude of state power as to effectively make any kind of action grounds for severe punishment. The question of what could be done was more fraught than ever before, especially after the issuance of Emergency Decree No. 9, which banned any campaign against the Yusin system and permitted law enforcement authorities to arrest and detain people without warrants. In practice the decree gave the government and its agents carte blanche to prohibit almost any activity conducted in a public space without warning or justification. This was particularly well reflected in police and museum officials' attitudes toward performance; more than any other artistic medium, performance provoked the most incidents of direct state interference. In almost all cases, the state did not provide a reason as to why an exhibition was shuttered or an artist put under surveillance.

The absence of justification in a society purportedly based on the rule of certain laws reflected an arbitrariness that rendered nearly any action suspect. In such a context, performance, or art centered on the process of executing a particular action or task, gained particular significance. Its relevance was intensified by the spectacle of legal enforcement that was as much intended to render viewers complicit with state mandates as it was intended to deter viewers from reproducing the prohibited activity.

The first of what would be seven iterations on a theme, *Body Drawing 76–01* was intended to be performed live in front of an audience. Yet it was the photographs that assumed a special significance, especially given that they were often taken to mirror, or at least allude to, photographs taken specifically for newspapers. Although seeing an actual performance is profoundly different from experiencing it through one or even a brace of still photographs, it bears keeping in mind that Lee Kun-yong and his closest associates placed as much, if not more, emphasis on the photographs documenting their activities. As Walter Benjamin declared, "[T]he audience's identification with the actor is really an identification with the camera."[6]

Lee relied on those who recorded, edited, and pieced together fragments of his works into composite form because he recognized that his audiences interpreted civil society, politics, and class through the visual culture created by the camera and disseminated in newspapers and, to a lesser extent, television. The renowned drama critic Han Sang-chul (Han Sang-chŏl) might have been discussing performance artists when he emphasized the need to reveal "the extent to which that considered as truth are in fact fabricated lies."[7] Likewise, how particular kinds of media affected the documentation of performances was central to the subsequent effect and agency of each performance. Together with the actual plywood board Lee used, the photographs Sung took of *Body Drawing 76–01* were publicly exhibited at the Publishing Culture Center in Seoul.

Equally notable is how this comparison openly foregrounds the image of the single, physical body as the crucible for thinking about the possibilities of action in Yusin Korea. As vividly reflected by the restrictions imposed on skirt and hair length, the state obligated its citizens to conform to a set of arbitrary norms. This in turn meant the systematic denial of personal autonomy; one must submit under pain of punishment. Such denial, however, begged the question of what actions in fact were permitted, which many Korean performance artists answered by investigating the connection between the physical body (*sinch'e*) and self-consciousness via a recognition of what the body could or could not do. Performance art in Yusin Korea thus encompassed larger questions regarding the nature of artistic agency, a critical task for a time and place so politically complex as to throw into doubt the viability of outright protest or critique.

Happening, Event, Incident

The social import of performance art in Korea is vividly manifested by the Korean terms used to refer to such works. "*Pŏp'omŏnsŭ*," the romanized term for "performance," was not widely used until the 1980s. Instead, the earliest performances, which took place in the late 1960s, were often called "happenings," a term likely borrowed from the US artist Allan Kaprow, whom the Korean press described in 1968 as an artist who proposed "unifying visual art and theater in the context of an environment" and whose works stressed "the process of expression" over the "outcome of such expression."[8] Happenings in Korea were variably defined as "spontaneously occurring incidents," as "struggles to leave the world of art for the society around it," and as "scenarios taking place within a designated place in real time."[9] The most important early happenings took place in December 1967 at the *Young Artists' Coalition Exhibition* (*Chŏngnyŏn chakka yŏllipjŏn*). Members of the Zero Group (Mudongin) and the New Exhibition Club (Sinjŏndongin) presented *A Happening with a Vinyl Umbrella and a Candle*. Participants held a vinyl umbrella and candle while singing "Blue Bird" (Saeya saeya p'arangsaeya), a popular folk song that allegedly began as a nationalist rejoinder to Japanese imperial ambitions toward Korea in the late nineteenth century.[10] The umbrella was set aflame with the candle, then torn and destroyed. In his overview of performance art in Korea, Lee Kun-yong alleged that the umbrella symbolized the "umbrella" of US military protection while the "Blue Bird" anthem was sung to remind audiences of present threats to Korean political and cultural sovereignty.[11] Some critics described performances like these as direct responses to what in the late 1960s was an intense pragmatism motivated by the state's relentless push for a fully industrialized economy. In 1968 Yoo June-sang (Yu Chun-sang) described happenings, or "shows," as the mainstream press sometimes called performances, as attempts to escape the "pressures of mechanization and pragmatism."[12]

In the 1970s, the term *event* (*ibent'ŭ*) was increasingly used in lieu of *happening* to refer to performances. On one hand, the change in terminology was strategic: Lee implied that publicizing an exhibition in this way would increase the likelihood that the performances would be recorded.[13] His friend Lee Kang-so (Yi Kang-so) claimed that using "an ambiguous foreign loanword like *event*" was a default response to the marginalized place of performance art in the Korean art world.[14] The insinuation was that by using such a term performances could be seen explicitly in connection to an expanded international art world.

Art historian Kang Tae-hi (Kang T'ae-hŭi) has claimed that the term was imported from Japanese artists, including those involved in Fluxus, the international, multidisciplinary network of artists whose works frequently involved written scores indicating how and when certain actions would be performed.[15] Another possible source of the term was the Japanese artist Suga Kishio, whose own "events" involved commonplace materials such as rope, stone, and wood. They took place outdoors and were seen by the Korean artist Kim Ku-lim (Kim Ku-rim) in connection with Suga's solo exhibition *Fieldology* at Gallery 16 in Kyoto.[16] Shortly thereafter Kim mentioned Suga's events to his friend Lee Kun-yong, who in roughly August 1975 became the first Korean artist to consistently refer to his performances as events.[17] As with many Fluxus event scores, Lee emphasized the sequence of actions. Yet his written notations were not formal scores per se but sketches visualizing what the performance might look like, with several resembling crude animation or film storyboards. In choosing to replace *happening* with *event*, Lee claimed that the former was too literal to adequately account for what he regarded as fundamental to performance: how the idea of place affects the capacity of bodily movements to express meaning, that is, to become gestures.[18] Here he diverged from Suga, who defined events as "a rejection of the idea of performance as a phenomenon arising from the movement of people."[19]

In his overview of key developments in 1960s Korean art, the critic Oh Kwang-su (O Kwang-su) argued that "the initial meaning of happenings changed as the actions undertaken [by artists] started to [more directly] reflect distinct social issues."[20] When Lee Kun-yong began to refer to his performances as "incidents" (*sakkŏn*) it was not long after a procession of sudden, short-lived, and often unpremeditated acts and conflagrations seemed to define the passing of time itself.[21] As Sung Neung-kyung observed, information was circulated as an accumulation of reported incidents.[22] For the average citizen, daily life became measurable in terms of discrete incidents: the January 21 Incident, in which a group of North Korean commandos almost succeeded in assassinating Park Chung Hee at the Blue House, his official residence; the Pueblo Incident of January 23, 1968, in which North Koreans captured a US Navy spy ship; and, most infamous of all, the October 17 Incident of 1972, in which Park declared martial law. At the same time, the state increasingly relied on kidnappings, executions, and torture to perpetuate its authority.

Many performances closely resembled incidents in what appeared to be an intentional attempt on the part of their executors to merge art with general Korean society outside state-mandated channels. In October 1968, Kim Ku-lim, Chŏng Ch'an-sŭng, and Chung Kang-ja (Chŏng Kang-ja) staged *Murder on the Han River* on the riverbank near the Second Han River bridge (known since 1982 as the Yanghwa Bridge) near western Seoul (fig. 6). Two holes were dug and a single artist placed in each. Partly buried in the sand, the artists looked as if they were being prepared for a live sacrifice.[23] Framed in close-up images, the bodies appeared frail but strangely resilient. More pointed still was *Funeral for Established Culture and Art*, staged by the Fourth Group, a casual association of visual artists, a fashion designer, a scriptwriter, a journalist, and even a Buddhist monk.[24] This performance symbolically took place on August 15, the holiday commemorating the date of Korea's liberation from Japanese colonial occupation. The Fourth Group intended the performance to mark the date on which Korean culture, too, would be freed from what the group called "the wrongheaded system of the establishment."[25] Five members (Kim, Chŏng Ch'an-sŭng, Chung Kang-ja, Kang Kuk-jin, and Son Il-gwang) decided to stage a "funeral" that would begin in Sajik Park in downtown Seoul, not far from the US embassy and home to another statue commissioned by the state, this one of Sin Saimdang, the Chosŏn paragon of womanly virtue.[26] A coffin shrouded in the Korean flag was to be carried from the park along Seoul's most heavily trafficked avenue to Kwanghwamun, the main gate of the main royal residence and, incidentally, where *Street Campaign* was abruptly halted by police three years earlier.

The choice of sites was not a coincidence; as Kim Ku-lim recalled some years later, the group "tried to erase the gap between the arts and the public" by bringing their works directly to the audience outside the sanitized context of an institution controlled by the state.[27] Yet the actual performance suggested that such erasure meant folding the performed acts into the very fabric of daily life. The methodical pace of the tightly arranged procession (whose participants were evenly separated by a distance wide enough to deflect accusations of wrongful public assembly, then a serious crime under Park's increasingly wary regime) contrasted with the fast,

Figure 5. Kang-kuk-jin, Chŏng Ch'an-sŭng, and Jung Kangja in *Murder on the Han River*, 1968.

free-flowing swarms of people enjoying a rare day off from work. Police took note of this slowness and quickly stopped the procession. After failing to convince police that the performance was in fact art, the group's members were found guilty of obstructing traffic and violating street laws. Legally speaking, the transgression was minor. But the repercussions were significant and even excessive. Kim Ku-lim recalled being harassed and followed by a police detective for about six months, while the Korean Central Intelligence Agency allegedly raided his father's house, an act so disproportionate to the potential infringement as to register as a unilateral show of state power over a private citizen.[28] It highlights the state's pathological unwillingness to accept the sight of a rival spectacle, however small or temporary.

Eventually the group disbanded, though not without attempting a finale. Intended to take place at the state-run Information Center on August 22, 1970, the event was canceled, with a "no exhibition" sign attached to the entrance alongside a poster advertising what would have been an upcoming exhibition of Chung Kang-ja's works. According to the critic Yi Ku-yŏl, there was a sign affixed to the poster reading, "This show will not be held as planned due to the orders of the authorities. As an artist, I join the audience in lamenting this state of affairs. Chung Kang-ja." Yi then entered the exhibition space to find the members of the Fourth Group in a state of "silence." Yi Kwi-hwan, the government employee responsible for the Information Center gallery, told Yi Ku-yŏl that the exhibition had been prematurely closed, largely because the members of the Fourth Group were notorious "violators of social order." After hearing this explanation, Yi went back to the artists, who allegedly responded, "We have nowhere to stand."[29]

In 1977 Lee's younger colleague Chang Suk-wŏn described events as themselves dependent on incidents rather than accidents (*sago*).[30] The latter were spontaneous and uncontrollable occurrences whose participants did not form any meaningful relationships with each other. Incidents, on the other hand, were occurrences governed by a certain kind of logic able to transform bodily actions into gestures that could get viewers to physically interact, and hopefully to relate psychologically to one another. This process was most likely what Lee meant when he defined his notion of the event as "a phenomenon of critique toward present culture and society."[31] His works involving the repetition of basic physical actions often appeared calculated to induce audience members to copy the same movements, thus encouraging a "collapse of the division between art and life."[32]

For performance artists to quibble directly with this division was to court state scrutiny. National Museum of Contemporary Art officials condemned performances as "heretical," a word that directly alluded to a Korean artistic establishment firmly committed to endorsing certain kinds of art—particularly figurative painting and sculpture—as orthodox.[33] Sung Neung-kyung alleges that a day before the opening of *Three-Person Event* at the Press Center in Seoul in 1976, he and fellow participants Lee Kun-yong and Kim Yong-min received a call from detectives "nervous" about what the "event" entailed.[34] Hannah Arendt has argued that twentieth-century police states were in part places where the limits of "the real" and "the possible" were replaced with a fictional world.[35] Yusin Korea was still far from being the kind of totalitarian regime of which Arendt spoke, but the replacement she mentioned would have been apparent for Korean artists familiar with the national documentary paintings project, whose subjects of economic and military glory coincided with what Arendt called the "totalitarian fiction" of seeing as possible, according to its ideological scheme, even that which is impossible. Producing works that focused on the limits of what a single person could physically achieve ran directly counter to the impossible fictions so vigorously promoted by a Yusin state immersed in its own views of progress.

The Matter with Medium

The suspicion directed toward performance as a medium may have also been affected by how Korean critics previously understood the origins of performance. An article published in the widely read *Tonga ilbo* newspaper described performance art as a phenomenon that had originated in "New York, the center of materialist culture," and was characterized by attitudes of "antitraditionalism" and "anticivilization," exemplified by artists' "penchant for using the waste of urban culture as materials for their works."[36] The specific use of the term *antitraditionalism* may have triggered alarm bells in the minds of state officials charged with upholding the image of a grand and continuous Korean tradition; an artist could be modern or even nontraditional but not antitraditional.

At issue here was a larger question of authority, which for Korean performance artists was greatly affected by a Korean art world establishment heavily supported by the state. Composed almost entirely by male professors of oil or ink painting based at either Seoul National University or Hongik University, the deeply stratified art establishment not only controlled the selection of works to be shown in such prestigious venues as the Kukjŏn but also access to state, and even private, sources of funding. In terms of artistic production, the establishment favored painting, a preference reinforced by a centuries-old bias against sculpture, whose relatively low status vis-à-vis painting was enhanced by its association with menial labor. As seen by the works chosen for the Kukjŏn or the forms of depiction taught at the university level, many established artists favored gestural abstraction of the kind that had been popular in the late 1950s.

By the late 1960s, however, younger artists were deliberately producing works that did not readily conform to the expectations of what painting or sculpture should look like. Many of these artists were graduates of painting departments whose collective refusal to only produce the kind of painted images on flat upright supports endorsed by the Kukjŏn could be taken as a rejection of the artistic establishment. Reflecting the inability of the prevailing artistic infrastructure to accommodate this refusal, their works were classified under the rubric "experimental" (*silhŏm*). Many of these works were made under the auspices of the many small artists' groups that proliferated in the late 1960s and early 1970s, including the A.G., founded in December 1969, and the S.T.[37] Largely comprised of graduates of Hongik University, groups like these brought together a number of artists that took as their objective "the investigation and creation of a new plastic order" that would "contribute to the development of Korean artistic culture."[38]

In 1967 there was another performance called *Street Campaign*. Twenty members of the Zero and New Exhibition groups took to the

Figure 6. Protest of the Zero and New Exhibition groups, Seoul, 1967.

streets to protest what they regarded as the conservatism of the Korean artistic establishment (Fig. 7). After congregating in front of Seoul's city hall, the artists went to Sejongno, Chongno 2-ga, Samilno, and then finally to Sogongno, all major thoroughfares in downtown Seoul. Eventually the procession was halted by police, who detained some participants for questioning.[39] As a protest, the event was more of a publicity stunt aimed at bringing city residents out to see the show. "Please come, free admission!" the placards promised. There were others too: "Contemporary art is friends with the public" and "National development begins with active promotion of the arts." Among the few photographs taken of the event, one shows a placard that read "artists who act," a legend that singularly resonated at a time when the status of the artist seemed particularly compromised.

Why "act" and not "make"? The wording is peculiar, especially given how the critic Park Yong-sook (Pak Yŏng-suk) defined a particular cohort of avant-garde Korean artists interested in performance and other media besides painting and sculpture who were active in the late 1960s and early 1970s. The editor of *Space (Konggan)*, the cultural journal that from its founding in 1966 until the mid-1970s was the preeminent outlet for art writing in Korea, Park described these artists as a group forged by the shared rejection of an earlier avant-garde legacy based solely on reifying the objecthood of painting.[40] He was likely referring to the institutional ascent of gestural abstraction known as Korean Informel, which first appeared in the late 1950s and came to dominate the kinds of artworks chosen to represent Korea in a burgeoning circuit of international biennials and exchange exhibitions. Nearly every student enrolled in an oil-painting department in a Korean university between the late 1950s and the mid-1960s received classroom instruction in Informel-type painting. The artist Pak Yŏng-nam claimed that the young artists who participated in performances did so partly to reject the canvas and, by extension, preexisting notions of art's possible functions: "[I]nstead of producing only decorative works, they wanted their art to jump directly into the field of life."[41]

The turn to performance was also facilitated by the international ambitions of the Korean art world in general. The critic Bang Geun-taek (Pang Kŭn-t'aek) suggested that performance in Korea partly arose from the interest some artists professed in earthworks, and especially outdoor works that involved hole digging or other forms of physical labor whose execution required only the most rudimentary of skills.[42] Though never explicitly cited, the focus on the physical body as both material and a metaphor of the self echoed the convergence of body art and performance present in the works of well-known overseas performance artists such as Yoko Ono, Vito Acconci, and Carolee Schneemann. Nam June Paik (Paek Nam-jun) was a popular subject in the mainstream Korean press as the first artist of Korean descent to gain prominence in the international art world. Throughout the late 1960s short articles eagerly reported on the "nude concerts" he staged with longtime collaborator Charlotte Moorman, with at least one insinuating that these works were partly responsible for the sudden appearance of performance art in Korea in 1967.[43]

Most important of all was the keen interest professed by artists like Lee Kun-yong in the works of the celebrated painter Jackson Pollock. For Lee, Pollock's appeal lay in how his works appeared to underscore artistic creation as less about "realizing one's ideas" than about the enactment of "bodily movements."[44] A prolific critic whose essays represent some of the most important published work on early Korean performance art, Lee claimed that it was the proliferation of Informel-type gestural abstraction in late 1950s Korea that first underscored the importance of gestures in the Korean art world.[45] His interest strongly recalls the argument Kaprow made in his seminal 1958 essay "The Legacy of Jackson Pollock," especially when the latter describes Pollock as moving away from "the confines of the rectangular field" in favor of "an experience of a continuum going in all directions simultaneously, beyond the literal dimensions of any work."[46]

But escaping the canvas was not as much Lee's point of departure as it was the sensory immediacy of creating a work in real time experienced by a live audience. For Lee performances involved more than "composing spaces or producing objects"; they also meant rethinking "the structures through which the world came to be realized."[47] In addition, the focus on the body in Korean performance generally was prompted by markedly different circumstances than were perhaps responsible for this focus in the New York art world. The turn to the body read as a tacit response to a society apparently based on restricting what it is the body could do. Expanded state surveillance and propaganda exhorting citizens to put the nation before the self fatally compromised the idea of personal space or sovereignty. As life in Yusin Korea became even more repressive, artists like Lee Kun-yong, Sung Neung-kyung, and Lee Kang-so focused on what went largely unnoticed: habitual actions everyone performed on a daily basis. In particular, their performances are notable for the degree to which they made plain their control over both the circumstances under which they performed these actions and how they were eventually transmitted to an audience through either carefully staged photographs or real-time occurrences.

Drawing the Lines of Engagement

The issues of both medium and political oppression were vividly conjoined in the early performances of Lee Kun-yong. Born in 1942 in Sariwŏn, Hwanghae Province, in what is present-day North Korea, Lee was among the first generation of Korean artists to grow up without direct memories of a colonized Korea. While he too suffered from the devastation of the Korean War, which permanently separated him from his birthplace, Lee's formative years were defined by the political ascent of Park Chung Hee beginning in 1961. While attending Paejae High School in Seoul, he developed a keen interest in linguistics and philosophy through a class on logic; the writings of Ludwig Wittgenstein moved the young Lee to paint a large portrait of the philosopher.[48] In 1963 he enrolled in the western (oil) painting department at Hongik University where gestural abstraction was perhaps most quickly absorbed into its curriculum.[49] By the late 1960s, works characterized as "Korean Informel" were routinely sent to represent Korea in large-scale international visual art exhibitions and festivals. That these delegations were funded and sponsored by the Korean government implicitly gave gestural abstraction the imprimatur of an official art.

By the time he graduated in 1967, Lee was among those younger artists exhausted by the endless production of Informel-type paintings. He addressed his situation by organizing his own group, the S.T., which he founded in 1969 alongside his friend the critic Kim Bok-young (Kim Pok-yŏng). Known officially as Space and Time and active until 1981, the S.T. was keenly proactive in studying information about overseas artistic developments in regular seminars moderated by the critic Yu Kŭn-jun and topics selected by Kim.[50] Especially popular was Joseph Kosuth's "Art after Philosophy" which was translated and circulated after the second exhibition of the S.T. in June 1973, and Lee Ufan's (Yi U-hwan's) *Search for Encounter*, parts of which were translated by the critic Lee Yil (Yi Il) for the group's October 1970 meeting. Lee Kun-young found intriguing Lee Ufan's critique of a culture "excessively" focused on the act of "making," a statement that struck a chord with him and other Korean artists disillusioned with the state's mandate for industrial production.[51]

Exhibitions comprised a large part of the S.T.'s activities. Held in spaces rented from both private galleries and buildings owned directly by the state, the S.T. shows often featured performance. Four of the seven known versions of *Body Drawings* were shown or performed at the fifth S.T. show, *Objects and Events*, at the Press Center in Seoul in November 1976. S.T. members also showed at the annual Taegu Contemporary Art Festival, which hosted the debut of some of the most important performance-based works in Korea.[52] Held from 1974 to 1979 and organized by a revolving committee of artists with little interference from local or national authorities, it took place in the southeastern city of Taegu where state scrutiny was noticeably less intense than what took place in the capital.

Central for performance artists in Korea was the issue of communication (*sot'ong*) with a public that ideally consisted of both artists and nonartists.[53] The emphasis was a thinly veiled criticism of the state's idea of communication that some artists saw as little more than a cacophonous inventory of catchphrases and statistics. "Living in the Korea of that time, I had no idea what it meant to live in a postindustrial society," recalled Sung Neung-kyung.[54] State benchmarks like "a GNP [gross national product] over three thousand [US] dollars" had "absolutely no meaning [for me]."[55] So fraught was the matter of communication that the critic Park Yong-sook openly commented that "the [artistic] language for refusal and communication became one and the same."[56] Fear of possible reprisals may have stopped him from naming the object of this refusal, but the implications were clear; only a few months earlier the state had violently quashed a nascent movement to defend the freedom of the press.

For artists like Lee Kun-yong, who came to performance at the height of Yusin surveillance, action first meant recognizing how state regulation and vigilance set the boundaries of what actions were in fact possible. The arrest of the Fourth Group members clearly illustrated that direct intervention in the streets was not viable. Neither was it possible for artworks to inspire the kind of collective action that would effect political change. Yet the limitations placed on action were no excuse for shirking what many performance artists implicitly regarded as their personal responsibility to do *something*. In many cases, this entailed making their works as physically and psychologically accessible to the ordinary, nonelite individual as possible. Several performance artists made an explicit point of inviting viewers not affiliated with the art world. Even more important was how they turned to bodily actions that were distinctly unspectacular. In Lee's case, this meant actions that were minor, tangential, and not "necessary."[57] It is no coincidence that most performances undertaken between roughly 1972 and 1979 involved little more than the repetition of very basic actions: scratching, erasing, eating, breathing, drinking, and walking. Small wonder, then, that many Korean artists and critics began to increasingly describe performance art as "*haengwi yesul*," literally "gesture art." Sung Neung-kyung observed that the repetition of a single gesture made it possible to "acknowledge gestures as gestures," which in turn permitted viewers to grasp a situation on their own without external interference, an important condition that had particular resonance in an age when personal autonomy was in short supply.[58]

Concurrently, these were actions ordinary viewers could easily follow and duplicate. Many performances were in fact documented in ways that encouraged viewers to reacquaint themselves with their own bodies. The intentionally sequential photographs of *Body Drawing 76–01* read, for example, like a step-by-step manual on how to reproduce the actions at home. These actions were about legitimating what ordinary individuals could do in marked contrast to the state, which constantly propagated impossible ideals that its citizens could never achieve even as a nation. In *Body Drawing 76–05*, which he undertook in the same group exhibition where he exhibited photographs of *Body Drawing 76–01*, Lee stands with his feet just far enough apart to admit a plywood panel onto which a paper sheet is attached (fig. 8). Propping himself up by placing his left hand on his left leg, he holds a piece of charcoal in his right hand, using it to draw lines on the paper from top to bottom. He begins by drawing a straight line that bisects the paper and then repeats the action until he reaches the

Figure 7. Lee Kun-yong, *Body Drawing 76–05*, 1976. (Courtesy of the artist. Photo by Sung Neung-kyung.)

side. As if uncertain of his own abilities or as if in defiant response to an invisible naysayer, Lee shouts "I will draw straight lines!" in an increasingly louder voice as the performance continues. But as the artist's hand moves closer to the edges of the paper, it is difficult to both keep his balance and draw straight lines. Contrary to the steadiness of the first line, those at the edges are deeply curved and most likely drawn at a much slower pace. At this point, Lee changes his phrasing to declare "I am drawing upright lines!"

In 1976, the year immediately following the Yusin state's suspension of numerous civil liberties, the issue of action was steeped in profound doubt. After performing *Body Drawing 76–05*, Lee was accosted by two government agents who took issue with the artist's change of language from "straight lines" (*chiksŏn*) to "upright" ones (*kodŭn sŏn*). "What does 'upright lines' mean?" they asked.[59] While the agents may have felt ill at ease with what "upright" might suggest in connection to a state apparently bent on suppressing even basic individual freedoms, for Lee the *Body*

Drawings series posed a broader question as to the scope of possibilities. Was it still possible to undertake even the most basic physical acts? Outright protest was futile, not because it would be short-lived or subject to punishment but because it would too easily play into an authoritarian culture that revolved around a polarizing, us-versus-them logic. More productive instead was to reinstill faith in the possibility of doing.

Consider *Body Drawing 76–05* through *On Certainty*, the collection of notes Wittgenstein wrote just prior to his death in 1951. Written in response to George Edward Moore's argument on behalf of common sense, *On Certainty* refuses the idea of self-evident axiomatic truths, a refusal that Lee and his colleagues would have found sympathetic. Their performance of actions so basic and ordinary as to be mimicked by almost anyone was undertaken in order to establish a deeper connection with an audience, not necessarily because such performances were "intrinsically obvious or convincing" (as Wittgenstein might say), but because audiences living under the restrictions of Yusin Korea would have recognized them as being among the few actions not subject to scrutiny or punishment.[60]

Or were they? One might believe that one could stand, stretch, or eat freely. But how strong could this belief be in a time and place where it was never certain what in fact was permitted. Lee remembers being accosted after performing *Body Drawing 76–05* by two government agents and asking them if it was a "crime" to "draw a straight line."[61] He and colleagues like Sung Neung-kyung performed such acts in order to confirm for themselves that they could, the possible consequences notwithstanding. That each performance is broken down into multiple photographs each showing a discrete act affirms the importance of experience. To borrow again from Wittgenstein, it was not enough to say "I know"; more crucial was to acknowledge one's experiences of a thing rather than accepting the claims made by human authority.[62] The significance of beliefs are embedded in one's lived experience in the world of people and things, a conviction performance artists in Yusin Korea seemed to share.

In an important essay published in the 1976 issue of *Tongdŏk misul*, the critic Park Yong-sook claimed that, while "events are comprised of basic actions, it does not follow that the continuous enactment of these actions must necessarily amount to a specific meaning or purpose."[63] This meant rejecting the purpose to which artworks had ordinarily been put, namely, the idea that artworks should represent something other than their constituent materials.[64] In Yusin Korea, where time was measured in five-year plans, quarterly gains, annual benchmarks, and other goal-oriented mark-

262 | Cultures of Yusin

ers, the distinct absence of purpose was significant. It was not exactly resistance, but it nevertheless offered a space within which to think about visual art beyond questions of practical function, progress, and use.

Lee Kun-yong condemned the iteration of explicit purpose as a form of narcissism.[65] He spoke harshly of what he described as the pointlessness of artists who deluded themselves into thinking that their works somehow addressed a phenomenon other than the artwork, declaring that an artwork addressing politics was really just a disingenuous means of blatant self-promotion.[66] What was possible was simply the rejection of meaning altogether in order to, in effect, emphasize "how" over "what."

On this point, the nonindexicality of his marks in the *Body Drawing* series is telling. His scribbles are hardly the result of technique; in fact, technique was the enemy, hence the deliberate shift from painting to drawing, a medium distinguished by its connotations of marginality. Drawing was never given the dignity of autonomy, particularly in Korea where it was long regarded as a preliminary step en route to the creation of a painting. Lee's interest in drawing can be seen as a refusal of this hierarchy and its implications: "I began drawing because of my fundamental suspicion concerning the history of art and its meaning," he wrote.[67] In his report of a group discussion held on the occasion of the fourth S.T. show in 1975, Park Yong-sook alleged that much of what passed for avant-garde art was in fact merely trying to confirm such a presence, by which he meant that the artists' agendas too narrowly revolved around the rejection of painting.[68] He stated that artists like Kim Ku-lim and Lee Kun-yong differed from their painting-obsessed colleagues by focusing on mark making rather than picturing.[69] Marks enacted in the course of painting were done to form a picture, a definition that anticipated the way fellow critic Oh Kwangsu defined "happenings" as an "escape from the trap set by the demands of the pictorial surface."[70]

For the fourth A.G. show in December 1975, and later for *Three-Person Event* in 1976, Lee performed *Logic of Place*. Before actually performing the work, he had a series of documentary photographs taken of himself executing it in stages. The first shows Lee drawing a circle on the ground using a long nail (fig. 9). The next shows him standing and pointing to the circle; during the actual performance he uttered the word "there" (*kŏgi*). He then entered the circle, shouting "here" (*yŏgi*). He next stepped outside the circle and pointed over his shoulder in the direction of the circle, uttering "over there" (*chŏgi*). Returning to the circle, he said "here," "there," and "over there." Finally he walked around the circle shouting "where" three times in succession, then disappeared.[71]

Figure 8. Lee Kun-yong, *Logic of Place*, 1975. (Courtesy of the artist.)

Photographs of the performance taken by Yi Wan-ho indicate several points from which we might access this work, the first of which is movement. The soft dirt of the Hongik University schoolyard yields obligingly to the combination of pressure and wood, the resulting incision in the sandy field appearing as indelible as a line engraved in stone. The permanence of the mark resonates against the words of members of the Fourth Group at their last exhibition: "We have nowhere to stand." The work concerns itself with how actions depend on their mediatization. In the photographs documenting *Logic of Place*, we see Lee from a distance and from the side. He points at the ground, which suddenly takes on a prominence not seen in most works. It is almost as if Lee is trying to compensate for the dispossessed members of the Fourth Group who had "nowhere to stand"; here Lee stands insistently and continuously.

The literalism of the performance was cousin to the tautologies of Joseph Kosuth, whose writings Lee and his S.T. colleagues encountered in

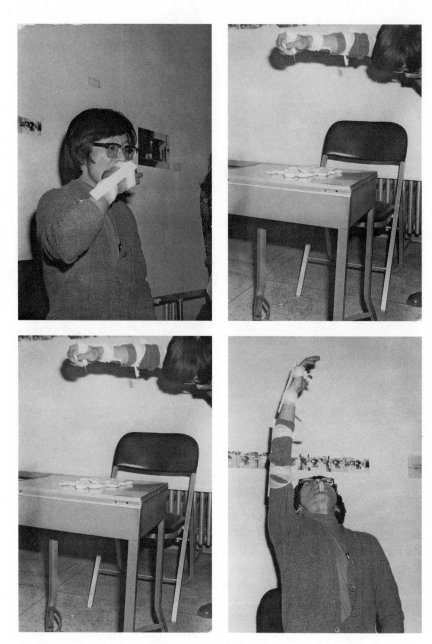

Figure 9. Lee Kun-yong, *Eating Hardtack*, 1975. (Courtesy of the artist.)

translation. But the marking, pointing, walking, and reciting in this and other Lee performances were intended to affirm what in fact was true: Yusin Korea "was a society of lies. Trying to figure out what in fact was true became the most important priority."[72] For him and his closest interlocutors, this meant getting viewers to think about what it was they were actually seeing. Lee recalled that during an actual performance audiences persisted in staring at the drawn circle, even after he disappeared from the scene. But the artist states that in repeating "where" his aim was "to question the idea of place."[73] So doing required making a connection between the viewer and the world in which he or she lived, a connection reified by the gesture—the pointing figure.

Lee himself described his performances as that which "happens when useless activity is pushed to its limit."[74] In many instances, it meant stripping any practical use from otherwise necessary actions. He performed *Eating Hardtack* on the evening of October 6, 1975, in a small gallery at the National Museum of Contemporary Art (fig. 10). Photographs show the artist eating a kind of hardtack (*kŏnppang*) that was a cheap and readily available snack food especially common in the Korean armed services. Pieces of hardtack were scattered on a plain wooden desktop. As the performance continued, he had an assistant wrap his right palm and wrist in bandagelike white gauze as if injured. Tied to Lee's hand, and later his arm, were thin, flat pieces of wood that acted like splints. They diminished his flexibility, therefore making extraordinarily difficult the otherwise simple act of picking up a small biscuit and eating it. As the performance progressed, the number of times Lee failed to put a biscuit in his mouth outnumbered his successes. Toward the conclusion of the performance, Lee had his upper arm wrapped so that he eventually surrendered all flexibility. In order to pick up a biscuit, he had to rise from his chair and bend his torso at the waist as if making a deep bow. He finally ate the hardtack by raising his arm, then dropping the biscuit in his mouth.

The effort seems disproportionate to the reward, an allegory for the increasing number of encumbrances that, circa 1975, conspired to make even the most basic and necessary actions required for everyday existence in Yusin Korea seem impossible. With his various limbs and body parts wrapped, Lee's movements were reduced to a series of attenuated gestures. What the audience thus saw was not Lee eating but Lee reproducing the act of eating.[75] The focus was on the action. After viewing the photographs of the performance that remain, one might also add that it was making visible the effort that went into an activity so common as to be nearly invisible. That Lee's hand, wrist, forearm, and even armpit were wrapped as if injured suggested that the act itself was painful.[76] So palpable was this impression that it blurred the divide between how Korean viewers might have otherwise separated art from life, thereby making it more likely that intentionally artistic gestures could have an actual social and even political impact.

Action Figures

Perhaps the most provocative challenge to the ostensible separation of art and life was *Bar in a Gallery*, a performance organized and conceived by Lee Kang-so in 1973 (fig. 11). Originally called *Extinction (Somyŏl)*, it took place for almost a week in June of that year at the Myŏngdong Gallery in Anguk-dong, Seoul.[77] The gallery's owner, Kim Mun-ho, was an early champion of experimental art, often inviting artists to show at his gallery without charge.[78] In a fairly large but indifferently lit space of about twenty-five p'yŏng (approximately eighty-three square meters), seven to eight wooden tables with accompanying stools are placed as they would be in a restaurant. Purchased from a small restaurant selling octopus in Mugyo-dong in downtown Seoul and placed directly on the ground, they came with signs that exactly resembled the signage of ordinary restaurants at that time. Brass kettles filled with *makkŏlli*, the treacherously delicious native Korean rice wine, sit on tabletops alongside dishes filled with typical bar snacks like dried squid, their contents waiting to be emptied. Labels advertising common dishes like stir-fried squid and clam soup are visible in the immediate foreground and the background. To the critic Kim Su-hyun (Kim Su-hyŏn), the furniture looked like so many "ready-mades."[79] Against the gallery's white walls, the tables and stools register less as functional objects than they do as freestanding dark wooden objects. Seen entirely in isolation surrounded by generous white space, a small rectangular sign almost commands the same kind of attention from the viewer as a painting might. The physical placement of the furniture and signs muddle the boundaries that ordinarily would separate such objects from their counterparts grouped under the headings "sculpture" or "painting."

The scene changed when viewers entered the gallery. Some were students; most were adult men in casual and business dress who sat on the stools. Many participants were artists personally acquainted with Lee. None were performers, and all appeared to chat freely. Were it not for the blank walls only occasionally enlivened by an incongruously small sign,

Figure 10. Lee Kang-so, *Bar in a Gallery*, 1973. (Courtesy of the artist.)

the scene would pass for any other casual lunch in downtown Seoul. Having viewers participate in performances was not without precedent; in 1968 Chung Kang-ja invited audience members to attach balloons to her body.[80] Yet *Bar in a Gallery* was the first performance to make audience participation absolutely central to its execution. On seeing the work, the dramaturge Oh Tae-suk (O T'ae-sŏk) declared theater "dead," a proclamation that acknowledged the dissolution of boundaries on which the idea of the medium had for so long depended.[81] Featuring a stage transformed into a bar and television studio, Oh's own groundbreaking play *May, 1980* seemed to regard *Bar in a Gallery* as a kind of permission to think about life through the lens of art.

If the performance was enacted to encourage viewers to think more specifically about life in Yusin Korea, *Bar in a Gallery* was perhaps most effective in bringing to the fore the ambiguities inherent in the relationship between performance and social class. Generally speaking, performance-based artworks were practically defined by their ability to draw large crowds, even to the point of obstructing nearby traffic.[82] The sheer volume of attendees alone was a distinctly subversive gesture in light of increasing state restrictions on any form of collective gathering. Free will was important; artists considered it a point of pride to have "repeat customers" who willingly returned to see their works.[83] Such assemblies were highly diverse in terms of age and occupation, and many audience members had no previous exposure to visual art, let alone performance.

Bar in a Gallery was no different. Although it took place for only a week, it drew a remarkably diverse audience in terms of occupation and age. A request for voluntary monetary contributions was posted near the gallery entrance to ostensibly cover the cost of the wine and snacks, which Lee replenished daily, but the work was in fact free for all.[84] Some viewers, however, were "befuddled" by the situation and left without participating.[85] Lee recalled, for instance, that some students visiting the gallery "ran away, so [the critic] Yoo June-sang wrote a sign proclaiming that "this work is process art, thus viewers are meant to participate [in it]."[86] The reluctance or confusion some viewers expressed toward Lee's pub reflected unseen divisions within what might otherwise be taken for granted as "the people" or "the public."

Lee stated that the idea for the work came from a meeting with an older friend at a *makkŏlli* tavern in his hometown of Taegu.

> The traces of cigarette butts, dishes, and cups on the tabletops made me almost feel the noise of the patrons who were there before me. I bought one of the chairs [from the tavern] and placed it in my studio. Then I bought all the chairs and tables and placed them in the studio, as well a large earthenware jar [a *changdok*, made for storing fermented foods like soy or kim-chi].[87]

Lee Kun-yong described the tables and chairs as having all but "faded from the present era . . . [so] the tables and chairs register as so much folklore."[88] Lee Kang-so himself commented that *Bar in a Gallery* was a gesture of recuperation: "[T]he [original] reason for calling it 'extinction' was because everything in the world disappears . . . [W]hen you have one drink, time evaporates so quickly . . . [and] every idea and life changes moment by moment, appearing and disappearing."[89] The kinds of chairs and tables used, as well as their configuration, recalls the *chumak*, the traditional pub-cum-inn that since the Koryŏ dynasty has served as one of the few genuinely public places open to all regardless of class. Lee actually used tables and chairs made from wooden boxes originally used by the US military, the kind that would have been found in a *chumak* during the years immediately following the Korean War.

Such furnishings, however, were anything but nostalgic. Even when seen in low-resolution black-and-white photographs, there is something concretely immediate about the textures, sounds, and look of the materials used. The wood from which the chairs are made is too rough, the dishes offered too common, the signs too crudely painted to belong to the small group of self-styled "restaurants" in 1970s Seoul. All belonged to humbler establishments serving a predominantly working-class clientele, one whose habits were distinctly at odds with the kind of haute bourgeois life widely promoted in lifestyle magazines.

But no matter how closely the work resembled a working-class pub, its contextualization in the four white walls of a gallery initially alienated some individuals for whom the idea of art may have been too closely entwined with the continued existence of a bourgeois elite. Visual art had long been allied to a particular class of urban sophisticates who often funded their activities through inherited wealth. The idea of art as being in part defined by its transcendence of the everyday was borne out by several artists. Performances could rely on everyday objects but could not become equivalent to them; as Lee Kun-yong wrote, "I am not interested in bringing art to the level of the everyday."[90] Indeed, despite their almost categorical exclusion from mainstream histories of art at that time, Korean artists involved with performance during the 1970s were among the most privileged of all cultural workers. Not only were they trained as visual artists, an education requiring a considerable amount of knowledge and social capital in a time when very few had such, but performance artists relied on photography to make their works known to a larger audience. Even in 1973, cameras were still relatively expensive, as was developing film.

Performance artists were themselves ambivalent about the role of class in their works. More than any other group of artists, they proactively sought to attract viewers from all walks of life but especially from the newly emergent middle class. "The absorption of contemporary Korean art depends on increased interest from the ranks of the middle class," argued Lee Kun-yong.[91] Yet early definitions of *performance art* in Korea vis-à-vis terms like *event* were inflected by a deep skepticism about the pragmatic aspirations of the middle class. One recalls, for instance, Chang Suk-wŏn invoking Harold Rosenberg's theories of the avant-garde in his essay on performances. Although he never mentioned Rosenberg's contempt for the middle class as the enemy of the avant-garde, Chang still harbored a strong intention to distinguish performance artists from what he saw as the bourgeois mind-set of other visual artists set on imposing their worldviews on a passive audience.[92]

More than any other group of artists, performance artists recognized that they were no better than their viewers. The idea of the artist as a celebrity or a heroic figure never took root in Korea as it did to varying degrees in North America, Western Europe, and possibly Japan.[93] In the mid-1970s, several magazines featured profiles that focused less on the artists' work than on their living arrangements: images of spacious studios filled with brushes and antique furniture were ready advertisements for the new aspirational—and largely inaccessible—culture of affluence such magazines tried to sell. Despite their privileged backgrounds, performance artists never featured in any of these layouts. Instead they channeled their energy into performances consisting of daily activities that most people could and did do, a project with tremendous political implications in a time and place when the state was constantly exhorting its citizens to be better than they ever could be. That performances were about audiences watching individuals undertaking even the most mundane activities also resonated especially with viewers accustomed to having their own quotidian routines monitored by various agents of the state. The sympathy inherent in these actions may explain why performances attracted larger and far more diverse audiences than the art of their peers working in other media.

Yet action seemed to go only so far, something that the Esprit Group seemed to understand in its own deliberate performances of stillness. Here the point was not a lack of action but the intentional choice to refrain from physical movement, or what might be described as conscious inaction. In lieu of a definite closing, let us turn to *Relay Life*, another work by

Figure 11. Lee Kun-yong, *Relay Life*, 1979. (Courtesy of the artist.)

Lee Kun-yong. It made its debut at the São Paulo Bienal, but its most compelling enactment may have been at the 1979 Taegu Contemporary Art Festival. It belonged to a group of performances that were held outside. Before us is the last stage of the performance, where Lee lies prostrate on sandy ground (fig. 12). Facedown, the full length of his body is visible only in profile. As our eyes adjust to the image, we notice a motley string of objects that appears to trail behind the man. Shirt, pants, belt, shoes, wallet, watch, and what looks like some bills and coins are all strung behind the body. It was a surrender of belongings, or, more broadly, worldly possessions, almost like a self-inflicted strip search: the work "comes from the idea that a single individual's life can be represented by his or her most everyday accessories."[94]

Relay Life illustrated what Lee's good friend Kim Bok-young described in 1979 as the hallmark of the event: the performers did not so much engage in a process of creation as they did in a process of arrival.[95] The performance began with the artist systematically and deliberately laying his belongings on the ground. Eventually Lee drops to the ground and lies still. No longer able to remain upright, he is utterly spent. The last image encapsulates Lee's earlier ideas about the necessity of the unnecessary gesture by proposing inaction as the most eloquent action of all.

The aesthetics of inaction proposed in *Relay Life* reflected what at the end of 1979 was a paralyzing impasse. For it was then that the Yusin era literally ended with a bang following the October assassination of Park Chung Hee. Lee's prostrate form reflects the toll of what had been a long winter of authoritarian rule. But unlike the spent bodies of the Esprit Group, Lee appears to be still breathing. Somewhere between taut and slack, his wiry body looks as if it might yet rise. The supine form we see was therefore not about finality or reaching conclusions; the accumulated violations of basic freedoms throughout the Yusin era made psychological closure impossible. Any pretense of objectivity was likewise doomed. But it was still possible to invoke the complex relationship between matter and action. For Lee and his comrades in performance, realizing this possibility was the only means of breathing in a time measured only by an infinite number of obligations and denials.

NOTES

Research for this article was supported by an Academy of Korean Studies (KSPS) grant funded by the Korean government (Ministry of Education) (AKS-2011-BAA-2102) and the Center for World Performance Studies at the University of Michigan. My thanks to Um Yoona for research assistance.

1. Hyug Baeg Im, "The Origins of the Yusin Regime: Machiavelli Unveiled," in *The Park Chung Hee Era*, ed. Byung-Kook Kim and Ezra F. Vogel, (Cambridge, MA: Harvard University Press, 2013), 234.

2. For a description of the national documentary paintings project and a discussion

of one of the works commissioned under this new emphasis on economic development, see Joan Kee, *Contemporary Korean Art: Tansaekhwa and the Urgency of Method* (Minneapolis: University of Minnesota Press, 2013), 213–20.

3. Article 1, Cultural and Arts Promotion Law, 1972.

4. For an overview of foundation activities, including annual amounts disbursed to support contemporary art, see Ko Ch'ung-hwan, "Han'guk misul 30 nyŏnsa munye chinhŭngwŏn misul kwallyŏn chiwŏn saŏp hyŏnhwangŭl chungsimŭro" [On thirty years of Korean art and the funding activities of the Korea Culture and Arts Foundation], *Munhwa yesul* (August 2003): 122–35.

5. Yersu Kim, "Cultural Policy in the Republic of Korea," *Studies and Documents on Cultural Policies* 38 (Paris: Unesco, 1976), 38.

6. Walter Benjamin, "The Work of Art in the Age of Mechanical Reproduction," in *Illuminations* (New York: Schocken Books, 1969), 228.

7. Han Sang-chŏl, "Ch'ohyŏnsiljuŭi ŭi yŏnŭksŏng" [The theatricality of surrealism], *Space* 156 (June 1980): 86.

8. "Kŭk ŭl kŏnnŭn chŏnwi misul: Sŏul ŭi h'ap'ŭning syo" [Avant-garde art toes the extremes: The happening shows of Seoul], *Chung'ang ilbo*, June 1, 1968.

9. Ibid. Also see "Haep'ŭning Han'guk sangnyuk" [Happenings arrive in Korea], *Sŏul sinmun*, May 9, 1968.

10. The lyrics of "Blue Bird" ask the titular bird "not to sit on the mung bean fields." "General Mung Bean" was a popular nickname for Chŏn Pong-jun (1854–95), a prominent leader of the Tonghak Peasant Revolution especially notable for being antiwestern and anti-Japanese. "Blue bird" referred to Japanese imperial troops whose uniforms were blue. The song became popular in the late 1970s among anti-Yusin demonstrators. Namhee Lee, *The Making of Minjung: Democracy and the Politics of Representation in South Korea* (Ithaca, NY: Cornell University Press, 2007), 58–59.

11. Yi Kŏn-yong (Lee Kun-yong), "Han'guk haengwi misul ŭi chŏn'gae wa kŭ chubyŏn" [The development of Korean performance art and its environment], *Misul segye* (September 1989): 49.

12. Quoted in "Kŭgŭl kŏnnŭn chŏnwi misul."

13. Yi Kŏn-yong, "Hangsang t'umyŏnghayŏra" [Always be transparent], *Space* (November 1977): 102.

14. Yi Kang-so (Lee Kang-so), "Naeirŭl mosaekhanŭn chakkadŭl" [Artists in pursuit of the future], *Space* (September 1979): 72.

15. Kang T'ae-hŭi (Kang Tae-hi), "1970-yŏndae ŭi haengwi misul ibent'ŭ: ST membŏ ŭi chakp'um ŭl chungsim ŭro," [Performance art events of the 1970s: On the works of the S.T.], *Hyŏndae misulsa yŏngu* 13 (December 2001): 10–11.

16. Ibid., 30.

17. Ibid., 31.

18. Yi Kŏn-yong, "Han'guk haengwi misul ŭi chŏn'gae wa kŭ chubyŏn," 48.

19. Quoted in Andrew Maerkle, "Kishio Suga: Between Potentiality and Fatality," Art iT accessed March 31, 2015, http://www.art-it.asia/u/admin_ed_feature_e/JB4M7fyAn HIN62SsFzUt/

274 | Cultures of Yusin

20. O Kwang-su (Oh Kwang-su), "60-yŏndae ŭi hyŏndae misul" [Contemporary art of the 1960s], Han'guk hyŏndae misul chŏnjip [Complete works of contemporary Korean art], vol. 20 (Seoul: Han'guk Ilbosa, 1979), 104.

21. Yi Kŏn-yong, "Chŏnwi misul 11 in ŭi yŏlgi" [The passion of eleven avant-garde artists], Kyegan misul 17 (Spring 1981): 76.

22. Sŏng Nŭng-gyŏng (Sung Neung-kyung), interview with Yi Tan-a and Kim Yun-sŏ, 22 myŏng ŭi yesulga, sidae wa sot'onghada: 1970-yŏndae ihu han'guk hyŏndae misul ŭi chahwasang, [Twenty-two artists in conversation with their times: A self-portrait of post-1970s contemporary Korean art], ed. Chŏng Yŏng-baek (Chung Young Baek) (Seoul: KungRee, 2010), 127.

23. The interest in death was especially notable in Practicing Death (1976), performed by Kwŏn Chŏl-in. Two assistants laid the artist on a stage, then took off his clothes, placed him in a coffin, and nailed it shut. The event was accompanied by a ten-day-long perpetual recording of news and weather reports.

24. The members as of summer 1970 were Kim Ku-lim, Chŏng Ch'an-sŭng, Pang Ka-ji, Chŏng Kang-ja, Kang Kuk-jin, Ch'oe Pong-hyŏn, fashion designer Son Il-gwang, journalist Yi Cha-gyŏng, scriptwriter Kim Chung-ong, and the monk Sŏgyajŏng. "Che 4 chiptan kyuyak" [The Fourth Group's regulations], typed unpublished manuscript. Yi Ku-yŏl Collection, Archives of Korean Art, 4–8. The group issued a set of "Regulations," which mimicked the format of the state's constitution. Like the constitution, the "Regulations" were divided into articles and paragraphs and made provision for national committees, upper committees, middle committees, and lower committees. "Che 4 chipdan sŏnŏnsik," [The Fourth Group's declaration ceremony], typed unpublished manuscript, Yi Ku-yŏl Collection, Archives of Korean Art, 11.

25. A detailed description of the performance, complete with alleged quotes from the artists, was published in the weekend magazine of the state-funded newspaper Seoul Sinmun (Sunday Seoul). "Kwanmego yesul hani kyŏnggwan utkijima" [Police don't buy art involving a coffin], Sŏndei Sŏul, August 26 1970, 12–13.

26. The commission was completed by Choi Man-rin, a professor at Seoul National University.

27. Kim Ku-rim (Kim Ku-lim), in conversation with O Kwang-su (Oh Kwang-su), in O, "60-yŏndae ŭi hyŏndae misul," 106.

28. Kim Ku-rim (Kim Ku-lim), interview with Yi Yŏng-chŏl (Lee Young Chul), Tangsin ŭn na ŭi t'aeyang: Han'guk hyŏndae misul 1960–2004 [You are my sunshine: Contemporary Korean art 1960–2004] (Seoul: Total Museum of Art, 2004), 278–79.

29. Held on August 22, this last performance was described by Yi Ku-yŏl in "Chopko p'aeswoejŏk in palp'yo kigwan,"[A narrow and enclosed institution for making announcements] Yesulgye (Fall 1970): 129–30.

30. Chang Sŏk-wŏn, "Ibent'ŭ, kŭ munje wa ŭimi" [Events, their issues and meanings], Hongdae hakpo, June 30, 1977.

31. Yi Kŏn-yong, "Han'guk haengwi misul ŭi chŏngae wa kŭ chubyŏn," 48.

32. Yi Kŏn-yong, "Han'guk ŭi ipch'e, haengwimisul kŭ charyojŏk pogosŏ" [A documentary report of object-based and gestural art in Korea], Space 156 (June 1980): 18.

33. Lee Kun-yong claims that KCIA agents physically beat him in December 1976. Yi

Why Performance in Authoritarian Korea? | 275

Kŏn-yong, "OB tŭl ŭi suda," in Kyŏnggido Misulgwan, *Han'guk ŭi yŏksajŏk kaenyŏm misul* (Seoul: Nunbit, 2011), 300.

34. Sŏng Nŭng-gyŏng, *22 myŏng ŭi yesulga, sidae wa sot'onghada*, 122.

35. Hannah Arendt, *The Origins of Totalitarianism* (New York: Meridian Books, 1958), 443.

36. Unsigned article, "Ŏndŏgŭraundŭ yesul (5): Haep'ŭning" [Underground art, no. 5: Happenings], *Tonga ilbo*, August 3, 1968.

37. The original members, along with Ha, were Kim Han, Suh Seung-won (Sŏ Sŭng-wŏn), Lee Seung-jo (Yi Sŭng-jo), Pak Sŏk-wŏn, Ch'oe Pong-hyŏn, Ch'oe Myŏng-yŏng, Yi T'ae-hyŏn, Kim Tchasup (Kim Cha-sŭp), Kwak Hoon (Kwak Hun), and Kim Ku-lim (Kim Ku-rim).

38. This statement was printed on the inside leaf of each issue of the group's magazine, *A.G.*

39. The procession was stopped by police in front of Kwanghwamun, the main gate of the Kyŏngbok Palace. Pak Yŏng-nam, "Han'guk silhŏm misul 15-yŏn ŭi palchach'wi" [Fifteen years of Korean experimental art], *Kyegan misul* 17 (Spring 1981): 92.

40. Pak Yong-suk (Park Yong-sook), "Silhŏm yesul, chuŏjin sidaerŭl chŏkkŭkjŏk ŭro sandanŭn il" [Experimental art, on living actively in one's present], *Space* 101 (October–November 1975): 77.

41. Pak Yŏng-nam, "Han'guk silhŏm misul 15-yŏn ŭi palchach'wi," 93.

42. Pang Kŭn-t'aek (Bang Geun-taek), "I chakkarŭl malhanda: Haengwi ŭi kwejŏk" [About this artist: The trajectory of performance], *Hyŏndae yesul* (July 1977), unpaginated.

43. "Ŏndŏgŭraundŭ yesul (5)."

44. Yi Kŏn-yong, *Han'guk misul tanch'e 100-yŏn* [A century of Korean artists' groups] (Seoul: Kim Daljin Museum, 2013), 237.

45. Yi Kŏn-yong, "Han'guk haengwi misul ŭi chŏngae wa kŭ chubyŏn," 48.

46. Allan Kaprow, "The Legacy of Jackson Pollock," *Art News* 57, no. 6 (October 1958): 26.

47. Yi Kŏn-yong, "Han'guk haengwi misul ŭi chŏngae wa kŭ chubyŏn," 48.

48. Lee Kun-yong (Yi Kŏn-yong), interview with the author, January 10, 2015.

49. Sung Neung-kyung recalls that he met Lee when both men decided to avoid the "charismatic" advocate of Korean Informel, Park Seobo (Pak Sŏ-bo), and instead "take refuge" in the class taught by the more permissive Lee Ma-dong (Yi Ma-dong). Sŏng Nŭng-gyŏng (Sung Neung-kyung), "'K'anbŏsŭ yŏ hŭndŭllyŏra" [Canvas, shake], *Gana Art* 49 (May–June 1996): 43.

50. Yi Kŏn-yong, *Han'guk misul tanch'e 100-yŏn*, 231.

51. Ibid.

52. For a concise summary of the Taegu Contemporary Art Festival, see Pak Min-yŏng, "1974-yŏn esŏ 1979 kkaji Taegu hyŏndae misulje ŭi chŏn'gae wa ŭimi" [The development and significance of the Taegu Contemporary Art Festival from 1974 to 1979], in *1960-70-yŏndae Taegu misul ŭi hyŏndaesŏng e taehan haesŏk* [An interpretation of the contemporaneity of Taegu art in the 1960s and 1970s] (Taegu: Daegu Foundation for Culture, 2013), 120–37.

53. Sŏng Nŭng-gyŏng, *22 myŏng ŭi yesulga, sidae wa sot'onghada*, 122.

54. Ibid., 123.

55. Ibid.

56. Pak Yong-suk , "Silhŏm yesul, chuŏjin sidae rŭl chŏkkŭkjŏk ŭro sandanŭn il," 80. Held on October 6, 1975, in the small gallery of the National Museum of Contemporary Art, the discussion's participants included Kim Ku-lim, Park Seobo, and Kim Bok-young.

57. Lee Kun-yong, interview with the author, August 25, 2014.

58. Sŏng Nŭng-gyŏng, untitled essay, in *4 in ŭi EVENT* [An event by four artists] (Seoul: Seoul Gallery, 1976), unpaginated.

59. Lee Kun-yong, interview with Sŏ Chŏng-im, "Chŏnhyŏ ssŭlmo ŏmnŭn il ŭl kŭktdanjŏk ŭro milgo nagal ttae kajang arŭmdaun yesul i naonda" [The most beautiful art emerges when activities having absolutely no purpose are pushed forward], *Article 38* (July 2014): 17.

60. Ludwig Wittgenstein, *On Certainty*, ed. G. E. M. Anscombe and G. H. von Wright, trans. Denis Paul and G. E. M. Anscombe, (Oxford: Blackwell, 1969), 21.

61. Lee Kun-yong, interview with the author, January 7, 2015.

62. Wittgenstein, *On Certainty*, 23.

63. Pak Yong-suk, "60-yŏndae ihu ŭi silhŏm misul," [Post-1960s experimental art], *Tongdŏk misul* (1976): 45.

64. Ibid., 45.

65. Yi Kŏn-yong, "Hangsang t'umyŏnghayŏra," 102.

66. Ibid.

67. Yi Kŏn-yong, "Segye wa ingan ŭl chŏnch'ejŏk ŭro ihaehanŭn pangbŏp ŭrosŏŭi tŭroing" [Drawing that is a method of understanding the whole of the world and humanity], *Hwarang* 26 (Winter 1979): 76.

68. Pak Yong-suk, "Silhŏm yesul, chuŏjin sidae rŭl chŏkŭkjŏk ŭro sandanŭn il" [Experimental art, on living actively in one's present], *Space* 101 (October–November 1975): 77.

69. Ibid.

70. O Kwang-su, "60-yŏndae ŭi hyŏndae misul," 104.

71. Lee Kun-yong, interview with the author, August 25, 2014.

72. Ibid.

73. Lee Kun-yong, interview with Sŏ Chŏng-im, "Chŏnyŏ ssŭlmo ŏmnŭn il ŭl kŭktanjŏk ŭro milgo nagal ttae kajang arŭmdaun yesul i naonda," 17.

74. Lee Kun-yong, interview with the author, August 25, 2014. An account of the performance is also given in Sŏng Nŭng-gyŏng, "'K'anbŏsŭyŏ hŭndŭllyŏra," 46–47.

75. Pak Yong-suk, "Silhŏm yesul, chuŏjin sidae rŭl chŏgkŭkjŏk ŭro sandanŭn il," 80.

76. Ibid., 79.

77. Lee Kang-so, interview with the author, January 11, 2015. The title was changed to *Sŏnsuljip* (a term used to refer to a casual drinking establishment) after hearing others constantly refer to the work as such. In English translations, Lee has referred to the work as *Bar in a Gallery*.

78. Ibid. Lee had met Kim when he participated in *Today's Artists*, a group show held at the gallery in 1971. For a brief summary of Kim Mun-ho's life and activities, see Kee, *Contemporary Korean Art*, 20–21.

79. Kim Su-hyŏn, *Yi Kang-so ŭi hoehwa: Tabŭllo wa hyŏngsang ŭi kongjon* [The paintings of Lee Kang-so: The coexistence of tableaus and images] *Yi Kang-so* (Seoul: Inkong Gallery, 1989), 5.

80. "Kŭk ŭl kŏnnŭn chŏnwi misul."

81. Lee Kang-so, interview with the author, January 11, 2015.

82. A policeman apparently demanded once that Lee Kun-yong explain himself after a performance attracted so many bystanders as to obstruct traffic in the Anguk-dong rotary. Lee Kang-so, interview with the author, January 7, 2015.

83. Lee said that in his solo show *Drawing and Event*, which took place at the Namgye Gallery, a small commercial gallery in Taejon, attention from local newspapers culminated in very large audiences. By the last day, there were so many people that they actually blocked the space of his performance. Yi Kŏn-yong, "Naega sanŭn kot" [The place where I live], *Hwarang* 25 (Fall 1979): 65.

84. To dispel any suspicion of profiteering, Lee deliberately limited the number of tables and chairs in the gallery: "Too many and people would think I was trying to make money like a real barkeep." Lee Kang-so, interview with the author, January 11, 2015.

85. Kim Su-hyŏn, *Yi Kang-so ŭi hoehwa*.

86. Lee Kang-so, interview with the author, January 11, 2015. See also Kim Sŏng-hŭi (Kim Sung Hee), *Yi Kang-so* (Seoul: Maronnier Books, 2011), 25.

87. Lee Kang-so, interview with the author, January 11, 2015.

88. Yi Kŏn-yong, "Han'guk ŭi ipch'e, haengwimisul kŭ charyojŏk pogosŏ" [A documentary report of object-based and gestural art in Korea], *Space* 156 (June 1980): 15.

89. Lee Kang-so, quoted in Kim, *Yi Kang-so*, 27–28.

90. Yi Kŏn-yong , "LOGICAL-EVENT," in *4 in ŭi EVENT* [An event by four artists] (Seoul: Seoul Gallery, 1976), unpaginated.

91. Yi Kŏn-yong, "Hangsang t'umyŏng hayŏra," 102.

92. Chang Sŏk-wŏn, "Ibent'ŭ, kŭ munje wa ŭimi."

93. Some Korean artists did try to cultivate a connection between themselves and celebrities. The boldest of these was Park Seobo, whose many moments of reinvention included shaving his head in anticipation of his participation in the second edition of the UNESCO-sponsored *Young Painters of the World* (*Jeunes peintres du monde*) exhibition in Paris. In December 1960, the daily *Min'guk ilbo* actually devoted a section to what it called Park's "Yul Brynner" look, as did *The Korean Republic*, which waxed eloquent on the parallels between the artist's "shiny head" and his equally bright future. Unsigned article, "P'yojŏng" [Expression], *Min'guk ilbo*, December 16, 1960. At the time of this incident, *The King and I* and the *Ten Commandments*, both films starring Yul Brynner, were enormously popular in Korea.

94. Yi Kŏn-yong, "Int'ŏbyu: 80-yŏndae hyŏnjangesŏ," [Interview: From the 1980s], *Wŏlgan misul* (November 1989): 47.

95. Kim Pok-yŏng (Kim Bok-young), "Yi Kŏn-yong ŭi tŭroing kwa EVENT chon e puchŏ" [On the exhibition of Lee Kun-yong's Drawing and EVENT], in *Lee, Guen-Yong Drawing/Event Exhibition* (Taejon: Namgye Gallery, 1979), unpaginated./

Conclusion

From Yusin Redux to *Yuch'e it'al*

Youngju Ryu

A painting, a parodied politician, and a case of malicious prosecution. Around a campy piece of pop art unfolded one of the stranger episodes of the entire 2012 presidential race in South Korea. This episode, which has turned out to be eerily prophetic in light of both the subsequent presidency and the historic impeachment of Park Geun-hye (Pak Kŭn-hye), provides a fitting point of entry for the final essay of a volume that has sought to illuminate the most authoritarian decade in South Korean history through a cultural lens. In these last pages of *Cultures of Yusin*, a controversial painting guides us into the heart of Yusin's conflicted legacy in the present and helps us reflect on the contemporary relevance of what this volume has explored in the context of the abortive end of the second Park presidency. Has the end of the Park Geun-hye era also brought the Yusin system to an end once and for all in South Korea?

The painting that became a lightning rod ahead of the heated 2012 election depicts a scene in a hospital delivery room where a middle-aged woman greets her newborn, her legs widespread and her face frozen in a grotesque smile somewhere between agony and ecstasy. A pan placed between her legs catches the messy afterbirth and a small notepad lies open on the floor by her side. The medical staff surrounding the new mother strike various poses: one holds up the baby for the mother to see, another gives the newborn a full military salute, and yet another looks directly at the viewer, holding up her fingers in a *V* as if posing for a photograph. The most striking detail in this wildly parodic painting is the newborn, who has emerged from the mother's womb bearing the visage of a middle-aged

Figure 12. Hong Sung-dam, *Golden Time: Dr. Ch'oe In-hyŏk Salutes His Majesty the Newborn*. (Courtesy of the artist.)

man and wearing an iconic pair of shades. Immortalized in Korean cultural memory by the famous photograph of the 1961 military coup, the sunglasses allow viewers to identify the newborn as Park Chung Hee (Pak Chŏng-hŭi).

The painting was exhibited in November 2012, a month before Park Geun-hye won a narrow victory over Moon Jae-in (Mun Chae-in) to become the eighteenth president of South Korea. A work of the *minjung* artist Hong Sung-dam (Hong Sŏng-dam), best known up to that point for his woodcut prints on the subject of popular resistance to military dictatorship, the painting was whimsically titled *Golden Time: Dr. Ch'oe In-hyŏk Salutes His Excellency the Newborn*.[1] The painting's satire operated on multiple fronts. The mother bore an unmistakable likeness to Park Geun-hye, a recognition further aided by a small notepad on the floor—a not so subtle allusion to Park's nickname, "Notepad Princess," itself a reference to the notepad she was purported to carry everywhere, which was said to contain all the names of her political friends and foes. The title of the painting was derived from *Golden Time*, a popular medical drama set in a trauma center that had aired on a major television network earlier in 2012. The fact that Dr. Ch'oe In-hyŏk, the fearless and dedicated head surgeon who bucks authority to practice humane medicine in the series, is portrayed as standing at full attention and saluting the infant Park Chung Hee in the painting was meant to highlight, according to the artist, "the trauma innate in all of us who lived through the Yusin era."[2] At the same time, the comical rendition of the dictator as a bare-bottomed infant undercut the very authority of the authoritarian figure. Indeed, the liberal use of popular cultural references to depict two of the most sacralized personalities in South Korean politics operated in the classic satirical mode in which the high is brought scatologically low and savagely ridiculed.

The outraged responses that the painting drew from Park Geun-hye's supporters, however, mostly had to do with its depiction of the presidential candidate as a mother. According to the artist, the inspiration for the painting had come from the unsubstantiated allegation reported in the media that Park had once given birth to a child out of wedlock, possibly with the cult leader Ch'oe T'ae-min, the father of Choi Soon-sil (Ch'oe Sun-sil), the so-called female Rasputin figure whose control over Park Geun-hye later led to Park's impeachment in 2017. In the socially conservative political environment of South Korea, such an allegation, if proven true, would have dealt a death blow to any candidate, but it was particularly scandalous for Park because of the cult of virginity that had developed around her. Even though her presidential campaign slogan highlighted her biological sex as "the prepared female candidate," Park was widely perceived to have forsworn the conventional joys of marriage and motherhood in order to "marry the nation," as it were. Fixed in the minds of her most fervent supporters—the generation old enough to have mourned the assassination of Park Chung Hee's wife in 1974 and Park Chung Hee himself in 1979—had been the image of Park Geun-hye as the "first daughter" doubly bereft. Her renunciation of wife- and motherhood thus had the effect of preserving her forever as a daughter at the moment of her most painful loss, and Park's campaign in 2012 was tremendously effective in translating the sympathy that such a figure would evoke among the older generation into actual votes. Even though the vociferous denunciation of the painting by Park's supporters was issued in terms of the painting's political manipulation of "even that most sublime moment of birth," the actual sacrality compromised by the painting was not of the fertile goddess but of the virgin queen.[3]

In Hong's painting, the daughter thus gives birth to her father. Ahead of a hotly contested presidential race, the political message of such a depiction was hardly subtle: a vote for Park Geun-hye would be a vote to resurrect Park Chung Hee. *Yuch'e it'al*, the title of the series of exhibitions of which the painting was a prominent part, made this message even more explicit. While *yuch'e i'tal* conventionally means to "exit one's body," as in "out-of-body experience," a clever substitution of the Chinese graphs for *yuch'e* in the exhibition's title rendered it a shortened form of *Yusin ch'eje* or "Yusin regime." The title thus came to mean "to exit the Yusin regime." Indeed, the exhibition declared its goal to be "the apprehension of the very nature and essence of October Yusin and a satirical and active reflection upon the many influences of Yusin that still cling to us, mind and body."[4] According to this curatorial statement, the cultural logics and manifestations of Yusin have persisted with stubbornness into our present, attaining a level of naturalization in the course of South Korea's breathless development. To exit from them, therefore, will require a truly out-of-body experience, a shock of recognition that a satirical work like Hong's painting can force on the scandalized viewer's consciousness.

The prescience of Hong's painting has become clear in the years since. In a much more literal manner than the curators of the 2012 show could have predicted, Yusin returned to the daily lives of South Korean citizens during Park Geun-hye's presidency, shocking them by its pure anachronism. For example, the green flag of the Saemaul movement (Saemaŭl Undong), bearing the three-leaf bud representing the three principles of diligence, cooperation, and self-help, as well as the word *Saemaul* written in a Korean font now known as the "Park Chung Hee script," returned to Seoul's urban landscape as part of an aggressive campaign to repackage the Saemaul movement as a global initiative. As the initiative's most enthusiastic ambassador, Park preached Saemaul's virtues in an address at the United Nations and marketed it as a Korean experience to be exported to the developing world alongside the latest videos of K-pop idols. In addition to sponsoring Saemaul training programs for representatives from the global south, Park's administration funded a number of large-scale commemorative projects, including the construction of a Saemaul theme park in the provincial city of Kumi, the birthplace of Park Chung Hee. The revivalist mood extended not only to policies and institutions but even to persons. Park Geun-hye brought the septuagenarian Kim Ki-choon (Kim Ki-ch'un), a former prosecutor who had participated in the drafting of the Yusin Constitution, out of retirement to appoint him as her chief of staff. An architect of the original Yusin Constitution during the father Park's presidency thus became the executor of Yusin Redux in the daughter Park's Blue House. From the fabrication of spy cases to the mobilization of right-wing groups for pro-government demonstrations, Kim Ki-ch'un's activities came to light as part of the scandal that ended Park Geun-hye's presidency. In an ironic twist of fate, Kim was finally arrested in January 2017 on the charge of creating and enforcing a blacklist of cultural organizations and persons critical of the government.

Other resurrections abounded, most notable among them the instrumentalization of anticommunism and the nationalization of history. In 2013 Lee Seok-ki (Yi Sŏk-ki), a national assemblyman from the United Progressive Party, was indicted on charges of plotting an insurgency in support of North Korea and violating the National Security Law. Found guilty of treason (naeranjoe) for holding a meeting in which one of his deputies discussed a plan to sabotage crucial facilities in the event of a South Korean war with North Korea, and of violating the National Security Law for, among other things, singing North Korean revolutionary songs, Lee was sentenced to twelve years in prison (later commuted to nine years). In the aftermath of this ruling, Lee's United Progressive Party was deemed unconstitutional and dissolved by the Constitutional Court. Members of the party popularly elected to the National Assembly were stripped of their seats. The entire proceeding marked the return not only of the laws that were at the heart of Yusin era state violence—treason, for example, was the legal basis of the 1975 judicial murder of People's Revolutionary Party members discussed in the "Introduction"—but the resurrection of anticommunism as a rationale for suspending the democratic process within the operations of the trifecta of government institutions that the original Yusin regime had used so effectively for its ends: the intelligence agency (the National Intelligence Service, formerly the Korean Central Intelligence Agency), the prosecution, and the courts.

Anticommunism also became the banner for an attempt to renationalize Korean history textbooks. In 2015, against strong and widespread opposition, the Park Geun-hye administration reinstated state-issued Korean history textbooks, citing the need to correct pro–North Korean biases and "masochistic" perspectives in the existing textbooks. A hallmark of the Yusin era, the state-issued history textbooks first went into effect in South Korea in 1974. As the first two essays in this volume have shown, the Park regime was keenly interested in mining national history for the narratives that would aid state-sponsored projects of national mobilization; history was a locus for the spiritual reformation of the Korean people. It was only in 2002 that the Korean education system began to move away from a nationalized curriculum based on a single, state-issued textbook. In seeking to readopt state-issued Korean history textbooks, therefore, the Park Geun-hye administration revived a mode of nationalist and anti-communist history education closely tied to the popular mobilizations of the authoritarian era. Even the rationale it provided for the change in policy echoed the Yusin rhetoric of enforcing uniformity in order to "protect students from the confusion caused by education based on biased historical perspectives." In the state-issued Korean history textbooks for the junior high and high school curricula unveiled in January 2017, the Park Chung Hee regime's authoritarianism is downplayed—the expression "dictatorship" has been changed to "long-term rule," for instance—while his achievements in the area of economic development are highlighted. In addition, the critique of pro-Japanese collaboration and Japanese colonial violence overall is significantly attenuated. Such changes strengthened the suspicion, already widespread in public discourse, that for the daughter Park, the office of the president was first and foremost a vehicle in her decades-long quest to restore her father's reputation.

They also lent credence to the characterization of the Park presidency as Yusin Redux. Such a characterization, in turn, raises a set of difficult questions. Beyond the personal motivations of a long-grieving daughter to see her autocratic father vindicated at the altar of the nation's modernization, even if it means rolling back time and short-circuiting the democratic process that had been firmly established in the decades since his death, how can we understand the political meaning of the Park Chung Hee era in the era of Park Geun-hye? To what extent did the violence of the Yusin era remain a basic point of reference for Koreans' views of themselves, whether as an original sin that set the country on the wrong path or a necessary evil in the country's ineluctable march toward development? And, in the final analysis, what might *Yuch'e it'al* necessitate in the time of Yusin Redux?

To address these questions, we might return to Hong Sung-dam's painting and note another dimension to its prescience. As discussed earlier, the title of the painting, *Golden Time*, was a whacky, parodic nod to the television series from which it drew its basic motif, but it later became a keyword and flashpoint of Park Geun-hye's entire presidency. The critical window of time during which an action taken might save a patient's life or condemn him or her to death, "golden time," became one of Park Geun-hye's favorite metaphors, peppering her speech over and over in relation to the economy, North Korea, and even the declining fertility rate of the country. Tragically, it also became a shorthand term for the Park Geun-hye administration's repeated failure to take appropriate action in the aftermath of national disasters. Despite Park's penchant for sounding the alarm and chiding her cabinet, the National Assembly, or even the Korean public for not sharing her sense of urgency about the fate of the country, her presidency will forever be remembered for the gross negligence and mishandling of national crises and the great loss of life that it failed to prevent. Such was the case during the Middle East Respiratory Syndrome (MERS) epidemic in the summer of 2015. Criminal negligence, ineptitude, and lack of oversight also led to the Sewol Ferry (Sewŏlho) tragedy of 2014. In that incident, only a paltry rescue effort was attempted during the golden hour when lives might have been saved. More than three hundred passengers, a majority of them high school students on a field trip, were told to stay below decks even after the ship had begun to tip, and as their stricken parents on land howled in horror as they helplessly watched the ship disappear, these students sank with the ship to the bottom of the sea. Much still remains unknown about the details and causes of the massive government failure that day, including the whereabouts of Madame President during the golden time for rescue—the seven hours after the Sewŏl Ferry began to sink.

Park Geun-hye's response to these tragedies was peculiar. Even though she was the supreme head of the executive branch, and therefore ultimately responsible for the failures of the government, Park's speech on the occasion of every crisis located that responsibility elsewhere, as though she herself were not part of the government. The South Korean press, opposition politicians, and even comedians noted the oddness of this pattern and took to calling it *yuch'e it'al hwapŏp* (out-of-body speech). Not simply a means of shirking responsibility, it was revealed that Park's speeches were delivered from a place outside the presidential office, at least as that office had been construed by representative democracy.[5] And yet the "out-of-body speech" of Park Geun-hye suggested that her authority sprang not from the people who elected her but from some realm beyond the common inefficiencies or vulgar fractiousness of the democratic process. To put it in Lacanian terms, it was as though there existed two subjects of Park Geun-hye's speech, the subject of enunciation and the subject of the statement. While the Korean public puzzled over the incongruity of the subject of the statement, the real discourse was actually unfolding at the level of the subject of enunciation.

A symptom that this indeed was the case during Park Geun-hye's presidency was the proliferation, whether in jest or utter solemnity, of a number of terms connected to Park Geun-hye that seemed to hail from a different era altogether. Ice Princess and Notepad Princess were two of Park's most popular monikers. The ruling party members took to calling Park's photograph "her esteemed noble portrait" (*chonyŏng*), demanding its return from a prominent politician who left the party during the National Assembly elections of 2016, as though the portrait of Madame President were itself a sacred object. Terms like *her ladyship* (*kakha*), *ten eunuchs* (*sipsangsi*), and *royal seal* (*oksae*) became part of the day-to-day political nomenclature. It goes without saying that these are old ceremonial terms suggesting a source of political authority that is monarchical; according to Rhyu Si-min (Yu Si-min), one of the most insightful pundits commenting on Korean politics today, Park Geun-hye as president excelled at one thing and one thing only, and that is diplomatic ceremony (*ŭijŏn*). If, as we saw in the "Introduction," Yusin was the proclamation of a political authority that did not spring from and was not beholden to the people, Park Geun-hye's *yuch'e it'al hwapŏp* can indeed be understood as a sign of the return of *Yuch'e* in the sense of the term used by the curators of the 2012 show as short for *Yusin ch'eje*.

Here we can recall the origin of the term *Yusin*. As discussed in the "Introduction," Yusin is the Korean pronunciation of the Chinese characters that make up the *ishin* of Meiji Ishin, or the Meiji Restoration of Japan. That the Meiji Restoration provided the inspiration and model for October Yusin is well known; in his own writings, Park Chung Hee made no secret of his admiration for the way Japanese oligarchs had managed to transform a collection of feudal domains into a modern nation-state in record time. If, however, the centerpiece of this political revolution was the restoration of the emperor to the supreme position of symbolic power without giving him actual political power, Park Chung Hee's imitation of Japan's imperial fascism contained an important difference. October Yusin restored Park to the position of supreme power not beholden to the people, but the separation of symbolic and actual political power did not occur. What resulted from this coincidence of symbolic and actual power was a cult of personality surrounding the autocratic ruler. This, for example, is how I understand the continued worship of Park Chung Hee as a demigod (*pansin panin*) by his most fervid supporters.

In this light, we can understand Yusin Redux as a restoration not simply of Park Chung Hee's Yusin but of the original Ishin in a purer sense.

The language of royal authority in which Park Geun-hye was shrouded and her habit of speaking out of body suggest her affinity to the Japanese emperor as an empty center of symbolic power. Less a servant of the people whose authority is contingent on actual processes and real performances than a sacral figure to whom the people owe their allegiance, Park Geun-hye the ice princess and virgin queen resided above the kind of demands that would hound a more ordinary Madame President—responsibility, accountability, culpability. It is perhaps not entirely coincidental that Park Geun-hye's typical response to the eruption of domestic problems that threatened her approval ratings was to exit the national body and embark on diplomatic missions abroad where the ceremonial nature of her power could be put on full display. While Park Chung Hee was an autocrat who wielded both symbolic and actual power, Park Geun-hye has been found out as a mere figurehead, a marionette on the strings wielded by Choi Soon-sil. In one of those ironies of history that turn out to be poetically just, cruelly so even, Park is suspected of having numerous procedures on her face administered by a variety of unofficial medical personnel. The major procedure that she repeatedly received is a species of facelift designed to eliminate the appearance of the deep creases that form around the mouth with age, also known as "marionette lines."

To demand the dethronement of this marionette, Korean citizens took to the streets in unprecedented numbers and sparked the political sequence that has now been officially dubbed the Candlelight Revolution. From October 29, 2016, to March 11, 2017, Saturday rallies in the Kwanghwamun area saw crowds that totaled some sixteen million. Gravity gave way to gaiety in many of these rallies as irreverent satirists made short work of Park, her puppeteer, and her many henchmen and -women, all of whom were seen and heard in parodied posters and songs. The "open mic for citizens" (*simin chayu parŏndae*) became the stage for registering dissent across age, class, and gender lines, from a fifth-grade girl proclaiming that "the president is no longer the president because she signed the power given to the president by the people over to Choi Soon-sil" (November 12, 2016) to a senior citizen belting out her indictment of Park on bribery charges to the tune of "Arirang," a song she cleverly titled "Geun-hye Arirang," following the refrain "Kŭne anida," which means "Kŭne (Geun-hye) is not" (November 26, 2016). Popular participation in politics expanded greatly as online and social media campaigns launched to publicly pressure members of the legislature to pass an impeachment bill had the unintended consequence of opening up direct access to these legislators. (In one widely noted instance, a high school student dissatisfied with his school's lunch menu texted the representative of his district, calling for an investigation of the inadequate oversight of the school meal program.) To put it in the striking terms Serk-Bae Suh used in his chapter on Christology and Korean literature in the 1970s and 1980s, Yusin Redux revealed democracy to be the gold-crowned Jesus, ossified and reduced to a "pernicious ritual." In order to clear a path out of Yusin and achieve *Yuch'e it'al*, the people constituted themselves in the square as a multitude (in the resistant sense of Hardt and Negri's formulation), as if exhorting each other: "It is not democracy that will save us—it is we who will save democracy, by battling, by creating, and by transmuting matter into spirit."[6]

As we have seen in this book, Yusin set in motion a political economy of modernization in South Korea that posited development and democracy in largely oppositional terms. To the extent that democracy and its fundamental premise of an individual subject of rights are integral to capitalist modernity, what Yusin sought was modernization without modernity despite the Park regime's incessant invocation of "modernization of the fatherland" as a slogan. Industrialization as mobilization, bureaucratic militarization of the everyday, and heavy reliance on what Gregory Kasza calls "administered mass organizations," such as the Saemaul movement, were all aspects of that central contradiction. The government's many projects of hypernationalization and the cultural work that accompanied them—the iconization of T'oegye discussed in Hwisang Cho's chapter, for example—are best understood as attempts to suture the splits and smooth over the dissonances produced by that central contradiction.

The cultures of Yusin examined by the essays in this volume were born within this context largely as responses to or symptoms of that central contradiction as well. Utopian visions of alternative collectivities guided some of them, as in the case of the science fictional imagination discussed by Sunyoung Park, and active collective antiauthoritarian resistance did take place in prominent ways even under Yusin's iron sky. But Han Sang Kim's study of the craze over "*my* sweet home" reminds us that utopian visions could be smaller in scale and acts of resistance even smaller and more ephemeral still—a cry of ecstasy in the dark of a cheap third-run movie theater at the sight of a body that defies regimentation, as discussed by Irhe Sohn, or seemingly meaningless motions choreographed into acts of performance that suspend the mad dash toward hypernationalist content and meaning, as Joan Kee has analyzed. And as Eunhee Park's examination of women's financial activities during the Park Chung He era shows, the repressiveness of the era sometimes had the effect of spawning innovation and new modes of sociality. The desiring subject capable of taking pleasure in individual acts of consumption was a category that never ceased to cause trouble for the Park regime, whether or not those acts can be seen as inherently dissident.

And it is the dismantling of the familiar oppositional relationship between development and democracy that suggests that Yusin Redux may finally have brought about the end of Yusin in South Korea. Throughout Korean history, in 1960 as in 1987, political revolutions followed an established pattern. A small radicalized group rises up in protest against the government, the government's attempt to quell the resistance results in greater violence, the state violence ends up fueling the spread of democratic ferment to the larger population, which then tips the balance over in favor of the protesters. Once the political change occurs, however, the masses return to their conservative ways and the remaining "vanguard" becomes even more radicalized in order to continue to hold onto the mantle of change, even after a major political change has occurred. In the process of *Yuch'e it'al*, however, a strange chiasmatic formation was glimpsed for the first time. The defense of democracy against Yusin Redux was broadly based from the start and remarkably peaceful throughout, and it was the conservative group that turned violent and militant, even radical. A hundred days into the new Moon Jae-in era, the multitudes that brought about *Yuch'e it'al* with their physical bodies in the square, as well as all their blogs, likes, Tweets, Facebook posts, YouTube videos, and Kakaotalk texts, had a new name—"collective intelligence" (*chiptan chisŏng*). "The people of Korea, it seems to me, are demanding direct democracy," stated Moon Jae-in during a press event on August 20, 2017. "As sovereign subjects, they are no longer satisfied with the form of indirect democracy in which they get to exercise their voting power only during the elections and must remain passive spectators of the political drama at all other times." The path to success for his government, argued Moon, would lie in whether it could go forward together with the "collective intelligence of the Korean people."[7]

Once again, it is on the grounds of culture that one finds prefigured the political sequence to come. In Hong Sung-dam's painting of 2013 called *Cherry Blossom Outing (Pŏtkkot nori)*, we see Park Geun-hye walking down a path strewn with cherry blossom petals, holding the child Park Chung Hee's hand in hers. During the five years of Park's presidency, the newborn of *Golden Time* had become a toddler. The blossoming cherry trees that line the boulevard are an unveiled reference to the famous

Figure 13. Hong Sung-dam, *Cherry Blossom Outing*. (Courtesy of the artist.)

promenade in front to the National Assembly Building in Yŏŭido that the architect Kim Swoo-geun (Kim Su-gŭn) once dreamed of making a nodal point in a modernist city of flows and thus a reference also to Park's political power as a president. Behind the trees peep black ops agents in shades. Accompanied by no one else and completely without fanfare, the father-daughter pair, now mother and son, walk away from their seat of power, their backs to the viewer, as toward a sunset.

By bringing back Yusin in a purer sense, Park Geun-hye the virgin queen became the mother of Yusin Redux, making it possible to bring about *Yuch'e it'al*. As an anachronistic—and highly private—campaign to restore her father's honor, Yusin Redux helped to dispel Yusin's original aura as a violent but effective nation-building project that the Park Chung Hee regime had crafted. The father thus privatized and infantilized can no longer be the father of anyone and certainly not the father of the fatherland. As a prescient statement of the post-Park era, Hong Sung-dam's painting has immortalized Park Chung Hee not as a national hero, a demigod, or even a fearsome dictator but as an unruly child in oversized military boots firing a toy gun that is still capable of squirting red paint in the eyes of a hapless head or two, all the while being dragged away by his still queenly mother.

NOTES

1. In 2014, Hong Sung-dam became a flashpoint for controversy once again when his painting satirizing Park Geun-hye's handling of the Sewŏl Ferry disaster was pulled by the curators of the Kwangju Biennale as too politically motivated to be included in the exhibition.

2. Yi Chae-jin, "Agi nannun Pak Kŭn-hye hubo, kŭrim sok agi ŭi chŏngch'e nŭn?" *Midiŏ onŭl*, November 18, 2012, http://www.mediatoday.co.kr/?mod=news&act=article View&idxno=106046

3. "Pak Kŭn-hye 'Yusin ch'ulsan' p'ungja kŭrim 'sikkŭl,'" *Hankyoreh*, November 19, 2012, http://www.hani.co.kr/arti/society/society_general/561259.htmln-hyen-hye

4. The curator's statement for the exhibition "Yusin ŭi ch'osang" (Portraits of Yusin), which comprise the third part of "Yuch'e it'al" series can be viewed at: http://www.alt-pool.org/_v3/board/view.asp?pageNo=1&b_type=11&board_id=837&time_type=&year

5. "The Republic of Korea shall be a democratic republic," reads Article 1 of the South Korean Constitution. "The sovereignty of the Republic of Korea shall reside in the people, and all state authority shall emanate from the people." The English translation of

the complete South Korean Constitution is available at: http://korea.assembly.go.kr/res/low_01_read.jsp?boardid=1000000035

6. The original quote, which also appears in Serk-bae Suh's chapter, is by Nikos Kazantzakis: "It is not God who will save us—it is we who will save God, by battling, by creating, and by transmuting matter into spirit." See Nikos Kazantzakis, *The Saviors of God: Spiritual Exercises* (New York: Simon and Schuster, 1963), 105–6.

7. Kim Tong-hyŏn, "Mun Chae-in Taet'ongnyŏng, 'Kungmin ŭn kanjŏp minjujuŭi e manjok mothae,'" *Asia Today*, August 20, 2017, http://www.asiatoday.co.kr/view.php?key=20170820010008766

Contributors

Hwisang Cho is Assistant Professor in Korean studies at Emory University. He recently completed his book manuscript, *The Power of the Brush: Epistolary Revolution in Early Modern Korea*. His research has been supported by the Andrew W. Mellon Fellowship of Scholars in Critical Bibliography at the Rare Book School, University of Virginia (2015–17) and the Andrew W. Mellon Fellowship for Assistant Professors from the Institute for Advanced Study (2016–17). His other works have appeared in the *Journal of Korean Studies* and the *Journal of Asian Studies*.

Joan Kee is Associate Professor in the History of Art at the University of Michigan. She is the author of *Contemporary Korean Art: Tansaekhwa and the Urgency of Method* (Minnesota, 2013) and curator of "From All Sides: Tansaekhwa on Abstraction," (Blum and Poe, 2014). A contributing editor to *Artforum*, she has written widely on modern and contemporary Asian art for various publications, including *Art Bulletin, Art History, Tate Papers, Modernism/Modernity, Positions: East Asia Cultures Critiques, Art Margins* and the *Oxford Art Journal*.

Han Sang Kim is Annette and Hugh Gragg Postdoctoral Fellow in Transnational Asian Studies at Rice University.

Won Kim is Associate Professor of Political Science at the Academy of Korean Studies.

Se-Mi Oh is Assistant Professor of Modern Korean History at the University of Michigan.

Eunhee Park is a PhD candidate in the Department of History at the University of Wisconsin–Madison.

Sunyoung Park is Associate Professor of East Asian Languages and Cultures and Gender Studies at the University of Southern California, Dornsife.

Youngju Ryu is Associate Professor of Modern Korean Literature at the University of Michigan.

Irhe Sohn is Assistant Professor of Korean Studies in the Department of East Asian Languages and Literatures at Smith College.

Serk-Bae Suh teaches Korean literature and culture at the University of California, Irvine.

Index

Note: Page numbers in italics refer to illustrations and tables.

Yusin regime (*continued*)
    political economy of, 5–8, 23
    propaganda, 18, 31
    slogans, 10, 22, 94, 122, 201
    as system of social control, 5–8
    See also Park Chung Hee

Yu Sŏn-yŏng, 11, 39
Yu Sŭng-jung, 209

Zero Group (Mudongin), 249, 254–55
Zhu Xi, 62–63, 66, 72, 84n8
Žižek, Slavoj, 243n29